WHA GAMEDAY

1972-1979 game program stories
from the archives of the
World Hockey Association Hall of Fame

edited by
TIMOTHY GASSEN

PCMP PRESS
P.O. Box 121
Tucson, Arizona
85702 USA

www.purple-cactus.tv

The logo of the WHA Hall of Fame is a registered trademark, used with permission.

www.WHAhof.com

ISBN 978-0-9797337-4-1

Manufactured in the United States of America

First Edition published June 2018

Front Cover: Goaltender Michel Dion, as painted by Robert Pelkowski in 1975 for a WHA Indianapolis Racers game program. Of all the fine artists who contributed to WHA programs, Mr. Pelkowski is the author's favorite.

Back Cover: WHA game program covers.

Thank you to the talented writers, editors, and media staff for 1972-1979 WHA teams and the WHA league offices. This publication is a tribute to their talents – especially those whose names were not attached to their hard work upon publication.

Thank you also to Curtis Walker for his kind assistance with this book.

TABLE OF CONTENTS

INTRODUCTION

Rest In Peace to the paper hockey game program.

For decades it was a ubiquitous game day companion for fans at pro hockey games, but now it is sadly replaced by electronic team web pages or smartphone updates. Slowly, from the 1990s onward, the paper game programs were reduced in page count, and then in physical size, and then in frequency of publication.

Then they were gone altogether.

Actual paper game programs once were king of the informational grapevine for hockey fans. At their peak – in the golden age of 1970s major league hockey expansion – they were full sized 8 ½" x 11" magazines, with color covers and 50-75 page interiors. They contained player rosters, and game schedules, action photos, and statistics.

And feature stories. They had so many fascinating feature stories.

Paper game programs were especially vital promotional tools for the fledgling 1972-1979 World Hockey Association. They not only provided advertising income for the home team, but they gave print space to include team-made feature stories about favorite players, opponents, or the league itself.

These features contain behind-the-scene glimpses about the personalities that made the WHA game possible – and that is why I love them so much. You must understand, though, that these stories were rarely hard-boiled news items written by independent news sources. They were positive in tone, and shied away from controversies. They most certainly were promotional in nature – but they also reveal so much humanity about 1970s major league hockey players and their WHA teams.

Many of the feature stories were written by team media relations staffers, though sometimes a local newspaper writer also contributed freelance pieces. The WHA also provided league-wide stories for teams to use, giving much needed copy to refresh program pages over the long season. Some game programs switched out stories and cover art for each game or week of games, while many teams switched content less frequently. Like many fans I often bought WHA programs for the exclusive cover art alone, even if the interior was unchanged from the previous game.

Game programs also remain some of the most readily available and affordable WHA artifacts to collect. With several dozen WHA teams and seven seasons of publication, you can do the math: there are many WHA game programs out there to find and cherish.

League staffer Walt Marlow penned many of the best pieces, first for the WHA offices and then later for the WHA Indianapolis Racers. You will see his photo and name often in the following pages. Marlow came from the world of newspaper sports reporting, and his parallel expertise as a promotional writer was a great resource for the WHA. Many other authors never saw their name in print, though – writing these program stories was just part of their team duties.

While WHA teams each created different programs, with their own unique graphic styles and editorial approach, many of them shared stories with each other. Often a program would carry at least one feature about the home team and one for the visiting squad – and then other teams would reprint those pieces throughout the season in their own publications. For that reason, in this book, we do not identify which specific team program the stories come from, because many times they would eventually be used by most other WHA teams, too. The stories are presented mostly in chronological order, from 1972-1979.

The WHA also printed their own promotional books and magazines, or created them in close association with other publishers. We have included here interesting features from WHA-made season preview and review magazines, and international game publications.

The Hockey Spectator newspaper also published during the WHA's first season and a half, from 1972 to the end of 1973. It was a fascinating large format newsprint tabloid, created in direct competition to The Hockey News. It gave fabulous, exclusive news coverage of the newly formed WHA – assisted by generous access from the team and league offices. We have included some highlights from its brief run here.

Other independent media, of course, also covered the WHA extensively, and we have included a few short pieces from the long-defunct Hockey Illustrated Magazine that gave the WHA much needed ink early in the league's existence. We end with some rare insights into the 1978 entry of Wayne Gretzky to major league hockey with the WHA Indianapolis Racers.

Together these feature story highlights from the 1972-1979 WHA era help paint a more complete picture of the people who populated this unique major league.

It is those people – those colorful, talented, rambunctious people – who make the World Hockey Association so memorable.

We are able to remember them now largely because of the late, great, paper hockey game program.

– *Timothy Gassen*
President, WHA Hall of Fame
Summer 2018

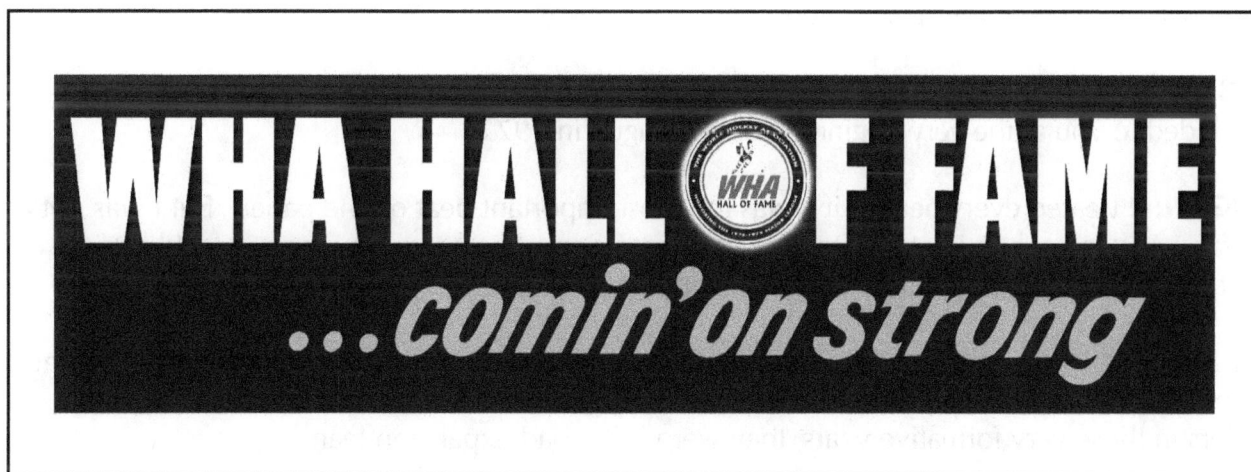

REPORTING THE WHA

an interview with sportswriter Bill Verigan about covering the early World Hockey Association

by Timothy Gassen

The New York Raiders were one of the founding 12 franchises to start play in the World Hockey Association's inaugural 1972-1973 season. The WHA made the ambitious decision to challenge the NHL directly in several major markets — Chicago, Boston, Minneapolis, Los Angeles and New York City – a miscalculation that eventually ended with all of those franchises either moving locations or folding operations.

The WHA would survive this initial miscalculation and become established in cities overlooked by the NHL, but in 1972 the New York market was seen as vital to the media acceptance of the new major league. A new arena on Long Island seemed to be the perfect fit for the WHA Raiders – a fact quickly also realized by the rival NHL, which hastily placed its expansion Islanders there. This forced the WHA into a busy Madison Square Arena, already the home of the NHL Rangers.

It seemed an impossible mission to gain a foothold in Manhattan in competition with the venerable Blueshirts, and this was quickly proven. The Raiders were almost immediately in financial trouble, and with new owners came a new name – The New York Golden Blades – for the 1973-1974 season.

The franchise limped out of New York City only six weeks into the WHA's second season to Chapel Hill, New Jersey, where they played the second half of 1973-74 on sub-standard home ice as The Jersey Knights. Amazingly, by then the franchise had accumulated good on-ice talent, and when the team relocated in 1974 as the San Diego Mariners they became competitive and credible.

Sportswriter Bill Verigan was the only New York City beat writer who witnessed the WHA Raiders' birth and struggles. He began his career with UPI and ended as the beat writer for the Newark Star-Ledger covering the NHL Devils. Verigan spent an amazing 28 years in between those posts with the New York Daily News covering auto racing, boxing, baseball, the NFL Jets and Giants – and the New York Raiders for the WHA's 1972-1973 inaugural season.

Verigan spoke with Timothy Gassen in December 2010 about his introduction to major league hockey with the WHA New York Raiders.

GASSEN: Would you talk about your perception of the Raiders and the WHA as this assignment was handed to you at the very beginning of the league in 1972?

VERIGAN: I treated every beat as if it was the most important beat on the paper. But I was not an NHL fan. And, so, when I got the Raiders as a beat, I sort of had empathy for it. And I liked the underdog attitude and everything that came with it.

And I sort of developed that, too, in covering them, and became sort of an advocate for the league. And, of course, the NHL had expanded and had brought in the Islanders at that point. And the Islanders in those very formative years, they were just a bad expansion team.

And I can remember the Raiders comparing themselves to the Islanders a great deal, and they would make fun of the Islanders by comparison, of course. But it didn't take long for the Islanders to become a dominant team and the Raiders to disappear from the scene.

GASSEN: Do you think if the Raiders could have been on Long Island instead of competing directly against the Rangers at Madison Square Garden that that franchise would've had a better chance in New York?

VERGIAN: Oh, I think it definitely would have. I think that the Raiders would have drawn much better and gotten a lot more attention out there. There would've been more excitement about the franchise if they had been able to move into the Long Island arena there.

GASSEN: Now, do you believe that's the only reason why the Islanders were put in that building at that time, to keep the WHA out of the brand new building on Long Island?

VERIGAN: I would think that they were trying to take as much existing talent away from the WHA as possible. And I really would say that there was a bit of that in that decision, quite frankly. It makes sense, doesn't it? That they would want to shut the Raiders out of that New York market.

GASSEN: Yes! Now, when I started following the league in its third year through the end of the WHA, year by year, the quality of the play really, really improved. By the mid-1970s — and I followed both leagues — I thought the leagues were extremely similar in talent. And I actually preferred the style of play in the WHA. But what were your impressions for this very first year of the WHA as the league was trying to find its footing, not only commercially, but on the ice? Can you talk about the style of play and some of your favorite players on that Raiders team?

VERIGAN: Well, the Raiders' style was pretty wide open. Camille Henry was the coach, and with the Raider players it pretty much was a free-for-all. With the Raiders you saw pretty much helter-skelter out there on the ice. Which was fun, and they had a very loosey-goosey attitude toward life and hockey.

The star of the team was unquestionably Bobby Sheehan, who had played for Oakland and California — for the Golden Seals.

GASSEN: Right.

VERIGAN: And he came to New York and he really had nothing except a gaudy, plastic, green suitcase that (Seals owner) Charlie Finley had given all the players. And those were pretty much his possessions at that point. And he moved in with me, and it was one of the most memorable events of my life.

There was another NHL player of some consequence named Billy Speer, who was a defenseman. But Billy Speer was a very free spirit, also. And quite overweight by the time he hit the Raiders. And his second occupation was being a hairdresser. And it was rather interesting, because when we would go on a road trip, he would always visit the hair salons, picking up tips. And, quite frankly, picking up (female) hairdressers in every town we hit, which added to the whole scene of the Raiders on the road.

But I would say that those were the two players that were the most memorable. The rest of the team, it was not a good team. And that was a tragedy for the league. If they were going to come to New York, they needed to come with a franchise that was going to be very competitive and play great hockey.

And they didn't. It was a bad team. Not mediocre, but bad. And Sheehan was a complete free spirit, and his pattern sort of followed the pattern of his career with the Raiders. He would burn himself out completely by the second half of a season. And he could be the leading scorer in the league for the first half of a season, which he was, on occasions, right up among those guys, both in the NHL and in the WHA. But by the end of the season, he'd be down in the middle of the pack. And it was not always in terms of the season. It was in terms of a game.

He would come out and he had long, blondish hair, and he was an American, and he was, at that point, I felt that he was the quickest and fastest player on the ice in hockey. And I had seen the NHL guys, too, and I felt that he was exemplary.

And once his career with the WHA ended, the (NHL) Rangers, years later, made the playoffs and needed somebody to provide a spark. And, lo and behold, they somehow dug up the name of Bobby Sheehan. And he came in and provided several goals and was just spectacular in those brief playoff appearances.

Probably, that's what his whole career should have been — it should've been 12 games, 12 playoff games instead of a full season. But he was just a loveable, likeable guy. He was at the bars every night in Manhattan. And I mean every night. And would be hung over for many games. But he was the image of the Raiders in that first year. Camille Henry, the coach, was just at wit's end. Of course, Camille had played for great (NHL) teams, and he had been a great player.

GASSEN: As the only New York beat writer following the WHA, you must have gotten a unique look at the league while following the Raiders on the road.

VERIGAN: And I will relate one road trip that we went on, which was typical. *(Verigan had written previously, with tongue in cheek, that "Those road trips never made it into the newspaper. My editor said he didn't want to kill the league or print pornography." – Editor)*

We started out — I guess it must have been about six games. And we started out in Minnesota. And I was the only writer who traveled with the team.

I was young, and they were young, some of them. And we were sort of kindred spirits out there on the road. And I remember walking to my room in the Minnesota hotel and I had the distinct scent of marijuana smoke billowing out from under a door where I knew one of the players — I didn't know which one. But one of the players was in that room. And I didn't think that would be a good idea in Minnesota in those days to have it be so evident that you could get a contact high just walking down the hotel corridor.

GASSEN: *(laughing)* Yes!

VERIGAN: So, I knocked on the door and low and behold, there was a party inside. I would say there were probably crammed into this room, oh, 30 people, including players and hairdressers and assorted others. And the lights were out, so it was hard to see who was there. And I joined the party for a little while, and they put towels down in front of the door so the fumes would not permeate the entire hotel.

But that was the first night of the trip, I guess. They went to Winnipeg next on that trip and they actually won. They had two games in three nights. I believe it was two games over a three-night period there, because it was a long haul. And they actually won the first game, which was a major accomplishment.

And Camille Henry made a very unwise decision of presenting the team with a keg of beer. And all of the players, they put the keg in the hall, and they all sat in the hall and drank beer. And, as chance would have it, there was a hairdressers' convention in the hotel. And Speer was in his element, and — anyone who came down that hall was — I mean, it was like a — they were sort of taking their virginity or whatever in their hands. And Camille realized he had made a serious mistake and comes up on the floor. And he was told that he was unwelcome. And he wanted them to calm down, and they did not exactly want to calm down at that point.

And they told him, quite frankly, that if he came on their floor again, they would throw him out of the window at the end of the hall. And they were on the third floor. So, he left.

The next morning, when I got up to go down to breakfast, I pushed the elevator button, and when it came up to my floor, I was greeted by Bobby Sheehan asleep on the elevator floor.

That night I don't think they got a shot on net for — it was more than well over a period.

Oh, and I might add, there were also some of the Winnipeg cheerleaders, they were pretty young women. I don't know if they would qualify as cheerleaders or exactly what their role was. But they were joining the beer party, too, that night.

And this made the Winnipeg management extremely angry because at least one of them was the daughter of one the owners of the Winnipeg team, and I don't think he appreciated having his daughter associate with these ruffians from New York who were really not on their best behavior.

GASSEN: *(laughing)* Oh boy...

VERIGAN: So, there may have been a pep talk in the Winnipeg locker room about the Raiders, too, before that second game. *(laughter)*

Then, the trip wound up in Los Angeles. And I have been with a lot of pro teams, and I have never seen a pro team where it looked like there was almost going to be a strip search of ever member of the hockey team.

I don't know if they had heard about Minnesota or what at that point, but it took hours to go through customs. And the players got to the hotel about 1:00 in the morning. And we stayed at the hotel where Bobby Kennedy had been killed.

I wasn't particularly sleepy, so, I decided to walk around and see if I could look around the area — in the kitchen, for instance, where the attack had occurred. And I was just wandering around the hotel. I walked outside for a few minutes, and I hear a rustling in a hedge. And so, I — I mean, I probably should have run, but I walked over to see what was causing it, and it was Camille Henry hiding in the hedge, trying to catch players leaving the hotel.

And I said, "Camille..." — and I was basically a kid, in comparison to Camille. But I said, "Camille, you know, that's not good. You can't hide in the hedge," I said, "Go to bed." And he took my advice.

But he was at wit's end by the time we had hit that stop on the trip. And I felt very bad for him. He was a very kind, nice, gentle man. And he was overrun by these barbarians on the team, who were just there to have fun.

GASSEN: It was a time of great change in how major league athletes and coaches dealt with each other. Coaches soon wouldn't get away with the iron hand like before.

VERIGAN: I remember a trip we made to Quebec, oh, three-quarters of the way through the season. And Herb Elk was the (assistant) general manager, and my room happened to be next to his room. I can remember hearing right through the wall of the hotel him saying, "Well, what am I supposed to do if we don't have any money to pay them?" It was payday, and the Raiders had run out of money. This was another tragedy for the WHA in New York.

If we wanted to look in retrospect, perhaps the Raiders set the entire WHA back a year or so, you know? As far as getting the recognition they wanted. I called him and I said, "I heard that the checks have all bounced for the team." I said, "What are you going to do?"

He says, "Well, I'm going to have to talk to them. And I really don't want to do that." He says, "I'm really a wreck." I said, "Well, you have to talk to them." I said, "You have to let them know that they aren't getting paid tonight."

And he says, "Yeah. What do you think I should do?" "Well," I said, "why don't you just call the captains up and talk to them and see what they suggest."

And he did. And the Raiders played that night. Played poorly. But those were, perhaps, my most vivid memories of the Raiders. Those were wild days for a franchise that was, without question, the most colorful, strange collection of players I ever encountered in my life.

GASSEN: Now, do you remember a defenseman on that Raiders team, Ken Block?

VERIGAN: Yeah. And there was also — there was a black player, one of the very few black players in hockey at the time.

GASSEN: Alton White was his name, wasn't it?

VERIGAN: Yes, it was. There were quite a few racial slurs and remarks, and he never — he was a very, very, very classy guy. I mean a super guy. And he never really was permitted to fit in with the Raiders in any way. They did not accept him, which was sad, because I thought he was a very gentle guy. But I felt that he had a potential that most of the Raiders did not have.

GASSEN: And The Raiders didn't have the time to develop their talent.

VERIGAN: Within a year they decided to change the name to the Golden Blades. And they really had run out of money. Madison Square Garden was a huge nut to cover.

GASSEN: Unsustainable.

VERIGAN: And they certainly could not do it with the — I wouldn't call them crowds. I would say with the "audiences" that they attracted, which were very, very meager. The dates that they were given to play in the Garden were horrible. Matinees on weekends! The Raiders were definitely a negative for the league.

GASSEN: Now, Bill, were you covering the team when they turned into the Golden Blades the following season, and then, later, into the Jersey Knights?

VERIGAN: No, I disappeared from the scene by that point. I really covered them for only that first year.

GASSEN: Did you have the opportunity to see the league later on, even though they didn't have a presence in New York? Did you ever see how the league had progressed?

VERIGAN: Yeah, I did. I saw it quite a bit. And, of course, when they eventually merged, they were on the par with the NHL, very competitive.

GASSEN: I believe so, too, yes.

VERIGAN: Yeah, they were exciting — they became an exciting league.

GASSEN: Did you go to Hartford when you were covering other events and you were in a town, would you go see a team? How were you able to see them?

VERIGAN: I did go to Hartford, and I did see them on TV a few times. As soon as they moved out of Madison Square Garden, the New York Daily News lost complete interest in them. So, we went from having them covered as a beat to being not covered at all. I doubt if the rest of their time in existence, if there were more than three or four stories on them.

The Rangers were the show, and even when the Rangers were not successful, they were still the show. They had extremely loyal fans, they sold out every game. They had a following that was rabid, and it's almost like even now, there's probably two Ranger fans for every Devils and Islander fan combined in the New York area.

GASSEN: Well, I think this was a vital mistake the WHA made in trying to put teams right up in direct competition in NHL cities. They didn't win one of those fights. It's amazing the WHA survived after making such a mistake. And I think they were surprised, actually, that they were most popular when they weren't competing against the NHL, and places like Edmonton and Winnipeg and Indianapolis embraced it as its own major league.

VERIGAN: And Quebec.

GASSEN: Yes, the Nordiques!

VERIGAN: All of these places that were hockey hungry and had no NHL franchises — they were dying for teams, you know? And they supported them. And probably — in retrospect, as I said, the decision to have a team in New York may have set the WHA back a year or so. The NHL was a very small, very, very small league without many franchises. So I kind of think if they (the WHA) had completely ignored New York, they would've been better off.

GASSEN: Talking about media opportunity, wasn't John Sterling, the longtime Yankees baseball announcer, the first-year radio play-by-play guy for the Raiders?

VERIGAN: That's right. Sterling may have been the most obvious vestige of credibility that the team had in that year. He was a big-time guy, you know? And a very nice man. And he was a very positive factor for the team.

The Raiders just simply did not have very much good, young talent. And they really were cheap.

But it was a fascinating period, and it was a great deal of fun to cover the league. And it was a good introduction to hockey for me.

THE WORLD HOCKEY ASSOCIATION
WHA
HALL OF FAME
HONORING THE 1972-1979 MAJOR LEAGUE

STORIES ABOUT
THE LEAGUE & TEAMS

Hockey's Incredible Happening

BY WALT MARLOW

Major league hockey, since 1968, has experienced attendance acceleration amounting to 113 per cent ----more than any other major league sport.

In the past eight years, the number of major league teams in hockey has skyrocketed from six to an incredible 32. Canada, the world's premier producer of hockey livestock, serves as home for eight of them.

Most startling in this unprecedented growth of a single sport, to be sure, has been the emergence of the World Hockey Association. In a mere two winters, the league that "couldn't happen" has clearly established itself as an integral element in the world's hockey structure.

First it was Robert Marvin Hull.

Then came the incredible unretiring of Gordie Howe and the meteoric rise of his two sons, Marty and Mark.

And as the league embarks on Year III of its' phenomenal journey into sports history, the newest magic name is William Francis (Frank) Mahovlich.

He joins six Swedish, and two Czechoslovakian imports, another 30 major league acquisitions, and the seizure of no fewer than 15 of the top graduating juniors in Canada.

"The magnitude of our growth over a mere two years is unchallenged in sports history," said President Dennis A. Murphy of the league he, in concert with Edmonton's Bill Hunter and Winnipeg's Ben Hatskin, launched in

Gordie, Mark and Marty Howe

the face of incredible odds in June of 1971. "We are no longer regarded as the other league, but rather an integral part of the world's hockey structure."

"While our procurement of players of major league stature represented expectations, our greatest gain as we enter this third season was in the category of graduating juniors and the caliber thereof."

"Franchise holders like Jimmy Pattison in Vancouver, Nick Mileti in Cleveland, Bert Getz in Phoenix, Bill DeWitt in Cincinnati, Jordon Kaiser in Chicago, Irv Kaplan in Houston, Bob Schmertz and Howard Baldwin in New England, Charles Nolton in Detroit, Richard Tinkham in Indianapolis and Wayne Belisle in Minnesota have hastened that day when it will be the WHA that has the abundance of super stars."

The elite harvested from last season's amateur crop included the likes of Pat Price and Ron Chipperfield by Vancouver, Dennis Sobchuk, Jacques Locas, John Hughes and Dick Spannbauer by Cincinnati, Gary McGregor by Chicago, Cam Connor, Dave Gorman and Dennis Olmstead by Phoenix, Bill Reed, Bill Evo and Barry Legge by Michigan, Paul Baxter by Cleveland, Real Cloutier by Quebec, Kevin Devine by San Diego, Terry Ruskowski and Don Larway by Houston and Craig Hammer by Indianapolis.

An examination of outstanding WHA

rookies of a season ago---like the Howe boys and Jim Sherritt (Houston), Wayne Dillon and Pat Hickey (Toronto), Frankie Rochon (Chicago) Tom Edur (Cleveland), Kevin Morrison (San Diego), Claude St. Sauveur (Vancouver), Michel Deguise and Richard Brodeur (Quebec) and John Garrett, Gord Gallant and Murray Heatley (Minnesota)---and it's readily apparent that the WHA, indeed, does have livestock of future super star quality.

"Our need for the established player has lessened considerably," says Murphy. "We're starting to produce new stars for new fans. The future strength of this league is in its' youth and the tapping of the vast European market."

Exploration of that overseas reservoir, to be sure, has already commenced with New England's signing of the Abrahamsson twins, Thommy and Christer---while Winnipeg lured four Swedes---Curt Larrson, Anders Hedberg, Ulf Nilsson and Lars Erik Sjoberg.

But it remained for Toronto's John Bassett, Jr. to generate international headlines with his capture of Czechoslovakian super star Vaclav Nedomansky and his teammate Richard Farda.

Nedomansky, 30, is known in Europe as "Big Ned", but doubtless will become "The Big N" of the Toros where he'll fit nicely with the "Big M" (Mahovlich).

Frank Mahovlich, Toronto Toros

Murphy, a virtuoso in sports organization, was the WHA's first visionary. While hockey scientists the world over prophesied disaster, the Californian who earlier had fashioned the master plan for the establishment of the American Basketball Association approached his task with evangelistic fervor---preaching the gospel of a new league to men of uncommon means in two countries.

Elimination of the reserve and/or option clause in contracts, which freed athletes from lifelong bondage to a single team, irrefutably represented the single most important act in the league's formation.

The momentous decision, rendered Nov. 8, 1972, by U. S. District Court Judge A. Leon Higginbotham in Philadelphia, freed Robert Marvin Hull and other distinguished major leaguers to function in the league of their choice.

Until then, of course, it was the Hull signing itself, on June 27, 1972, that skyrocketed the WHA into sports page prominence.

Hatskin, chairman of the league's board of trustees and an instrumental force in bringing about this fall's historic WHA series with the Soviet Union, engineered the phenomenal coup with a $2.75 million contract for hockey's greatest left winger. The Golden Jet was now a Winnipeg Jet.

"Certainly that was the play that altered our early image," reflected Murphy, "The skeptics developed nervous disorders when Bobby came aboard."

The Hull acquisition, aside from the image impact, also touched off an avalanche of fresh signings, 28 within a period of a week. They included the likes of Gerry Cheevers with Cleveland, Ted Green with New England and Bobby Sheehan, now on the roster of the Edmonton Oilers.

With the signings came a number of nuisance litigations, none of which had any significant bearing on curtailing the league's growth.

Then there was the WHA's $50 million anti-trust damage suit against the 57-year-old National League. It, to be sure, was not to be confused with nuisance.

It climaxed February 19, 1974, in an out of court settlement, 32 months from when the league filed articles of incorporation in June of 1971, with the NHL picking up the tab for WHA legal costs in the amount of $1.75 million. More importantly, the settlement represented recognition of the WHA by the NHL, with both leagues agreeing to a series of exhibition games, honoring of each other's contracts, etc.

"This is a major step to the co-existence of the two leagues," said Murphy, a graduate of the University of Southern California, who had taken

Gordie Howe

Bobby Hull

over the presidency two months prior following the abdication of Gary Davidson. The latter had collaborated with Murphy, Hunter and Hatskin in the WHA's birth pains.

"It had been our position from the beginning that we can co-exist with the NHL, and that both leagues can retain their individuality," added Murphy, "Elimination of what was a perpetual reserve clause without having to go to trial represents total victory over what we started."

By now, of course, the WHA's sovereignty was no longer a matter of conjecture.

The incomparable Gordie Howe, along with his two sons, Mark and Marty, had joined the ranks of the Houston Aeros to mark the first time in history of any major league sport that a father had played alongside of two sons.

"Howe's signing alone was a coup rivaling that of the Hull signing," reflected Edmonton's Hunter, "But for his two boys to join him, two future super stars, today stands as the most monumental event in the history of hockey. The chances of it happening again are a million to one."

Proclaiming that while there's a little snow on the roof, there's still fire in the furnace, hockey's living legend-- 21 months in retirement to the

contrary---orchestrated the Aeros to the Avco World Trophy.

And like Hull in the WHA's baptismal year, Gordie emerged the MVP and a first team all-star. Not even son Mark, rookie of the year at 19, is convinced that his ol' man is 46.

A testimony to Howe's greatness was evident at the annual Charley Conacher Memorial Dinner in Toronto this past May when he modestly captured the audience with two standing ovations.

Announcing that hockey had become so much fun again that he would play another season, he attributed his MVP honors to the fact that he had sired two sons to cover up his mistakes.

Mistakes? All he did was score 31 goals and contribute 69 assists.

While it would be a friendly exaggeration to suggest that the WHA, in two seasons, has attained the stability representative of long established leagues, there are unmistakable signs for the unwavering belief of success exhibited by the league's 15 franchise holders.

Of monumental significance this season is the fact that the WHA has established an all-Canadian division of Vancouver, Edmonton, Winnipeg, Toronto and Quebec. In essence, Canada now has it's own major hockey league for the first time in history.

The WHA's Western Division is comprised of Houston, Michigan, Phoenix, Minnesota and San Diego, while in the East it's New England, Chicago, Cleveland and Indianapolis, with Cincinnati taking up residence a year from now.

Meanwhile the Stingers, headed up by the aggressive Bill DeWitt, Jr. have assigned their signed players to other clubs in the league.

Indianapolis and Phoenix, plus the shifting of the New Jersey franchise to San Diego and Los Angeles to Detroit, represents the league's new look this season. Not to be overlooked, of course, is the new look in playing facilities, too.

Certainly Edmonton's new 16,000 capacity Coliseum will enhance the WHA's immage, as will Cleveland's new Coliseum and Hartford's new arena which will become the home of the New England Whalers, who won it all in the first historic season.

"Our potential now is limitless," says Murphy, who first teamed with Hunter and the Canadian contingent five months into the league's talking stages. Thereafter, it was a story of perpetual motion.

"Funny, how a lot of critics, people who should know better, said we'd never hit the ice. But the only critics that really count are the guys and gals who pay the shot."

"Our credibility is of their doing."

GARY DAVIDSON AND THE WHA

By Lee Meade

It seems unlikely there were any historians on hand, with paper prepared and pencils poised, when a young Southern California attorney decided maybe the best way to run a major professional sports league was without the pesky reserve clause.

What is known, however, is that a withering bolt of legal lightning struck the world of professional sports when Gary L. Davidson announced the World Hockey Association would operate without a reserve clause or an option clause in its player contracts.

Davidson's approach to the controversial reserve clause was direct and to-the-point.

"I believe if a major league is to be truly successful, it has to be a league that holds the interests of the owners and the interests of the players in the same esteem."

Davidson went ahead with the largest player draft in the history of professional sports, and when it was over the 12 WHA teams had screened every professional, amateur, intercollegiate and junior hockey player in the world.

A Chicago hockey writer predicted the WHA's chance of success was bleak because it "lacks three things: players, arenas and television."

So, armed with Davidson's theory the reserve clause was illegal, the 12 WHA teams signed more than 70 players from the NHL, giving each of them the only opportunity in their hockey-playing lives to improve their position by considering an alternative contract proposal.

Arenas suddenly became available to the new league. Some, were there to be rented. The St. Paul Civic Center—a $19 million hockey showplace of the world—was built. Others were renovated and provided with hockey facilities for the first time.

No professional sport has achieved success until it had network television exposure. In the WHA's first year, Davidson negotiated television contracts in two nations—with the Columbia Broadcasting System in the U.S. and the Canadian Broadcasting Corporation in Canada.

Davidson, at 38, was five years older and wiser than when he cut his teeth in organized sports as the first president of the American Basketball Association. Drawing from that experience, he had answers for every question and solutions to every problem.

With each passing week, the WHA gained credibility. On Wednesday, October 11, 1972, the WHA dropped its first puck.

Davidson had called the shots all the way.

Where did it begin? How did it come to be?

It began in a dream, at least as early as 1967. That was when Dennis Arthur Murphy of Fullerton, Calif., was planning the ABA, and, in the back of his mind, thinking ahead to the WHA.

Four years later, it was Murphy, again, who telephoned Davidson to tell him of his idea to start the World Hockey Association. On July 10, 1971, Articles of Incorporation for the WHA were filed in Delaware and By-Laws were drawn with Davidson, Murphy and Donald J. Regan, a law partner of Davidson's, as officers.

Born in Missoula, Mont., August 13, 1934, Davidson moved to California with his mother when he was in first grade.

At Garden Grove (Calif.) High School, where he was an A student, Davidson lettered in football, basketball, baseball and track. He was an All-League second baseman and American Legion junior baseball All-Star.

For 15 years, since graduating from UCLA Law School, he has played on a team in an AAU basketball league in Santa Ana.

He's also a tennis player of note and can hold his own on a handball court.

A partner in the law firm of Nagel, Regan and Davidson, Gary has learned the value of surrounding himself with competent partners and delegating responsibilities.

He is Chairman of the Board of General Residential Corporation, President of Mammoth Sports, Inc., and Chairman of the Board of SIS, Inc.

A devoted family man, he lives with his wife, Barbie, and their four children in Laguna Beach.

"Creating the league was more fun and more satisfying than the everyday job of running it," he said. "The operation phase is a major job, however, and you are required to solve a lot of problems.

"Before, when the league was being formed, everyone was pulling together," he continued. "Now, these same people are adversaries and they all rightfully want to win."

Davidson is greatly impressed by the integrity of his partner-owners in the WHA, however.

"They'll try to wipe each other out on the ice, then ask if there's anything they can do to help when the game is over," he said. "The association has been an enriching experience for me."

Davidson runs the league with quiet discipline.

"I make my decisions on what I believe is best for the WHA," he said. "Personalities don't enter into it.

"We hoped for and worked hard to achieve parity within the league, and I think we have it," he declared. "The caliber of play has been of a level that no one denies our claim to being a major league. I heard one television commentator suggest that a series between a couple of our teams and the NHL champion probably would be a six-game match, and he wasn't at all sure which would win.

"I'm satisfied we've come a long way in one year. We've organized a league, signed more than 300 players, played a 468-game schedule, negotiated national television contracts, started an international properties and marketing subsidiary and had our position on the rights of players to determine their own destiny upheld in court. It's been a great first year.

"I'm not a hockey man, but I've seen enough of it to realize it's the fastest growing sport in the world. I see a true World Series of hockey in the future, with our champion competing against teams from Europe and Asia."

And the NHL?

"That depends a great deal upon the NHL," he answered. "We're not seeking a merger with them. We just want the right to compete in the major league marketplace. The courts have already told us we have that right.

"We're ready to play them on the ice, too."

The Exciting Difference

Hockey, it has been said, is a game combining all the elements—grace, speed, emotion, violence.

The purists said there just wasn't any room for improvement. But that was before the WHA came along.

World Hockey's rulebook, for the most part, duplicates that of any other professional league. There have been, however, several innovations that give the WHA a distinctive flavor.

Take, for example, the WHA's overtime format.

Over three seasons, there have been 191 overtime games, with 127 decisions rendered as against a mere 64 ties.

Beyond overtime and its attendant drama, other areas where WHA rules differ from other professional leagues are in *OFFSIDE PASSES, CURVATURE OF THE STICK,* and the *THIRD MAN RULE.*

OFFSIDE PASS

In other leagues, a completed forward pass that crosses two lines is ruled offside unless the 'receiver' was in the same area of the ice as the 'passer' when the pass was made. In the WHA, a player may pass the puck from inside his own blueline to a teammate beyond the center red line, providing the puck precedes the player across the center red line and the receiver takes the puck ahead of his body. The rule is designed to bring about more quick breaks, but at the same time preventing a player from floating beyond the red line awaiting a breakaway pass.

STICK CURVATURE

The National League restricts the curvature of the stick blade to half an inch, mainly for the reason that goaltenders complain that curved blades represent an unfair advantage for the shooter adept at making the puck do tricks. The WHA has an allowable curvature of an inch and a quarter, resulting in more difficult shots for the goaltenders.

THIRD MAN RULE

The WHA's *"third man rule in an altercation"* is somewhat more realistic than in other leagues where an automatic game misconduct is issued.

Depending on the actions of the *"third man"* WHA officials have the option of issuing *NO PENALTY, A TWO-MINUTE MINOR, FIVE-MINUTE MAJOR* or *10-MINUTE MISCONDUCT.* A game misconduct applies to second time violators in a single game.

The WHA

Gary Davidson's Second Success Story

It began in the Never-Neverland of man's imagination. Some sportwriters christened it the Wishful Hockey Association. It held its first draft meeting just across the street from Fantasyland in Anaheim, Calif.

But the World Hockey Association has survived the laughter, the pessimism and the indifference. It is now a viable, tangible member of the major league sports scene.

And from Day One, the man at the top has been Gary L. Davidson, a Southern California attorney who's been through all this before.

After organizing the American Basketball Association in 1967 and serving as its first president, Davidson moved into hockey last year and the WHA is the result.

Which makes Davidson 2-for-2.

The WHA is "for real." The league is now firmly entrenched in 12 strong cities, is nearing the 100 mark in announced player signings and is converting skeptics daily.

Bobby Hull's signing with the WHA is testimonial to this reality, to Davidson and to the men he found to become partners in the new league.

Davidson, President of the WHA, professes no great hockey knowledge.

"That's what general managers and coaches give an organization," he says.

He does recognize the astounding rise in popularity of hockey in the United States and elsewhere in the world, and he expects the WHA to find the road less grueling than did the ABA.

"For one thing," he says, "hockey outdraws basketball tremendously. It's a much faster sport.

"I see the WHA reaching parity with the National Hockey League within three years, and I'm talking about the top NHL clubs. I see a European Division and an Asian Division coming within the next four years."

A 37-year-old graduate of UCLA Law School, Davidson does not approach professional sports like the former athlete he is. Rather, he calls himself a professional financial manager who puts together financial packages for professional sports and other business ventures.

"I don't practice law anymore," Davidson says. "I'm basically oriented to do financing."

Davidson's close friend and partner in founding both the ABA and the WHA is Dennis A. Murphy, now President and General Manager of the Los Angeles Sharks.

"Because of our prior experience in the ABA," explains Davidson, "we figured we had more experience than anybody in the world."

Blonde and boyish, Davidson looks a good deal like motion picture actor Robert Redford. He is a physically active man, the result of years of athletic competition.

18

WHALER WELCOME — Howard Baldwin (right), president of the New England Whalers, welcomed Davidson to the club's executive offices in the Statler Office Building when Gary came to Boston to view the Whalers' operation first hand.

For 15 years, he played on a team in an AAU basketball league in Santa Ana, Calif. WHA Legal Counsel Donald Regan and Assistant Legal Counsel Tim Grandi are members of the team, which won the Orange County championship two years ago.

Davidson also is a tennis player of some note.

At Garden Grove (Calif.) High School, where he was an A student, Davidson lettered in football, basketball, baseball and track. He was an All-League second baseman and American Legion baseball All-Star.

Born in Missoula, Mont., August 13, 1934, Davidson and his mother moved to California when Gary was in first grade, following his parents' separation.

"I am a firm believer in the value of athletics," he says. "I know they helped me stay on the right track."

Working in the WHA offices means avoiding Davidson on the building's main floor. Less physical staffers know if the WHA President spots them they will have to walk the five flights of stairs up to the league suite. Davidson shuns the use of elevators for so minimal a trek.

A partner in the law firm of Nagel, Regan and Davidson, Gary is the originator of the WHA's unique position on the reserve clause and option clause. The new league has neither.

"I believe if a major league is to be truly successful," he says, "it has to be a league that holds the interests of the owners and the interests of the players in the same esteem."

Davidson still owns a minority interest in the ABA's Dallas Chaparrals. He also is Chairman of the Board of General Residential Corporation, a firm that builds residential care homes; President of Mammoth Sports, Inc., a leisure recreational land development company, and Chairman of the Board of FIF, Inc., a temporary employment services company.

His mother works for him at General Residential and now, as he contemplates the WHA's future, he can look from his office window onto a spot where once there was a supermarket. His mother was a cashier in that supermarket.

But that was many years and two leagues ago.

THE MAN

BEN HATSKIN

Louis Hatskin's success as a businessman, devotion as a husband, and guidance as a father, are a matter of record. Here was a man, who in 1911, with his wife Annie Cohen, had travelled almost 5,000 miles from Proprask, Russia to Winnipeg. Starting from scratch his wooden box plant business was coming along nicely. They were blessed with two fine sons, Benjamin, born in 1918 and Ruben, six years his junior. The family were beginning to enjoy the good things of life after years of struggle.

The year is 1931. Ben is now 13. His father would prefer that his affinity for

HATSKIN

sports gave way to culture and the arts. However, no amount of parental persuasion could force him to take lessons on the violin and mandolin. Looking back Ben says "can you imagine a baby hippopotamus playing the fiddle. After all I weighed about 185 pounds on a 5'8'' frame.'' Close friends of Ben's claim he told his father "the music I love to hear is played on a cash register.''

About the same time, a cousin, now doctor Joe Ludwig, was taking art lessons. Before he knew what was happening, Ben was enrolled in the class but was preoccupied with the sketching of dollar bills and the more the merrier. Besides, Saturday mornings were hardly the time for art lessons. As captain of his midget soccer squad his presence was required elsewhere.

Tagged "Fats" by his boyhood pals, extra poundage never prevented him from being a "good serious athlete." Still carrying too much weight, "not because he has a big appetite but he's a nibbler," Ben's physical activity is now restricted to an occasional round of golf.

Ben Hatskin's passion for sports, if anything, has grown stronger through the years. In many ways it has set the pattern for his life.

Certainly his grades at Ralph Brown and Aberdeen Schools, and St. Johns Technical High School would not have earned him a scholarship at Oklahoma University. Nevertheless, Ben Hatskin was one of the first Canadians to win a football scholarship south of the border. That was in 1938 after his rookie season with the Winnipeg Blue Bombers. His prowess on the gridiron had been established with YMHA and Deer Lodge Juniors, the latter city champions.

The war cut short his stay at Oklahoma. Upon returning home he suited up again with the Blue and Gold. He centred two Grey Cup champions, 1939 and 1941, in his 6 season tenure with the Bombers. As a high school football coach with Kelvin, one of his players remembers him "as a helluva good one."

The man who negotiated a two and a half million dollar contract for a single hockey player himself signed to play a rigorous season of pro football for $100.00. That was 1937, his rookie season. By 1939 his worth had risen to $900.00. Unlike the rest of his teammates who took periodic cash advances throughout that season, Ben decided to take his in one lump sum at the end of the campaign so he could buy a car. Unfortunately the coffers were

bare and all GM Joe Pyan could pay him was $280.00. That was one of the few mistakes Ben has made in his lifetime.

Not many greenhorns can get into the horse racing dodge and come out of it better than even.

In 1944 Ben and Les Lear, a boyhood friend and football teammate, formed a stable. Their blue and white colors raced the western circuit for quite a few years. In 1957 Ben went out on his own with Hatskin's Farms. His stable of 15 horses raced on some of the best tracks south of the border.

Master Palynch set a track record in winning the 1959 Louisiana Derby at New Orleans. That rates as the stable's major victory and was worth $50,000 to Ben Hatskin.

The passage of time and some millions of dollars later prove how well Ben planned his own fate.

The Hatskin family sold their plants in Calgary and Winnipeg, and their lumber camps,. after almost a half century in the wooden box and corrugated paper box business. Ben and brother Rube shifted their interest, business acumen and money into a number of companies: James Realty—Hatskin Containers—Lodge Investments and Triangle Acceptance. In 1966 they bought Universal Music which is the largest juke box distributor in the three prairie provinces. He's been in half a dozen other businesses over the last decade.

Now's as good a time as any to answer the question "what makes Ben Hatskin tick and why is he a success?"

"Ben has a fierce pride. It pushes him to the ultimate, supreme effort in any undertaking. He's protective and a friend forever to those he likes." So says Cecila Rasch a vivacious, cultured woman who has known Ben for 35 years, the last 26 of them intimately as Mrs. Hatskin.

One thing you can bet on. The Winnipeg Jets and hockey won't be the final chapter in the life of Ben Hatskin.

But until he moves on to other ventures Ben "sees this thing as the most exciting and fantastic challenge of my life."

Brother Rube analyzes him this way: "Ben is a soft touch. He'll go a long way with someone he likes. Determination, pride, aggressiveness: they're his main characteristics. Having a summer home, lying around doing nothing, vacations, they're not for him. He has to be active—mentally if not physically, although it was both when he was younger."

Dave Simkin, a longtime friend comments "Ben has big shoulders, he can take it. Criticism, unkind or untrue allegations, roadblocks, disappointments, don't seem to faze him. Or if they do, you'd never know it."

Let's hear now from Big Ben himself. "I talked to Clarence Campbell about getting into the NHL before the second expansion. He called me back and said we'd need a rink seating a guaranteed 16,000 and $7.2 million entry fee. When the idea of a second major league originated I was all for it. I figured it was maybe the only chance our city would ever have to go major league in any sport. The WHA became a reality and its success became more and more important with each passing day. After all we got in deeper and deeper and besides we had something to prove to the disbelievers who were by far in the majority."

About Bobby Hull, the Superstar with Chicago Black Hawks. "I felt we'd get a good percentage of NHL players. But getting a superstar like Hull would mean instant-league in the minds of the public and the news media. Also it would cause other players to take the WHA seriously. There are only 3 or 4 superstars in hockey. All but Hull were tied up. He was our trump card. We went after him and we got him."

It wasn't that simple and there undoubtedly are pit-

falls ahead. Jets executive manager Terry Hind says "Ben can take on a number of problems covering a wide range of matters, without making a production of it, he also has a good memory. Ben doesn't cultivate people—no phony airs, no showing off, and he's not a back-patter or glad-hander. You take him as he is. I wish people could know him for the good guy he is."

It's time now for the hockey chapter. Ben's love for hockey goes back to the 1930's when he was a pretty good defenseman in juvenile and junior brackets. But Hatskin's name first came into real prominence on the local hockey scene 6 years ago, when he entered the Western Canada Junior Hockey League with the team now known as the Winnipeg Jets. Despite a feud with the CAHA the league flourished and Ben ended up bank-rolling at least three other franchises under the table to put it on its feet. Today the W.C.H.L. is a thriving 12 team operation.

Playing the godfather to an entire league is ironically similar to what he's doing now.

"Ben Hatskin has been the strong man in our embryonic stages and much of the progress of our league can be credited to him." That tribute comes from World Hockey Association President Gary Davidson.

THE AVCO WORLD TROPHY

Epitome of that which is the best.

That's the Avco World Trophy, emblematic of World Hockey Association supremacy.

And, like its Stanley Cup counterpart, the Avco Trophy already has experienced a history of turmoil.

Due in Houston this past May when the Aeros and Chicago Cougars were battling for the WHA championship, the Trophy disappeared in transit from a trophy house in Boston where it had been undergoing extensive repairs from a prior mis-adventure.

On the day the Aeros swept to the WHA title, the Trophy . . or rather what was left of it . . . was discovered seven hours before game time in a Houston airport freight shed.

It was in three pieces.

And to compound the problem, it was a Sunday.

A WHA official, following a series of frantic phone calls, finally found a silversmith who agreed to try and make the prized hardware presentable.

He was able to smooth out enough dents and afix detached parts to have the trophy ready for its historic journey around the Sam Houston Coliseum ice surface carried high by Aeros' Captain Ted Taylor.

The WHA championship trophy was designed for Avco by noted Canadian artist, Donald W. Murphy, well-known painter and sculptor who specializes in early Canadian. A resident of Toronto, he is senior vice-president and creative director of Vickers & Benson Advertising Ltd.

Design construction of the Avco Cup encompassed many problems, the largest of which was the floating globe buried in lucite. The lucite acted as a lens which defused the light and affected the apparent shape of the globe. The problem was ultimately solved after four separate castings of the lucite.

The only metal compatible with lucite is silver plated Britannia, and while the globe appears to be three and a half inches in diameter it in actuality is 5 inches high and 3 inches wide.

The final product was silversmithed by Henry Birks & Sons of Canada at a cost of approximately $8,000. Design fee for the trophy ran in the area of $5,000.

The trophy stands 3½ feet and weighs 75 pounds.

And hereafter, when the AVCO WORLD TROPHY travels, it'll be accompanied by an adult.

WAND AND A WALLET INSPIRED JET MIRACLE

By: Reyn Davis

Fairytales can come true . . . it can happen to you . . . when you're young at heart.

Frank Sinatra sang the song and made millions. Ben Hatskin is spending as much trying to show it really does work. Providing, of course, he has a little help from his friends, the people of Winnipeg.

This was a homespun miracle, founded and funded by people who resolutely believed that Winnipeg was prime, unbroken territory for major league hockey.

It began with a charter membership in the World Hockey Association. Even the crusty president of the National Hockey League, long the dominant force in the sport, said he would welcome the new league.

Clarence Campbell cited the birth of the WHA as a welcome source of employment for "seniors and semi-pro players."

But the WHA had other plans . . . plans which spoke more of the hope than fact. They were after professionals and they wouldn't stop short of the NHL.

Yet who really believed in Winnipeg that enough nerve, let alone money, could be generated out of that little hole in the wall in the Arena, to launch the tremendously touchy business of attempting to stock a team with players off the rosters of the hallowed NHL?

It was a moving experience on the rainy morning of Wednesday, May 24 when the Jets proudly announced the signing of their first National Leaguer — goaltender Ernie Wakely.

Two days, it was windy but sunny when a nattily-garbed Joe Daley announced that he too, had signed. Now the Jets had two excellent goalies.

The days that followed brought more names into the picture. Larry Hornung, a defenceman, signed. Then Bob Woytowich, Danny Johnson and Ab McDonald.

Others had their signings announced less triumphantly than the board room press conferences in the Arena. But the aura of excitement continued through the summer heat as the Jets, every 10 days or so, added new names to their roster.

Norm Beaudin . . . Bob Ash . . . Milt Black . . . Wally Boyer . . . Cal Swenson . . . Joe Zanussi . . . Garth Rizzuto . . . Dunc Rousseau . . . Bill Sutherland . . Jean-Guy Graton . . . Steve Cuddie.

But the man everybody was watching was Bobby Hull, the highest active scorer in the NHL and the man Associated Press hailed as the player of the decade.

Many thought it was a publicity trick, Hatskin chasing Hull to all corners of the continent for their "coincidental" meetings.

Then Hull responded one day when he told Bob Verdi of the Chicago Tribune that, yes, he was thinking about leaving the Black Hawks if Winnipeg met his price.

Hull came to Winnipeg for a few days on a Cross-Canada promotions tour. Unlike other cities he visited, he spent his free time in Winnipeg touring the city and the country-side, looking for a home.

Finally, after miles of tapes and newsprint, the $2.75 million contract was agreed upon in a roadside motel on the outskirts of Denver, Colo., high in the mountains. Hatskin came back to Winnipeg saying he was "99.99 per cent sure" Hull would sign.

The day was June 27 and it began early. Hull flew into Winnipeg from Edmonton in the cover of the night, caught a couple of hours sleep at the International Inn, then shuffled back to the Airport at 6:30 a.m. where 40 newsmen from all parts of Canada were waiting for the first leg of the most spectacular signing ceremony ever held in hockey.

The morning was still young in the Twin Cities when Hull stepped out of the Trans-Air turbo-jet to embrace his wife, Joanne, and three of their five children — Bobby Jr., Blake and Brett — who had arrived only minutes earlier on a flight from Chicago.

A 1938 Rolls-Royce was waiting to lead a cavalcade to the proud old Minnesota Club, where the biggest press conference in the state's history was poised and ready to rush the news to two countries.

Hull signed a cheque for $1 million — the down payment on behalf of the league. He used 11 pens, each one representing one of the teams other than the Jets.

Then it was back to Winnipeg for another parade, another press conference and finally a public ceremony at the corner of Portage and Main. There, he was accorded a hero's welcome by more than 5,000 cheering bystanders.

Weeks later, he became a national issue when he was blackballed from playing for Team Canada.

And there would be the entanglements of the courts attempting to determine if Chicago Black Hawks had any claim to hold him. He missed the first 15 games of the schedule but the team charged into an early lead in the Western Division with the Golden Jet perched beside the bench.

Strangely enough, the club leader was Chris Bordeleau, a slick little centre who also bolted the Black Hawks to play for the Jets.

Bordeleau signed almost too late to grasp the full attention he deserved. He waited for a better time . . . on the ice in full view of the paying customers.

Three amateurs were turned pro to round out the roster. Brian Cadle, possibly the most popular junior who ever played for the Jets, made the club on guts alone. Then there was the big Duke Asmundson, who instantly won a job playing the point on the power-play, and finally Gordie Tumilson, the 148-pound package of fiery desire who made the team as a third-string goalie.

But most important of all, the team and the league got off the ground.

Really, it was a veritable fairy-tale come true.

The WHA's Troubleshooter

By Walt Marlow

From counter intelligence to administrator of the World Hockey Association, that's affable James W. Browitt, a man who, you suspect, knows far more than he pretends. He is a listener with perception, a tuned-in man.

The phenomenal success of the WHA can be attributed to many, but few will deny there is no job tougher than that of the league administrator.

In abbreviated form, he is WHA President Gary Davidson's No. 1 troubleshooter.

When problems arise among the league's 12 owner spokesmen, or lesser internal grievances develop, Browitt is the man who irons out the wrinkles.

In essence, Browitt has taken over where WHA co-founder Dennis Murphy left off when he stepped out of the league office to concentrate on giving Los Angeles a representative collection of Sharks, as president and general manager of that club.

Admittedly, the WHA is off to a far greater start than scientists of the game dared forecast. The reason for the skepticism, at least in Browitt's view, is not without cause.

"There are promoter types that always seem to go hand in hand with the new enterprise," calculated Browitt, "but they were weeded out early in the WHA, to be replaced by the genuine businessman types before the season ever started.

"Because of that fact, we've done in months what other leagues required years to accomplish."

Long a student of sports administration, Browitt, 51, was aware of the mistakes that surfaced in other leagues and has been quick to implement measures to avoid them.

"The key to stability," he cautions, "is playing sites. Within three years, our difficult arena situations will be turned around."

Meanwhile, it's Browitt's view that hockey has not yet penetrated the surface, despite the impact of the long-established NHL on the American sports public.

"It's the game that everybody is just starting to discover," he matter-of-factly declares. "Hockey, for all of its heritage, is still an unfamiliar game to millions of Americans.

"We're embarking on a new era."

A graduate of Military Intelligence at Fort Custer,

Mich., Browitt served 12 years in the Army. As a chief special agent in the counter intelligence corps, he spent six years in Korea and Japan after four campaigns in the Pacific.

Okinawa and Saipan were among his residences.

He can read, write and speak Korean.

"I got far more out of the service than I gave," Browitt is quick to point out. He also dismissed his CIC experiences as a personal chapter in his life not to be exploited.

Following his military career, Browitt was executive director of Freedom Hall in Louisville, which hosted a number of major national sports events, including the NCAA basketball finals four times.

A charter member of the Kentucky Athletic Hall of Fame, he was president of the Kentucky Derby Festival in 1966.

Browitt is now a resident of fashionable nearby Tustin with wife, Irene, and two daughters. A son, Joe, is in the Coast Guard.

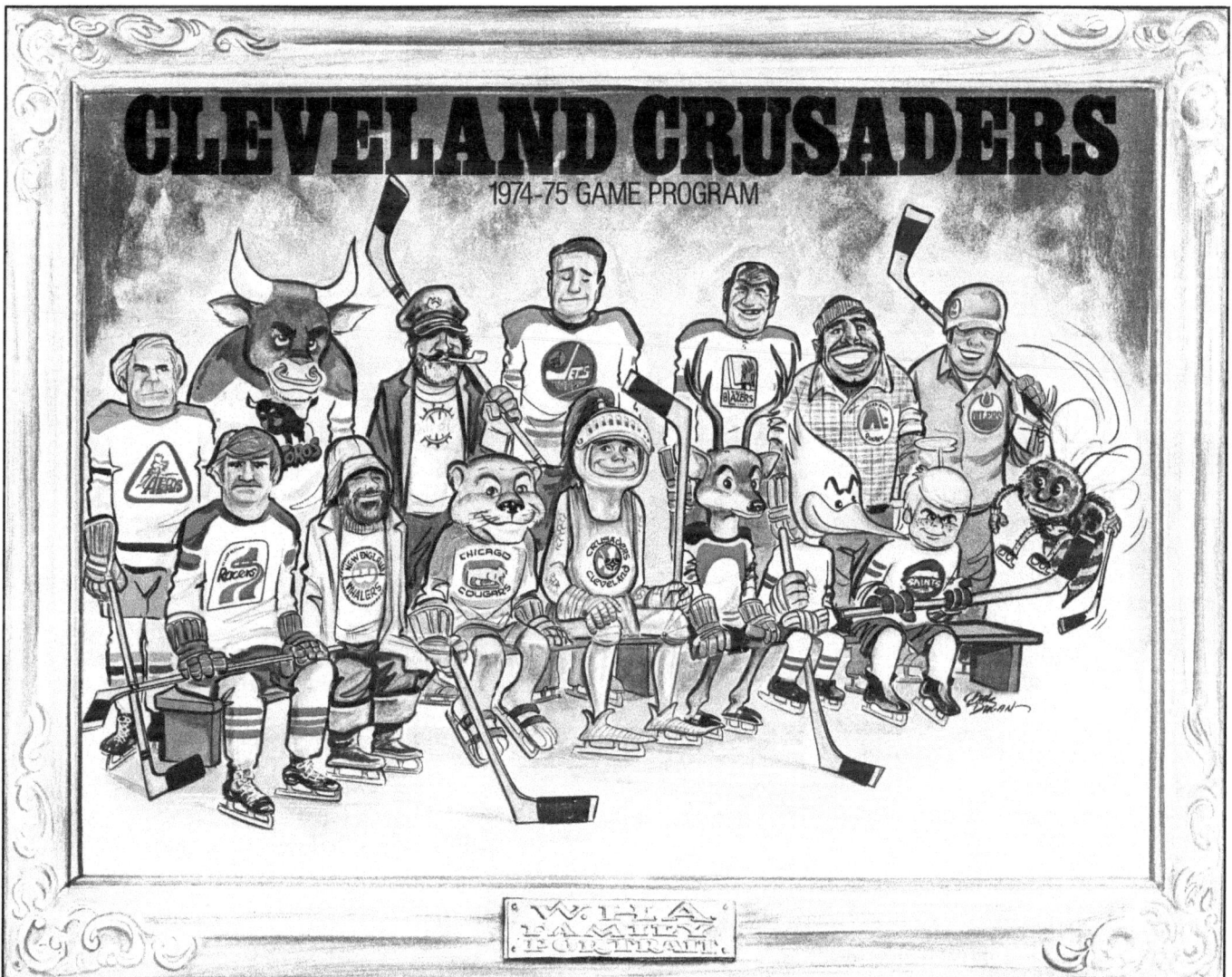

OCT. 12, 1972 —

"A NIGHT TO REMEMBER"

by Art Dunphy

In 1984, or sometime thereafter, when someone calls "Ask The Globe" and inquires: When was the first Whalers (league) hockey game played in Boston?, the reply will be, Oct. 12, 1972. And you were there!!!

To some sports fans, the significance of this event might blend in with "first nights in sports", such as the Boston Bruins first game at Boston Arena in November of 1924 or the Celtics first game, also at the Arena, on Nov. 5, 1946.

However, neither the Bruins nor the Celtics had to face the odds that the Whalers faced when Howard L. Baldwin, and John Coburn Jr., first had the brainstorm last October that Boston should have a second major league hockey team.

Even the most optimistic fan had to be taken back by the first announcement that New England had been awarded one of the 12 franchises in "a dream" . . . the World Hockey Association.

As some observers at Kitty Hawk, I'm sure, replied . . . "it will never get off the ground."

But Baldwin and Coburn — both of whom at the time were under 30 and armed with a good deal more than optimism — managed to accomplish what few if any believed possible.

Tonight's game here at Eddie Power's "House of Magic" is the fulfillment of Baldwin's and Coburn's dream. What's more, the capacity crowd of some 15,000 hockey fans that are on hand here tonight is in itself proof that they were correct in their assumption that Boston would support more than one major league hockey team.

The obstacles that the two faced trying to start this club staggers the imagination. To mention but a few . . . financing, staff, players, a place to play, credibility and acceptability.

In retrospect, it almost looks easy. But don't make the mistake of telling either Baldwin or Coburn it was a snap. The financing they accomplished through personal resources and the addition of several other persons to the inner circle of investors, including one Robert J. Schmertz, Godfrey Wood and Bill Barnes.

The staff grew by association and reputation, beginning with the acquisition of Jack Kelley, the highly successful coach of Boston University, in January of this year.

Kelley's "jump to the WHA" lent the first degree of credibility in the press to the new venture. His reputation as an outstanding coach and a prudent man did much for the Whalers . . . and was one of the first indications to the public that Baldwin et. al. meant business.

Kelley took care of the "tactical" side of the organization chart, while Baldwin handled the "administrative" appointments.

Together they built a staff and a team that has earned the respect of most people in hockey, both within and without of the WHA.

In the process they also gained a degree of credibility with the press and acceptability with the public that is in itself a sports phenomenon. What other new professional team — in the AFL or ABA for instance — ever sold 90% of their season playing capacity before the first game was played? And what other new sports team ever enjoyed the press respectability in Boston that the Whalers have been afforded during their infant months?

This is still pretty much of a "show me" town when it comes to the representatives of the Fourth Estate, whether they are members of the keyboard fraternity or the electronic media. But still, the Dick Stockton's, Don Gillis', Dick Dew's, Kevin Walsh's, Bob Gamere's, Larry Claflin's, Tim Horgan's, and Bud Collins', etc., have been extremely generous in their reporting of Whalers' news.

Their support to a great extent was responsible for the subsequent demand for Whalers' tickets. Or was it the demand for tickets that led to the support in the papers?

IN FEBRUARY representatives from the 12 league franchises met in Anaheim, Calif., to conduct the first player draft for the WHA. Many felt it was a joke when Bobby Hull, Derek Sanderson, Pie McKenzie and Ted Green were drafted. Handling the selections for the Whalers were (left to right), Asst. Gen. Manager and Dir. of Player Personnel, Ron Ryan, President Howard Baldwin and Vice Presidents John Coburn, Jr. and Godfrey Wood. Jack Kelley was tied to the proceedings via a "hot line" from his Boston office. Within a few months, the Whalers' list was translated into possibly the best team in the new league.

But now is the moment of truth. The night that many said would never happen . . . couldn't happen. The WHA begins play and a full house is on hand to witness this memorable event in "God Bless Orr Country."

Tonight's pairings certainly wasn't an accident either. No sooner had Jim Cooper gained Pie McKenzie's signature in Philadelphia when Howard Baldwin was on the phone to Ed Fitkin at the WHA's headquarters in California saying that he wanted to open the Whalers' home season against the Blazers. The subsequent signing of Derek Sanderson by the Blazers helped to fan Baldwin's enthusiasm even more. The league agreed and here we are tonight . . . tomorrow night it's a return match (for obvious reasons) in the City of Brotherly Love.

It will be interesting to see in the months ahead whether you fans still greet McKenzie's aggressive style with the same degree of enthusiasm that was so apparent here at the Garden in years gone by. Will Derek still be the idol of the teeny bopper set? Will Jim Dorey still be regarded as a bad guy?

The one thing that will probably remain constant is the love and admiration that has characterized Ted Green's professional career here in Boston.

The numbers for the most part remain the same. The color of the jerseys have changed, and certainly the loyalties are different. It's a whole new ball game starting tonight. The skeptics said it would never happen. Clarence Campbell said it couldn't happen. But you are here, and we know differently. The WHA is a reality. Dreams do come true.

29

THE SHARKS ARE HERE

By—Tim Rutten
President Southern California Hockey Writers Assn.

Any new sports organization is a challenging proposition. This is double true of the Sharks. Not only are they a new team in a new league but they must buck the "establishment". Still, the Shark's future is promising. Los Angeles is a "winners town". They may grab a big share of the fans attention.

The Los Angeles Sporting Press also pays a large part in the club's chances of success. Sport coverage is a "Chicken and the egg" proposition. No one is quite sure whether an interesting team brings about good coverage or whether good coverage creates an interesting team.

But, the Sharks have already taken over a large share of the hockey news in the L.A. media. This may be due partially to the novelty of a new enterprise such as the WHA. General manager Dennis Murphy and his staff have also been working overtime on a plan for community envolvement and a series of suburban press conferences to aid in providing fans with information on the club.

An unexpected plus for the new club has resulted from the NHL All-Stars' embarassment at the hands of the Russian National Team. The Soviet's performance seems to have buried the long-cherished belief that the NHL was the only legitimate theatre of big league play.

Los Angeles may be in a position to capitalize on that funeral. One of the WHA clubs to draft European players. the Sharks have three on their roster. including goalkeeper Antone Gale and centerman Zoltan Horvath. With the Russians the talk of most hockey circles. these players could turn out to be unexpected drawing cards.

"I really wasn't too hot on these European fellows when we drafted them", says coach Terry Slater, "especially because I'd never seen them myself. But, after the way the Russians have played I'll be taking a close look at them all."

Slater himself may be quite an attraction. An admirer of the late Vince Lombardi, he brings an outstanding minor league coaching record and a masters degree in educational physchology to his new job. Articulate and colorful, he is also highly quotable.

"We're going to be a big team and rough team," he says, "and we're going to fight. I'm not going to have any sissys on my club. Hockey, like Gordie Howe said, is man's game".

The team becomes a reality at first draft session. Right to left: General Manager — Dennis Murphy. Coach — Terry Slater, Broadcaster — Gary Morrell. Board Member — Fred Beckham.

Rumors were floating around a few weeks ago that the Sharks are moving to Kansas City. They no doubt came about when Dr. Arthur B. Rhoades arrived in town and immediately huddled with Murphy at the Sports Arena. When Dr. Rhoades got back on the plane for Kaycee he was a substantial owner in the Sharks.

"No way do I have any intention on moving this club out of Los Angeles," emphasized the good doctor. "Shucks, I spend half my time in California and I feel certain we will make it here."

Coupled with the WHA's innovative scheduling and rule changes, a fiery coach, a solid sprinkling of NHL vets and the behind the scenes work of Dennis Murphy, the man who started the whole thing, it should make for an interesting first season.

SHARKS ARE HERE . . . Sharks pros join rookies and amateurs in the team's initial practice session, Oct. 1, at Norwalk Ice Rink.

RAIDERS' FUTURE CAME EARLY

By BILL VERIGAN

The future of the Raiders arrived even before Year One began in the World Hockey Association. It arrived by cars and buses with an eager smile at an ice rink in Brick Town, N.J.

The future includes a law student, an insurance trainee, a disillusioned hockey player from the Eastern League and more. Dressed in longjohns and skivvies, they bent to touch their toes to trainer Fraser Gleeson's chanted cadence a month before the season began.

To them, it was somewhere over the rainbow — a chance to play in the World Hockey Association. Only five or six could make the Raiders for the start of the first season; the rest would be somewhere besides Madison Square Garden, perhaps in the Eastern League.

None of them came to the camp with the idea of being cut, yet somewhere along the way a few dropped out and a few others knew their time hadn't come by looking at the competition.

When Camille Henry spoke of them, however, he looked as proud as a fresh father.

Ian Wilkie was one who drove into camp. He was 23, a goalie who attracted attention in the juniors, a law student, and he had the kind of face that attracts a fan club filled with the fairer sex. "He's beautiful," is the way one potential member described him before seeing him play. "It's too bad he's married. It's too bad he has to wear a mask."

He came to camp saying "I'm through with travelling in a bus. I decided that in the juniors." He had given up the idea of making the NHL because he hated buses, and he knew how many times he would have to ride in them to minor league games before finally getting to the top.

"I went to the Canadiens' camp twice," he said, "and there were 13 goalies. The first year, I was the leading goalie in camp, but I could tell I wasn't going to make the team because they had made up their minds to send us down before we ever came to camp.

"Instead, I went to law school at British Columbia and played hockey there."

When the Raiders drafted him, he was only mildly surprised. He had expected to be drafted by some WHA team on the basis of his junior hockey reputation with the Edmonton Oil Kings, but he didn't realize his reputation reached as far as New York.

"I decided this was what I wanted," he said. "Ken Dryden was doing the same thing, keeping up with his reading at law school while playing with Montreal. I enrolled at Rutgers, and looked around for a place to live. I didn't come with the idea of riding buses again."

There were others, too, among that group of eager players. Wally Olds, one of the new American breed of hockey player who graduated from Minnesota and played defense on the silver medal Olympic team, was one. So was Brian Morenz, who played for Bobby's Orr's old junior team, the Oshawa Generals, and got tired of explaining in training camp that his distant cousin, Howie Morenz, played in the NHL and died before he was born.

These were players who were drafted, known quantities before they came to camp, but there were some like Frank Grace who had to make a telephone call to the Railers' office in order to get their tryouts.

At Cornell, the handsome redhead was a star good enough to attract attention from Detroit, but instead of going there he became an executive trainee for the Prudential Insurance Company when he graduated last year.

In the early days of the Raider camp, he worked at night after practice and even pitched insurance policies to the other players. But one day, his picture turned up in a newspaper with a caption telling how he was trying to make the Raiders.

"I've got to go to the office tomorrow and tell them I'm here," he said. "I thought I could do both jobs, and I hope they'll understand. But even if they tell me to choose one or the other, I'll be back in camp tomorrow. This is something I have to do now; insurance will always be there later."

He left camp to go to the office, and Henry didn't know if he'd ever come back. But when he returned the next day, Henry said, "He's got what it takes—inside."

Of all the players in camp, perhaps Jamie Kennedy was filled with the most doubts about making the team. He was 26, older than most, and his brother, Forbes, had been an NHL firebrand who was busted for bouncing around officials.

Although Jamie would never say it, others suspect his brother's reputation might have hurt his chances of making the NHL. His nose had been shoved slightly to one side during his seasons in the Eastern League, and his confidence had been shoved slightly to one side, too, the result of three fruitless trips to NHL camps.

Of all the players in the camp, however, perhaps Jamie wanted a job with the Raiders the most. He called being drafted his "second chance at life."

Every time the Raider scouts went to watch the Jersey Devils last season, Kennedy knew they were there, and in a game against Syracuse he got two shorthanded goals and an invitation to camp. It meant he might not have to do construction work again in the summer, and maybe he could spend more time at the race tracks.

"But I've been through all this before," he said. "They still consider me an amateur although a guy can make better than $250 a week in the EHL, and if his team makes the playoffs he can really do well. What I've always wanted is to play in places like Madison Square Garden and Boston Garden, though.

"I look around and know I might not be there at the start of the season, but wait. I'll be there before the season's over."

AND THE BAND PLAYED ON

In short, the WHA not only has survived its first uncertain year, it's now on its way to a confident second season with expansion plans already set for the future.

As Bobby Hull now says, "We've made believers out of a lot of people," but the tune wasn't all that melodic at the start. Bobby himself was frustrated by court orders as the first season started last fall and the Winnipeg Jets' famous player-coach was kept off skates for the first 15 games before the courts ruled the NHL's binding reserve clause illegal.

It didn't sound good in Philadelphia either, where the Blazers were delayed opening their home season when the Zamboni cracked through their arena's inadequate ice surface. There were discords in New York, too, where the original Raiders' franchise quickly ran out of money. But the team played on with the support of the league, and now is healthy again under new management.

Important to note, perhaps, is that the WHA opened with 12 franchises and ended its first season with 12; that while attendance was a disappointment in some sectors (Winnipeg, Ottawa, Philadelphia, Chicago), the overall average was better than 5,000 and advance sales for the 1973-74 season indicate a solid improvement.

Personnel-wise, the WHA chose to label the Boston Bruins' Derek Sanderson a superstar and

They laughed when Gary Davidson sat down at the piano a couple of years ago and played a little thing he called "Here comes the World Hockey Association". They sputtered and stuttered and frowned last summer when Bobby Hull came over from the National Hockey League's Chicago Black Hawks and began humming the WHA tune.

They ran to their lawyers and begged the courts to "stop the music!" when other NHL stars rushed in to join the chorus.

But the music played on, and except for a sour note or two here and there the melody is on its way to becoming a solid hit.

he was lured to Philadelphia in a multimillion-dollar package. He turned out to be a mistake and both he and Blazer goalie Bernie Parent have been returned to the NHL.

But others, such as J.C. Tremblay, Gerry Cheevers, Wayne Carleton and Hull, provided the harmony which carried the WHA tune its first year.

Launching a new season, the WHA abandoned Philadelphia and its fickle fans for Vancouver, and Ottawa for Toronto. Chicago shifted to the league's Eastern Division, with Vancouver new in the West, and another 20 or so former National Hockey Leaguers are strengthening rosters throughout the league.

The spirit and determinated optimism of the WHA was nowhere more evident during the off season than in Chicago where the Cougars, refusing to fold under the weight of the league's worst first-year record (26-50-2), went on a spending binge and landed more NHLers (four) than anyone else while announcing firm plans for a new arena.

From their NHL rival Chicago Black Hawks they stole premier defenseman Pat Stapleton as player-coach; and they added teammate Ralph Backstrom, longtime star center with the Montreal Canadiens; defenseman Darryl Maggs, another former Hawk who played for California last year, and Cam Newton, a promising

young goalie who had been languishing in the Pittsburgh Penguins' system.

As Cougar president Walter Kaiser succinctly put it: "We intend to build a winner in Chicago." These daring moves have not gone unnoticed by Chicago fans; season ticket sales were heading toward 6,000 as the new season opened.

Also grabbing summer headlines were the Houston Aeros, who grabbed Marty and Mark Howe from Toronto of the Ontario Hockey Association in a surprise pro draft move, then startled everyone by luring their famous father, Gordie, out of retirement to play with them. Houston, which finished second to Winnipeg in the WHA West at 39-35-4 last year and ousted Los Angeles from the playoffs before losing to the Jets, thus should be a stronger gate attraction as well as improved on the ice.

Elsewhere around the WHA, here's how things shape up:

East — The AVCO World Cup champion New England Whalers, who took the league's best record (46-30-2) into the playoffs and knocked off Ottawa, Cleveland and Winnipeg all in 4-1 series, surprisingly changed coaches, with Jack Kelley concentrating on the general manager job and moving assistant Ron Ryan up as coach. The Whalers, who were tops in attendance with an average of almost 10,000, also added NHLers Al Karlander

from Detroit, Don Blackburn from Minnesota and Hugh Harris from Buffalo.

Cleveland's Crusaders, second to New England at 43-32-3, boasted the WHA's toughest defense with 239 goals-against but presented netminder Gerry Cheevers with the defensive brother act of Wayne and Larry Hillman, getting Wayne from Philadelphia and Larry from Buffalo of the NHL.

Philadelphia overcame its player problems, which included crippling injuries

JEAN-CLAUDE TREMBLAY

33

AND THE BAND PLAYED ON

to John McKenzie, Parent and Sanderson before the latter's defection, to finish third at 38-40 and enjoy the distinction of being the only team not to have a tie game. Trades with the New York Raiders netted high-scoring Ron Ward and goalie Pete Donnelly, and the shift to Vancouver is delighting the league. Well over 8,000 season tickets have been sold.

Ottawa (35-39-4) won the tight battle for fourth place but despite making the playoffs the Nationals were so poorly received in the Canadian capital that the move to Toronto already had been effected before they lost to New England in the first round. Now the Toros, they have picked up veteran defenseman Carl Brewer from the NHL St. Louis Blues. They will be plagued by poor home facilities but reportedly have sold more than 3,000 tickets for their 5,000-seat arena.

Quebec (33-40-5) expects to move up with the acquisition of young stars Rejean Houle and Dale Hoganson from the Canadiens and Serge Bernier from the Los Angeles Kings. Nordiques' attendance, excellent last year with a 7,000-plus average, is projected higher, with 7,000 seats already sold.

New York's Raiders (33-43-2) now are the Jersey Knights. They dealt with Chicago for goalie Jimmy McLeod in an effort to lower their league-leading goals-against total of 334, and added scoring punch with the acquisition of Andre Lacroix and Don Herriman from the Blazers.

West — Division-leading Winnipeg (43-31-4) mostly is staying with its winning hand, but coach Hull hoped to bolster his defense by getting Jim Hargreaves from the Vancouver Canucks and trading for Toronto Toros' Ken Stephanson. Fan support has perked up since rumors that the team might move, but the Jets must do better than half fill their 10,000-seat arena.

The Los Angeles Sharks, third last year at 35-37-6, surprised by luring Canadiens' young star Marc Tardif, and they dealt with Edmonton for center Ron Walters to further improve their attack.

Alberta (38-37-3), now the Edmonton Oilers, beat the Minnesota Saints in a one-game showdown for the final West playoff berth before bowing to Winnipeg. Their changes include winger Brian McKenzie from Atlanta of the NHL and Ron Climie from Toronto of the WHA. They also hope to have star Jim Harrison healthy all year.

The Saints got winger Mike Walton away from the Boston Bruins and defenseman Rick Smith from the California Seals. They hope playing the full year in their new arena will be reflected in increased attendance.

Davidson, the happy tunesmith, is looking ahead with optimism. "The quality of play should be up this year, as well as attendance. We got more fine talent from the National League, and the WHA should be evenly matched again.

"And we'll be even stronger next year when we add Cincinnati, Indianapolis and Phoenix to our league."

4th Annual World Hockey Association

ALL STAR GAME

1976 WHA All-Star Program

Price: $2.00

Winnipeg Jets History

by PAT YANKOSKI

The Winnipeg Arena looks like a cement block deposited on open ground. It's not a spectacular arena, but its hosted numerous hockey games, circuses, rock concerts, and car and boat shows. But hockey has usually been the main attraction at the arena, and its even more so now the Jets are here.

Today is a game day. Last-minute fans are lined up at the box office trying for a seat. It's only two in the afternoon, but already the smell of warm popcorn fills the air as empty boxes are filled in anticipation of the night's crowd.

Ramp 5 leads out to centre ice area. Right now the ice is shiny, waiting for cold steel under leather boots. Rows of seats march up to the ceiling. The caretakers have cleaned the aisles of debris so the fans can have a fresh start.

At one end of the rink, a picture of the Queen looks down over it all. And there is silence. Silence that in a few short hours will be interrupted with cheers of "Go Jets, Go", "in the corner, in the corner," "shoot, shoot, what're you waitin' for?" After the echoes of the game die away, and the last player has left the dressing room, there'll be silence again.

Everything is ready, but a glance at the clock shows an old score. It reads: Home 5, Visitors 3. That means a Jets win. What will it be tonight?

When the World Hockey Association was formed, it created a war with the NHL, brought skeptics to their knees, and eventually robbed many NHL teams of players. But to the hockey fans of Winnipeg, there was something else the WHA did — it brought professional hockey to Winnipeg— a city that had been scoffed at by Clarence Campbell and told that a professional team could not exist here.

The opening of the NHL's 1971-72 season was marred with stories about the new league. Although the WHA wasn't operating fully yet, it was already stealing headlines. The NHL fathers laughed, and their supporters laughed even louder. But Winnipeg and Ben Hatskin hadn't yet pulled their rabbit out of the hat, and when they did, Bennie had the last laugh.

In spite of all the publicity, one thing the new league didn't have was credibility. Maybe they had financial backers, but what they needed was credibility in the eyes of the hockey fans—because fans don't go to the game to see bank accounts, they go to see talent and good hockey.

Hatskin went to the NHL for his big coup —Bobby Hull. Hull is one of the superstars of the game, and Hatskin knew if he could sign Hull, he could give the league some much needed credibility. If Hull signed, then other players in the NHL would also jump.

Apparently the rest of the teams in the new league felt the same way, because they each threw in $100,000 to make up the initial $1,000,000 which would be given Hull just to sign.

The city of Winnipeg found itself in the middle of a heat wave on June 27, 1972, but that didn't stop the thousands of people who came to watch Hull put his Golden Jet signature on the contract that would make him a Winnipeg Jet.

The crowds started to gather early in the afternoon at the corner of Portage and Main where Bobby was to do the deed at 5:00 P.M.—the height of rush hour. And the people stayed and waited. When Bobby finally arrived in a 1934 Rolls Royce, the crowds cheered and clapped. Winnipeg was ready to accept the ex-Chicago Black Hawk with open arms.

With Hull tucked firmly away, Ben began recruiting more talent for the Jets. He wanted to concentrate mainly on players from Winnipeg and Manitoba. Thus when the WHA held its first player draft in February of 1972, such names as Ted Green, Joe Daley, Ernie Wakely, Bob Woytowich, Wayne Chernecki, Jim Hargreaves, Larry Bolonchuk, Ab McDonald, Milt Black and Freeman (Duke) Asmundson were on the Jets' draft list. All were native sons of Manitoba.

By September of 1972 the Jets had a team ready to start the season. But, as everyone suspected, the Chicago Black Hawks weren't going to let their best box office draw be spirited away. Legal action kept Hull from playing the first month of the initial season for the Winnipeg Jets.

By November, Hull joined his linemates of Beaudin and Bordeleau. By the end of the season, this unit, which was dubbed the "Luxury Line", was the highest scoring line in the WHA with each member getting 100 points or more.

The original Jet line-up went as follows: Joe Daley, Ernie Wakely, goal; Bob Woytowich, Bob Ash, Joe Zanussi, Larry Hornung, Steve Cuddie, defense; Chris Bordeleau, Wally Boyer, Bill Sutherland, Danny Johnson, Cal Swenson, Brian Cadle, centre; Bobby Hull, Dunc Rousseau, Ab McDonald, left wing; Norm Beaudin, Garth Rizzuto, Jean Guy Gratton, Milt Black, Duke Asmundson, right wing.

For the first season, the WHA was divided into two divisions—east and west. The Jets, playing in the West, easily wrapped up first place. They made it to the finals of the Avco Cup play-offs, but were beaten by the New England Whalers in five games.

For the start of the 1973-'74 season, the Jets took their training camp to Kenora. The season progressed with more humdrum than the first, and Winnipeg fans were not filling the arena quite as Hatskin wanted them to be.

This time, the Jets finished in fourth place, and were then wiped out in the play-offs by the Houston Aeros in four straight. The Jets were in trouble, but more was to come. Ben Hatskin decided to sell the Jets.

The price tag was around $4 million, and possibly buyers were located in Milwaukee, Detroit and San Diego. But Winnipeg decided it wasn't going to give up the ghost so fast. Perhaps visions of another Winnipeg Whips disaster made people think twice. It was one thing to lose a baseball club, but for Winnipeg to lose a hockey team—unheard of, especially when one man was certain Winnipeg wanted her team to stay.

Bob Graham, president of Inter-City Gas Ltd., decided to launch a "Save the Jets" campaign to raise $1 million for a down payment on the team. The full price had now come down to $2.3 million.

During the campaign, people were asked to buy memberships at $25.00 a piece or make founders' loans. The campaign worked beautifully. The money was raised, with 4,158 Winnipeggers coming up with $133,912.50. An additional $625,974.67 was brought in from 249 individuals and businesses who made founders' loans. With this money and the $300,000 from the city, the down payment was reached. The Winnipeg Jets became the only publicly owned professional hockey team in the world.

In the meantime, overseas connnections were coming up with interesting new players for the coming 1974-75 season. Dr. Gerry Wilson had interested the Jets in some former members of the Swedish Nationals. By May 4, a release came through stating the Jets had signed two young Swedes—Ulf Nilsson and Anders Hedberg. Two more Swedes—Lars-Erik Sjoberg and Curt Larsson along with Finnish players Heikki Riihiranta and Veli Pekka-Ketola rounded out the international scope.

The European players nicely complemented the Canadian guys on the team. The line of Hull, Nilsson and Hedberg became especially successful and popular. Each member scored at least 100 points.

A significant change came over Winnipeg fans during this last season. In spite of finishing out of the play-offs, the Jets had given some good and entertaining hockey to their fans. People began to realize that perhaps this wasn't "bush hockey" after all, especially when you have a record breaker like Bobby Hull on the team.

By the latter half of the season, the Jets were selling out their home games. What a glorious sight—no longer did Houston draw the only crowds to fill the building. It was a noticeable change. One which called for Bobby Hull to "pull in his horns" as he says, and give Winnipeg credibility as being a city able to support its own professional hockey club.

HOCKEY HISTORY...
WHALERS STYLE

from Boston to Hartford

By Bob Neumeier

To some of us (somehow my advisor hoodwinked me into minoring in European history, pre-Napolean), the pursuit of history is as dry as a peanut butter sandwich on dark rye, with no milk. Others somehow revel in leafing through sturdily-bound classics, foaming over The Crusades. The Second Battle of Bull Run, the Lindbergh kidnapping, and any and all written remembrances of past events. I fondly recall my ninth grade Ancient History teacher Miss Binder (as in three-ring) spraying our class with saliva (the kids in the front row needed unbrellas) with so much graphic enthusiasm, recounting the heroic exploits of Xerxes, Attila, and Helen of Troy (we got the **real** story on Helen in college). So it is with history.

Although the history of the New England Whalers may not be as swift as Sherman's march to the sea, as stimulating as Copernicus' theory of the sun, as stirring as Patrick Henry's speech to the Virginia House of Commons, as stingy as Marie Antoinette, or as sad as the administration of Richard Nixon, it is most interesting and unusual in its own right. I'll be the first to admit that Theodore White need not be summoned for his personal observation, nevertheless the birth of a professional sports franchise is noteworthy, especially in a league trying to buck an establishment figure, the National Hockey League, a league whose roots are dug into the heart and soul of previous generations. Thus, this historical record merits our attention.

It all began, like everything in life, with an idea. Ideas are commonplace, but good ideas, and more importantly, successful ideas are less common. When two gentlemen, Howard L. Baldwin and John Coburn Jr., decided to pitch for a World Hockey Association franchise in October, 1971, they had to believe their idea was a good one. They had no idea it would be a successful one. But here Baldwin sits, four short years later, with a shiny office in the spanking Hartford Civic Center and a championship banner flying atop the arena roof. But before you look at this venture as an idyllic, yellow-brick-road, fantasy, keep in mind that Baldwin and Co. spent many sleepless nights wondering if the New England Whalers Hockey Club Inc. would become a bona fide reality.

Like all new businesses, the franchise intitially needed capital. Coburn contacted Godfrey Wood, an ex-Harvard chum, about the idea and the need for investors. Bill Barnes soon joined the Baldwin-Coburn-Wood triumvirate and the franchise was granted by early WHA leaders. So the group had a professional hockey team. All that was needed was a coach, players, and a place to play.

Based in Boston, the group turned to historic Commonwealth Ave., a Boston tradition as familiar as beans and franks on Saturday night, to find their coach and general manager.

Jack Kelley, as Irish as St. Patty himself, appeared to be a natural selection. Well known in the Hub for his workmanlike hockey machines at Boston University, Kelley won back-to-back NCAA championships with the Terriors, just prior to his Whaler signing. His overall record of 206-80-8 could not be excused.

Yet, pessimists abounded. Hockey critics questioned the ability of a coach accustomed to the emotions of youthful college kids to adjust to the pragmatic nuances of big-time pros. To help with this task, Kelley lured a college coaching adversary, Ron Ryan, to aid and abet the hockey cause.

While Kelley and Ryan began their search for players, Baldwin announced the acqustion of the now deceased Robert Schmertz of New Jersey as a prime financial backer, the man who also backed the NBA Boston Celtics.

Patriots' Day in Boston, a day usually reserved for the Boston Marathon and a Red Sox morning game, found a new announcement edge into the sports pages.

Larry Pleau, a Greater Boston native skating in the organization of the Montreal Canadiens, placed his John Hancock on a WHA contract, the first player signed by Kelley and the Whalers. From that very day until tonight, Pleau has been a classy symbol of the squad, a quiet, businesslike professional . . . a guy who can impress on and off the ice.

The management of the Toronto Maple Leafs, a group who poo-pooed the existence of the WHA, soon got caught with their pants down as the Whalers inked their entire defensive Kiddie Korps, Rick Ley (presently captain), Brad Selwood, and Jim Dorey, now with the Toronto Toros. Kelley, a great proponent of defense, banked the club's success on these blue-liners. They did not fail.

By then, the names began flowing like fine wine. Ted Green, a perennial Beantown favorite was named captain and players of the calibre of Tim Sheehy, Tom Webster, Al Smith, Tom Williams, and Paul Hurley signed contracts. The battle lines were thus drawn.

On October 12, the Boston Garden was filled to the brim as the Whalers spotted the then Philly Blazers a two-goal lead before rallying, 4-3. Fittingly, Larry Pleau scored the first winning goal. But above and beyond the euphoria of the 4-3 victory, the mere existence of the game . . . the mere fact they dropped the puck before a huge crowd, just had to be a great thrill for Baldwin, Coburn, Wood, Barnes, Kelley, and Ryan and all the other dedicated front office personnel that sweated blood to see that first night become a reality.

From that point on, the first year was pure magic. The Whalers battled Gerry Cheevers and the Cleveland Crusaders tooth and nail during the regular season, before winning a home and home series to insure an East Division championship. The Whalers jogged in the playoffs, sweeping to the playoff championship was little opposition.

Personal highlights? Well, Tom Webster popped in 50 big goals, finally escaping a damnable personal injury jinx. Lithesome Terry Caffery surprised many so-called experts, by accounting for 100 points, most ever by a rookie. And the unpredictable one, Al smith, played simply spectacularly in goal during the playoff series.

So, how do you succeed after success?

This question was placed squarely in the lap of Ron Ryan, after Kelley opted to abdicate his coaching duties to concentrate on the front office. Ryan also did not disappoint. His troops again repeated as divisional winners, with consistency their byword. Not once did the green and gold lose more than two straight, maintaining first place since day one of the season.

1973-74 could be called the season for the French, as left-winger John shunned his tab as just an honest

hustler and became a point scorer, so much so that he led the club in total points. Included in this French dressing was a four-goal game against Toronto and a five-assist performance against Los Angeles.

But with all this hockey poop, one inescapable fact remained. The club simply could not draw at Boston Garden. With the primary focus riveted on Orr, Esposito, and the Bruins, the Whalers played game after game before a small but very loyal band of fans. But there were not enough of them to continue the club's operation in Boston. Rumors and rumors about pending moves circulated through the Boston papers, certainly an unsettling effect on Ryan's troops, who read more about where they were going than who scored the goals the previous evening. But yet they doggedly hung together and won that regular season championship.

Finally, a move was announced, prior to the playoffs that year. A group from Hartford, Ct. led by Don Conrad of Aetna Life and Casualty successfully negotiated with Baldwin and the Whalers, and the Whaler leader decided that this area was indeed a fertile one. A new arena was under construction, the fans seemed hungry for major league sports. So the decision was finally reached. Goodbye, Boston, Hello, Hartford.

That the 1973-74 playoffs did not turn out so well can ostensibly be traced to a number or reasons, **reasons** not excuses. For one, the club was forced to play the games at the venerable Big E in West Springfield, an arena known more nostalgic AHL memories rather than room to maneuver. It was a perfect fit for the tight checking Chicago Cougars, who parlayed a waiting game with a number of Whaler injuries to post a memorable seven-game playoff victory.

Last year proved to be an instant replay of 1973-74 with one very big exception. Yes, the Whalers did cop the divisional championship. Yes, the Whalers did get knocked out of the playoffs in the first round (by Minnesota). But above and beyond all this, the Civic Center opened. The Whalers, transients for almost a year, had their own home. And there is no place like home. Buoyed by enthusiastic fans and a beautiful facility, the Harpoonmen posted the best ice record in the WHA and their 4-3 OT win in the inaugural against San Diego will be forever cherished.

But any historical record must touch upon another, albeit negative, happening. Coach Ron Ryan, feeling the intense pressure a coach only knows so well, collapsed suddenly in a Toronto airport runway in the wee Sunday morning hours after his troops had salaamed to the Winnipeg Jets, 9-3. Fortunately, after, holding their breath for several uncertain days, Jack Kelley thought it best to return behind the bench. And that is where he now stands, while the fully recovered Ryan is working in the front office.

In retrospect, these individual incidents and events appear to me to be almost secondary. It is the mere fact that Baldwin and Co. were able to begin it all in the first place, to do what everybody thought they could not. Namely, begin from a couple of idealists kicking around an idea to where they are today. With a team ready to skate before you're very eyes.

Got all that?
You sure?
OK, they'll be a quiz on Friday.

THE COLLEGIANS COME OF AGE

By Nate Greenberg

Y ou've heard it a thousand times. The names and places differ, but the story lines almost always remain the same. The hard-working scout is scouring the "bushes" of Canada, from neighborhood ponds to midget leagues in search of players who appear to have the stamina — the size, speed, shot and, most of all, desire — to someday play professional hockey.

A teenager catches the eye of a scout, who immediately keeps close tabs on him. At the proper age (presently it is 20 but once was as young as 16) the scout will hopefully add his name to the club's negotiation list so, ostensibly, no other team can deal with the player.

Next, it is on to the amateur leagues. From that day on, the game of hockey becomes the way of life. You eat, drink and sleep on skates and nothing — including an education — gets in the way.

A professional hockey player is born. There was no other route for the aspiring professional to take — until recently.

Colleges in this country began stepping up their hockey programs to be sure, but an education also was becoming more and more important to each and every person. Together, it was enough to interest many Canadian teens in attending college and playing hockey there as opposed to playing junior hockey exclusively.

Only a handful of collegiate hockey players, such as Red Berenson (Michigan) and Lou Angotti (Michigan Tech), had advanced to the pro ranks until about five years ago, which is not to say there weren't more collegians capable of playing hockey on the professional level.

"I've felt for the last 15-20 years that there have been collegians worthy of a pro career," says Jack Kelley, General Manager-Coach of the New England Whalers and himself an all-east defenseman at Boston University, where he became one of the most successful college coaches in the nation.

"The only problem was that major league hockey consisted of the then six team National Hockey League and there was no place for so many talented skaters to go. Now with expansion in the NHL and

TIM SHEEHY – B.C.

FORMER COLLEGIANS now under contract with the New England Whalers include (l. to r.) John Danby, Bob Brown, Ric Jordan, Tom Earl, Mike Hyndman, and Toot Cahoon. All but Earl are BU graduates, while Tom played his collegiate hockey at Colgate.

the arrival of the World Hockey Association, things are beginning to open up.

"Of course, there are many more college hockey players now," continued Kelley. "Back when I played, you were lucky if you had two lines and two defensemen or sometimes three lines and four defensemen. Now there are peewee and midget teams in every city and town in Massachusetts alone."

Kelley is a strong believer that colleges will become the life line for professional hockey and showed it when he signed 12 players with college backgrounds to professional contracts with the Whalers.

Five players who'll wear the dark green and white colors played under Kelley at BU — defensemen Bob Brown and Ric Jordan, center John Danby and forwards Don Cahoon and Mike Hyndman. Four others played against Kelley's clubs at Boston College — defenseman Paul Hurley and forwards Kevin Ahearn, John Cunniff and Tim Sheehy. Forward Tom Earl and goalie Geoff McMullen of Colgate and forward Guy Smith of New Hampshire round out the slate.

What motives the Canadian teenager with pro aspirations to forego junior hockey, where you admittedly still have an edge in making it with some pro clubs, in favor of college?

"Canadian young men are finding out that there's more to life than a hockey rink," says one ex-collegian in his mid-20's. "You have to think of the future. What happens if you are injured early in your hockey career and unable to play again. What are you left with?

"Not too many years ago, you'd go back to Canada and find some kind of work which usually didn't pay that much, but you were able to survive. Those days are almost gone. A college degree is becoming more

and more essential. Very, very few would consider beginning college, or in some cases, finishing high school, once they'd been away four or five years.

"And the brand of hockey in colleges today is real good, as far as I'm concerned. I've played in the minor leagues for a short time and my college experience really didn't handicap me. Sure, there were certain guys who had a lot more game experience than me because they played junior hockey, but everything considered, I still think college hockey is great. If I had to do it all over again, I'd still go to college."

The only problem facing collegiate hockey at the moment — and it really hasn't started to formulate on a very great scale as yet — is the signing of undergraduate players by the professional teams.

Many collegians hear of the enormous figures being bandied about recently by hockey clubs. They also hear and read of their stature as a collegian. They are one or two years away from graduation and figure, if the money is right, they can always finish their schooling in the off-season.

Some decide to turn professional and retain an agent. The moment they do so, they become ineligible for NCAA play. The signing of a professional contract, therefore, became just a formality.

"I'm all for the professional leagues establishing a rule that says no team can sign a collegian until his class graduates," notes Kelley. "I personally would like to see boys complete their college education so as to have that security when their playing days are over. It's the kids that get the agents, not the team."

Whatever, the rise of the collegiate hockey player is a new chapter to an old story on the building of a professional hockey player. You'll probably hear it a thousand times.

YANKEE GO HOME!
CANADA

Sheehan · Marty Howe

By MIKE LAMEY

It is not quite a full scale invasion yet, the type of assault made by the Allies at Normandy, but the American hockey player is becoming more of a factor in a profession that once was almost an exclusive Canadian club.

An American was a rarity in the National Hockey League in the founding years. Players such as John Mariucci, Sam Lopresti, Frankie Brimsek, Bobby Dill and Cully Dahlstrom were almost aliens in a sport Canadians claimed as their own.

Tim Sheehy · Mark Howe

But the formation of the World Hockey Association along with the expanded youth programs in Minnesota, Michigan and the New England area, the Americans started to make inroads.

Today there are more than 70 Americans playing pro hockey in the WHA, NHL and the minors. Of the 70-plus, more than half are in the big leagues, 23 in the WHA and 16 in the NHL. And this does not include the current crop who were drafted this past season.

In former years the training grounds for the big leagues were the Canadian junior leagues such as the OHA, QJHL and WJHL. They still provide most of the pros today. But more and more players are being developed in the American college system and lately junior leagues.

Larry Pleau

A look at the Fighting Saint roster gives an excellent example of the college productivity. Ron Busniuk came from University of Minnesota-Duluth, Bob Boyd from Michigan State, George Morrison from Denver University, Murray Heatley from Wisconsin, Mike Curran from North Dakota and Mike Antonovich, Bill Klatt, Gary Gambucci and Jack McCartan all from the University of Minnesota.

The day may even come to pass when an American All-Star squad will challenge the Russians as the two Team Canada teams did this fall and two years ago.

Mike Curran

Although big named stars such Hull and Howe or Esposito and Orr would be out, the Americans could form a respectable roster with players such as Tim Sheehy, Bobby Sheehan, Gambucci, Antonovich, Klatt, Curran, Dick and Bob Paradise, Kevin Ahearn, Henry Boucha, John Cunniff, Robbie Ftorek, Stan Gilbertson, Phil Hoene, Paul Hurley, Tommy and Butch Williams, Pete Donnelly, Doug Volmar, Craig Patrick, Larry Pleau and Tracy Pratt.

There are a couple of other youngsters who would qualify for that team, too, Mark and Marty Howe. The Howes were born in Detroit and have dual citizenships thus enabling them to also play for Team Canada this past fall.

Volmar · Antonovich

DID YOU KNOW

Mike Curran was the first player signed by the Fighting Saints. Wayne Connelly was first NHLer signed.

The Yanks are Coming

The last time the United States invaded Canada, during the War of 1812, some of the soldiers mutinied, others fired on each other in the dark and the Canadians referred to their week of service as a "party of pleasure."

Now there is another U.S. invasion. The Yanks have established a beachhead in one of Canada's most prized sanctuaries, professional hockey, and aren't about to let go.

There are 10 U.S. players in the National Hockey League, and the World Hockey Association has 20.

Mike Antonovich, 5' 8", 160-pound left wing for the Minnesota Fighting Saints is on the team with the largest number of U.S. players (10) in pro hockey. He hails from Minnesota, where hockey is strong, and has played at three levels of the game there in the last four years.

First he made all-state three times and led Greenway of Coleraine, a regional high school embracing a dozen northern mining towns, to two state titles. Then he brought the University of Minnesota its first Western Collegiate title in 16 years, followed the next season by a trip to the NCAA finals. He left school to turn pro after his junior year.

The Saints' coach, Glen Sonmor, who had recruited Antonovich for college hockey signed him.

A lifetime center, Antonovich at first seemed lost at a new position on a line with a rookie center and a variety of right wings, but he had scored 17 goals by February and his first hat trick on Jan. 20. "If you're little, sometimes you have some extra quickness," Antonovich says. "I think it's an advantage." He scores most often on rebounds and deflections, and after each goal he does a dance.

It is easy to attribute the success of Antonovich and others to the sneering catchword, 'expansion'. But expansion doesn't account for so many good U.S. players, such as the Saints' goalie, Mike Curran, who was an Olympic star, or New York's Bobby Sheehan and New England's Larry Pleau, who are among the WHA's leading scorers.

The first big break for U.S. players came in 1967, when they raised the hockey draft age from 18 to 20. Many Canadians decided to use the extra years to begin college in the U.S. When Canadian scouts crossed over to watch their native products waste time before becoming eligible for the pro draft, they discovered that sourth-of-the-border hockey was better than they had expected. And so, in the last two drafts 43 players were picked from U.S. colleges, including many of the once-scorned natives.

All but two members of the U.S. World Cup team are Minnesota-born or bred. The feeder programs in Massachusetts and Michigan are comparable, but Minnesota has 55,000 players in organized programs, more than one-fourth the U.S. total, and an unmatched 80 indoor rinks.

Minnesota hockey, many feel, is equivalent to Canadian until the high school level. This is where Canada moves ahead. A top Canadian teen-ager has what might generously be described as an abbreviated high school education. He will play some 300 games between the ages of 16 and 19 in September-April leagues reserved for the best players. But at least in Minnesota, U.S. high school hockey is improving apace.

The backlash from all this activity is that more U.S. players are bound to turn pro before finishing college or playing on the national team. "You want to play for God and country—or a $50,000 bonus?" asks National Coach Bob Johnson. More fearful is the prospect of junior leagues raiding the high schools and creating the classic dilemma of the Canadian who is almost but not quite good enough to play pro. "What could be worse than being a mediocre 21-year-old hockey player with a ninth-grade education?" asks the Saints' western Canada scout, Roy Kelly.

For the Mike Antonoviches, such risks undoubtedly seem worthwhile.

"I think I would have worked in the mines and played baseball if I hadn't got a hockey scholarship," says Antonovich, who was an All-State third baseman in high school. He grew up in Calumet, a town on Minnesota's iron range.

The Antonovich family still lives in the small frame house where Mike's mother Eleanor gave birth to him without benefit of physician 21 years ago.

Small-town legends grew up around Antonovich, legends of how he was better than bigger and older boys and how he skated every day until dark. There were tales of his cockiness. "Mike was really a modest kid," says his high school coach, Bob Gernander, "but he had an arrogant way about him." From the time he led Greenway to its first state title as a 5' 4", 122-pound third-line sophomore, Mike no doubt felt it was necessary to throw what weight he had around.

Perhaps because of his reputation for roughness, Mike never made All-America, though he led Minnesota from third-period ties and deficits to 13 wins his freshman year and from a three goal third-period disadvantage to an overtime win in the NCAA semifinals in his second year. The magic ran out in his junior year, when he injured his knee. With a pregnant wife and no chance of remaining academically eligible, he did not have to vacillate about turning pro. "I could have gone back to school," he says, "but you want to get in at the ground floor. I just went to school to play hockey." Antonovich is anything but cocky now, being understandably preoccupied with learning his position and surviving against bigger men.

"Every time a Mike Antonovich takes the ice for the Saints, it helps hockey all through Minnesota," says Roy Kelly. "The kids on the high school teams look at him and realize that if they work hard enough, there's a place for them in pro hockey, too."

"In a few years there's going to be an explosion," says former Minnesota and Olympic Coach John Mariucci. "Why? Because we have numbers. Coaching's getting better, we have a 12-month program and rules are getting better, too." He paused. "And when we cross the color line, it's gonna be great."

Mike Antonovich

Frank Comes Home: More NHLers Follow

Frank Mahovlich

When Frank Mahovlich dons his Toronto Toros jersey, the World Hockey Association will have three of the five men in hockey history who have scored 500 or more goals in their career.

The "Big M" with 533 goals joins Houston's Gordie Howe (807 goals) and Winnipeg's Bobby Hull (657 goals) in this select circle.

Mahovlich, who played the last three years with the Montreal Canadiens, has been in the major leagues since 1956.

Besides his tenure with the Canadiens, Big M spent 12 years with the Toronto Maple Leafs and three seasons with the Detroit Red Wings. While with the Red Wings, he played on the same line with Gordie Howe.

Mahovlich, who won the National Hockey League's Calder Memorial Trophy for the Rookie-of-the-Year, will add much — not just to the Toros but the entire WHA.

The World Hockey Association started this season with everybody asking, "What are they going to do for encores?"

In 1972 the WHA plucked Bobby Hull from the Chicago Black Hawks; in 1973 the Houston Aeros lured Gordie Howe out of the comforts of retirement; and continuing the super-star trend, the Toronto Toros this season grabbed hometown hero Frank Mahovlich from the prestigious surroundings of Montreal's Forum.

The signing of Mahovlich by the WHA is a significant move. In less than three years, it now boasts the talents of hockey's three all-time greatest scorers.

But that is not the entire story.

Other top NHL names have made the jump, and with them, many new young faces destined to carve their names into the hockey annals.

Here are just a few of those new faces WHA fans will witness:

Gerry Desjardins

Paul Henderson

Joining Frank Mahovlich with the Toronto Toros for the 1974-75 season is Paul Garnet Henderson.

A 12-year NHL veteran, Henderson comes to the Toros from the rival Maple Leafs, after having spent many outstanding years with the Detroit Red Wings.

An interesting note, Henderson was involved in the trade that sent him to the Leafs and Mahovlich to the Red Wings.

Henderson's best season was in 1971-72 while with the Leafs, when he placed 38 goals in enemy nets.

Along with the Big M, Henderson will add needed experience and strong offensive punch to the Toros attack.

The newly transplanted Michigan Stags (nee Los Angeles Sharks) will have an old NHL vet in Gerry Desjardins as a new net minder.

Signed from the New York Islanders, the new goaltender has also played with the Los Angeles Kings and the Chicago Black Hawks.

Thommy and Chris Abrahamsson

If the immigration laws don't change any time soon, the New England Whalers now have two men with major league potential.

Thommy and Chris Abrahammsson, twin brothers who have played for the Swedish Nationals, have both been inked to multi-year pacts by the Whalers.

Chris, the elder son by five hours, is a goaltender who has played more than 500 games during his 11-year career. He was named to the Swedish National team seven times.

Chris has played in six World Games and the 1972 Olympic Games in Japan.

Thommy is also an 11-year veteran of his home town club, Leskand. He captained his squad to the team championship in Sweden the last two years and has played in four World Games and the 1972 Games in Japan.

An offensive defenseman, Thommy scored 26 goals and gathered 35 assists last season. At the conclusion of the 1972-73 campaign, Thommy received the Golden Puck Award as Sweden's best hockey player.

No stranger to the New England area, Fred O'Donnell joins the Whalers after spending almost two full seasons with the Boston Bruins of the NHL.

The Whalers signed O'Donnell from the Vancouver Canucks after he was traded to Vancouver by the Bruins at the tail end of last season.

The young right winger will be a real asset to the Whalers.

Fred O'Donnell

Danny O'Shea

A strong centerman who had spent six years in the NHL, Danny O'Shea is no stranger to Minnesota. O'Shea, who was signed by the Fighting Saints from the St. Louis Blues, spent nearly three seasons with the North Stars of the NHL.

In addition to his stints with the Blues and the North Stars, O'Shea spent time with the Chicago Black Hawks.

His best year in the majors was his initial year with the North Stars in 1967-68 when he garnered 15 goals and 34 assists.

Al McDonough

Joining the forward wall of the Cleveland Crusaders, Al McDonough comes from the NHL Atlanta Flames. The five-year hockey veteran has also spent time with the Pittsburgh Penguins and the Los Angeles Kings.

While with the Penguins, McDonough scored a career high 35 goals in 1972-73.

Dave Dyrden

To bolster the goaltending crew of the Chicago Cougars, Dave Dryden has been lured away from the Buffalo Sabres for the 1974-75 season.

Dryden, who has played both for the Sabres and the Chicago Black Hawks, is the brother of Montreal Canadien ace goalie, Ken.

45

THE PEOPLE'S TEAM

by Debbie McArthur

The course of the Jets looked rough last spring. If the money couldn't be raised, it looked like a crash-landing was inevitable which meant sure death to the hockey club in Winnipeg. Rumours of hijackings to Miami and other American cities were widespread. All in all, the fate of the Winnipeg Jets was a precarious one until the people of Winnipeg in a united effort raised the necessary funds to insure that their hockey club would stay where it belonged.

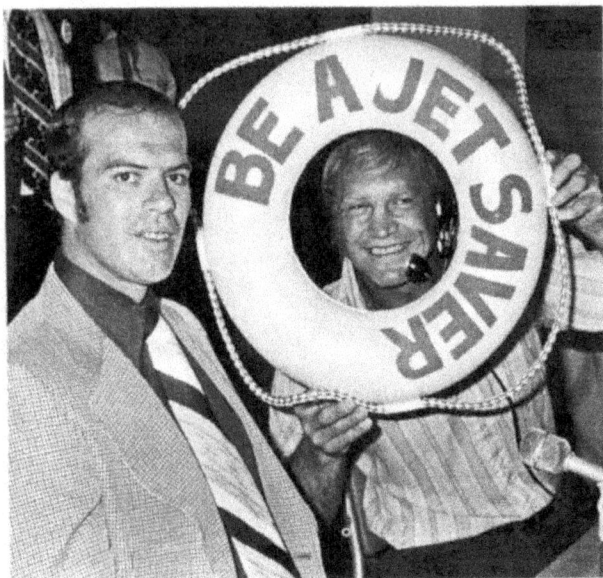

The panic began in January 1974, when it became known that Ben Hatskin and the Simkin family were selling the Jets hockey team and it became painfully aware that there were no serious local offers.

Ben Hatskin was justifiably worried. He had used a lot of money and elbow grease to get the WHA franchise in Winnipeg, even though many critics had said that our city wasn't ready for a Professional hockey team. As owners, he and the Simkin family just couldn't afford to see the team in the red for another year, but they genuinely wanted the Jets to stay in Winnipeg.

With the same thoughts in mind, a "Citizens Committee" was formed to ex-plore different means of financing the acquisition of the Jets Hockey Club as a community-owned professional team. Encouraged by the prospects of keeping the Jets in Winnipeg, the owners offered the club to the community for $2.3 million. Hatskin had said that the asking price would be $3.5 million or higher for a private transaction.

That $2.3 million figure meant that $600,000 would be needed for a sufficient down payment with $300,000 for working capital with the outstanding amount re-payable over eight years with 9 per cent interest. With all the calculations down on paper and with what they thought was a pretty good plan, the committee, a group of earnest businessmen began to drum up support from the public.

Early in the planning stages for financial support, the Premier of Manitoba, Mr. Ed Schreyer, implied that the provincial government would lend a fiscal hand to help keep the team in Winnipeg. Using that as a basis, the Committee designed a plan by which the City of Winnipeg would be asked to loan, interest free, an amount of $300,000 to a non-profit corporation to be

46

formed on behalf of the community. This amount was to be matched by the Province and the public supporters in similar amounts.

It looked almost fool-proof, especially after the city granted the loan and added a rider that Council was authorized to pick up one-third of the cash flow deficit should such occur. Of course, all of this was contingent on the fact that the Province would match the offer. Crunch. The Provincial Government bowed out saying they found it impossible to provide direct assistance. They did however give indications that they would give the company the rights to a lottery. Although the lottery is a future means of support for the club, the score had changed and the Committee had to organize a new set of plays.

Evidence of growing public support in local newspapers and talk shows made the Committee revise their figures to an ominous $600,000 to be collected from the public. After giving the group a five week extension, Hatskin wanted the final decision made no later than July 1, 1974.

With little time left, one of the most successful promotional jobs was accomplished with the Save the Jets campaign. Information brochures were printed and large ads in the newspapers explained the program and asked the support of everyone in Manitoba.

Speeches were made to explain the amount of revenue and benefits to the community, the Jets provide. By the actual starting date of the campaign everyone knew the predicament of the Winnipeg Jets hockey team.

Bob Graham, spokesman for the local group, outlined the new proposals designed to raise the funds.

"We will approach large businesses and certain individuals to try to obtain $1,000 interest-free founders' loans. We will also go to the general public to sell membership shares."

The membership shares cost $25.00 for individuals and $100.00 for families. Being a non-profit corporation, subscribing members are not entitled to any interest or any other return on their subscription. On the other hand, with founders' loans, should the company generate sufficient surplus cash, decide to dissolve or sell the WHA franchise, holders of these notes are entitled to repayment of the loan. Both subscription and founders' loan members are granted the right to one vote when it comes time to elect the Board of Directors.

Graham and the other members of the Committee were gaining confidence in the ability to raise $600,000. It had been hinted that there were several businesses ready to offer $25,000 donations. It was

time to put the "Save the Jets" campaign to work.

Monday morning, June 10th, the Marlborough Hotel looked like Grand Central station during Christmas vacation. Typewriters, adding machines, secretaries, and a radio station were just part of the new scenery that transformed the hotel into "Save the Jets" headquarters.

Peter Warren, CJOB's investigative reporter was using his most persuasive rhetoric to lure the people downtown to the Marlborough to make their contributions. And they started coming . . . a little at a time until the room was packed with the folk from North Kildonan and Sunny St. James and Brandon and Dauphin and all corners of the city and province.

There was a $25.00 membership pledge from one of the youngest Jets fans going, an eight day old baby. Another rather odd donation came from a one year old German Shepherd. No one is quite sure how the dog will vote at the annual meeting, but the important thing is that someone cared enough to take a membership in its name.

The first day clearly indicated that people of the city of Winnipeg enjoyed having a professional hockey club bear their name and they'd put up a good fight to keep it here. Day one of the campaign

showed a collection of $106,000 toward the goal.

It was a good turnout by the public, but corporate aid was less than inspiring. Oscar Grubert, one of the teammates in the organizational power play of the Save the Jets campaign, expressed concern when he said, "When you see this many people giving $25.00, you start asking 'where are the firms?' A lot of businesses who aren't involved yet should get involved."

In the days that followed a variety of money-making schemes were enacted by conscientious Winnipeggers. Office collections, car washes, and baseball games were just some of the programs initiated to Save the Jets. Every little bit helped bring the goal closer in sight.

After nine days and only 12 days left in the running, the fund had reached $206,000. Campaign chairman Graham applauded the outstanding support from the public sector and small businesses. The corporations were still being stubborn and the Committee still had not received word from the city about their $300,000 interest-free loan.

With only four days to go, the figure left to raise by the end of the week was $280,500. Graham, trying to keep a level head, wondered where a couple of hund-

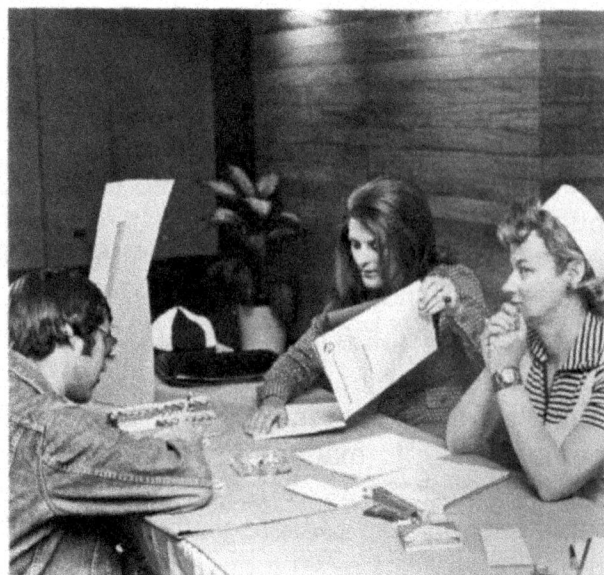

The Story of the Toros

"Bassett's group bought 90 percent of the team for an estimated $1.8 million. They either outbid or outmanoeuvred a similar group which Bill Ballard had apparently formed"

When Douglas Michel, a Toronto electrical contractor, settled his new pro hockey team into Ottawa and named them the Nationals, he wasn't really expecting round-the-block lineups for tickets. His team, like most in the World Hockey Association—a league born an almost indecently short time after its conception—boasted a lineup of had-beens, hadn't-beens and might-bes.

Originally the club was to have played in Hamilton, but that city's council made too many financial demands on Michel, who had had enough financial demands made on him already. By August 1972, six months after purchasing the franchise and the personnel required to put a team on the ice, Michel sold majority interest in the Nationals—an estimated 80 per cent—to Buffalo aerospace millionaire Nick Trbovich. That insured at least that the team would be able to get through its first year. Some prospective franchises would fold before the season got underway—Miami Screaming Eagles (the name alone would have done it), Calgary, and Dayton, Ohio.

One of the first things Michel did was to secure the services of Allan J. "Buck" Houle. (The last name is French, properly pronounced like Rejean's but usually improperly pronounced as Hooley. Houle's grandfather came from France to the U.S., and settled in Johnstown, Ohio. He was around for the Johnstown Flood, which persuaded the family to settle in Niagara-on-the-Lake. The Buck part came to be during Houle's softball-playing youth: he came out of a batting slump just as the Jack Benny radio show, *Buck Benny Rides Again,* was being aired. "Buck Hooley Hits Again", the kids decided.)

Houle had spent most of his working lifetime in the employ of Major Conn Smythe and/or the Toronto Maple Leafs. Even during the war he was under Smythe's command. From 1948 on he coached, managed, administered and scouted in the Leaf organization. He was general manager of the 1964 Marlboros, considered by many to have been the best junior hockey team ever assembled. Certainly they were the biggest team, outweighing their nearest rivals, the Chicago Black Hawks, by an average of nearly 20 pounds per man. He managed the Victoria Maple Leafs for three years after that, then returned to the Marlies for two more seasons.

In 1969 Houle went to Hockey Canada as general manager of the National Team. He was supposed to be on loan from the Leaf organization, but he never returned to it. Michel, who had become involved with Hockey Canada and knew Houle, asked him to come to California with him in the spring of 1972 to help him draft a team for the WHA. Houle did, and became Nats' general manager. It was

pretty tough slugging, he remembers. There was one player (unnamed) he wanted badly, and Al Eagleson, the player's lawyer, gave him 60 days to come up with the money, some $30,000. When Trbovich was brought in, the money was made available, but unfortunately it was two days too late.

The Nationals, after attempting to lure Dave Keon away from the Maple Leafs—and paying him $50,000 (which was never returned and is now a matter before the courts)—settled for three former NHL players, Wayne Carleton from California, Guy Trottier of the Leafs, and Les Binkley from Pittsburgh. They could best be described as journeymen, and none could be counted on to fill an arena. In the WHA, however, they would acquit themselves admirably. Carleton, whom Stafford Smythe once called the best junior he'd ever seen, scored 42 goals and added 49 assists; Trottier had 26 goals and 32 assists. The other players were minor leaguers. Billy Harris, the ex-Leaf who'd played on three Stanley Cup winners in the 1960's, and who had more recently been coaching in Sweden, was signed as coach.

The Nats were about as popular in Ottawa as a ninth month of winter. For the first half of the season, when they were getting regular thrashings, a crowd of 1,200 people commonly rattled around in the 9,500-seat Civic Centre arena. Later in the schedule, when the team started to win, the fans burgeoned to maybe 3,000. On a big day (like when Hull and the Jets were in town) they'd get 4,000. Average attendance was about 2,000; for the rest of the WHA—according to the league offices—the annual average attendance was about 5,000 per game, better than the 3,500 anticipated by Gary Davidson before the season began. But only two teams made money, and the Nats dropped an estimated $1 million.

Early this year, the word was out that the Nats were looking to move, and Milwaukee was oft-mentioned. The possibility of Toronto increased weekly as 1973 wore on, and as John F. Bassett (on one hand) and Bill Ballard (on the other) began having meetings with Trbovich, and with Davidson. On April 5, 1973, Ballard called a press conference at Maple Leaf Gardens, which his father owns and of which he is vice-president, to announce the Nats would play their WHA playoff games at the Gardens—and, as far as he was concerned, the team would play out of the Gardens in 1973-74. Trbovich, who was there, allowed that his options were still open.

The Nats had a good finish, winning 12 of their last 15 games to grab fourth place in the Eastern Division. They were knocked out of the semi-finals by league-champion New England Whalers in five games; but the Whalers needed overtime for two of the victories. The Nats' record was 35 wins, 39 losses, and

tour ties.

The team would never return to Ottawa. The financial problems and squabbles with the city over arena rentals—now a matter before the courts (the city is suing)—plus the crummy support, plus the fact that a Toronto sports consortium bought the franchise, kept the team in Toronto.

Bassett's group, Can Sports Inc., bought 90 percent of the team from Trbovich for an estimated $1.8 million. They either outbid or outmanoeuvred a similar group which Bill Ballard had apparently formed. The Gardens, Ballard insists, never had any intention of buying the Nats; he was representing outside interests. After Bassett's group won out, Ballard offered the team a three or four year deal for the use of the Gardens, but it was turned down. Bassett's argument was, essentially, that the new team needed to establish a separate identity in Toronto, something it couldn't do playing out of the same house as a Canadian Institution, the Toronto Maple Leafs. Also, Bassett realized that a half-filled Gardens—say 9,000 people—is worse than a wholly-filled rink seating maybe 5,000; very bad for morale, as the team learned in Ottawa.

Perhaps more important though is Bassett's intention to create a major sports complex, probably somewhere in the west end, or in Mississauga. The hockey team, naturally, would be the basis of such an undertaking; he figures the rink could be ready by January 1, 1975. For this season Can Sports first approached Metro Toronto for the use of the CNE Coliseum, even offered to increase its capacity from 6,000 to about 9,500, but red tape made that venture unattractive; so the directors pulled out and managed to get the 4,800-seat Varsity Arena for most (30 of 39) home games.

While all this was going on the Nats, who of late had become known as the Gnats, the No-Names, and the Orphans, were transmogrified into the Toros by the creative people at Vickers and Benson Ltd., the advertising company; V and B's president, Bill Bremner, is one of the Toros directors. The image was changed from the greyness of civil servantism—the Nationals—to fiery, aggressive bulls-rampant.

The team improved itself, signing Peter Marrin and Wayne Dillon from the Marlies, Pat Hickey from the Hamilton Red Wings and Jeff Jacques from St. Catharines. In fact, it was the only WHA club to secure anybody from the top-30 NHL draft choices. Brit Selby was traded for, and Carl Brewer—who started training camp in the best condition, at 35, of his checkered career—signed on, vowing to prove something to the hockey fans of Toronto. Thanks to the perceived battle between the Bassetts and the Ballards for the team (read: sports superiority in Toronto) the Toros became widely and well-known in a short period of time.

RACERS IN RETROSPECT

(R) Bob Woytowich - No. 5, and (L) Bob Sicinski, team up to assist Andy Brown, on ice, as he stops an opponents goal attempt.

So you think Noah had it bad, huh? Forty days and 40 nights of rain.

Well, consider the Indianapolis Racers of 1974-75. They went through 172 days of almost unrelenting thunderstorms.

Or did it just seem that way?

There's no getting around the fact that the Racers' first World Hockey Association season was dismal. Just 18 victories and three ties in 78 games defy any lesser adjective.

The emphasizing adverbs would be a league-record 13-game losing streak early in the season, a 10-game slide at the end, just 216 goals scored and 338 allowed.

Those were tangible elements that made the first season seem a lot longer than the 172 days it took to play 78 games.

At one point, it seemed possible that the season wouldn't be half that long. Indiana Professional Sports, Inc., which was awarded the franchise in October 1973, was the single most positive influence on the Indianapolis sports scene since Carl Fisher built the Indianapolis Motor Speedway in 1908-09. The group of local sportsmen had the courage to gamble on a new American Basketball Association and founded the Indiana Pacers. They were the moving force behind the construction of Market Square Arena. And when no one else seemed interested in helping out, they took the plunge alone to bring the Racers and hockey back to the Circle City.

The group always was a lot longer on civic pride and courage than it was on hard cash. And about the time the Racers were leaving the launching pad, the shortage of the latter was overhelming the last reservoirs of the former.

Fiscal crisis moved rapidly into catastrophe in November and the last born--the Racers--were the first to feel the bite. By the end of the month IPS simply couldn't meet the payroll any longer. It's possible that the WHA might have had to take over the club for the remainder of the season and had no new owners been found by season's end, the Racers might have been unceremoniously disbanded--as were the Chicago Cougars and Baltimore Blades.

It's also possible the club might have been shut down right on the spot. The WHA already was loaded down with the problems in Chicago and Detroit where the soon-to-be Blades were performing as the Michigan Stags. Trying to carry three ailing clubs at one time might have been too much for the other league teams.

Fortunately, it never came to that. Paul Deneau, an architect and real estate man from Dayton, Ohio, purchased the club from IPS on Dec. 5. The purchase marked the turning point for the Racers both off the ice and on--though the latter wasn't immediately noticeable as the team lost a 5-3 decision to Chicago on the MSA ice that night, defeat No. 12 in that 13-game nightmare.

Deneau's first move was to convince WHA Executive Vice-President James W. Browitt to join the Racers as president and general manager. That gave the club something it had lacked--a man with a solid hockey background in charge of the front office.

Once on hand Browitt started moving immediately to get players who could make the Racers competitive on a major league level.

Faced with a money crunch from the start, IPS had gone with players it could afford. Some had talent; others didn't. One experienced observer described the first Racers ad "big, sluggish and mean." Only the last seemed inappropriate.

On the sum, the club had forwards who could check but, with the exception of Bob Whitlock, none who could score--at least with any consistency. The defense was either too small, too mistake-prone or both.

When Deneau purchased the club, its record stood at 4-20. It had generated only 51 goals (a 2.13 a game average) and had allowed 113 (4.71). It had been shutout five times.

Browitt's first moves were aimed at shoring up the leaky defense. Some help arrived from resources already on hand--Ken Desjardine, the best of the blue liners on the roster, returned from a broken heel that had sidelined him for six weeks.

But Browitt's own efforts also started to pay off. Within a week after assuming his post, he had acquired Dick Proceviat from Chicago and before the turn of the year Bob Woytowich came in trade from Winnipeg. In January he added Ken Block from San Diego for Jim Hargreaves in a deal that gave up muscle and youth for finesse and experience.

By mid-January, those three, Desjardine and Bill Horton had welded into an effective backguard that made life a little more bearable for goaltenders Andy Brown and Ed Dyck.

Bob Whitlock, the 1974/75 leading scorer with 31 goals is congratulated after scoring one of them.

The front lines weren't ignored. IPS already had made some moves that helped in the last days of its proprietorship, trading for Brian McDonald from Michigan and calling up rookie John Sheridan from Mohawk Valley.

Browitt's first move was to get center Joe Hardy from Chicago in December. But the big scores didn't come until late.

The biggest came during the All-Star meetings at Edmonton when he finally culminated a month of negotiations by acquiring center Ron Buchanan from the Oilers. The rangy pivot had left the Canadian Division club a month earlier asking to be traded to a U.S.-based team.

Fans on their feet as they enjoy one of the thousands of exciting moments offered by Racer action, win (or) lose.

He reported out-of-shape and played the last six weeks with a broken knuckle, but his contributions immediately made him the Racers' most valuable forward.

Soon after Bucky got here, Browitt was able to come up with the right wing to complement him. Murray Heatley had twice been available to the Racers under IPS' ownership but neither time did they feel they could afford him. When the Minnesota Fighting Saints came around a third time, Browitt jumped fast.

Heatley made the most of his limited time here, scoring 15 goals in the last 27 games.

By season's end, the Racers were a competitive club, one that was perhaps seven games better than those final 18 victories. Among those 57 losses were 17 by one goal, including seven in overtime. Furthermore, the early part of the year had put the Racers too far behind to have any playoff hopes by March. That produced a letdown that was only accentuated by a schedule that had them on the road for their last six games.

And, though it was short on victories, the Racers' first WHA season did not lack for thrills many of which came before their ferociously loyal and patient fans at Market Square Arena.

In fact, the fans would have to rank as one of the biggest thrills of the season. "They're the greatest," was a description used by friend and foe alike. Virtually unexposed to hockey for more than a decade, they came in ever-growing numbers, making up in enthusiasm what they lacked in knowledge of the sport. By season's end they had averaged an incredible 7,906 a game.

At times they clearly carried the Racers above where they were prepared to play. No night was it more graphically demonstrated than on March 7 when the crowd picked up the club and literally carried it back from a three-goal deficit to tie Baltimore 4-4. That the local heroes quickly died once more in overtime did nothing to cool their fervor.

But that fervor still had its seed on what happened on the ice. And there were nights--not many--when there were thrills aplenty. A sampling would include:

Nov. 7--Andy Brown turned in as fine a 20 minutes of goaltending as anyone is ever likely to see in the third period and defenseman Roger Cote seemed to be every place as the Racers shut out San Diego, 3-0.

Nov. 9--Just two nights later, the Racers came from three goals down in the last seven minutes to tie World Cup champion Houston on the Aeros' ice as Joe Robertson got the evener with 1 second remaining. In overtime Gary Bredin's rebound shot gave the Racers their first road victory and only overtime triumph of the year.

Dec. 8--The Racers finally ended that 13-game losing streak with a hard-working 5-3 triumph over San Diego.

Dec. 22--Gerry Moore refered to this as the Racers' best game. Checking tightly all the way, they stunned the Eastern Division-leading New England Whalers, 2-1.

Jan. 16--This was Guaranteed Win Night and more than 10,000 customers came out to accept the Racers' dare that they would win or the next game was on them. No one went home unhappy or with a free ticket as the Racers won, 4-2.

Feb. 1--This was perhaps the most beautifully played game of the year, one that not even a 2-1 loss to the Quebec Nordiques could dampen. It was fast-moving and exciting all the way with the Nordiques' brilliant defenseman J.C. Tremblay the difference.

Feb. 20--The Racers pounded Minnesota goalie John Garrett with 49 shots and only a superlative effort by the cage cop kept more than six of them from going in. The 6-1 triumph may have been the Racers' most decisive of the year.

Feb. 21--The next night Andy Brown posted his second shutout of the year as the Racers, not quite as intense as the night before, dispatched the Cleveland Crusaders with businesslike ease.

Mar. 8--It was a rough game almost from the opening whistle and late in the second period it exploded into a full-scale brawl that involved both benches and coaches. The Cleveland Crusaders got a 6-5 victory and the WHA got a new one-game record for penalty minutes--228.

There were other thrills and other chills. But now they belong to the past. And as a wise man once said, "The past is prologue."

So it is with the Racers. On with the Second Season.

"First and Ten", one of the many battles they endured in their 74-75 efforts.

Blueline Magazine, 1975

The Iron Goaltender

by Lockwood

There were two different roads which could have brought Ron Grahame to San Diego. But he chose a third, and his arrival was anything but welcome. To the rest of the world, Grahame is a pleasant, soft-spoken young man of 24 — respectful of his elders and properly modest. To the San Diego Mariners, he was to become a figure of the utmost frustration and dismay. In four games, four painfully short games, Grahame ended abruptly what had been a truly remarkable year for the Mariners.

This nomadic team pitched its World Hockey Association tent in San Diego after fruitless last-place stops at New York City and Cherry Hills, N.J. In the Southern California sunshine, the Mariners bloomed into an outfit which finished second in the WHA's Western Division and upset heavily favored Toronto in the first round of the playoffs. Enter Grahame. Exit Mariners.

In four games, San Diego peppered the young Houston goaltender with 154 shots. Only five wound up in the net — four of those in the final game. Forget the Howe family. Grahame had personally knocked the Mariners out of the playoffs. "Ron has to be the difference in this series," said Houston coach and general manager Bill Dineen. "I don't think I've ever seen this kind of goaltending over a stretch of games. "To face it one night has to be bad enough. But to face it night after night has to be pretty frustrating." Indeed. "It's obvious we were up against a goaltender that just wasn't going to be beaten," sighed Mariner player-coach Harry Howell. "There's not much you can do about that." Except to reflect on what might have been. Grahame, you see, might have been wearing a San Diego uniform two years earlier. He might also have arrived with the Mariners from New Jersey. They try not to think about it.

The whole thing began while Grahame was performing for Denver University, where he was named an All-American his final season. Another member of that club was Peter McNab, son of the man who served as general manager of the Western League San Diego Gulls. Max loved to watch Peter (now with the Buffalo Sabres) play. As a result, he also saw a lot of Grahame. When the slender goaltender graduated, McNab was there. When Grahame, surprisingly, was not selected in the National Hockey League draft, Max added his name to the Gulls' negotiation list. Grahame was selected in the WHA draft, however. That's where the plot thickened. He was tapped by the New York Golden Blades, a team which became the Mariners two moves later. But the Blades showed little interest in signing their draft choice. Instead, his rights were traded to Houston for Ray La-Rose, a journeyman defenseman now out of the game. So it became a bidding war between the Gulls and the Aeros. Minor league team against major league team. It was no contest. "I really respected Max McNab very much," Grahame remembers. "I really kind of wanted to play for him. But I came to Houston for economic reasons. They were able to offer me more money, so I went there."

His first year was spent mostly in the minors. The Mariners, meanwhile, were in exile in New Jersey. Then Grahame arrived in Houston while the team which once drafted him arrived in San Diego. It was a successful regular season for both. Grahame had the league's lowest goals-against average and made the all-star team. The Mariners finished second with a closing rush. Strangely, although they inhabited the same division, the two met only once during the regular season — San Diego taking a 5-4 overtime victory. "The Mariners have a tendency to be a physical team," Dineen explained. The coach took a look at Grahame's slight frame and chronic sore knees and started Wayne Rutledge five games out of six, which happened to be the same number that San Diego won. "Wayne is a little more physical," said Dineen. "I thought he'd be better able to take care of himself." But by playoff time, bad knees or not, it was Grahame all the way.

The first two games were played in San Diego, due to an arena conflict in Houston. The shots in the opener were 35-35 but Houston won, 4-0. That, the Mariners were to learn, was just a sample. It was game No. 2 which decided the series. San Diego had 48 shots, the Aeros 23. But Houston scored goals 25 seconds apart in the second period and won, 2-1. "The kid was just fantastic." said Dineen. "He was unbelievable," said San Diego's Andre Lacroix, the league's leading scorer. "That's the best game we've played all season," said Howell. "And we lost it." "He saved us," Dineen elaborated. "San Diego outplayed us badly but he just wouldn't let them win." The series shifted to Houston for the next two games, but it seemed there was little left for Grahame to show the home folks that the people in San Diego hadn't already seen. He thought of something. In the opening period of Game No. 3, the Mariners outshot Houston, 16-12, and came off losing, 2-0. The final score was 6-0.

In three games, 180 minutes, Grahame had faced 117 shots and let in one. The Mariners had come to believe he was really four feet high and six feet wide. Ron's only human moments came in the fourth game, when he gave up four goals after breaking a skate in warmups. But Houston got five, the last in overtime, and it was over. Even Grahame couldn't quite believe it. "I was very happy with the way I played," he admitted. "I can't play any better than that. But I was a little lucky, too. There were some times I didn't even see the puck. I just kicked out my leg and hoped." Lucky? Maybe. But luck seems to follow talent. "If it's possible for a player to come of age in one series, I think that's what happened to Ronnie," judged Houston defenseman Poul Popiel. "We came within a goaltender of being even in this series," felt San Diego general manager Ron Ingram.

Instead, the Mariners went home. To think about the road Grahame might have taken.

Top: Aeros — Ron Grahame
Top Left: Roadrunners — Jack Norris
Center Left: Nordiques — Serge Aubry
Bottom Left: Racers — Ed Dyck

CLUBS LIVE AND DIE ON THE HOME FRONT

By Jim Kernaghan

Well beyond the roar of the arenas, the slip of skates on ice and thump of pucks against boards, a burgeoning form of Canadiana is observed, ritual-like, every day.

Small boys with glistening eyes throughout the nation, like the princes of industry, negotiate complicated transactions, barter, trade, gamble. The monetary system is hockey cards.

This stock market of cards is merely a manifestation of a larger truth. Only in Canada could this economy-in-microcosm exist. The phenomenon is a matter of evolvement.

There are financial concerns, to be sure, but the emergence of a purely Canadian Division in hockey, in the World Hockey Association, is something that evolved almost as if fore-ordained.

It's in the very nature of the nation that the five-team grouping has risen so rapidly and will continue to do so.

To those who insist they have no interest in the game, it remains a common denominator. To those smitten by hockey it is irretrievably inter-twined with the Canadian psyche. Hockey is Canada; Canada, hockey.

To argue is difficult, if not impossible. Of the three most successful Canadian films made, two are about hockey – Paperback Hero and Face-off, both of which thrived in Canada, and both produced by John F. Bassett, Jr.

There have been songs of Canadian hockey stars – Gordie Howe and Bobby Hull, to name two. Poems have been written about the game and it

Two of hockey's all-time greats, Bobby Hull and Gordie Howe, are shown admiring a number they've both made famous — No. 9.

has been the subject of art works from the greatest to the least celebrated.

If a civilization can be understood by its cultural contributions, hockey in Canadian art stands foremost of any sport in any nation in the world.

Ask any Canadian this question: What were you doing when Canada beat the Soviet Union in the final game in 1972? Chances are, most people can recall vividly.

That's important.

So it is that an essentially Canadian league, one within the governmental confines of a larger league, has

evolved. It has filled a vacuum. The Canadian Division was needed.

Why not sooner? Simple. Financial considerations, meaning cutting up more shares of rich television money, precluded the rival National Hockey League to go beyond Toronto and Montreal for two decades and when it did, only to Vancouver.

The Canadian Division of the 14-team WHA is not only a geographic possibility, with Calgary in the West and Quebec City in the east as its perimeters, there are indications that the scope could be widened — to British Columbia once more and even the Maritimes.

The operative word in the Canadian Division is rivalry. Meaningful confrontations are the fuel on which the division is succeeding.

A decade ago, you'll recall, any Saturday night game at Montreal Forum or Maple Leaf Gardens was a showpiece, an event which started to take shape Wednesday and which people didn't stop talking about until after the game was over — whether they watched it live, in a bar or in the middle of a house party.

The seeds of such meaningful sports fare have been sown again in Canada and the Canadian Division scheduling has been arranged to this end.

Take Toronto Toros and Quebec Nordiques, who'll meet 14 times before the shooting is over. There are elements of traditional Anglo-French rivalry, a clash of disparate styles, rustic Canada vs. Hogtown.

It's rich, that rivalry, and is sauce to what has become, in three seasons, a series of dramatic confrontations, a consideration reflected in crowd attendances.

This is no less true of Edmonton Oilers and Calgary Cowboys, a duel slightly different, like cousins feuding. The pride of each city is at stake, after all, once more in a long series of escalating one-upmanships on the part of each.

Winnipeg Jets, the eastern westerners, battle on two fronts and have their own built-in audience grabber. He's Bobby Hull, of course, whose unmatched on and off ice charisma could pack them in in Afghanistan.

With scheduling designed to heighten these rivalries, one important fact leads to better basic hockey. For one thing, the teams are playing before the most knowledgeable fans in the world: for another, they can't afford to lose.

In an 80-game schedule, any team in hockey can easily take a subconscious coast if it isn't careful. No Canadian Division team can afford it because, in essence, everything is a four-point game.

Each team in the division has carefully done its homework and none is without personalities and stars. Hull, the man who made the league credible, stands out with Winnipeg.

Frank Mahovlich and Paul Henderson made Toronto Toros a reality: Rejean Houle, Serge Bernier, Marc Tardif and J. C. Tremblay stabilized Quebec, Norm Ullman, Bruce MacGregor, Dave Dryden in Edmonton.

As the number of top-flight Europeans and rookies who've joined the division will attest, Canadian cities can compete with any in scouting and landing the players they want.

The Nordic horde of Winnipeg, with Anders Hedberg and Ulf Nilsson leading the 9-member pack of Swedes and Finns, have brought a new dimension to the game. Toronto followed up with a pair of Czechoslovakians, Vaclav Nedomansky and Richard Farda.

Calgary's Ron Chipperfield, Mark Napier of Toronto, Real Cloutier of Quebec, Peter Sullivan of Winnipeg and Peter Morris of Edmonton are just a few of the top rookie signings.

Joe Crozier, with Calgary, is the dean of Canadian Division coaches and, at the same time, one of the deans of pro hockey coaching ranks. New approaches to the game have been brought by Bobby Baun and Clare Drake, rookies, and Bobby Kromm has shown in Winnipeg he has belonged in the majors for a long time. Jean-Guy Gendron, Quebec mentor, has, in two seasons, established himself as a thinking man's coach.

Bobby Hull, Winnipeg Jets, WHA's most valuable player 1974-75. Hull scored 77 goals last season to set a major league goal scoring record.

Aside from seeing traditional rivalries grow, fans are still able to assess the WHA as a whole, since each of the U.S.-based teams plays twice in every Canadian Division city.

But the Canadian clubs live and die on the home front. It's impossible for a Canadian team to be below .500 and entertain thoughts of a playoff berth. And playoff berths are in themselves intriguing.

Therefore, it could evolve that four of the five Canadian Division teams have a shot at the playoffs. Last season, two division champs, Houston Aeros from the West and Quebec Nordiques from the Canadian, met in the final with Houston repeating as Avco World Cup champions.

The Canadian Division led the league in total attendance last season with 1,840,061 for an average of 9,436 with Edmonton boasting five 15,326 sellouts, leading all clubs with an average crowd of 10,722.

Andre Lacroix, San Diego, All-Star centre and WHA scoring champ 1974-75 with 147 points (41-106).

Toronto Toros were second with a 10,437 average with Quebec (9,406) and Winnipeg (8,586) third and fourth.

Considering the arena plans underway, those are solid bases upon which to work. Edmonton, with its Coliseum, one of the finest facilities in the game anywhere, needs no changes. Nor do the Toros, playing out of Maple Leaf Gardens, although the Toronto entry still has not given up seeking means to build its own arena.

In Calgary, plans are underway for an expanded Corral and both Quebec Colisee and Winnipeg Arena can be expanded readily.

Hockey's future is intriguing, to say the least. In our unsettled economy, the game is undergoing changes like it never saw in the previous 50 years.

There is reason to suppose that the five Canadian clubs are best equipped to weather the storms and that this sport we love to call our own will be even more so in the future.

Phoenix Roadrunners home ice, 1975

NO LONGER DOORMAT, RACERS SEEK TO TURN TABLES ON RUNNERS

FIVE GAMES INTO this season the Indianapolis Racers made a coaching change, and almost immediately their fortunes seemed to turn around. Under last season's mentor, Gerry Moore, the Indianapolis sextet won their first game of the season against Denver in the Mile High City, somewhat surprising since they'd only copped four road decisions all last year. But after that heady success, they lost four straight, including a couple at home and Jacques Demers, who assisted Pat Stapleton in Chicago last year, stepped into the breach. The turnabout was apparent to all. Demers wanted his club to play a close checking systematic style of hockey and they responded well, so well in fact, that when they trimmed the Whalers in Hartford a couple of weekends ago they moved up out of the Eastern cellar for the first time (excluding, of course, their opening night victory).

In addition to following Demers' disciplined style, the Racers present several other problems to opponents. They have a new toughness, represented by several additions to the team. Defenseman Kim Clackson, a 20-year-old rookie out of the WCHL, the same spawning ground for Roadrunners Cam Connor and Barry Dean, has been among the penalty leaders all season, and at his current pace would amass well over 500 minutes. Couple of weeks ago Clackson set a WHA record by receiving eight penalties (4 minors, 3 majors and a game misconduct) for 33 minutes, which would also have been a league high if it hadn't been for 36 minutes received in one game by Derek Sanderson four years ago.

The Racers can score also, and in center Randy Wyrozub they have a gem of a playmaker. Wyro, as an example, scored three powerplay goals within a 1:46 span earlier this year for a league record for that sort of thing. Bob Whitlock potted 31 goals last season, Ron Buchanan had 16 in just 32 games for Indy, Nick Harbaruk, Murray Heatley, Bob Sicinski, Brian McDonald were all around the 20-goal mark.

Defensively, Pat Stapleton, Ken Block and Bob Woytowich are all savvy veterans and in goal maskless Andy Brown remains one of the games most courageous performers. Swedish International star Leif Holmquist also has been performing well.

Last season both the Roadrunners and Racers were expansion teams, but the Phoenicians swept the six-game series in one-sided fashion, administrating two shutouts and pummeling the Racers once, 12-2. Those days are past. Coach Demers will see to that tonight.

In action last year, Roadrunner John Gray draws a crowd and sticks get high as goalie Andy Brown goes sprawling. Below, despite checking of Bob Woytowich, Michel Cormier deflects puck past Brown, one of 12 to escape him in that March 1 blitz.

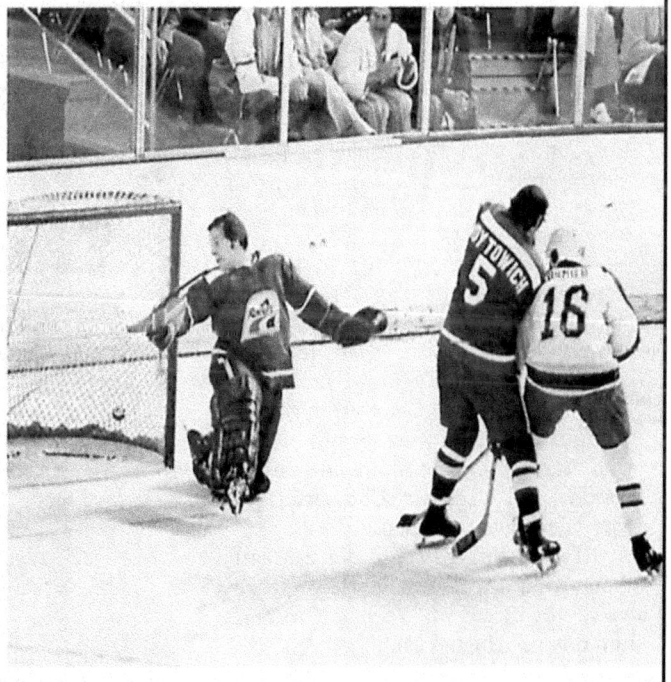

Aeros

Best in the

W.H.A.

by Rich Burk

Gordie Howe stood at center ice, the joy and relief of a second straight Avco World Trophy smoothing the lines of weariness and 47 years.

When the Great One stepped to the microphone in Quebec's Colisee after the clincher, he told the crowd, "Les Aero sont la."

The pronouncement was not lost on the French-Canadian fans. For that matter, it wasn't lost on teams in the World Hockey Association, either. If the Aeros weren't it, who was?

For two years in a row, nobody was more efficient during the regular season or the playoffs. Houston's two-year record is 101-50-5 for the regular season. The playoffs? The Aeros are 24-3.

"The idea is to put together 12 wins as quick as you can and then get the hell out," Houston defenseman Poul Popiel said.

The Aeros definitely had the potential to put together 12 wins in a hurry. Houston coach Bill Dineen went into the playoffs with a stacked deck — four lines capable of scoring, the league's best defense and the Numbers 1 and 2 goaltenders in the WHA.

Dineen had something else going for him, too.

"We're hitting our peak now, just about the right time. We're playing about as well as we can," he said.

During the regular season the Aeros played almost every style game. Slow it down and Houston would outwait you. Speed it up and hasten the end. Play a little loose and get murdered.

The Aeros scored a record 369 goals during the regular season and added 599 assists. Houston allowed only 244 goals. The Aeros won their first game and then dropped four in a row. After that, Houston never lost more than two in succession.

That was the kind of momentum Houston had for the playoffs.

Still, Dineen was genuinely worried about Cleveland, the first opponent. The Crusaders had a losing record, but they also had Gerry Cheevers in goal.

Houston right wing Frank Hughes, who scored eight of his 48 regular season goals against Cheevers, knew why Dineen was worried.

"If Cheevers gets hot he can carry them in a short series. He's the guy we've got to get to. We've got to break him down," Hughes said.

2nd Round Playoff — San Diego vs. Houston

Above: Papa Howe   Left: Ron Grahame

Cleveland coach Jack Vivian agreed that Cheevers was an important factor — but maybe not as important as Ron Grahame, Houston's rookie goaltender.

Grahame led the league in wins with 33 and had a 3.03 goals against mark, tops in the WHA. What he didn't have gave Vivian confidence. Grahame had never been in a playoff game before.

"Grahame is a good goaltender, but there's no way of telling how he's going to react to this. Cheevers has been through it before," Vivian said.

It appeared Vivian knew what he was talking about when the series began in Houston. Jim Harrison scored 15 seconds after the game got started and Grahame appeared anything but settled.

Cheevers had his problems, too. The Aeros bombed him for eight goals as the Cleveland defense played poorly. When it was over, Houston had an 8-5 win and a 1-0 series lead.

Cheevers and Grahame were more in command in the second game as the Aeros escaped with a 5-3 victory. Houston didn't cinch the win until Mark Howe hit the empty net with 32 seconds to play.

"Houston knows it's been in a hockey game now. I don't know if we can do anything more than guarantee them a couple of good games at our place, but we won't quit," Vivian said.

The Cleveland coach was half right.

The Crusaders made it, 2-1, with a 3-1 win in the third game of the series and the first in Cleveland. Mark Howe got Houston's only goal, his fifth in three games. A pair of power play goals in the last period was what Cleve-

Above: San Diego — Andre Lacroix, 7; Houston — Larry Lund, 13

Below: Stick Exchange — Wayne Rivers, San Diego — Murray Hall, Houston

land needed, however.

"We didn't play that bad, they just played that well. If we keep playing like this, we're going to be all right. We won't lose too many more," Dineen said.

The Aeros continued to play well when the teams played the fourth game of the series. The Cleveland defense, which had performed well in the third game, fell apart and Cheevers was saddled with a 7-2 shelling.

Mark Howe got the hat trick after Murray Hall wrapped up the win with two early goals. Playoff goals are nothing new for Hall. Nobody has scored more in the WHA tournament.

But Mark Howe was moving up fast.

"I'm not doing anything different. They're just leaving me open because of my dad," Mark said. "I get the puck and all I have to do is shoot."

Dad, of course, is Gordie Howe, who appeared to be holding rehearsals for Cleveland team pictures. Two sometimes three, Crusaders were always near him when he came on the ice.

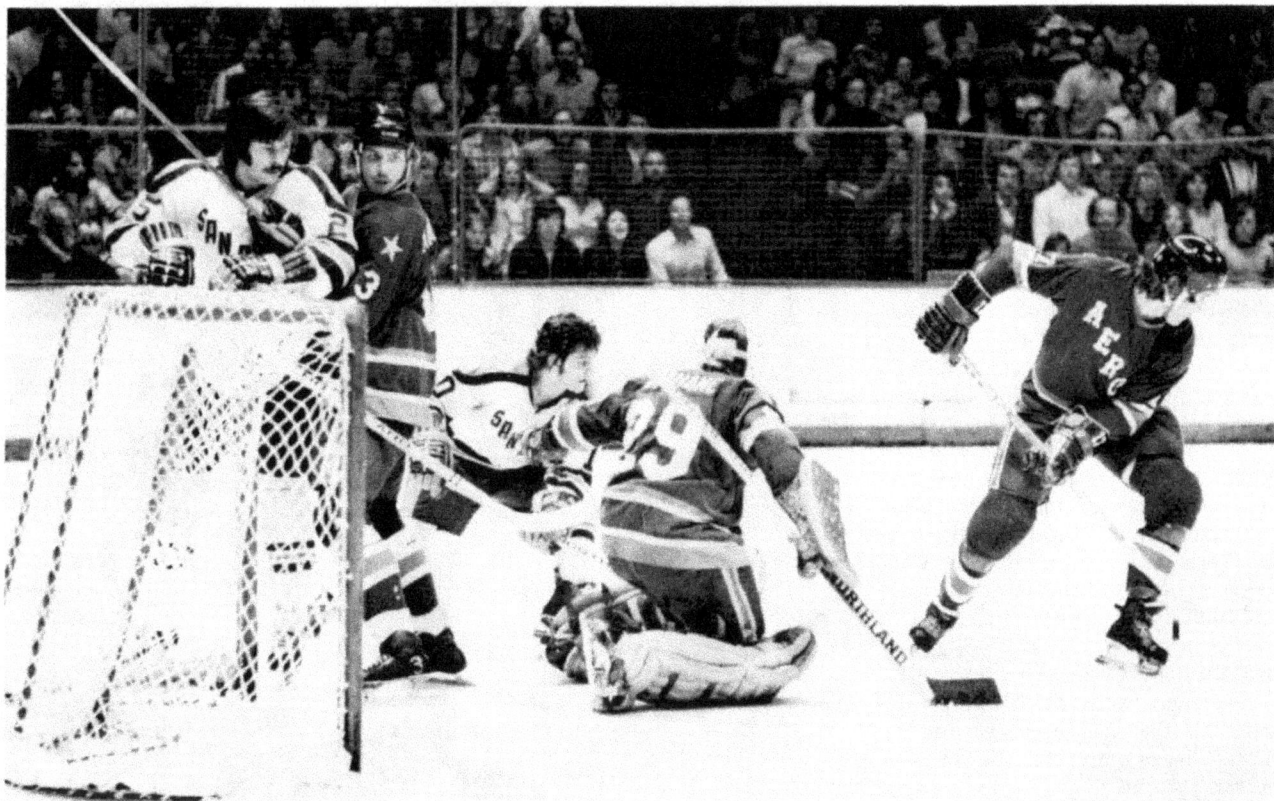

Second Round Playoff — San Diego vs. Houston — Series total: Houston — 4 games; San Diego — 0 games

'I really haven't noticed," Gordie said.

Hall was aware of the order of things. He knew Mark was hot.

"I hope our plane goes down so I can keep my lead for awhile," he joked.

The Crusaders went down in the fifth game of the series, though not without a fight. Cheevers, who surrendered a trickler to Gordie in the first minute, played his best game of the series.

Houston didn't get any breathing room until Ted Taylor scored late in the third period.

"I don't think we played that badly. We just ran into a fine team. Houston didn't get to be No. 1 in the league for nothing," Vivian said.

Cheevers complimented Grahame, who had grown progressively stronger.

"He showed it was wrong to mention he hadn't been here before. He's going to do all right," Cheevers said.

Houston now moved into the second round against San Diego and Dineen had a new worry.

The Mariners won five of the six games the teams played during the regular season. Most of them weren't close games, either. Andre Lacroix, the San Diego center who led the WHA in scoring, said it didn't mean a thing.

"Houston has too many good players for us to take them lightly. Both teams have players who can score. And we can't take a team that has Gordie Howe for granted," Lacroix said.

"We have a lot of people who can score and Houston has a lot of people who can score. The team that wins will be the team that stops the other team."

So it loomed that Grahame would be a big man in the series. When the Cleveland series was over, the rookie laughed and pointed out, "Did you notice how the goals went down? That it went 5-4-3-2-1? I was getting more confident and comfortable as we went along."

The next step, logically, was a shutout. Naturally, Grahame got it.

The Aeros were forced to begin the series on the road because of an ice show. Dineen didn't like the idea, but he was resolved to get a split, knowing

Above: Ron Grahame and Gordie Howe

Team Captain Ted Taylor carries AVCO cup

four of the last five games would be played in Houston.

Grahame accommodated him with a 4-0 win the first game.

"When that happened I knew we had a chance to win both of them," Dineen said.

The Aeros were perfect in the first game, beating the Mariners with a solid position game. Then Grahame, working on two bad knees, was near perfect in the second game as Houston took a 2-0 edge.

Grahame injured his right knee midway through the season and required a wrap on it for every game. The left knee went sour at the end of the second period of the first game.

If the knees troubled him, Grahame didn't have time to think about it. San Diego fired 48 shots at him, but only one passed. Two second period goals, one set up by Gordie Howe, stood up.

The frustration mounted for the Mariners in the third game. San Diego controlled the early action, but Grah-

ame and the Aeros controlled the scoreboard.

When it was over, Houston had a 6-0 win and a 3-0 lead in the series. All the Mariners had was one goal in 127 shots.

"What can you say after you've said that. Grahame is the difference, obviously," Mariner coach Harry Howell said.

San Diego broke Grahame for four goals in the fourth game, but the Aeros won in overtime as Jim Sherrit scored after 27 seconds.

Gordie kidded, "In all the years I've played I've never had a goal in sudden death. Tonight I didn't even touch the puck."

Now only Quebec remained between the Aeros and another title. For a number of reasons, the Nordiques never had a chance.

It began badly for Quebec as hotel accommodations vanished under a flood of 40,000 conventioneers. The Nordiques moved like gypsies, three times

in three days.

"It didn't help us. And we are not used to this heat, this humidity. We should have started the series in Quebec," Nordique coach Jean-Guy Gendron said. "Anyway, we did better than people said we would just getting this far."

Gendron's team was down one game already after a 6-2 loss in the opener of the finals. But he was already talking like a man who was beaten.

Houston upped its lead to 2-0 in the series with a 5-3 win. Quebec's only hope was home ice. In three years the Aeros were only 1-7-1 in Le Colisee and Houston rarely played well in Quebec.

Grahame promptly shut out the Nordiques, the first time in three years Quebec had not scored at home. It was the third shutout for the rookie and the clincher in his bid for the first Gordie Howe Trophy as Most Valuable Player in the playoffs.

The playoffs were then marred by legal confrontation between the Aeros and Canadian Amateur Hockey Association. The group tried to confiscate Houston's uniforms and equipment.

The move grew out of a dispute over money owed to the junior hockey governing body. The Nordiques, who guaranteed payment, probably wished they hadn't when game four was over.

The 7-2 win was almost anti-climactic. The Aeros and the rest of the league knew it was coming. Taylor quietly asked Gordie if he wanted to carry the Trophy around the arena since this would be his last chance.

"No, you do it. You're our captain," Gordie said.

When it was over, Gordie helped present the trophy named in his honor to Grahame. Then he returned to the cramped dressing room to take part in the celebration.

"We didn't even think about it, that this would be his last game. I guess we all knew it, but nobody wanted to say anything," Grahame said. "He acted like it was just another game."

There will be one more game. On November 5, Gordie will play against Minnesota when the Aeros open their brand new arena. He'll play because he promised he would.

The End

Below left to right: *How Sweet It Is* — Murray Hall and Rich Preston

If it hasn't worked it wasn't for lack of trying

By GEORGE BILYCH

The Calgary Cowboys rode into town in 1975. In the intervening months they've kept the airlines in business.

The Stampeders had an airlift of major proportions last season but it did not totally overshadow that of the Cowboys. The same has been the case this year but with a half dozen games remaining in the schedule it's still much too early to put those statistics on the board.

It would appear that Joe Crozier's modus operandi runs along the lines that to get the most out of your players you keep the competition for jobs keen. If it hasn't worked it wasn't for lack of trying.

In the season that was 1975-76 the Cowboys went through 37 players. Only the Edmonton Oilers will top that this year.

Some, mind you, were up just for the proverbial cup of Sanka. People like Dave Gilmour and Ken Desjardine are hardly memorable, each playing in only one game. Ron Walton was up for a couple, Vic Mercredi for 3.

The Cowboys of last season surprised a lot of people with their strong finish, particularly when they eliminated the highly-favored Quebec Nordiques in the semi-final round of the Canadian Division playoffs.

They were the darlings of the Calgary hockey faithful last April, playing in front of nothing but sellout houses against Quebec and Winnipeg in the playoffs. It hasn't happened since.

The Cowboys this season have failed miserably in their attempts to generate that same type of civic involvement this year. They got off to a miserable start, losing their first 6, and never did fully recover. It's been a dogfight the past three months as they try to bump the Oilers from the fourth playoff spot.

It's been something of a shock to Crozier that the people who were consistently getting the job done a year ago have faltered this time around. That probably explains why there are currently only 11 players remaining from last year's roster. Even more surprising may be the fact that 11 players who performed in the highly-successful playoff run of last April are no longer around.

It might be interesting to note what has happened to the heroes of last spring.

Five of them are in the league in enemy uniforms. Danny Lawson was traded to Winnipeg; Gavin Kirk went to Birmingham for a draft choice, subsequently traded to Edmonton; Rick Sentes was made a free agent and joined San Diego; Francois Lacombe rejoined Quebec when his contract expired; Pat Westrum rejoined Minnesota, later to be shuffled to Birmingham.

Three others—Bob Leiter, Duane Rupp and Harry Howell—retired. Howell became an assistant manager with the NHL Cleveland Barons. Rupp was named playing coach at Rochester of the American League while Leiter returned to the everyday business world in his native Winnipeg.

Rick Jodzio has been commuting all season between Calgary and the minors, be they either in Tidewater or Erie. He's logged more miles than anyone else.

Bernie Lukowich, currently with the AHL Hershey Bears, has spent all season in the minors. Considering the financial uncertainty in Houston, that may be more reassuring than being with the Aeros, the team that owns his WHA rights. Wally Olds spent the winter playing in Europe.

Only one other player, goalie Ed Humphreys, is still in the major leagues, making a comeback with the Quebec Nordiques.

It has been this sharp drop in offensive production that has plagued the Cowboys this season. A year ago they scored 307 goals, a figure topped only by 4 teams in the 12-team league. Unless there's a sudden explosion in the remaining 6 games, they could finish some 70 goals off that pace.

The biggest impact this has made involves their road record. The Cowboys scored 145 times on the road last year, this performance guiding them to 16 wins and 2 ties. Needless it is to delve into the corresponding figures this season.

The most amazing feature about their road record is that they still are in the playoff hunt.

All of which points out the true Jekyll and Hyde traits of the current edition. Last season they won only 65% of their home games, this time they're travelling at a 77% clip.

DENEAU'EM IS TO LOVE'EM

Some architects dream of erecting an edifice taller than Chicago's Hancock Building. Others envision the world's longest bridge or lengthiest tunnel.

Paul Deneau has a simple little dream. He'd like to build a winning hockey team for Indianapolis.

In less than a year since he appeared as a December "angel" to save the financially floundering first-year Indianapolis Racers, he busily has been applying new mortar to a sagging — and seldom winning — foundation.

Many of the bricks assigned coach Gerry Moore last year turned out to be crushed stone. Deneau has not supplied a super brick such as a Bobby Hull or Gordy Howe, but he gave the go-ahead to general manager Jim Browitt and coach Moore to go after some solid blocks such as veteran defenseman Pat Stapleton.

While away from the playing ice, Deneau has been busy, too, seeking what he considers a basic to a strong operation . . . primarily local participation and money.

Deneau is an out-of-towner — Dayton — who has become an in-towner much of the time the past months. First he lived in a down-town hotel, then rented an apartment. His time during the summer was spent in Indianapolis during the week and in Dayton on week-ends, a drive east on I-70 of about 2-1/2 hours.

To further his ties with Indianapolis he has applied for an architectural license in Indiana so he can practice his trade here. Additionally, he has a daughter attending Indiana University, again strengthening his association with the Hoosier state.

Still Deneau didn't back off. One of the first moves he made after assuming control and appointing Browitt g.m. was to oust player personnel director Chuck Catto.

Catto and Moore were at odds over how to run the team and this dispute had divided the players. With Catto gone, Moore became the coach he was supposed to be and the Racers showed much improvement through the second half of the season.

Deneau has put in countless hours in the past year working to improve the situation, but everything hasn't gone along as smoothly as he had hoped. Still he admits that when he came into the operation he was willing to lose considerably in the first two years. He hopes to see some financial daylight by the end of this season.

More victories than last year's 18 and competition for a playoff berth certainly will help in this area.

Deneau lives in a Dayton division he designed. The fenced grounds include a swimming pool that is enjoyed by his family, which, in addition to the daughter, includes a son. He considers his dog a part of the family, too.

Always battling a weight problem, the 47-year-old Deneau enjoys golf, when he can find the time, fishing and spectator sports. At the hockey games he acts the role of not only owner but fan.

Architect and sports entrepreneur, Paul Deneau wouldn't mind being a cheerleader for a winning team. That's his design for the Racers.

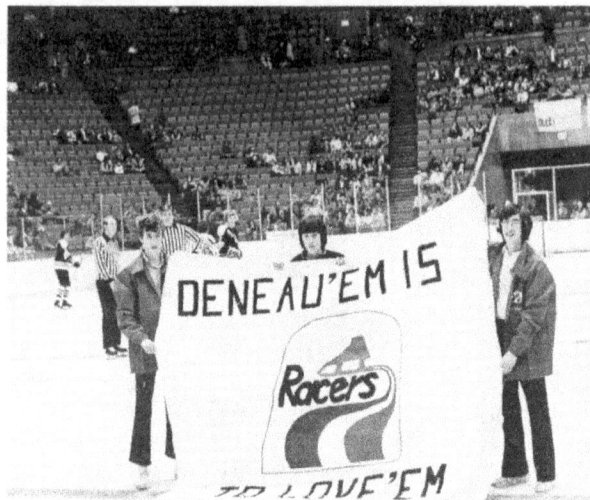

Of course, many who knew of Deneau might have expected an instant miracle upon his arrival. He was the man who purchased the Houston franchise in the World Hockey Association and gave it the impetus to capture two straight WHA championships.

That impetus came in the form of Gordy Howe, recognized as one of hockey's all-time great players. Sons Mark and Marty were signed first and then Gordy was lured out of retirement to play with them. The elder Howe was eager to join his sons but not so eager that he didn't accept a $1 million bonus.

Houston, though successful, was a long way from Dayton and Deneau had to face the problem that he couldn't operate his building business in Ohio and his hockey business in Texas without finding a twin. He sold his interest in the Aeros.

But his love for the game, acquired when he was stationed at the Boston Naval Shipyard and watched the Bruins, never wavered. He originally wanted to put a WHA team in his hometown, but could not convince the city fathers to construct a major league-sized arena.

Meanwhile, the word got out that Indiana Pro Sports, Inc., the group that put together the Racers as an adjunct to the American Basketball Association Pacers for Indianapolis bright, new Market Square Arena, was experiencing deep financial difficulties. Here was a major league hockey team available and reasonably close to home.

Paul Deneau, a mystery man to most Hoosiers, became the Racers boss at the team's lowest ebb last season. The Racers were in the throes of a 13-game losing streak and the night Deneau saw them for the first time may have been their rock-bottom worst. They were beaten by Deneau's former team, Houston, 10-0.

Racer's Engine

These four men could well be the driving force that will power the Racers to their first W.H.A. checkered flag.

L - R. Jacque Demers, Coach; Jim Browitt President and General Manager, Pat "Whitey" Stapleton and owner Paul Deneau.

This pic was taken when Stapleton's acquisition was announced. Demers and Stapleton were Chicago Cougar cohorts.

At age 31, Jacques Demers thought he had plenty of time to decide what his ultimate goals in hockey were. And director of player personnel for the Indianapolis Racers seemed like a perfect in-between job bridging managing and coaching.

It included some of the elements of front office management, some of the direct player contact of coaching and a heavy dose of player evaluation that is elementary to both jobs.

So Demers turned down an offer of the Quebec Nordiques coaching job and a position with the Montreal Canadiens to sign a two-year contract with the Racers as player personnel director last summer.

But it took only 4½ months for Demers' future to rush up to meet him. It arrived late on Oct. 18 when Racer President James W. Browitt relieved Gerry Moore as coach of the Racers following a 6-4 home opening loss to the Denver Spurs, a defeat that dropped the club's record to 1-4.

Browitt's choice to replace Moore was Demers.

Becoming major league hockey's youngest coach came as "a shock" to Demers. "I had no idea this was going to happen until 15 minutes ago (before a hastily called press conference)," he said.

"I'm sorry it happened this way for Gerry. I did everything I could to help Gerry and I really wish things could have worked out differently."

From a personal standpoint, Demers accepted that the coaching job could be a mixed blessing, "an opportunity but also a potential setback for my hockey career."

But if Demers realized the pitfalls of moving from the press box to the bench, he was willing to give his new job his best shot and he moved quickly to remodel the Racers into the image he thinks will turn them into winners.

At the first practice after assuming command, he completely reworked Racers' forward lines and installed his own system of play. When things weren't done to his satisfaction, he stopped play, pointed out the mistake and had the task repeated.

His quick and sure grasp of the reins made an immediate impression on Browitt, who originally had named Demers as only an interim replacement for Moore.

But after watching Jacque's assumption of responsibility, the club president quickly decided he had his man. Less than 48 hours after the change was made, Browitt dropped the "interim" from Demers' title.

"We liked the way he has taken hold of the team," said Browitt, "so he is our coach."

Demers was making no promises of immediate salvation of the Racers. "Changing coaches doesn't mean any miracles," he said. "It doesn't mean we are going to go on a 20-game winning streak.

"It will take two to three weeks for me to remodel the club to the way I want it. It's going to be like going back to training camp all over again."

JACQUE DEMERS
"NEW RACER SKIPPER"

A gentleman above all else, Demers went out of his way to point out that the changes he felt necessary did not represent a reputation of the way Moore had done things. "No two hockey coaches look at the game in exactly the same way," he said, "and I have to do things the way I think is best."

Demers faces two unique problems as major league hockey's youngest coach: 1 — Several of his players are older than he is; 2 — One of his players was his boss a year ago.

Demers sees neither as an insurmountable problem. "There really is tremendous pressure because there are some older players than me on the club," he says. "But any player who wants to cause me aggravation will be gone. I don't want them to like me, just respect me."

And as for now coaching Pat Stapleton, from whom he was an assistant with the Chicago Cougars, Demers says, "Pat put me where I am because he gave me the chance to help him in Chicago. I know Pat will work with me now because he's man enough and smart enough to do it."

Despite his limited major league experience, Demers has a solid hockey background. After a knee injury cut short his playing career while he was a center for Notre Dame de Gras Junior A team in the Montreal Junior League, he moved into amateur coaching.

The highlight of junior coaching career came with the Chateauguay club in the Richelieu Junior League. During the 1970-71 and '71-'72 seasons, he compiled an incredible 83-17-9 record and was named coach of the year after winning championships both years.

He then joined the newly minted Cougars in the new World Hockey Association as chief scout. From there he advanced to director of player personnel and Stapleton's assistant, handling the bench coaching chores while Whitey was on the ice.

His proudest achievement while with the Cougars was scouting, drafting and then signing Gary MacGregor. The swift pivot scored 99 goals in his final year of junior hockey, but many scouts took that with a grain of salt because they came in the high-scoring Quebec Major Junior League where defense often is more a rumor than integral part of hockey.

Demers, however, was convinced that MacGregor had the makings of a superstar and convinced the Cougars they should make every effort to sign him. They did and MacGregor, who went to Denver when the Chicago club folded, has more than lived up to Jacque's expectations. Last year he finished as the Cougars' leading scorer with 44 goals and 78 points to finish second behind Winnipeg's Ulf Nilsson in rookie-of-the-year balloting.

It was that kind of eye for talent that attracted the Racers to Demers in the first place. That's also a pretty good recommendation for a coach.

TED MC CASKILL   JACQUES DEMERS   BRIAN CONACHER   JAMES BROWITT

30 days in march

Astonishing! That's the one word that described the Racers last season when they streaked from last to first in the twilight of the schedule to capture a division championship.

The headline says this is about the "Thirty Days In March".

To which could be added, "more or less".

For our story actually begins on Feb. 22 and stretches to April 6. But the meat of the saga comes during the 30 days (okay, you purists, 31) of March.

It is the incredible drive of the Indianapolis Racers from last place to the World Hockey Association's Eastern Division championship in six short weeks.

As our story begins, there is absolutely no indication it can have a happy ending. For Feb. 22 was the absolute nadir of the Racers' second season in the WHA, a day when all hopes of making the playoffs seemed dead.

The Racers had met the Phoenix Roadrunners on the Market Square Arena ice. It was a game the Racers just had to win to stay alive in the Eastern Division race -- or so it seemed.

And they had lost it, 6-5. The defeat left them seven points behind Cleveland and Cincinnati who were tied for second and the last playoff spot. Only 20 games remained and 12 of them were on the road. There just didn't seem to be any way to close the gap.

But if all about them were writing the Racers off, they hadn't given up on themselves. In fact, they were sitting in the dressing room, as Al Karlander put it, "talking over what we had to do to make the playoffs".

It helped that they had six days off in which to put things back together.

And by the time the Racers took to the ice again at New England Saturday, Feb. 28, they had an opening. For on that day, the Minnesota Fighting Saints, unable to meet a payroll, ceased operations. Before the Racers needed to finish second in the Eastern Division to make the playoffs. Now a third would do the trick.

The first step through the newly opened door was tentative. The Racers tied the Whalers 4-4. But in it was proof they hadn't given up. New England solved Leif Holmquist for two quick goals and still had a 4-2 lead entering the third period. But the Racers kept coming and got the evener from Rene Leclerc at 18:40 of the third period.

The next day they were in Cincinnati where they hadn't won against the first-year Stingers. By 6 p.m. they had. Hugh Harris scored twice and Brian Coates, just recalled from Mohawk Valley to replace Frankie Rochon who had broken his wrist the night before, got another as the Racers downed the Bees, 5-2.

Sharing the hero's mantle was goaltender Jim Park, also just up from Mohawk Valley to replace Dion whose bad back would bench him for two weeks.

So as they entered the "30 days of March", the Racers were still fourth, but moving. They were six points behind Cleveland, seven down to Cincy and nine back of New England.

And they had seen this war movie on an off-night in Hartford. There was this character played by Donald Sutherland who kept talking about feeling "positive waves". Now entering the homestretch, so were the Racers. . .

MARCH 2 -- But right off on the wrong foot. It was Phoenix again -- this time in the Valley of the Sun. And those new positive waves were short-circuited by the Roadrunners, 5-2. But this was a Western Division road game, one they didn't figure to win anyway, so nobody was too upset. Ahead lay the vital four-point games against Eastern foes.

MARCH 4 -- Earlier in the week, Cincinnati Coach Terry Slater had called Brian McDonald "Porky Pig". Tonight he ate those words raw as Big Mac scored twice to provide the margin of victory as the Racers whipped the Stingers 3-1 at Market Square Arena.

MARCH 6 -- Rematch time again in Riverfront Coliseum, and the Racers made it three victories over Cincy in seven days. Nick Harbaruk's 20th goal of the season tied things in the second period and Bryon Baltimore's first goal as a Racer gave the Indy Icers a 3-2 victory at 9:42 of the third period.

MARCH 7 -- Those positive waves still were erratic. Cleveland goaltender Bob Johnson didn't feel them at all as he turned aside 32 of 33 Racer shots in the first two periods to key the Crusaders' 5-1 victory at MSA. So a week into March, the Racers were still spinning their wheels. The loss left them six points back of Cleveland, seven behind slumping New England and eight down to new leader Cincinnati. But those spinning wheels were about to get traction.

MARCH 11 -- Michel Dion returned to action and produced the big stops -- including three 2-on-1's in the second period -- to key a 3-1 victory over Toronto. Nick Harbaruk and Rene Leclerc scored in the second period and Michel Parizeau in third for what was to be the start of something big.

MARCH 12 -- It was back to Cincinnati, but by now the Racers were beginning to like Riverfront Coliseum. They pounded five goals past Paul Hoganson in the first 10:59 and breezed to a 6-3 victory over the Stingers.

MARCH 14 -- Phoenix returned to the scene of the February 22 crime and for 38 minutes it looked like more of the same as the Roadrunners broke out to a 4-1 lead. But Brian McDonald breathed some life into the cause with a goal at 18:29 of the sandwich session. That set the tone for a third period that was as good as the Racers had ever played. Michel Parizeau, Rene Leclerc, Reg Thomas and Hugh Harris all produced goals as the Racers pulled out a 6-4 triumph. The assist on Harris' lamplighter into an empty net went to a newcomer in the Indy livery. Dave Keon, former captain of the Toronto Maple Leafs, had been left without a club when Minnesota ceased operations. A day before, the Racers had given him a home and in his first appearance he started paying his way. And the Racers had Cincinnati and Cleveland within reach. Just two points away now.

MARCH 17 -- New England had returned to first place in the East but after a 5-2 victory in the Hartford Civic Center, the Racers had them in their sights, too. Now only three points separated first from last in the East. Michel Parizeau had two goals as the Racer power play connected three times.

MARCH 18 -- The four-game winning streak ended, but the unbeaten string reached five as the Racers came from behind to tie San Diego 4-4 and close within a point of Cleveland and Cincinnati and within two of New England. Dave Keon got the tying goal at 5:02 of the third period after the Mariners had opened a 4-2 lead in the first 30 minutes.

MARCH 20 -- It was back to Hartford for the second time in a week -- and it was another tie. This one was a brilliant goaltenders' battle as Michel Dion stopped 40 shots and the Whalers' Bruce Landon 43 in a 1-1 standoff.

MARCH 23 -- It was a game that almost wasn't and almost unbelievable when it was played. Six hours before the faceoff it looked like the Racers-San Diego tilt would not go on. The Mariners were in the hands of the league since March 19 when owner Joseph Schwartz missed a payroll. If they didn't get assurances of pay they wouldn't play, the team said. Finally, at midafternoon they got it. The game itself was out of fiction. The Racers were down 6-3 after two periods and had exactly 0 shots on goal in the second stanza. But Rene Leclerc scored twice and the Racers added singletons from Michel Parizeau, Reggie Thomas and Darryl

Maggs in the third period to post an incredible 8-8 tie.

MARCH 25 -- It was back to Indianapolis and 10,783 showed up at MSA to see if the Racers could end their string of ties at three and run their unbeaten streak to eight against the defending AVCO World Cup champion Houston Aeros. The answer was yes, but it was close. For the fourth game in a row, they went into overtime, but this time Rene Leclerc pulled the trigger on a 35-foot breakaway slap shot that beat Ron Grahame at 5:07 for a 4-3 victory. Now only one point separated Indy from Cincinnati, Cleveland and New England.

MARCH 26 -- Two down and one to go. A 3-2 victory over the Crusaders in Cleveland moved the Racers into second place but New England beat Calgary to hold onto first. Hero of this piece was Captain Ken Block who went the final 6:40 at left defense after Pat Stapleton drew a game misconduct for disputing a penalty call too strenuously.

MARCH 28 -- FIRST PLACE! A 3-1 victory in Hartford boosted the Racers' unbeaten streak to 10 and moved the Racers by the Whalers and into the top spot for the first time in their brief history. Al Karlander scored twice against his ex-mates and Brian McDonald once. Michel Dion produced several big saves, the best of which came against Rosie Paiement with less than 30 seconds to go and just before Karlander iced the issue with an empty net tally.

APRIL 1 -- MSA was packed with 13,465 who came to watch the Racers wrap up a playoff berth. But it was not to be. Houston, perhaps finally taking the Racers seriously, got a big night from the immortal Gordie Howe to post a 4-1 victory. The grand old man scored twice and dominated the game.

APRIL 2 -- A day late, but not a dollar short, the Racers wrapped up their playoff spot with a 3-1 victory over Toronto in Maple Leaf Gardens. It was a big night for goaltender Jim Park who, for the first time as a pro, was playing in his home town -- especially since the Toros had refused him a tryout in December when the Racers had released him temporarily.

APRIL 3 -- Now for the first place and the first sellout in Racer history -- 16,040 -- was on hand at MSA to see Indy's darlings do it. Only New England spoiled the party. Still seeking to wrap up a playoff spot themselves, the Whalers played with an excellence born of desperation to post a 5-2 victory. Of course, it helped that the Racers were playing their third game in three nights while the Whalers had been resting for three days.

APRIL 4 -- The final day. Game 80. And the Racers finished in fine style with a 4-2 victory over the Whalers at Hartford. Darryl Maggs and Blair MacDonald got them away to a fast start with first-period goals. The 35-39-6 record left them in first place by a point over Cleveland. But the Crusaders had a game left and it was at home against the still unpaid Mariners. There was hope but not a lot.

APRIL 6 -- It happened. Unpaid, but not unprideful, the Mariners refused to go through the motions. They played to win and win they did, beating Cleveland 3-2 on Ray Adduono's goal at 7:49 of overtime. Goaltender Ernie Wakely, so often a pain in the neck to the Racers, turned aside 57 Crusader shots and the Racers were Eastern Division champions.

Some may say they backed into the title because Cleveland had to lose for Indy to claim the top spot. But that's arguable in the face of the facts. Down the stretch, the Racers went 12-4-4 in their last 20 games.

That's not backing into anything.

LIFE IN THE SHOOTING GALLERY

by Doug McConnell

Bobby Hull scores a lot of his goals with nothing more than his reputation, contends Phoenix Roadrunner goaltender Gary Kurt.

Ron Grahame and Wayne Rutledge of the Houston Aeros, Ernie Wakely of the San Diego Mariners and Kurt's teammate Jack Norris more or less agree with him.

All agree that he still owns hockey's biggest shot but he has a lot of rivals.

Quebec's Serge Bernier and Marc Tardif ... Houston's Gordie Howe and sons Mark and Marty and teammate Frankie Hughes ... Calgary's Danny Lawson ... Cincinnati's rookie Claude Larose ... Toronto's Tom Simpson ... New England's Tom Webster ... Phoenix' Pekka Rautakallio and Cam Connor ... and Hull's teammate Anders Hedberg, to name a few.

"You know Hull can rifle the puck," explains Kurt, "so you have to be prepared for him and sometimes he gets a lot of cheap goals that way.

"He has the goaltender really uptight for a big shot all the time. He scored four goals against me in two games and three of them were flub shots. He didn't get everything into them."

"He's got a guy so up on edge when he shoots. You're overkeying him all the time. If you don't do that, you probably have a better chance with him, but when he does get the good one away, then you probably aren't set for it."

"The guys (forwards and defense) respect Hull," said Grahame. "They don't necessarily freeze up but they're not as loose as they would be playing somebody else and he gets around them and lets a good shot go where another player, the defenseman might be able to block him or steer him into the corner."

"He's the most determined," adds Norris. "If he makes up his mind he's going to score, he'll either put it past you or through you.

"Hull is just so strong, he gets so many good shots from 10 feet straight out.

In a scramble, he gets the puck on that big hook of his and just throws it at you; he doesn't shoot it and it's usually on the top corner."

Hull has a lot of rivals, says Rutledge, but not under game conditions.

"Nearly everybody, if given enough time, will shoot hard," said Rutledge. "In a practice, all our guys shoot the puck well, but in game conditions some guys get the puck away better.

"Take a Hull for instance. He generally always gets a good shot away.

"To me, Hull is not slapping the shot as much. He's wristing it more. There are some guys who shoot a heavier shot, the slapper, but he's more effective with his wrist shot and he lets it go in stride.

"Hull's always been more effective with the wrist shot than the slapper but he'll generally let the slapper go from outside the blue line when he knows he can't

get through the defense."

Wakely refuses to admit Hull gives him any more trouble than any other player.

"I think if you psych yourself out that somebody scores a little more often against you," said Wakely, "then you could put yourself in a precarious situation and you're defeating yourself before you even play that opponent. Consequently, every time the guy gets the puck, you're being unstable and every time he shoots you're bobbling and juggling it and first thing you know, they're going by you into the net."

Grahame had Quebec's Marc Tardif and Chris Bordeleau, and Roadrunner defenseman Pekka Rautakallio from Finland, and Winnipeg right wing Anders Hedberg from Sweden high on his list of shooters.

"Tardif is hard and accurate," said Grahame. "Bordeleau's the same way."

"The fellows from Europe are pretty good because they shoot in stride," points out Grahame. "Most of the Canadian and American fellows, when they're going to shoot, they stop skating. The kids from Europe, they come down and come around the defensemen or they're skating around the corner and they're still skating when they shoot it, which is a little confusing to some of the goaltenders because they haven't seen that before."

"Simpson is probably as close to Hull as anyone for a hard shot," said Norris. "I just don't know where he gets the power, the way he shoots. He seems so relaxed. He looks like he's just getting rid of it and it's on you, fast and heavy and it hurts."

"Simpson is unbelievable," adds Norris' teammate, Kurt. "He doesn't seem to get that many shots away in a game, but I know he's given me trouble for three years now. He has the quick release and the short backswing."

"After Hull and Simpson, there are a lot of guys," says Norris. "Serge Bernier has a good shot, but there are 50 others.

"Bernier is just one hell of an all-around player. He's terrific with the puck. He doesn't telegraph what he's going to do. He makes plays off balance, forehand, backhand, it doesn't make any difference. He's strong and can go over anyone.

"He's also the kind of guy who, when things are not going right, he seems to have so much desire and determination, he'll keep at it until he gets the job done. Other guys might say the hell with it. I have a lot of respect for him.

"Danny Lawson (Calgary) shoots crazy pucks. He shoots them rolling and they come at you like knuckleballs. Most guys try to make another move to get the puck down and usually somebody is on them by then, but Hull and Lawson just drive it and it's a hell of a shot to stop. You don't know whether it's coming at your throat or your toes.

"Wayne Rivers was really shooting the puck well last year," Rutledge said of the San Diego right wing who has been hampered all this season by a back injury. "He was always tough for me."

"On the San Diego team, Gene Peacosh is another player who always seems to be in the right place at the right time, like a Johnny Bucyk, who you never see, yet you look at the scoresheet after the game and he's always got a couple of goals or something. He seems to have that instinct of where to go and he picks up that loose puck and the next thing, it's in the net.

"Peacosh is generally on the corner. Some guys shoot the puck harder than him but he's more accurate than some of those hard shooters.

"The most difficult to stop is the guy who gets the shot away quick, more so than the guy who has the hard, heavy shot you might have time to get your body in the way in the time he takes to wind up. Line up with the puck right between your eyes and it cuts out a lot of your moving one way or another."

Rutledge notes a lot of strong young shooters coming along. "Larose for Cincinnati really shoots the puck well," says Rutledge, "especially for a little man. You wouldn't think he could get that much behind it. The thing about Larose is that he's generally down low, like a Frankie Hughes.

"Hughes gets a lot on his shot and it's tough because he's always along the ice."

Connor is another strong youngster with a booming shot but he hasn't been a big goal producer.

"He needs time to get it away," points out Norris. "There can't be anybody around him. If he can wind up, he

can shoot with the best of them, hard and heavy. Hull and Simpson get their's away with guys draped all over them. Cam's big, though, and he's young."

Connor tore Grahame's glove off with one drive from the blue line, whipping it back into the net.

"I didn't have my hand in the glove," recalls Grahame. "He let it go and it caught the top of my glove. He has a helluva shot but I didn't have my glove on properly."

"Hughes has the best shot on the Houston team, besides Mark and possibly Gordie," says Wakely. "He's very accurate, although I'd say most of his goals seem to come from garbage collecting, hanging around the side of the net.

"They have kind of a buzz-saw line (the Go-Go Line) and they're in and around the net a lot. It seems more of their goals come from the scramble area."

"Mike Walton (Minnesota) is another one who is tough in front of the net," says Rutledge. "He's like Andy Hinse on our team.

"I'm thankful I don't have to play against Hinse. He likes to get in there and bother and bump and pull the feet from the goalie and everything like that.

"The little rat, he even does it in practice. Andy is just a complete little pest. He just bothers the defense so he's not only screening the goaltender, but so is the defenseman.

"A lot of guys don't like to stand in there. You hit them across the ankles and they stay away for a while. That's Andy's game, though. Johnny McKenzie (Calgary), too.

"Andre Lacroix is good in front, too. He's a shifty little hockey player. He relies on his wingers, but if he can't make a play to them, he generally just slaps it from 35-40 feet.

"You've also got to watch out for that little Robbie Ftorek with Phoenix," adds Rutledge. "What a worker and he's so quick.

"Webster (New England) is so fast. He gets a real head of steam going. I don't think he knows what he's doing half the time himself, but he's got a good move coming in off the wing and he can hold the goaltender and shoot or he has a quick deke."

"I haven't played against Larry Lund (Houston), but you can see he's good with the puck," says Grahame. "He gives it off to Andy or Frankie and he's really good with it himself. He's really amazing.

"Richie Leduc in Cleveland is pretty good with the puck," says Grahame, "and Davey Keon (Minnesota) is a real hustler, a forechecker. You've got to be alert all the time when he's in there because he could pick it off with his stick or have it hit you and he'll be right on top of you.

"Mark, most of the goaltenders will tell you, shoots the puck well and Marty has come along real well. I don't think he did anything to work on it over the summer, but he's really firing it from the point.

"Gordie has lost some off his shot, but Hull probably has, too. Gordie is just so accurate. He shoots low and puts it just where he wants to put it."

"He's always shooting for the corners," points out Rutledge. "He never shoots at the goaltender. After practice, he'll just stand there and try to hit the post so many times."

It's the reason he's also put the puck between the pipes more than any other player in history.

'75-76 Stinger Season in Capsulated Form

By John Hewig

EDITORS NOTE:

(*Going into last year's premiere season, the Cincinnati Stingers were said to be one of the best thought out Major League Expansion teams, ever, in any sport. Coaches, General Managers and Hockey experts all agreed that the Stingers were going to have a talented, youthful team, one that had been virtually handpicked during the previous two years.*)

In the month of October Cincinnati was introduced to Major League Hockey with a 6-4 victory over the Edmonton Oilers. The first ever Stinger goal on Coliseum Ice was scored by Captain Rick Dudley, at 0:12 seconds into the second period. Just eight seconds later, Dudley set a WHA record by scoring again at the 0:20 second mark.

The Stingers finished the month of October perched atop the Eastern Division of the WHA, and critics began to believe. Jacques Locas, Claude Larose, Dennis Sobchuk and Rick Dudley were the names that kept popping up, along with Dave Inkpen, Pierre Guite, John Hughes, and Ron Plumb. As an expansion team, the Stingers raised eyebrows throughout Cincinnati, a sports minded city that had previously been unfamiliar with either the team or the sport.

In November the Stingers extended their winning streak on Coliseum Ice to 6 games before dropping a 3-2 decision to the Minnesota Fighting Saints. Included in their wins were victories over the defending Avco Cup Champion Houston Aeros (twice), the Calgary Cowboys, the San San Diego Mariners, and rival New England. On Sunday, Nov. 9th, the Stingers drew over ten thousand fans as they defeated the Whalers 5-2, avenging a loss to New England in Hartford on November 6th and at the same time, establishing a dominance on home ice over the Whalers that would continue throughout the season.

On November 21st, Cincinnati came from a 7-2 deficit in Toronto against the Toros to tie them at 7-7 with five goals in the final period, only to have Rookie of the Year Mark Napier win it for the Toros with a goal at 19:28 of the final period. The Stingers continued to be bogged down by what was to be their worst slump of the year, and defeats at the hands of the Winnipeg Jets, Quebec Nordiques and Toronto Toros dropped them out of first place as December approached.

Not to be by-passed would be the fact that Cincinnati had lost both of its' regular goaltenders in the latter part of November, and as the Stingers went to Cleveland on December 3rd, John Kiely had been called up to play in the nets. (he had been playing for the Stingers' top farm club, the Hampton Gulls of the SHL)

Jaques Locas scored some big goals against the Racers last year.

Kiely responded with a 5-3 victory over the Crusaders, a win that was sparked by third period goals by Locas and Larose, Dudley, and Dennis Sobchuk.

After that game, Stinger Rick Dudley was prompted to say that he was going to call Kiely "Moses" from now on, because according to Dudley, John had 'led the Stingers out of the wilderness'. That was on a Wednesday, and the following weekend, 'Moses' proved that 'Duds' was right. He played two games on Coliseum Ice and won them both. On Sunday, December 7th, John proved that his victory in Cleveland was no fluke by beating the Crusaders again, this time by a score of 3-1.

Cincinnati then departed on a five game western swing that was to culmi-

nate just five days before Christmas. After a disheartening loss to the Aeros in Houston, the Stingers beat Phoenix and tied San Diego in overtime. After losses in the last two games before returning to the friendly confines of Riverfront Coliseum, Cincinnati's Head Coach, Terry Slater remarked that he felt that his team had to learn to settle down and 'just play fundamental hockey with a lead going into the third period'. "My team is so young that they get ahead by a goal and they are cocky enough to think that they can score whenever they want. I feel that this is a great team of the future, but part of learning (and that is what they are doing right now) is to be able to sit on a one goal lead, and they haven't learned that yet."

It's like having ten young colts in your stable" Slater went on to say, "and they all just want to go full speed all the time. It takes a lot of coaxing."

Coaxing Slater did, and when Cincinnati returned from their West Coast trip, they beat the Mariners on the 18th of December, and then they conquered the Whalers 4-1 on Dec. 20th.

By now Cincinnati had acquired goaltender Paul Hoganson from New England, and 'Hogy' was to play a very prominent role for Slater for the final four months of the year. As the Stingers began to turn the corner into the New Year, they were wrapped up in the closest race in Major League Hockey, with all four teams only a matter of a few points away from each other. Going into 1976, the Stingers were just 2 points out of first place, behind New England.

Among other things, the month of January brought with it the nominations of the All-Star Teams, picked by the News Media throughout North America.

Stinger rookie Claude Larose was the only Cincinnati player chosen to play in the annual classic, and although Claude deserved the award richly, (he had 22 goals and 16 assists at the time, which was good enough to lead all rookie scorers) many people wondered out loud why defenseman Ron Plumb and right winger Rick Dudley weren't chosen to represent the Stingers also.

At any rate, Cincinnati greeted the New Year with a spark of enthusiasm by beating their first two opponents in '76, and those two victories pushed the

Stingers to within one point of first place. After losses to Minnesota and New England before and after the All-Star game respectively, Slater's crew rebounded with a 4-0 shutout in Indianapolis over the Racers, a victory that was a combination of tremendous goaltending (Hoganson was in the nets) and taking advantage of scoring opportunities. Guite and Larose led the Stingers with a goal and assist each.

January 21st, the Stingers continued their dominance over the Crusaders by beating them for the fourth consecutive time. The 24th of January proved that the New England squad (which had won the Eastern Division of the WHA every year since its inception in '72) was not such a 'whale' of a team by beating them again, this time by a score of 6-3.

In February, Cincinnati dropped three decisions on the road before beating the Whalers in Hartford on February 13th, 5-1. That victory was to spark the Stingers on to a seven game winning streak, their longest of the season. Included in that seven game winning stretch were important victories over the Racers on St. Valentine's Day (Stinger rookie Claude Larose scored the winning goal with just 32 seconds left in the third period) and a 5-4 victory over the Calgary Cowboys in overtime after coming from behind with two third period goals that were scored late in regulation time.

During the winning streak a freak accident occurred to right winger Pierre Guite that was to affect the outcome of the Stingers final positioning in the league standings. On Feb. 20th, Guite lost his balance while heading back towards the Stinger net and crashed into the right goalpost, breaking two small bones in the lower portion of his back. He was to be lost for the season.

Nearing the end of February, the Stingers were sitting in first place and waiting for the Houston Aeros to invade the Coliseum for a Saturday night game. The Aeros left Cincinnati with a 4-2 victory, and the next day the Racers also beat Cincinnati on Coliseum Ice 5-2, dropping the Stingers from first place.

The month of March brought more bad news as first the Crusaders, and then the Racers (again) beat Cincinnati and sent them tumbling into third place, just three points ahead of Indianapolis in the Eastern Division standings. As the race for playoff births tightened even more, the Stingers found themselves in a position that dictated either being successful on the road (something that hadn't come easy all year) or watching the league playoffs from the sidelines.

Six out of the last nine games were on the road, and even though Cincinnati had beaten Houston March 20th (in front

The injury to Winger Pierre Guite hurt Stingers playoff drive.

of over 14,000 fans) a four game road swing that began the next day (the 21st, up in Cleveland) was to spell fourth place for the expansion Stingers. Cincinnati dropped 3 out of the four games, with their only win coming in Phoenix by a score of 5-4.

With three games remaining in the regular season, the Stingers now had to win two of the three to insure a playoff spot. They dropped a 7-2 decision to the Roadrunners on Coliseum Ice (first ever Business Man's Special in Professional hockey) and consequently they were faced with beating Cleveland both times in a home and home series which ended the regular season.

As far as Stingers fans are concerned, the song "This Time We Almost Made It" would pretty well say it all. Head

Coach Terry Slater pumped his players to the limit on "Fan Appreciation Night" here in Cincinnati and they responded with a well earned 6-3 victory. That night Dennis Sobchuk grabbed the three goal 'Hat Trick' and goaltender Paul Hoganson literally stood on his head to keep the Crusaders at bay.

Sunday, April 4th, Cincinnati roared to 3-0 lead in Cleveland, but the Crusaders came back to tie the Stingers and eventually went on to win 6-3. The season was over, and the Stingers had run out of 'ifs'.

"It hurt so much to lose that last game up there, especially since we were leading" commented Slater during this year's training camp, "but looking back

Dave Inkpen (getting congratulations from No. 8, Claude Larose) scored the winning goal against Houston, March 20th, in front of over 14,000 fans.

on it now, it might just be the very thing that will make our kids give it that 'extra effort' needed to get into the post season playoffs this year.

Looking ahead just a bit, this season's Stinger team will be the youngest ever in Major League hockey, with an average age of just twenty three. Off season acquisitions (Richie Leduc, Bryan Maxwell, and Dennis Abgrall and Blaine Stoughton) plus the top notch job of both Jerry Rafter (Director of Player Personnel) and Flo Potvin (Head Scout) in obtaining Peter Marsh, Barry Melrose, Greg Carroll, and Jamie Hislop (graduating juniors from Canada and the University of New Hampshire) should "improve the team 35 to 40%" according to Executive Vice President Bill DeWitt, Jr.

"It will be quite a year" remarked Slater as he headed back onto the ice to put his troops through another training camp practice. He couldn't have put it in any better way. ℰ

Dennis Sobchuk grabbed the "Hat Trick" on Fan Appreciation night.

Racer Crisis Every Night

Photo by Mary Ann Carter
THE RACER BENCH REFLECTS THE WINNING HABIT

Eyebrows are being arched around the hockey map.

The Racers are for real. They have turned the WHA East into a feverish finish, and nobody's laughing -- particularly in Cincinnati, Cleveland and New England.

The men of Coach Jacques Demers, as this prose is constructed, have lost only twice in nine starts. They're two points back of the Crusaders and Stingers and a mere five behind the Whalers.

And while the disbelievers perspire, Racer followers -- like the players themselves -- have been captured by playoff mania. In the case of the players, a first place finish represents $50,000, second place $25,000 and third place $17,500.

Looking beyond San Diego tonight, the Racers have home dates left with Houston (twice) and the New England Whalers in the regular schedule finale April 3.

At this juncture, that looms as the biggest game of the year. It might be wise to give thought to ticket purchases now. Exclusive of last night, the Racers still have four games left with the Whalers -- all of them vital keys to who finally resides in first place.

Playoff tickets, to refresh memories, go on sale for the general public March 29. Season ticket holders can pick their's up starting March 22.

The playoff structure calls for the second and third place teams in the East to meet in a best-of-five series with the winner going against the first place club in a best-of-seven.

The ultimate winner goes against the Western Division champion (Houston, Phoenix or San Diego) for the American sector title, with that winner in turn facing the Canadian Division champion for the Avco World Trophy.

The playoffs are what as known as the 'second' season, and the Racers to a man confess that they'll be there.

The Racers have 10 to play, six of 'em on the road. To suggest that all are critical would be an under-exaggeration. The margin for error has been reduced to nil.

Some people talk of the Racer charge to the wire as a "Miracle Finish." Better you should describe it as an "Honest Effort" by a team that refused to be written off.

It's worth noting that of the 24 men on the Racer roster today, 12 of them were plying their trade elsewhere when the season started.

For men like Renald Leclerc, Michel Parizeau, Bryon Baltimore, Darryl Maggs, Francois Rochon, Brian McDonald, Hugh Harris, Blair MacDonald, Kerry Bond, Michel Dion and Davey Keon joining a new team in the course of a season represented a special challenge.

This was especially so in the cases of Baltimore, Maggs, Rochon and Keon, who suffered much strife before their former clubs were beset by a cash deficiency.

Coming to the Racers represented the opportunity to salvage a dismal year, and they mean to make the most of it.

Then there is the case of the goaltender Dion who came out of the minors 34 games into the season to emerge a strong candidate for rookie of the year honors. Fearless Michel ranks today among the finest young goaltenders in the game. There are those who'll testify he's the best in the WHA.

When the WHA media gets around to voting the all-star team and individual awards, there are a number of Racers worthy of more than casual consideration.

Beyond Dion as an all-star and rookie of the year, there's defensemen Pat Stapleton and Kenny Block, both worthy of all-star and MVP votes; Keon as an all-star and the most gentlemanly player award, and then there is Demers -- certainly a heavy in the coach of the year balloting.

The Demers 'System' to this point has resulted in the least number of goals allowed and a highly entertaining product with a team that has seized the imagination of Indiana.

"We've had to experiment all season for the winning combination," concedes Demers. "Our plans called for some new faces, and the moves have paid off.

"When you get down into the final weeks of a season, momentum becomes a big factor. We've got it going for us. I would like to think we're peaking at just the right time."

Back on February 5, Claude Bedard -- the noted Quebec writer and broadcaster -- said of the Racers following a 4-2 victory over the Nordiques:

"That team will be in the playoffs. And once in, they'll be extremely dangerous. The Racer style is geared for playoff hockey. They have the defense and goaltending -- the vital elements to win a series."

As a prophet, Bedard is to be reckoned with -- and he'll get no argument from the Racers.

Racer PRIDE Has Turned The Tide

The Road To The O'Keefe Cup

By PAT YANKOSKI

The sound of purring lawn mowers can be heard all over the city. Golfers have been on the greens for weeks now. The annual Shrine Circus has come and gone. And hockey is still making headlines in the local papers.

It's been a long season for the Winnipeg Jets. Last August saw the squad get their skating legs in shape for the European training camp and a season which extended to 81 games instead of 80.

An improved team and a better record left the Jets with top honours in the Canadian division. Winnipeg's fourth season out also provided the fans with some new faces.

Mats Lindh and Willy Lindstrom made up the new imports. Teddy Green, a veteran defenseman finally decided it was time to come home. Bill Lesuk jumped leagues to put his skating legs to work in the confines of the Winnipeg arena.

Lyle Moffat proved to be an excellent trade from Cleveland. Les Canadiens' loss was Winnipeg's gain when shifty Silky Sullivan decided he would score his goals for the Jets.

The well-travelled Larry Hillman came to add his defensive abilities to the team. Minnesota Fighting Saints dissolved and Gerry Odrowski was picked up. The player without a team—Bobby Guindon, found what he was looking for.

The coaching reins were taken over by Bobby Kromm, a man who doesn't take to losing, and a winning team was moulded. Along with a few memorable hockey moments.

As was the case March 10th when the Nordiques waltzed onto the ice wearing boxing gloves, but left with their pants down after a 10-3 loss.

Heartbreakers too. Like the 5-4 loss in Houston. Three goals by the Aeros in 91 seconds to erase a 4-2 lead at the end of the third period.

And a few humorous moments. Especially during one Toro-Jet match-up when the 6'1" Nedomansky encircled his arms around the torso of little Sjoberg in an affectionate hug.

First place was a great finish for the team, but they hadn't officially sewed it up. The play-offs would determine which team had their name engraved on the O'Keefe Cup—symbol of supremacy in the Canadian Division.

The contenders in the first round were the Edmonton Oilers. Their fourth place finish gave them the right to meet the Jets. Something which didn't sit well with Coach Kromm who maintained they had no business seeing play-off action.

The Jets, with an impressive eight victories over the Oilers during regular season play, still gave the Edmonton club healthy regard.

April 9th was the first game. Even though the Oilers scored three, it wasn't enough to stop the Jets who fired seven goals past a shaky Dave Dryden.

The game was not a sell-out. Something which Bill Hunter said was the fault of a coach who ridiculed the series.

The second game of the series saw Dave Dryden turn in a brilliant show of goaltending to hold the Jets to four goals after 61 shots in three periods. It would have been early showers for the Oilers had Dryden's superb play not sent the game into overtime.

You have to be good to be lucky, and the Jets were all of that. Only 54 seconds had to be played before Ulf Nilsson secured a victory with a 40 foot slapshot. A dramtic finish to a very close game.

The Jets Joe Daley was ejected from the game during the first period after chopping Oiler's Patenaude on the shoulder with his stick. Curt Larsson was called on to finish the game. Jets' number one goalie was subsequently suspended for the third game of the series.

If anyone was worried about the third game, they needn't have been. As Billy Robinson said, "That's the Curt I saw play against the Russians." A solid performance by Larsson in the absence of Daley lifted the Jets to a 3-2 decision.

Hedberg and Sullivan turned in goals for Winnipeg before the Golden Jet came up with the winner in the last twenty minutes of play. Hull's goal and Larsson's 27 saves gave the Jets an insurmountable lead in the seven game series.

The Oilers were down but not out. Teams have come back from a three game deficit before. But not against opponents like the Jets. The fourth match-up was a 7-2 runaway for Winnipeg. The nails had been driven down in the coffin lid—and the hockey season was over for Edmonton.

The Oilers were humbled in four straight games. But while the Jets and Oilers were doing battle, the Calgary Cowboys had literally been fighting to win their series over the Quebec Nordiques.

Brawls were more common than goals, and both teams rosters were shortened by game misconducts. But when the last drop of blood was scraped off the ice, the Cowboys emerged victors after only five games.

So this would be it. The Cowboys and the Jets for the O'Keefe Cup and the right to be the Canadian representative in the Avco Cup finals. The Cowboys decided to try playing hockey, but man for man, they couldn't hold up to the Jets. A 6-1 loss was the only reward the Cowboys received in the initial match-up with the Jets. They did manage though, to prevent Daley from keeping his shut-out.

The second and third games were more evenly matched, but each time the Jets emerged winners. The scores were 3-2 and 6-3. The tide turned against the Winnipeg team for the fourth game. Jet fans watching the game at home were not happy to see their team beaten 7-3.

And neither were the Jets happy themselves. Skates were sharpened, the ice readied and some 8,700 Winnipeg fans poured into the arena for the fifth game of the series. It was do or die for the Cowboys.

A 0-0 tie at the end of the first period was giving a lot of fans the jitters. Loyal supporters were given a break at 7:23 of the second when Anders Hedberg's speed paid off once again in a goal. First blood was drawn by the Jets. The Cowboys would never get on the scoreboard.

Another goal from Hedberg at 1:36 of the third period plus another one from the stick of Willy Lindstrom two minutes later was all the Jets needed to keep Calgary at bay.

This time Daley was not to be denied. He had his first play-off shut-out of the year. And the crowd began to chant, "We're Number One."

The first team to have its name engraved on the 92-year-old punch bowl would be the Winnipeg Jets.

Captain Lars-Erik Sjoberg did the traditional skate around the rink with the prize held aloft in his arms while the fans stood and applauded the victors.

The Jets celebrated and deservedly so. But after the last champagne cork had popped and sweat lade uniforms peeled off, the Jets looked forward to a rest. They didn't want a vacation.

But an 18 day lay-off is what they received. And now it's Houston and Winnipeg in the Avco Cup Finals. If the series goes seven, then the last game will be played June 1. If the Jets can regain their momentum, the chances for a victory are good.

WHA- a fully established big league.

WALT MARLOW
WHA Director of
Press Relations

By Walt Marlow

It's been three years since those celebrated inventors, namely Dennis Murphy, Bill Hunter and Ben Hatskin, detonated the biggest explosion in the history of hockey.

Critized without restraint, they were said to be in need of cerebral attention for leading accomplices on what most assuredly represented a perilous journey that would result in loss of haberdashery to all.

"They'll never hit the ice" was the most popular denouncement. When 12 teams did, the detractors---choking on their morning cups of coffee---piously hallucinated "they'll never last."

Only in Toronto, Montreal and Vancouver, it was foolishly philosophized, would major league hockey flourish in Canada. Cities like Edmonton, Winnipeg and Quebec, it was argued lacked the citizenry and affluence synonymous with stature.

Tonight, on the occasion of the World Hockey Association's third All-Star Classic---A Salute to Team Canada '74---Messrs Murphy, Hunter and Hatskin can offer irrefutable evidence that the skeptics and negative thinkers were caught with their rompers out of adjustment.

It was WHA players exclusively that comprised the make-up of Team Canada '74 in a historic series with the Soviet Union---a distinction, doubtless, that provoked a renewed wide-awakening from sea to sea in two countries.

Team Canada involvement not withstanding, however, WHA impact on the sports world in less than three full seasons hasn't exactly been microscopic.

The league has been the architects of two of the most unique happenings in the history of any sport, has triggered an avalanche of new arena construction and qualifies as the first major league ever to acquire talent from behind the Iron Curtain.

"The magnitude of our growth is unchallenged," states President Dennis Murphy. "We are no longer striving for recognition. Total stature was attained this past off-season with the acquisition of another 25 acknowledged major leaguers and our dominant role in the signing of preferred amateur graduates."

The elite harvested from last season's amateur draft included the likes of Mike Rogers by Edmonton, Ron Chipperfield and Pat Price by Vancouver, Dennis Sobchuk, Jacques Locas and John Hughes by Cincinnati, Cam Connor, Dave Gorman and Dennis Olmstead by Phoenix, Don Larway and Terry Ruskowski by Houston, Ron Ashton by Winnipeg, Gary Mac Gregor by Chicago, Real Cloutier by Quebec, Jim Turkiewicz by Toronto, Craig Hanmer and John Sheridan by Indianapolis and Kevin Devine by San Diego.

It has been noted that the WHA has a total of 65 rookies in action this season, comprising 22.7 percent of the active rosters.

"Our need for the established player has lessened considerably," says Murphy. "We're starting to produce new stars for new fans. The future strength of this league is in its' youth and the tapping of the vast European market."

Exploration of that overseas reservoir, to be sure, has already commenced with New England's capture of the Abrahamsson twins, Thommy and Christer, while Winnipeg lured four Swedish and two Finnish stars---Curt Larsson, Anders Hedberg, Ulf Nilsson, Lars-Erik Sjoberg, Heikki Riihiranta and Veli Pekka Ketola.

It remained for Toronto's Bassett, however, to generate international headlines with his seizure of Czechoslovakian super stars Vaclav Nedomansky and Richard Farda.

The pattern of the WHA has been a single signing each year of monumental magnitude. First it was Robert Marvin Hull, then the Gordie Howe family, followed by Frank Mahovlich, of course, represent the three most prolific goal scorers in the history of the game.

But even more startling is the fact that the WHA in its' third year has experienced an attendance increase of upwards of 70 percent over the first season.

A crowd of 10, 11 or 12 thousand that first year represented a happening. Two winters later, they have become downright common---particularly here in the Coliseum where there have been four in excess of 15,000 and the average is in the 12,000 category.

Bill Hunter, the stylish and loquacious vice-president and general manager of the Oilers, justifiably takes the stance that further dialogue relative to Edmonton's major league credentials is a study in ignorance.

Pressure is the constant companion of the referees and linemen...

LIFE
IN A STRIPED SHIRT

By Mike Armstrong

It has often been asked if hockey officials—referees and linesmen—are born or made. Bill Friday, Referee-in-Chief of the World Hockey Association, thinks it's a combination of both that makes a good official.

"A referee must have good judgement on penalties and I think that's inborn. He has to make quick decisions and he must be right. If he has that, we can teach him the rest," Friday said.

"I think we have good officials in the WHA—the best available".

Friday, along with Director of Officials, Bob Frampton, scout various officials' schools during the summer and pick out the best who are then invited to attend the WHA officials' school conducted by Frampton and Friday.

On their scouting missions they look for size and excellent skating ability. "Officials must be good skaters", emphasized Friday, "and size commands respect from the players. Referees and linesmen must have the respect of the players".

The ideal referee should work four or five years as a linesman at the major league level and follow that term of experience as a referee in the minor leagues for the same period of time.

"You can't let a man into the major league too quickly. He has to learn by experience to be in command all the time and develop the respect of the players", said Friday.

If aspiring linesmen have the size and

good skating ability, the rest can be taught. Some are brought up from the Ontario Hockey Association and the World Hockey Association is developing its own people.

"We have some good kids coming up", added Friday.

The Referee-in-Chief feels a 20-year old has the best chance of making it as an official. "It's a tough job and they have to be dedicated. Our officials are on the road more than the players".

Once selected by Frampton and Friday, it's off to WHA officials' school...and it's not all ice work. They must know the rule book inside out and there are written tests on the rules. The school is tough to complete and not all make it.

The World Hockey Association has an agreement with the North American Hockey League and provides referees for all regular season and playoff games.

"There is no substitute for actual game conditions and the officials gain valuable experience in the NAHL.

In past years referees or linesmen of the WHA would be given assignments as referees. However, this year, they are either referees or linesmen", Friday said.

Pressure is the constant companion of the referees and linesmen, whereas, the players' pressure might be 15-20 minutes per game. The officials are under constant pressure for 60 minutes and in some cases, overtime.

"Ron Asselstine, one of the brightest

stars in our plans, asked to be relieved of his duties as a referee earlier this season and is now doing line work. Hopefully, Ron will be back next season as a referee, as he has all the ingredients to be a great one", Friday said.

Assignment of game officials is a big problem. "The problem is to keep everyone happy so that clubs don't see the same referee too many times. All WHA officials have their assignments three weeks in advance and the only changes made are due to illness or injury".

Friday pointed out that the main ingredient in being a good official is consistency. "Consistency is the main factor. That comes from experience. If you let some things go in a game, you have to let them go all the time. If you call everything, you have to call everything all the time. An official can never let the players get the best of him".

"Some can quote the book—they know the rules—but you can't teach them how to call penalties. That comes from experience, instinct, inborn, whatever you want to call it. Some have it and some don't".

The WHA employs six referees, including Friday, and 12 linesmen.

Friday, a veteran of 16 years as a major league referee, is quite proud of the WHA men he works with.

"I'd match our officials with those in any league", Friday said.

San Diego Mariners' Coach (Ron Ingram)

What are your impressions of the league so far this year?

I think the league this year is probably the greatest in comparison to parity in what I've seen over the five years that I've been connected with it — three years in the league and two years running the minor league system for different teams in the World Hockey Association. I think we are closer to parity now than the National League ever dreamed of being.

What is your feeling on a merger? Would it really help? Is it the answer?

I definitely think that a merger is getting closer and closer everyday. My own personal feelings on the merger would be that the National League, I think, sees fit that it should happen because I think they can read between the lines, and if we don't have a merger between the NHL, I think what is going to happen is that some of our people in the WHA are going to opt to go to the international league games with the Soviet Union, Czechoslovakia, and I think that would definitely hurt the draw in the National Hockey League.

How about San Diego? What's the difference for you as the coach working with this management as opposed to the past?

Well, every player that I've asked to obtain, they've tried to obtain for me. I think that they've given an honest effort in trying to build a competitive hockey club with the players that were available. I still think we have a ways to go to be a championship hockey club, and they have given me a free hand to do it. In the past I had a free hand to operate this hockey club, but I had no facilities in the way of bank accounts.

You say that right now we are not the caliber that you think is necessary to have a championship year? What is needed in your mind to get it to that level?

Without stepping on everybody's feet, and you have to be very careful with mentioning names, but I think that we are probably a real good centreman away. Because you make a trade for another centreman, or you make a purchase of another centreman, he may not be the centreman you want. But I feel that any time I can trade or purchase a player and improve my club by one percent in any position, then it is a good move. Because when you look at the percentage of players that come out of the juniors that make it to the big league, then you are doing a big job just to improve your club by one percent. I think we need another defenseman and another right winger.

Have any players surprised you this year with their play?

Well surprises don't come easy. I think I'm happy with the play of a couple of people that we purchased on the way or traded for. I can say I am disappointed in a couple situations also. I am very disappointed in the effort I got from Gregg Boddy. I was disappointed in the fact that I had to trade him. I still feel that he is an excellent hockey player. I think I am very pleased with Tony Cassolato. Some of my rookies I brought up — I realize I'm going to have to go along with some of these kids while they learn. I think we made a hell of a deal in Shmyr and I'm disappointed in Pinder.

How about the rest of the positions? How do you look at the other teams in our division as playoff potential?

Well, the rest of the teams in our division — I think Edmonton really has improved themselves. They are going to be heard from before this season is over because they are starting to put together a real strong hockey club. The changes they've made were all for the best. I think that Winnipeg is starting to round themselves back into the situation where they are the champions they were last year. They are not going to sit idly by while we are in first place as that is the position that they want. We also want it, so it should be a great season and will make for great competition. Houston is obviously concerned about their hockey club, because they have made a lot of last minute trades in the last few weeks . . . trades that some thought would never happen, and I think that they are aware of the fact that our division is strong, and San Diego and other teams are getting stronger. I think Calgary is stuck in a situation, where, because of the smallness of the arena and dollars, they can't put a good team together that is a real great contender until they can move into a building where they can draw more people and have more flexibility in purchasing players. I think Phoenix has hurt themselves in some of the trades they have made. I am over here, and I'm not in Phoenix, so I can't tell you what is behind them, but they all look like dollar trades to

me, and I don't think they've done their hockey club any good at all.

When you play a team like the Russians and create quite a bit of interest in the city, and obviously we had a sellout for the night, how do you prepare for that? Do you consider that game just another exhibition as far as you are concerned? Does it have any more meaning to you than a regular season game or vice versa?

It has great meaning because you are playing what we feel is the cream of the crop as far as European hockey teams go They have millions of people to draw from, so we have to look and say that the Russian hockey players that they brought over to play the game in San Diego and the rest of the league, on this tour, were the best possible players they could assemble. They had a great amount of time to do it. They just finished playing in a big tournament for the championship before they came over here, which they won, and they knew they were coming to play us and they didn't want to be defeated at all. I believe someone made the statement, and I don't know who, that they came over here intending to win every game and snow us under as much as they could. I think when they got over here, they were surprised that we had the competition we had. I know I talked to some of the referees that refereed some of the games, and some of the people that were at the game in Quebec, incidentally, which the Russians lost by a fairly large score, and the comment from the Russian coaches and some of the Russian Hockey Federation people was that they probably had the best competition ever so far in playing the WHA teams even including the National Hockey League teams this year, in the competition we gave them on this tour.

How about the style of Winnipeg and Houston as principal rivals. Do they differ a lot from yours — philosophy-wise, coaching-wise?

Yes, in Winnipeg they play a European style of hockey. I really don't know who is teaching it to them. I think it is the foreign players who are bringing it over and bringing the system into being, because all their lines don't play that way. We play against the number 2 line or number 3 line and there are a lot of Canadian players on it, and they play the spread out hockey that we play . . . Up and down the wing type thing. We play against the European line and you get that circular motion all the time. I think that Houston plays basically the same type that we play. They try to overpower you. They use the muscle and stick a little more than we do, because they have a different type of personality. I made one mistake this year, very visible to myself and that was believing that the WHA would hold up the violence rules and I built my club that way, and since that time, since the start of the season and part way through it when I felt we were getting abused I made some changes. I brought McNamee back in, who probably was the best fighter in the league, and I think just his presence alone has won a couple of hockey games.

How strongly do you feel on the violence in the league?

I don't think the league is very violent this year except for a couple of teams. I think it is being over played and I'm going back to 25 years when I've seen the cycle go. One year you would walk in and the referees and the league will tell you they are cutting down on violence this year and if there is any high-sticking, there is going to be suspensions, and they curb it pretty well, and all of a sudden the fan interest drops off, then they think of something else. Well, it's not exciting enough so they take out the icing rule and put in another rule. And it changes every five years, as the cycle goes and as the fans drop off, and they change the rules, and about every 8-9 years you get back to the point where they come up with the old Philadelphia Flyers and the Boston Bruins, Syracuse Blazers and the teams that only lost 5 and 6 games during the season because they had a real tough hockey club, and no one wanted to come and play in their building.

What do you think about referees in this league and the quality?

I think the referees in this league do as good a job as they possibly can under the circumstances. One of the biggest problems in the business today is getting good officials. I think the officials that we have right now are as good as we could possibly get at this time. There are a lot of leagues and a lot of referees being used. I don't think we have any training program, especially with the World Hockey Association being the youngest of all the leagues. I think that our scouting staff for referees needs to be improved.

HE'S THE MAN WHO LOOKS FOR TALENT

FLO POTVIN IS *ALWAYS* ON THE GO

For Flo Potvin, head scout for the Cincinnati Stingers, travel is a way of life.

"I do a lot of traveling, all over the United States and Canada," said Potvin. "I was with the team last year (when the Stingers went to Europe) and I seldom miss a college game and the juniors in Canada."

The position entails travel and last year, Flo saw more than 160 hockey games as he searched for the players he feels might be of benefit to the team.

He rarely spends time in the office because of the demands of his job, but then he wouldn't have it any other way.

"I don't think I'm the type of guy to stay in the office," said Potvin. "I see 150 to 165 games a year, and I like that. I'm still learning and I enjoy what I'm doing right now."

Wherever Flo Potvin travels, he is in search of talent, perhaps for a left winger, a defenseman or a goaltender, and with him he always takes charts on which he can write what impresses him about a specific player.

There are two skills in a hockey player which Flo Potvin says he is always looking for and a player must have.

"The first thing you look at is his skating," he explained. "Then, it's puck control and passing and anticipation. I really insist on passing, especially a defenseman. It's a thinking game and you have to think fast."

Of all the positions on a hockey team, goaltender requires a special concentration because he is the final line of defense when the play comes to his end.

Flo Potvin looks for certain things when he watches a goaltender.

"I look at the goaltender," he said. "I look to see if he follows the play to the left, to the right, even when the play is at the other end.

"It's a tough job. He talks to the defenseman, how he can cover the angle. I look to see how he covers the net, what he's going to do with the goalpost, if he's too deep in the net or not far enough. Most of the time, a goaltender won't give up a loose puck in front of the net, especially when he plays a good skating club."

Flo Potvin might well have been an outstanding hockey player but he suffered a serious injury at the age of 19 and his playing career was over.

It was then that he turned to the management side of hockey. Flo served as head scout, coach and general manager of the Verdun Maple Leafs during the

ON THE ICE Stingers scout Flo Potvin handles matters on the ice as he conducts a practice at Riverfront Coliseum.

1960s. Later, he joined the Montreal Canadiens, for whom he was a scout, and he also worked with the Chicago Cougars of the WHA.

In the spring of 1975, Flo joined the Stingers as head scout, and in the past three and a half years he has shown the same dedication and style which characterized his work when he was with Montreal, Chicago and Verdun.

During the 1977-78 season, coach Jacques Demers told Flo the team needed toughness. With that thought in mind, Flo went to the American Hockey League in search of such a player.

"We needed a tough guy," Flo recalls. "The first game I went to was in Springfield. There were fights. I looked at his size. He won the fights. Then I walked to the lobby.

"I put Paul Stewart on our list, and I talked with Binghamton," continued Flo. "I call up Bill DeWitt and he says

bring him in for a tryout. He came down to the tryout and he's on the team. His name's Paul Stewart. He's a fighter, and the name of the game is win. I like a guy with pride, guts and drive."

When not working as a scout with the Stingers — which isn't often — Flo relaxes by playing softball in Canada, or touring the links for a round of golf.

The nature of his job means Flo Potvin travels extensively, living out of hotel rooms and being on the run constantly, and whenever he checks into a hotel there is something Flo always does.

"Television is my favorite sport," he joked. "As soon as I open the door in the hotel room, I turn on the television. I especially watch Johnny Carson."

For Flo Potvin, a man whose constant travels take him in search of hockey talent for the Stingers, it is the only time he relaxes. ℭ

ICEMAN ON THE HOT SEAT

J. JEANMARD

Herb Holland interviews new WHA President, Bill MacFarland

The World Hockey Association took more steps to benefit itself last summer than perhaps it had in its four previous seasons.

Not by player signings, though. There were no Bobby Hulls or Gordie Howes last summer, as had been the case in years past. Instead, the league brought solid new ownership in to some of its troubled cities—San Diego, Edmonton, Minnesota—and finally coaxed Bill MacFarland into the presidency.

MacFarland's name long had been prominent in discussions when conversation turned to possible successors to the long-vacated post, empty since Dennis Murphy resigned after the 1974-75 season.

After a shakey season under the guidance of board chairman Ben Hatskin, MacFarland, president of the Phoenix Roadrunners and former Western Hockey League chief, was persuaded to take the job.

The problems were obvious—the WHA's image had suffered immeasure-able damage as the result of two franchise failures in midseason and another at the end of the season. Officiating in the league was criticized more than the weather and players were getting hospitalized (or arrested) for uncontrolled violence on the ice.

Rules have been changed and money has been pumped into the league since then, but MacFarland still has his work cut out for him. Nobody knows it better than he...

HOLLAND: You had been offered the presidency before but had balked. Why?

MacFARLAND: I was slow in accepting the position for two reasons. One is personal—my family. After 20 years we moved to Arizona with a young family and we were very happy there. It was just difficult to move again within two years to Toronto.

HOLLAND: Is that where league offices will be permanently located?

MacFARLAND: I think so. We'll take a look at it in a city that doesn't have a WHA franchise. I think it's important to promote the WHA in Canada and in the United States, but the WHA has benefitted more really in the Canadian cities because of the enthusiasm connected with the Canada Cup participation by WHA players, who did very well by the way.

Robbie Ftorek (Roadrunners) was MVP of the U.S. team and Bobby Hull (Jets) along with Bobby Orr, were the two outstanding players on Team Canada.

And some of the foreign players in the WHA did very well for their national teams. Anders Hedberg played well for Sweden as did Thommie Bergman (both Jets). Kids like Pekka Rautakallio, Seppo Repo and Juhanni Tamminen who are with Phoenix did a great job for Finland.

But we have to maintain an ongoing PR job in Canada, so I would think we'll stay in Toronto. We might open another office in the United States to promote the WHA in the eight American cities.

HOLLAND: Getting back to the original question—what made you decide to take the presidency of the league?

ICEMAN INTERVIEW

MacFARLAND: Well I'm a lawyer who has a history of getting in and out of hockey, and I always seem to bounce back into hockey somehow in between periods of private practice.

I really have a feeling for the game and I really enjoy the people in it. It's a little more exciting than probating wills and filing divorce cases.

I did balk for a while because I didn't want to assume a responsibility to the WHA unless I had the authority to assume it. It was a little tug and pull in that area but I think Mr. (Ben) Hatskin and myself have things resolved as to who does what and who has the authority.

HOLLAND: Well, who does what and who has the authority?

MacFARLAND: I have the authority to operate the WHA and I answer directly to the board of directors and not to the board chairman. So I am really working for the 12 WHA teams and nobody in particular.

Ben Hatskin has been elected to be chairman of that board and he does what the board sees fit for him to do. But the operating of the league is mine and I feel I have carte blanche within the operating budget of the league to do as I see fit.

HOLLAND: What does that budget allow you to do?

MacFARLAND: Well, I'd have to say the operating budget of the league is just over minimal to make the improvements we have to make in the league.

I think we have to spend a little more money in public relations to promote our league as an institution. Much the same as General Motors would publicize a new car it's putting on the market. And then the dealers publicize their own outlets. I feel we have to do the same thing between the league and the 12 member franchises. There has to be more money spent to improve the image of the WHA.

Plus we have to spend some money to improve the overall officiating in the league. We should spend a little more money in referee development and in supervision of referees. Right now we have no supervisory staff whatsoever.

So those are some of the areas, plus a little better communication within the league operation so that the clubs have a set of rules to live by and they know the rules will be enforced. I think everybody will be happier with a stricter structure than we've had in the past.

HOLLAND: How do you feel the league's enforcement of its bylaws has been laxed?

MacFARLAND: I don't think it's so much laxity in enforcing the bylaws but it's been a problem of not having very definitive, all-encompassing rules for the league. There's a 50-year history of operation in the NHL and there are leagues like the American Hockey League and the Central Hockey League that have operated for years and have developed rules by trial and error.

This is a young league and has attempted to adopt its rules by trial and error over a four-year period. But it hasn't really taken the time to sit down and put those rules into a legal form that the president can follow and enforce.

It's kind of been shoot-from-the-hip up until this point in time because the rules haven't been there. They haven't been able to enforce the rules because they just haven't been there.

I don't think it's a laxity in enforcement, it's a problem of not having any rules to enforce with a constant standard.

HOLLAND: Over the summer the league brought in new ownership which apparently will help last year's problem franchises. Where do the problems still exist?

MacFARLAND: I think now the 12 WHA teams have adequate financial backing in that the people behind them have the capital to go over the long haul. That's not to say that if things don't improve or if profit isn't forthcoming in any reasonable amount of time that people won't stop putting money into the teams. In the past we've had groups which have depended greatly on gate receipts to exist and didn't have equity capital for the long haul. Let's face it, everybody can't win every year and the teams with the lowest attendance are really going to have problems.

We're in 12 pretty good cities now and we have been competitive. I think during the league's history the teams have been competitive. That's been the one saving factor for the WHA—that there hasn't really been any disparity in team talent like there is in the NHL. I think it's going to be a long time before Washington and Colorado can win 20 games a season. We don't have that problem in the WHA.

But there will be some cities on the lower end of the attendance ladder that will feel problems.

HOLLAND: Hockey on the whole has been badly hurt without the American television dollar. Are there any deals forthcoming to get major league hockey back on the air and get those dollars coming back in?

MacFARLAND: Television is an important part of it, but it's important from two aspects to the WHA. The other "second" leagues that started in football and basketball, had to fight established leagues with a lot of television revenue to use against them. But we're not in that position. So we're bucking the NHL strictly on gate receipts.

We're also trying to establish ourselves on TV, probably regionally first— the NHL is trying to build its own network and we're probably going to have to take that same approach. The major networks have struggled with hockey. They've found it very difficult to televise. It always will be because the object of the game—the puck—is so small and moves so fast. In baseball, football and

continued on next page

basketball it's really easy to pick out the ball on the playing area.

Hockey aficionados really don't understand this but if they'd stop to look, they'd realize they follow the play by the movement of the players and not by the puck. To get new people interested in hockey via television is very difficult if they have to follow the puck.

But I don't know what the future of hockey on television is. What we'll probably do is figure the possible revenues as being minimal and try to operate our clubs based on possible gate receipts.

HOLLAND: Is this possible, considering the enormous overhead costs involved in operating professional sports teams today?

MacFARLAND: As long as there are two leagues bidding for top talent, and management is willing to pay the price, it's going to be a problem. My personal feeling is that vis-a-vis merger, which I think is a long way off, the most sensible thing for both leagues to do is to attempt to get a common draft. But as everybody knows, the courts have picked away at other sports and have recently ruled the college football draft was a restraint of trade and a violation of antitrust laws.

But a common draft is the first logical step and the second is a playoff between the two leagues for a champion.

HOLLAND: Are the NHL owners in a position now where they can ask the WHA to make an offer?

MacFARLAND: No they're not. Even if they wanted to, and I'm not sure they do, they couldn't, because they've just entered into a five-year agreement with the NHL Players Association which precludes merger. The clause, I gather, would make all NHL players free agents in the event of a merger.

So the NHL is locked in there, but I don't think that precludes interleague games, playoffs and a common draft.

HOLLAND: This hasn't been a good year for the WHA in terms of player signings, has it?

MacFARLAND: I think there are two factors there: 1) the reduction in the number of players under contract and 2) the reduction of the rosters to 18. I think the past two years the WHA has done very well in the junior market. But that's going into ground for ore in a very costly manner. I don't think you can do it every year. Some teams are going to get back into it. Really we haven't gotten too deeply into the junior market this year but neither has the NHL. This junior crop wasn't as good as the one two years ago because of the 18-year-old signings two years past.

I know Phoenix had to stay out of the junior market because it had signed two bona-fide first-rounders of NHL teams in Barry Dean and Cam Connor and it's too expensive to do that each year. But Cincinnati has done well in the junior market three years running and Houston seems to have done pretty well also.

HOLLAND: You mentioned before that the NHL needs to see a year of solid operation from the WHA to begin to consider a deal. What does a year of solid operation include?

MacFARLAND: I would say a year with no midseason franchise failures, a year of the teams meeting their commitments to the players under contract and a year of everybody showing up for every game scheduled. Last year we had problems with Denver, Ottawa and Minnesota folding in midseason. We had teams replacing teams in the schedule, and I think that destroyed public confidence. A year with solid operating teams will have a positive effect on our overall image and prestige.

HOLLAND: How far away from where you'd like it to be is the WHA today?

MacFARLAND: I think this is a long term project. If we have the funding to do the things we have to do, I think we can have a competent officiating staff by the end of the second season, with adequate supervision and no part time officials. We'll have the players, general managers and coaches properly indoctrinated a little bit.

As far as the PR aspect of the league, I think it will be an ongoing thing. It's going to improve as long as our franchises remain stable. You can't sell people with all the promotion and advertising you can drum up if it's a bad product.

If it's not a good product, you just can't sell it. •

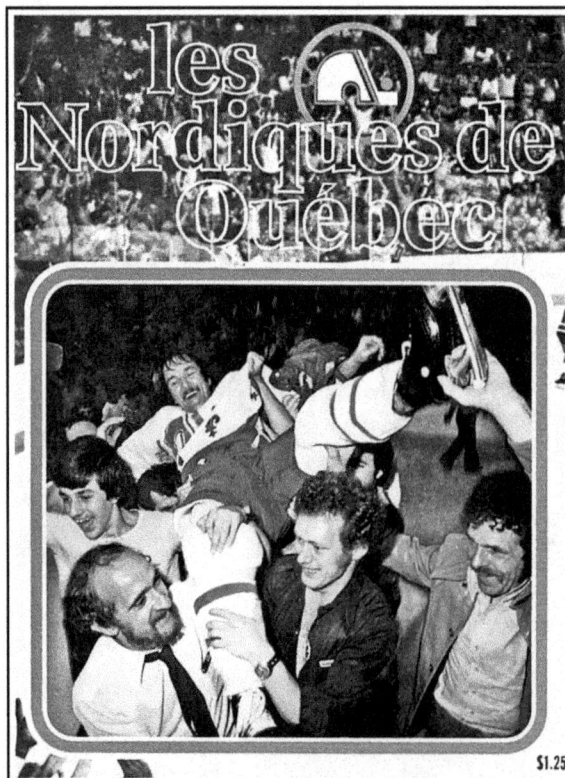

les Nordiques de Québec

$1.25

WHA
HALL OF FAME

NHL – VERSUS – WHA

By GEORGE BILYCH

EXPERIENCE
EXECUTIVE
COULD
BE HELPFUL
IN ANY
MERGER TALKS

WILLIAM H. McFARLAND
PRESIDENT - WHA

You can sense that the various team owners in hockey's two major leagues are starting to breathe a little easier these days. An end to the Five Year War may not be very far away.

Since the World Hockey Association became more than just an idle dream of Gary Davidson's, life has been virtually one perpetual nightmare for the owners. It brought with it wildly escalating salaries and a series of court battles, all of which had the affect of creating a haven for players, their agents and numerous lawyers throughout the land. The owners, many of whom heretofore had been reaping rich dividends annually, were suddenly feeling the pinch.

There is little doubt that the haughty attitude of the National League as much as anything else was responsible for the WHA's stubborn refusal to knuckle under despite suffering heavy financial losses in most areas. While some of the original WHA franchises never got off the ground, others who did went belly-up after a year or two of fruitless operation. Franchise shifts, some in mid-season, became commonplace. But despite all the dark days and the many predictions of doom, the WHA showed it had the resourcefulness to keep coming up with people willing to gamble their money in a second major league.

It must be heartening to the few of the WHA originals who are still in business that they're finally gaining acceptance by the NHL.

As it prepares to enter its fifth year of operation the WHA appears to have gained the type of financial stability that its proponents only dreamt of a half-decade ago. And with the exception of the Calgary Corral, all are housed in major league surroundings.

It's apparent the National Hockey League has finally got around to recognizing as much. Whereas talks of merger and/or compatible coexistence have almost emanated from within WHA ranks in past years, it's only recently that the NHL has re-echoed similar thoughts for public consumption.

Stan Fishchler, the eminent New York hockey scribe who for many years has followed the NHL closely, brought it out into the open in an interview with NHL vice-president Don Ruck. In an article appearing in The Sporting News, Ruck predicted that an absorption of WHA teams, similar in style to the recent pro basketball agreement, was "inevitable."

Ruck acknowledged that the NHL had erred in not embracing more Canadian cities during previous expansions but added they would be welcome in the future.

"I could see Quebec City, Winnipeg, Calgary (if a new arena is built) and Edmonton as possibilities," said Ruck. "In the United States they also have good cities ready for big league hockey, such as Cincinnati, Indianapolis and, perhaps in the distance, Houston."

Ruck went on to say that something similar to what happened between the NBA and ABA was inevitable in hockey.

"WHA owners must realize that year after year they can't keep pouring a million and a half dollars down a rat hole. Something is going to have to give. But the fact remains the WHA has a lot of cities with spending power."

That should be heartening news in a lot of WHA precincts but league vice-president Howard Baldwin of New England indicated he was not in accord with the idea of incorporating only part of the WHA.

"The only acceptable thing would be an absolute merger with total unanimity on the part of the NHL, the WHA and the players' associations," said Baldwin.

Whatever, there are definite signs that the two factions indeed are getting closer together. This year there are 13 exhibition games scheduled between teams of the rival leagues. Eight WHA and five NHL teams are involved, an indication there's been a large degree of compatibility achieved already.

Actually, they embarked on inter-league exhibition play back in 1974 when seven games were played but this program was discarded last year, presumably at the insistence of the respective players' associations. The players made a similar request this season but this time the owners stuck by their guns. It's a solid hint that total peace may not be far down the road.

While merger may still be years away, Calgarians now know full well what is required if they're to be a part of any big league hockey setup in the future. Now even the NHL is on record as saying Calgary would be considered as a future candidate should the city get a major league building.

There's proof enough the WHA is capable of surviving on its own. It's up to Calgary whether it wants to be a part of hockey's big time. If it does, some initiative in providing a facility will have to be shown in a hurry.

BOBBY KROMM EATS, DRINKS AND SLEEPS HOCKEY.

On a recent visit to Houston, Winnipeg superstar Bobby Hull was asked about Jets' coach Bobby Kromm. Hull leaned against a wall, his face breaking into a sheepish grin. After a few moments of silence, he found the right words.

"Krommie, well, he's a very intense individual who wants to win all the time," replied Hull, who has observed numerous coaches in his 20 years of professional hockey. "Krommie's a great student of the game. Like in a restaurant, he'll be diagraming plays with salt-and-pepper shakers. He'll also pour some sugar and map strategy in it."

Hull hesitated as he remembered his years with the Chicago Black Hawks and the National Hockey League's revolving door for coaches.

"Krommie's a very dedicated person," Hull continued. "He has control over everything he does. He's a good tactician and he expects everybody to give 110 per cent all the time. He's a

hard-worker and a winner, and he won't accept less from those around him."

Indeed. The key to the success of Bobby Kromm is that he is a driving force who eats, drinks and sleeps hockey. It is hard for him to accept the fact that others don't take the game as seriously as he does.

Kromm, the World Hockey Association's coach of the year when he helped Winnipeg win the AVCO World Trophy last season, is demanding and controversial with a flair for flamboyance.

"I'm what you could call a little fiery," says Kromm, who has been called a lot of things by his contemporaries, not all of it good. "But I've mellowed a lot, and I've learned through my immaturity. I'm very strong-minded and strong-willed, and I expect the very best from my players. Sometimes I expect too much, and as a result, I can get myself in trouble."

Kromm's personality did cause trouble in late December. The Jets had represented Canada in the Izvestia Tournament in Moscow. They returned and immediately lost to Quebec, Houston and San Diego. There were rumblings of discontent in Winnipeg.

Reports said the players were disenchanted with Kromm's constant pressure. Naturally, Kromm was displeased

with the losing streak and what he thought was a lack of effort.

Something had to be done, one way or another. The Jets were hosting Houston Jan. 2. Winnipeg stood 0-2-1 against the Aeros going into the game. Kromm had exhausted his supply of salt-and-pepper shakers. He needed something drastic. He found it.

Minutes before the Houston-Winnipeg game, Kromm used a few choice words on his players and stormed from the dressing room, leaving the coaching duties to injured defenseman Lars-Erik Sjoberg.

Kromm's departure had a lasting effect on the Jets, who soundly defeated the Aeros, 5-2. Kromm returned the next day, and the Jets resumed their normal pace, that of winning consistently.

"Krommie felt something drastic had to be done," said Hull, "and he did it for the betterment of the team. It worked, too. We got over that little hump, and things fell back into place."

Kromm's personality helped the Jets escape their slump.

"Bobby Kromm is the Billy Martin of hockey," says a Winnipeg sports writer. "He's the kind of guy that has to be the total boss. When he has control, he can do things his way. Who can argue with success?"

WHA HALL OF FAME

ILLUSTRATION BY MELISSA GRIMES

Kromm is like Billy Martin in other ways, too. Early in the season he had an argument with Edmonton coach Bep Guidolin. Kromm decided the best answer could be found in Fist City. Later, Kromm disagreed with Quebec coach Marc Boileau. After some heated exchanges, Kromm was ready to mix it up.

"I'm certainly not going to change my convictions," says Kromm, who lacks size but not the heart for his many confrontations. "I always say what's on my mind, and oftentimes I disagree with a lot of people.

"Some people may not agree with my ways and means, but I don't let it bother me. I think I have to be fair, stern, tough but honest. Oh yeah, I think there is a time and place for fun, too."

Houston's Bill Dineen is the only original WHA coach to survive into the league's fifth year. Dineen and Kromm have contrasting styles. Dineen is easy-going and well-liked by his players and his opponents. Yet both coaches are winners, and both receive respect, which is one characteristic a coach cannot win without.

"I think Kromm is an excellent coach," says Dineen. "He's a unique person, and you can't knock his style because of all the success he's had.

Bobby's the kind of person that if a player doesn't do the job, Bobby lets the guy know it in no uncertain terms. He stands up for what he believes in. I admire a guy like that."

The road to a major league coaching position was a long and rocky one for Bobby Kromm, who traveled much of the United States and Canada as a minor league player and coach. His final stop before the WHA was Dallas, where he coached the Chicago Black Hawks' Central Hockey League affiliate.

"I worked for the Black Hawks for nine years, and I think I spent a little too much time with them," admits Kromm, who thought he would be Billy Reay's successor in Chicago. "I had hoped the Black Hawks would consider me as the heir to Billy Reay when they decided to make some changes.

"It became evident three or four years ago they weren't going to make any changes then, so I decided I couldn't die in Dallas. I missed a lot of opportunities and turned a lot of people off because they said I had Black Hawks stamped on my rear end.

"When the chance to come to Winnipeg arose, I thought it was a good time to break my ties with the Black Hawks. The Winnipeg job has worked out for the best."

Throughout this season, there have been rumors that Kromm will jump to the NHL next season as coach of the Detroit Red Wings.

"Let me say that I'm very indebted to the Jets," Kromm says. "Also, I owe a lot to Rudy Pilous, our general manager, the players and the fans. I'm sure when the season is over and all these rumors have been cleared, I'll be staying in Winnipeg."

While Kromm remains in Winnipeg, the Jets continue to win. He has outstanding players with whom to work, but it takes a special kind of coach to mold a team, especially a team with such superstars as Hull, Anders Hedberg and Ulf Nilsson.

"I think my position of never being a major league player has helped," Kromm says. "I've always studied the game, and I learned that the first thing about being a coach is that you have to earn the respect of your players.

"The reason the majority of great players who have tried to coach have failed is because everything comes so naturally for them. It's hard for them to adjust to others who don't have the natural ability that comes easily."

Kromm is well-versed in international hockey, and he has built the Jets

Bobby Kromm

with numerous European players.

"The foreign players are very dedicated and they don't mind hard practices," says Kromm when comparing the North American and European players. "They accept hard work rather easily, much more so than our players. They get results from hard work, and they don't mind paying the price. They believe if they're in excellent condition, they can exploit all their abilities, and those are the kind of players I like."

A credit to Kromm's coaching ability can be found in Winnipeg's success.

"I have to have two styles of hockey," he says. "It's not a stereotyped system where you have a basic philosophy. We have a combination European-Canadian game, and if things are going well, I can cope with it. We've done very well with the combination style, but if we don't do well, we'll go back to one style and carry on from there.

"It is a little difficult coaching two types of players. The Europeans' skills are probably a little better than ours, and their basic fundamentals are, too. Our players are position players, and you have to have special players to play the combination game. Luckily, I've got those special players."

Like every coach, Kromm has his ideas about improving the game.

"When the WHA cut the rosters from 20 to 18, it cheated the fans," he says. "When you play three games in four nights, you need the extra players. The players are tired, so the fans don't see the best brand of hockey.

"Injuries in games hurt, too. I'm just vehemently against the roster reduction because you end up taking the extra guys on the road, so it doesn't cut expenses. It's better to have them suited up on the bench than in the press box just watching the game.

"Another thing I'd like to see is the two leagues get together and eliminate some of the poor franchises. I'd like to take the best 18 in the National League and the best six in our league and put six teams in a division and have four divisions."

"We need realignment with a common draft. Each team would go into the draft able to protect 12 players and two goaltenders, and that way you would get parity when the weak teams could draft the unprotected players from the strong teams.

"We'd have good competition then, and competition brings fans to games. If we don't do this, the fans don't come. The fans are getting cheated because they can't see the best hockey possible."

Many of Kromm's outbursts have resulted from the rough tactics used against his teams. Because violence is not a part of the European game, opposing teams often try to intimidate the Jets. Naturally, Kromm sticks up for his players.

"I don't mean to be complaining all the time, but sometimes I just think the violence thing is overdone," he says. "I like hardnosed hockey, don't get me wrong. But if you're a fan and you pay nine or 10 dollars to see the good players, and if a good player gets knocked out because of too much violence, then you get cheated in that area, too. A hard body check to an Anders Hedberg is a good play, but I don't think two guys should be trying to rub out a player on the boards.

" I don't like the stick stuff either. Like hacking on the ankle and calf. This is the kind of stuff we have to control, all the things that are overdone. Hockey is a rough, tough game, and it's tough enough without having to take all this other crap."●

WHA Vs. NHL: Same Game

It was once said that the World Hockey Association would never make it, that the product would never measure up to that of the long established National League.

Many of the game's intellectuals were still making those observations as recently as a year ago.

Today, such dialogue is relatively extinct.

Admittedly, there are still a few newsmen in North America beating the tambourine on behalf of the NHL.

But not many.

Christie Blatchford, featured columnist for the Toronto Globe & Mail, one of Canada's foremost newspapers, tells it like it is. You'll find the observations most enlightening.

TORONTO, ONT.

Face it, folks.

There really isn't much difference between the World Hockey Association and the National Hockey League, not anymore. When the two leagues each send one of their best clubs into town, as they did last weekend, it takes a picky man (or a relative of Harold Ballard) to still spot the big and blatant contrasts of a few years ago.

They simply don't exist, not after three long seasons the WHA spent learning the ropes.

Even the small differences between the leagues, some of them so visible only a month or so ago, are disappearing.

As an example, the announcer who calls the Toro play-by-play has either been replaced or sedated — his whining keen has recently become a deeper and more acceptable squeal.

And the calibre of hockey? Well, have a second look at what we saw last weekend.

WHA at its best

On Friday night there were the Toros, still locked deep in their divisional basement, but playing (at least for two periods) as though their 5-12-2 record was a matter of accident and not a reflection of the club. True, they played against a Winnipeg Jet club that was weary from two previous games, and true, too, the Toros eventually lost, 5-3, to the Jets.

But, for the first two-thirds of the game, it was good professional hockey — not just good hockey for the WHA, but good hockey, certainly better than some of the yawners Leaf fans have had to watch in recent years.

The Jets are not only a first-place team, but a first-class one, and they got the best out of the Toros. The WHA also gave Toronto fans the prettiest goal of the weekend, a Vaclav Nedomansky-Richard Farda combination that the pair tried once without success and simply repeated a moment later for a goal.

The Toros also got outstanding efforts from two of their baby-rookies, 18-year-old Mark Napier and 22-year-old Peter Marrin. Marrin, especially, has learned a lesson from his time in the minors, and is now one of the team's never-quit players.

It is a lesson that the league itself has also learned; after sugar-coating its product in gimmicks and give-aways for several seasons, the WHA is now selling hockey.

As much quality

On Saturday night, the normally mediocre Leafs pulled a similar trick, playing above their heads, in perhaps their best game of the year, to tie Philadelphia Flyers 1-1. Flyer coach Freddie Shero had deliberately muzzled his club's usual style in honor of the Ontario Attorney-General, and Leafs made Flyers play their type of hockey, which is fast. (Like the Toros did the previous night, Leafs slowed in the third period, holding onto the tie thanks only to Wayne Thomas and his goaltending.)

It was the fourth time the two Toronto clubs have played back-to-back games, the Toros on Friday, the Leafs the next night. (Total attendance for the two games, incidentally, was 27,327.) There are 13 more such doubleheaders scheduled for the rest of the regular season and while not all of them will be as good as the most recent one, it is likely, in the end, that the WHA will have given us as much quality hockey as the NHL.

It is time, then, to stop pretending that the WHA is a Mickey Mouse operation — and the only one in town. In the diluted world of professional hockey, the league can hold its own, offering as much good stuff and as much of the other as the NHL.

Time, gentlemen

In fact, the real remaining difference between the two leagues may very well be in the way in which they are regarded in the press box. (On Friday night, for a top WHA game, the press box was almost empty. On Saturday night, for an NHL game of similar calibre, it was jammed.)

Long accustomed to the NHL and unwilling to admit that another league can sometimes be just as good, sports reporters are still, in their hearts, refusing to acknowledge the WHA — or at least, as Toro coach Bobby Baun says, looking for underdog characteristics.

It's time, really, to give up that kind of thing, NHL owners and supporters cannot cry any longer, gleefully, "Vive la différence".

Most of the time, there isn't any.

STORIES ABOUT PLAYERS

'GOLDEN JET' LEADS HIS CLUB TO COLISEUM FOR FIRST TIME

There's nothing more to say about Bobby Hull that hasn't already been said by columnists in magazines, newspapers, all of the electronic media and person-to-person. Except, perhaps, 'thanks."

A gentleman in every way on the ice and off; gracious almost to a fault; modest and yet confidently aware of his talents and abilities. It was Bobby who made the WHA an "entity" and stopped the scoffers and doubters. And it still is Hull who commands attention wherever he, and his club, goes.

And it is Hull who still is the dominating force when the Jets take the ice. In the first meeting between these clubs this season, all Bobby did was score three goals — including the game-winner after 9:19 of overtime — and add two assists in the Jets' 6-5 victory. And it was the same Hull who commanded the checking attention of little Bobby Mowat in the following game which was won by Phoenix, 3-1. Mowat put the checking shackles on Hull, holding him to just one shot on goal during that game and Phoenix netminder Jack Norris handled that perfectly. Next time out, however, Bobby took his frustrations out on Michigan, putting 17 shots on net and scoring four goals for the third time in his WHA career.

Hull is averaging a goal per game, a remarkable pace so far. Coach Rudy Pilous (Bobby is the "playing coach") has him paired with a couple of Swedes, center

Ulf Nilsson and Anders Hedberg, and the three compliment each other's styles completely in speed, playmaking abilities and selflessness. All three are complete team players.

It was Pilous who called his Jets a "smorgasbord" this past summer before training camp even began. Between the Swedes (Nilsson, Hedberg, goalie Larsson, defenseman Sjoberg) and Finns (defenseman Riihiranta, center Ketola) Pilous can serve quite a buffet (noun) while buffeting (verb). But Hull is the catalyst.

So let's give a warm welcome to Bobby and let's also treasure the 4000 "Bobby-and-the-microphone" posters (courtesy of Avco Financial Services and Frontier Airlines) distributed tonight.

Rudy
Pilous

Bobby Hull

ALTON ON THE MOVE

By STAN FISCHLER

He toured the Catskill Mountain "Borscht Belt" and pounded the pavements in shopping centers from Livingston Mall, New Jersey, to Huntington, Long Island. If you didn't know better, you'd think Alton James White was running for president, instead of right wing for the New York Raiders.

The only Black player in the World Hockey Association and only the second in big-league shinny, White spread the WHA gospel, answered questions and made himself very much a part of the local scene.

"I was surprised by the whole experience," White said. "Here I was just out of Providençe in the American League and people came up to me knowing who I was right off the bat. Of course, wearing the Raiders' jersey didn't hurt."

Because there are so few Negroes in Canada, only a handful have made it up the organized hockey ladder. During the late Forties an all-Black line comprised of the brothers, Ossie and Herbie Carnegie, and Mannie McIntyre dominated the powerful Quebec Senior Hockey League skating for Sherbrooke.

Both Art Dorrington and Alf Lewsey stickhandled in the minor pro leagues but only Willie O'Ree climbed all the way to the National Hockey League, playing for Boston in the 1960-61 season. A year later O'Ree was shunted to the minors. Now it's Alton White's turn at the top.

"I have no doubts that I can hold my own with anybody," said White. "I've got a lot of confidence in myself. During the summer I spent a lot of time with the coach (Camille Henry). He ex-

pects me to be quick and aggressive and go into the corners. Sure the competition will be tough, but I expect to rise to the call."

Inevitably, White has been assailed by questions regarding his skin color. Has he been the victim of prejudice? Have enemy skaters singled him out as a target because he is Black? Does he think of himself as a latter-day Jackie Robinson. Unfortunately for story-thirsty newsmen, the answer inevitably is in the negative.

"We might as well face the facts," said White, "and the fact is that I haven't had any more trouble than any white hockey player. Some fans have needled me, sure. But what hockey player hasn't been needled? The barbs have been typical and not be-

cause of my color."

During a visit to the Branch Brook Park rink in Newark, Alton encountered some young, Black skaters.

"They impressed me with their ability," he said. "A few of the boys had gone to hockey schools in Canada and came home quite accomplished for their ages."

More and more young Negroes are taking to hockey in the metropolitan area. A regular ice hockey program is conducted at Central Park rink near 110 Street and Fifth Avenue in Harlem and street hockey programs have become part of curricula in places such as The Cathedral School in Manhattan where Michael Lockett, a Black gym instructor, has more teams than he can handle. Newark also has a program.

These young fans are part of the audience to which the Raiders are addressing themselves. They'll come, too, particularly if the WHA sextet is a winner.

"We've got a solid club," said White. "The goaltending is good and that may turn out to be the key to our success in the long run."

Then again, Alton James White might help turn that key. He waited many years for this chance and, for a time, thought he'd be buried in Providence where he played for four seasons without getting the big-league call.

"It was nice and comfortable playing there," he recalled. "The fans were pleasant and the living was good. But I've never had second thoughts about the move I made to New York. I was never more anxious about making good in anything in my life than I am now with the Raiders!"

Lacroix returns ... to glory

By Frank Bertucci

ANDRE LACROIX

Before Bobby Clarke, there was Andre Lacroix.

When there was only the Flyers, Lacroix was the hero, the future superstar, the player who would make the Flyers an NHL power.

Lacroix is still a local hero, but it took the Blazers to make him a superstar.

"This is the first time in the last two years that I've really felt like playing hockey," Andre says. "The last two years, all I did was pick up my paycheck every two weeks. Now I'm always the first one on the ice."

Two years ago, Andre sat in Vic Stasiuk's doghouse. And when Stasiuk was replaced by Fred Shero as Flyers coach, nothing changed.

"I never got to know Freddie," Andre says, "but all of the Flyers really like him. I don't know what the problem was, maybe it was in management."

So Lacroix was shipped to Chicago for Rick Foley, who promptly replaced him in the Flyer kennel. With the Black Hawks, Andre found himself skating with Bobby Hull. After awhile, he found himself skating alone.

The word out of Chicago was that Lacroix couldn't skate. If Andre Lacroix couldn't do anything else in ice hockey, he could always skate. And now that he's on a line with Danny Lawson, he has begun to fly.

In the Blazers' first 39 games, Lacroix had 22 goals and 35 assists for 57 points, putting him among the WHA's top three scorers. Lawson had 28 goals, tying his career NHL total. And Don Herriman, on left wing, had 16 goals and 19 assists.

"This year I'm freer on the ice," explains Lacroix. "I'm doing more tricks with the puck, the way I like to play. It's the first chance I've had to do that in a while."

The last chance was 1967-68 when he had 41 goals in 54 games with the Quebec Aces, then in the AHL. He was called to the Flyers, and finished with six more goals. He had 24, 22 and 20 goal seasons the next three years, and then fell to four last year.

"I jumped to the WHA because of the money," he admits. "I was originally drafted by Quebec, which was fine because that's where I'm from. But now I live in Philadelphia, so when I got the chance to play here I had to take it.

"Billy Reay told me not to jump because he planned to use me a lot more this season. But then he didn't protect me for the expansion draft. Bill Putnam called me from Atlanta and said he was going to draft me. (Putnam is president of the Flames, and the original president of the Flyers.) But I told him not to waste a draft choice because I was so close to making a deal with the Blazers. I have a lot of respect for Bill and I owed him that much.

And Andy was reunited with another original Flyer, Bernie Parent.

"The Flyers had the best goalies in the league that first year, with Bernie and Doug Favell," says Andre. "Then they started trading everybody for defensemen."

For Lacroix and the rest of the Blazers, Christmas wasn't on time this year. Between Dec. 22 and Jan. 1, they were on an 11-day road trip through six cities, including games in Los Angeles, on New Year's Eve, and New York on New Year's night. It was a special hardship for Lacroix because his wife had given birth to their first daughter, Chantal, two days before the team left.

"We were going to celebrate before I left, but then my wife was in the hospital having the baby. So we decided to celebrate Christmas on Jan. 2. It's going to be like this for the next three years, because the Ice Follies will be using the Civic Center each Christmas."

Andre still expects the Blazers to be playing after the regular season ends.

"We were leaning on Bernie too much at the beginning," he feels, "and I think most of us came to training camp out of shape. The other teams were playing a little harder against us, too."

"But now we're coming on. Our line is playing good and Bernie is back. Believe me, he's been the difference in a few games already."

So has Andre Lacroix.

BLAZINGS . . . Rookie Michel Boudreau twisted ligaments in his right knee and will be on crutches until early January...Lawson's four goal game against Andre Gill of Chicago on Dec. 20 was his second this season. He scored four against Gerry Cheevers in Cleveland Nov. 1, ... Parent had started 16 straight games since his return Dec. 1. Marcel Paille had to finish three...Ron Plumb has become one of the league's top scoring defensemen, with five goals and 26 assists in 39 games.

94

A Bargain at $200,000

By Bob Schlesinger

Those of us who must wage a constant battle just to raise funds for an occasional visit to that lap of luxury—the meat counter at the supermarket—may find it hard to accept that someone with a $200,000 salary could be a bargain to his employer.

But, judging from what has gone on thus far, Cleveland Crusaders President Nick Mileti, who has contracted to pay goalkeeper Gerry Cheevers that not insignificant sum for each of the next seven years, according to court records, may be accused of driving a hard bargain.

In front of the nets, Cheevers' performances have been divisible into two categories, routinely spectacular and spectacularly spectacular. In fact, there's a tendency for reporters to occasionally reduce Cheevers' contributions to one sentence: "Cheevers was flawless, as usual" in order to make room for the telling of the heroics of the rest of the Crusaders.

While it has been said that statistics are like a bikini, in that what they reveal is interesting, but what they conceal is vital, the stats on Cheevers tell at least part of the story.

He has recorded two shut-outs and six victories in his first seven games, allowing only 11 goals.

But that alone isn't what has made Cheevers an instant favorite among Cleveland hockey fans, who have some expertise on the subject, having seen such goalkeepers as Johnny Bower, Emile Francis, Les Binkley, Ernie Wakely and Gary Kurt stop off here for a year or more with the Barons on their way to the big leagues.

The man who minded the nets last year as the Boston Bruins blasted their way to the Stanley Cup, is the ultimate ramblin' and gamblin' man among goalkeepers.

He seems to consider everything on his side of the Cleveland blue line as within his domain, often leaving the crease by 10 or 20 feet to scoop up a loose puck and direct it to one of his teammates, or to attack a break-away rival forward and stifle him before the enemy can launch his shot.

"I'm not a conservative type goalie," Cheevers says, "If I see a chance to go out and spoil the shooter's opportunity, I'll take it."

Fortunately, that gambling instinct is combined with what has so far been a totally accurate ability to gauge when such tactics will be effective rather than suicidal and embarrassing.

Cheevers also acts as traffic cop for the Crusaders, letting his mates know what the enemy forecheckers are up to and which routes are open through which to launch an attack.

"He's like having a coach right out there on the ice," said veteran defenseman John Hanna.

And if enemy forwards attempt to lean on Cheevers in the crease, or take a cheap shot at him as they're going by, it's not at all unlikely that they'll wind up attempting to achieve the probably impossible feat of digesting the big goalkeepers stick, tape and all.

Were Gerry a different kind of guy, it's probable that others on the team might resent his fame and fortune.

But he's lavish in the praise of his teammates, always ready to go to bat for them, on or off the ice, and willing to take, as well as dish out, the inevitable barbs that are flung around the locker room.

So he has emerged as one of the most popular players and one of the leaders of a team which has developed an incredibly fine esprit de corps in the short time It has taken the Crusaders to jump out to the top of the Eastern Division standings.

Crusader Coach Bill Needham, a man of few words, says flatly "We've got the best goalkeeper."

And nobody in these parts is inclined to argue at all with that statement.

Much Travelled Larry Hillman Defenseman Bar None

By STEVE KLEIN, Director News Media Information

When Larry Hillman played on his fifth Stanley Cup champion as a Toronto Maple Leaf in 1967, he was only 30 years old, a veritable youngster on a team that included Bobby Baun (31), Marcel Pronovost (37), Tim Horton (37), George Armstrong (37), Terry Sawchuk (38), Red Kelly (40), Allan Stanley (41) and Johnny Bower (43).

Seven years and 6th Stanley Cup championship later, Larry Hillman is 37—"Only 37," he'll tell you—and looking forward as a Cleveland Crusader to a 7th championship, the Avco World Trophy awarded to the World Hockey Assoc. champion.

"When I played for Toronto," Hillman remembers, "all the defensemen were over 30, and we were playing for one of the best six teams in the world. Why, two or three were around 40. But age never seemed to hit guys like Allan Stanley and Tim Horton."

Perhaps it is because most of those Maple Leaf teammates were older, or because the old 6-team National Hockey League is now little more than nostalgia that Larry Hillman seems even older than his 37 years, 20 major league seasons and 17 professional hockey teams. Barely a dozen of hockey's greatest names have played as long and no hockey player has belonged to as many teams as Hillman.

"In one season alone, I belonged to 5 NHL clubs," he claims with a smile thinking back to 1968-69. That was the second year of expansion, and Hillman had known only one team, Toronto, for the previous 8 seasons.

"Punch and I had a little dispute over a little money," Larry says of his first and only professional holdout with Toronto General Manager and Coach Punch Imlach. "Punch was always A-1 and fair, but he always got the better of you. That year, after 4 Stanley Cups and 8 years in Toronto, I de-

cided I was going to get my way. Money wasn't really the issue—it was a matter of principle. Punch always got his way, and I wanted to turn it around. I made a stand for what I believed in, which basically came down to what I thought I was worth. But it

was either his way or face the consequences. I took a chance."

After sitting out the first 24 days of the 1967-68 season, Imlach got his way. But after the season, one in which the defending Stanley Cup champions finished fifth and out of the playoffs, Hillman was sent on his way to the New York Rangers on waivers.

On the same day (June 12) he was waived, however, he was drafted by the Minnesota North Stars, and that's where Larry started the season. But 12 games into the 1968-69 campaign, Montreal's Terry Harper broke his leg, and the Canadiens obtained his rights as a fifth defenseman to join Jacques Laperriere, J.C. Tremblay, Serge Savard and Ted Harris.

Hillman's 5th team that season was Pittsburgh, but he never got to play for the Penguins. When the Canadiens made their deal, Pittsburgh complained that Larry had not been waived out of the NHL Western Division. After a loss to California the night of their objection, the Penguins were in last place and they claimed Hillman. So Montreal had to trade yet another player. (Jean-Guy Legace) to the Penguins before Larry was really a Canadien. He rewarded Montreal with steady defensive play that contributed to an old habit, the Stanley Cup, in the spring of 1969.

Larry Hillman became a professional 20 years ago, on March 5, 1955, signing with a dynasty at the end of an era, the Detroit Red Wings. Although he played only 9 games with Detroit that season, 3 of them were playoff games, and his name was engraved on the Stanley Cup with those of Gordie Howe, Alex Delvecchio, Red Kelly, Terry Sawchuk, John Wilson, Bill Dineen, Tony Leswick and Ted Lindsay.

For Larry Hillman, then 18 years old, playing on a championship team with Ted Lindsay had to be a dream come true.

"Ted was from my home town, Kirkland Lake (Ontario)," says Larry, "and he used to take players like Dicky Duff and me skating 90 miles north in Timmins. In the summer, we would see Ted in his big Cadillac with his buddies like Gordie Howe, and the desire to play in the NHL was instilled in all of us early.

"We had 4 choices then. We could work in the mines like all our fathers had, we could go to school for an education, we could learn a trade or we could play hockey. It was more fun to play hockey."

It was also more work. "There was a National Hockey League of 6 teams then," Larry says, "and we never thought it would change. To be one of those 120 players, you really had to work at it. Just to be a 5th defenseman or penalty killer meant something then."

Close to two-thirds of Hillman's professional career was spent in pre-expansion hockey. It was a different game, and with a 5th the number of jobs there are today, it took a special kind of dedication, not to mention ability, to be a major league hockey player.

"In our day, hockey was our living," Hillman says. "No young kid was going to come up and take the bread and butter out of our mouth. You either made it with the club you belonged to or you were sent to the minors. Management held all the strings. Today, the players hold all the the advantage.

"For 18 years, I signed with NHL teams. I had no option. The year I signed with the Cleveland Crusaders (1973-74), I talked with 5 clubs including 2 in the National League. That was unheard of before 1967, but expansion has put the player in the driver's seat."

For 7 of the 8 seasons Larry Hillman played for the Maple Leafs, he started the year in the minors (6 times in Rochester, once in Springfield).

"One year, the Leafs kept Al Arbour and sent me down. Another, it was Kent Douglass, and he ended up rookie of the year. Ted Lindsay used to say that there was only one place to play, the NHL, and I had it in my blood. So any time I was sent down, I wanted to do my best to get back as soon as I could. It was easy to get discouraged—there were openings, usually because of injuries, for only two or three guys to come up a season. I would work that extra time after practice (he still does), and I was always prepared.

"Douglass has that tremendous year, but for the next two or three, I always ended up and Douglass down by the middle of the season. I think it was because I was a better 5th defenseman than Kent. He had to play every other shift to be effective, but I was satisfied just to play at all."

For Hillman, the competition in Toronto was tough. "I don't think we changed defenseman for 10 years," he says, recalling players like Stanley and Horton, Baun and Carl Brewer and later Marcel Pronovost. When down at Rochester, Hillman had teammates like Mike Walton, Jim Pappin and even a goaltender named Gerry Cheevers with the same problems.

Hockey was different game in the pre-expansion days. "Games were tighter played," Hillman points out. "There weren't many games over 5 goals or many decided before the 3rd period. And before they changed the power play rule (a penalized player had to remain off the ice the full two minutes until 1956), a team like Montreal could end a game during a penalty and there would be no catching them.

"Teams had great compatability then. The cities weren't so spread out, and often, we'd travel by train. You lived with each other, and you lived with a game and the way you played, good or bad, for days. If you had a grudge against a player or team, you knew you'd be seeing that team in a week or so. There were some great rivalries then, but it's something that you can't maintain today with air travel and schedules that separate teams by months at a time."

In 20 years, Hillman has known many of the game's great personalities—and characters. Larry puts Gordie Howe, Henri Richard and Jean Beliveau at the top of his list of personalities, and Eddie Shore at the top of his list of characters.

"Anyone who knows Gordie will tell you he's two different people on and off the ice," says Larry. "I know how Gordie was day one, and I know how he is day 20, and he hasn't changed.

"Beliveau and Richard are in the same class as Howe. The same things were instilled in all of us at an early age. Hockey was our living, and despite the changes expansion has brought, the game is still played the same way, and played best by those who play it that way."

Larry probably learned how to stay ahead of the game during the 1962-63 season, most of which he spent playing for Shore in Springfield.

"Eddie was the master of creating unheard of situations," says Larry. "He was man of ever changing moods. If he felt blowing up balloons for Ice Capades or washing his Cadillac was part of your job, you blew up balloons or washed the car. Otherwise, he fined you. And if Eddie caught you close to a curfew and said you were late, you were late, no matter what all the clocks in the world said. Usually, it would be 10 or at the most, 15 minutes. I've kept my watch 30 minutes ahead since that season in Springfield. I call it "Shore time." He hasn't caught me yet."

And at 37, 20 professional seasons and team No. 17, time hasn't caught Larry Hillman yet, either.

"Kirk adds class —On ice and off"

By JOHN SHORT

Gavin Kirk was talking about why he is glad to be playing with Edmonton Oilers instead of either Birmingham Bulls or Calgary Cowboys in the World Hockey Association.

As he spoke, he gestured toward Bob Nevin, the veteran obtained from the NHL to help provide stability in the Oilers' changing fortunes.

"We were playing in Calgary and it wasn't going so well," Kirk said. "We ultimately lost 3-0.

"But once I looked up and I saw Nevin hurrying to get back as a checker—so I figured I had to get back, too.

"Hockey players know how great Nevin has been and still is," Kirk continued. "When he's still not in shape and he's working harder than anybody, you realize there's no excuse for you not to do the same thing."

Nevin broke his collarbone in his 2nd game as an Oiler. He was out almost two months and came back as soon as the break healed, although he was not in top shape.

"The only way to get into condition is to play your way back," says Nevin. "I still like to play; anything beats sitting, especially when you see little things you might be able to do to help the team."

Kirk didn't mention any names when he spoke about his stay at Birmingham, where he was one of the club's top point-getters, as usual.

"I don't know why I was traded. All I know is that I was told I'd be sitting out for awhile; I don't think I was playing badly."

He said the big difference between Birmingham and Edmonton is that leadership is provided on this team.

"Nobody helps you in Birmingham," he said. "The veterans, stars, don't take control the way you might think they should.

"Here, it's different. I can see that although I've only been here a short while.

"Everybody works to help everybody else. It's the kind of thing that makes it fun to play.

"I'm looking forward to staying a long time."

It was surprising that Kirk became available, with Tom Simpson, in a trade for Tim Sheehy just as it was surprising—to everybody but Kirk—that he went to Birmingham at the start of the season.

"I didn't want to go back to Calgary," said Kirk who would not elaborate in detail on his dispute with General Manager Joe Crozier.

"I knew I wouldn't be going back."

The dispute started in the playoffs last year against Quebec Nordiques when the Cowboys pulled off the biggest playoff upset in several seasons.

"I was one of the leading scorers against Quebec," he said. "Then, in the final against Winnipeg, Crozier told me I wasn't playing.

"He didn't give me a reason, just said I hadn't been playing well enough. I don't know how he could say that when I'd had a good series and we had won it.

"Nobody likes sitting on the bench, but I know if I'm not playing well, it's likely to happen. If I get a reason, I can live with it, but it's hard to sit down when you think you're going well.

"That was part of it. There were other things I don't want to talk about.

"All I know is I'm glad to be here."

Bep Guidolin, Coach and General Manager of the Oilers, is glad to have him.

"His track record says he's a player.

"You notice, every time there's a loose puck in our end, he's the guy that gets it. Those are little things to some people, but not to coaches and not to me.

"He can play winning hockey and he's young. That makes him someone to build around and that's what we're trying to do here—build from the ground up."

EXCITEMENT IS SPELLED "SHEEHAN"

By BEN OLAN

Early last season, the California Golden Seals, who had been averaging about 3,500 spectators, billed their National Hockey League game with the Boston Bruins as a "Battle Between the Bobbys—Sheehan and Orr," and more than 10,000 people attended the contest in the Oakland Coliseum.

After the game Milt Schmidt, the Bruins' general manager, asked Garry Young, his Golden Seals' counterpart, if Sheehan might be available in a trade. "No way," Young said sternly. "If we traded Sheehan, the people here would murder us. Bobby is excitement and, man, that's what we need here."

Sheehan, the 5-7, 155 pound center from Weymouth, Mass., is bound to be Mr. Excitement for the Raiders. "The fans will really take to his speed an razzle-dazzle style," predicts Marvin Milkes, the Raider's general manager. "With the Garden crowd behind him he'll really be flying."

At 23 years of age, Bobby is in his fourth year as a hockey professional. He was turned pro by the Montreal Canadiens in 1969. The flying American played in 16 games for the Flying Frenchmen that year and 46 more for the Canadiens' Montreal farm team in the American Hockey League. The following season he played in 29 games for the Canadiens, collecting six goals and five assists. He was sold to the California team on May 25, 1971 and scored 20 times for the Golden Seals last season.

"Bobby could be for my hockey team what Vida Blue was to my baseball team," Charlie Finley said about him last year. Finley owns the Seals and the Oakland A's.

"Sheehan," commented Emile Francis, the Rangers' general manager, "skates like a bat out of hell. You just wind him up and turn him loose. If you're standing still, he'll go by you four times."

And Carol Vadnais, the former California defenseman now with the Bruins, stated, "Sheehan's the fastest. Every time he's on the ice, just listen to the fans. They go crazy."

Sheehan once was in a position to accept a hockey scholarship to a college in the U.S. Instead he chose to go to Nova Scotia and play junior hockey. The first few weeks in Halifax were rough. The Canadian boys were using Bobby like a Yo-Yo. "In the States," he points out, "you could get away with skating with your head down. But not in Canada." The Canadians made Sheehan the target of many practical jokes. However, he relates now, "They stopped the jokes when I knocked down a door they had locked on me."

He received his room, board and $12 a week. "I couldn't live on $12," he remembers. "Fortunately there was a race track next to the hockey rink in Halifax. I made real money at the track." On the ice, Bobby captivated the crowds but antagonized the management. He scored 153 goals in two seasons despite numerous suspensions, fines and other assorted disciplinary measures. "Somehow I always seemed to be in the middle of everything that happened," he explains.

Sheehan, who eludes opposing defenseman as if by magic, had everything to do with the emergence and disappearance of one Bob Terry. "My high school team in Weymouth had a rule that you couldn't play for any outside club," he recounts. "Well, they only had a 14-game schedule and that wasn't enough for me. So I hooked on with a team 30 or 35 miles north in New Hampshire. I borrowed my buddy's name, Terry, and no questions were asked."

Bobby wasn't caught either when he stepped a bit out of line while playing for the St. Catharines team in the Ontario Hockey Association, the top Junior A circuit. The rap against Bobby, if it can be called that, is that he was a swinger with the gals as well as a hockey stick. "We used to play

on Sundays when I was with St. Catharines and then be off for three days," he remembers. "So, after the Sunday game, I'd slip across the river into New York and have some fun. Team management didn't like it too much. But I never hurt myself. Never did anything the night before a game. But can you imagine? They even put a detective on me one time."

He adds, "I have a good time wherever I go. People asked me if I liked Oakland. There are girls there, same as any place else. But New York is really my kind of town. If I had been drafted by the Islanders I'd have to have given it a lot of thought. But the Raiders will have one of the best teams in the WHA and I'll be getting a lot of opportunity to play."

Sheehan indeed was one of the best players on the West Coast last season. At one point, Young, the Seals' G.M., said, "Bobby is one of the fastest players in the National Hockey League. And I think he's the best American-born player in the history of the

continued on next page

... ANDY BATHGATE

Not all that Andrew James Bathgate has done for hockey is found in the goals and assists columns. Much of his contribution can be found in the hands and on the feet and faces of hockey players from Thetford Mines to Salt Lake City. Wherever organized hockey is played, there is a touch of Bathgate.

Would you believe that he, and not Stan Mikita, perfected the first curved stick. Or that Bathgate had the final hand (actually, it was a backhand) in the permanent adoption of face masks by professional goalies? Or that this same innovative Mr. B picked up a tidy piece of change last year by devising and patenting a detachable counter-weight which fits on skate blades to build better leg muscles?

Read and believe.

Stan Mikita, the Chicago Black Hawk centre, always gets the credit for introducing the curved stick into the National Hockey League, a step that introduced Bobby Hull's slapshot, and paranoia to the goaltending profession. But the fact is, Bathgate was fiddling with curved sticks when he was an amateur at Guelph in 1951. And it had started even before that, playing road-apple hockey in the streets of Winnipeg.

He says, "You know how it is when you're a kid, playing with old equipment. You get that frozen road-apple and hand-me-down stick that may be warped or splintered. Well, I noticed that sometimes the stick blade would be warped and it would have a bit of a bend in it. With that little bit of a curve, you could tuck the road-apple away and keep it away from everyone.

"When I got to Guelph, I started deliberately bending the blades of my sticks under a door, just to give them a slight hook. I liked the results and I kept doing the same thing when I got to the Rangers but I didn't tell anyone about it. Well, one weekend, the Black Hawks came to New York for a Sunday game after a long road trip. It would have been around 1954, I guess. Mikita had been on the road a long time and he had run out of sticks so he asked the Ranger trainer if he could borrow some of ours. The trainer gave him two or three of mine, the ones I had put the hook into. Mikita took a couple of his boomer shots and the hook in the stick made the puck drop. He got a couple of goals that day that sold him on the curved blade. From that time on, everyone said he invented the curved stick."

Bathgate didn't invent the goalies' face mask, but he struck the blow for the freedom to use them.

In 1959, Jacques Plante of the Montreal Canadiens' was acknowledged as one of the greatest goalies in history. He was also recognized as one of the most fragile. Playing goal bare-faced, as was the style of the time, Plante had picked up 200 stitches in his face, his skull had been fractured, both cheekbones had been broken and his nose had been broken four times. Every injury had come from stopping a puck with his unprotected head or face.

In the desperation of self preservation, Plante devised a crude face mask and began using it in practices. He asked coach Toe Blake if he could wear it in games, but the traditionalist Blake flatly refused to condone such namby-pamby behavior.

On November 1st, 1959, in Madison Square Garden, the Canadiens and Rangers were scoreless in the first period. Andy Bathgate came out of the face off circle to Plante's left and ripped a 25-foot backhand through a crowd of players. The screened shot caught Plante flush in the face, slicing open his nose and his cheek. Covered with blood, groggy, Plante was taken to the dressing room for stitches while the game was held up. Twenty minutes later, a grim Plante said to Blake, "I don't go back in unless I wear the mask." There was no spare goalie available, so Blake, the traditionalist, had to give in. Plante wore the mask for the rest of the game and the rest of the season.

The rest is history.

Bobby Sheehan continued

league." Another time after the swift-moving center had played brilliantly against the Vancouver Canucks, Young commented, "There aren't many players like Bobby who lift you out of your seat the way Bobby Orr does." And still on another occasion after he had scored twice against Pittsburgh, Penguins' coach Red Kelly stated, "The way my guys were moving Sheehan looked like he had on double jets."

How does a New England boy get to the NHL and then to New York with a brand new World Hockey Association team? "You've got to skate and skate," he explains. "In Canada they call kids like that 'rink rats.' I guess that's what I was in this country. I bet I skated on every pond and lake in and around my home town."

No doubt about it, Garden spectators will enjoy watching Bobby Sheehan skate. He's fast, clever, colorful and mod. The Raiders are pleased that he made the 3,000-mile jump.

— DON BLACKBURN —
Blackie, 1,000 and Counting

By BOB NEUMEIER

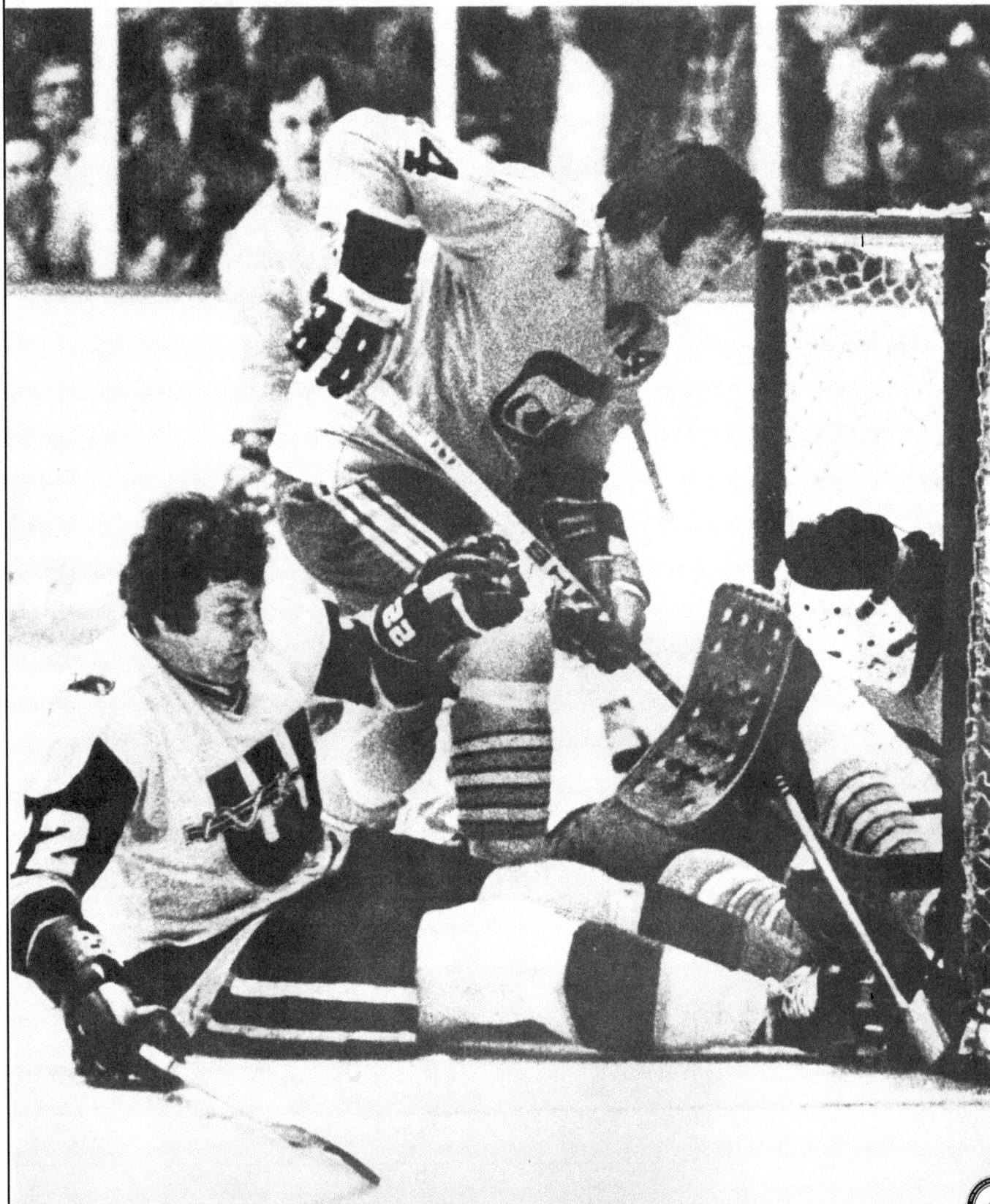

They call this man Blackie.

No, this Blackie is not the scraggily-faced, ornery hombre who stuck up the Wells Fargo stagecoach each week on the old television serials. Nor is he the cunning detective of the 1940's who earned the monicker Boston Blackie from those seedy, movie tough guys.

No, this Boston Blackie is left-winger-center Don Blackburn of the New England Whalers, who has the knack of scoring the important goal. But clutch scoring is nothing new for the popular veteran. While skating for the Philadelphia Flyers in 1967-68, Blackie scored a Stanley Cup overtime goal against the St. Louis Blues, a feat Don ranks high on his long list of hockey thrills.

Another of Blackburn's greatest thrills received the most limited publicity. For on a brisk January eve in Toronto, the 35-year-old forward skated in his 1000th game as a professional hockey player.

"No, I never imagined I would ever play that many games," Blackburn said with the kind of sheepish Robert Mitchum grin that has helped win Blackie a top spot on the Whalers' totem pole of popularity.

The 17-year-old veteran credits conditioning and good, old-fashioned enthusiasm for the reasons for his longevity. "I just love this game," enthused Blackburn, "and I've been lucky enough to be relatively free of injury. I work hard in practice to keep in good shape and I love playing with this particular club."

You could fill a closet with the number of sweaters Blackburn has worn in his long and winding hockey road. Originally drafted by the Boston Bruins in 1956, Blackie has ridden the roller coaster of a hockey journeyman.

From the exhaustion of minor league bus rides to the euphoria of scoring key major league goals, Blackie has skated for 13 different clubs before joining the Whalers this season.

"Players are skating longer now," Blackburn theorized," and I believe there are several reasons why. I credit Punch Imlach with establishing the concept that older players can be of value to a hockey club. When I first broke in, general managers would start phasing you out when you reached 30 years of age. But when Imlach started to win Stanley Cups with players 35, 36, 37-years-old, people in hockey realized that an experienced player can help a club." And Don Blackburn has helped the New England Whalers.

The line of Blackburn, center Tom Williams (since lost in expansion), and right-winger Tom Webster was the club's most consistent scoring line in the latter stages of last season. But when injuries knocked out Williams and Webster during the play-offs, one might have expected Blackburn to fold up his hockey tent and wait for a new season.

But skating at center with new wingers Hugh Harris and Tim Sheehy, Blackburn tied for the club playoff scoring mark, a credit to the veteran's versatility.

Does Blackburn have any thoughts of retirement? "Right now, I still have a season left on the two-year contract I signed with the Whalers a year ago June," said Blackburn. "As long as I stay in shape and play the game competitively, I'd like to continue with hockey."

Detective Boston Blackie will probably be playing on the Late, Late Show long after this Blackie hangs up the old skates. But judging from the interest and performance of Don Blackburn, this Blackie will be featured in prime time for a few years to come.

KEN DESJARDINE

Racer Defense Man

Ken Desjardine, the Racers 27-year-old defenseman, is in his third year as a major leaguer and in his fifth season of professional hockey.

The handsome, 6-foot, 185-pounder comes to the Indianapolis Racers from the Quebec Nordiques via the World Hockey Association Expansion Draft which was held last May in Toronto, Ontario.

Ken is a consistent performer who plays his position well. A real hard worker around the blueline, Ken always seems to be where the action is. He has good speed, is an excellent stickhandler and moves the puck well enough to become a bigger scorer than his past record indicates.

A 1970 graduate of Michigan Tech University where he majored in Business Administration, Desjardine entered the pro ranks after skating three seasons with the Huskies in the highly regarded Western Collegiate Hockey Association. Ken inked his first pro contract with the Toronto Maple Leafs of the National Hockey League and was dispatched by the Leafs to their Tulsa farm club in the Central Hockey League where he played 132 games over a two-year span. He had 5 goals, 31 assists and 208 minutes in the penalty box during his stay with the Tulsa Oilers.

In February, 1972 the newly-formed World Hockey Association held its Player Selection Draft and Ken Desjardine was selected by the Quebec Nordiques. He accepted their offer and remained two seasons for the Nordiques.

With the Indy Racers this season, Ken took his regular turn on defense until he was sidelined by a fractured bone in his left heel. He sustained the injury October 27 during some heavy third-period action in the Racers 5-3 victory over the Quebec Nordiques that night. In the process of checking Charles Constantin, Nordiques left winger, both Desjardine and Constantin hit the ice with Ken sliding heavily into the boards . . . skates first. X-rays taken following the injury disclosed the fracture that has kept him out of action the past three weeks (10 games including tonight's). He is not expected to be back in uniform for at least another three weeks.

Ken was born in Toronto, Ontario on August 23, 1947 and currently makes his off-season home in Oshawa, Ontario, just a short chip shot from his native Toronto. In the summer months and between his work at hockey schools, he likes to spend his leisure time on the golf course or on water skis.

During the season Ken and teammate Steve Richardson live in a house they rent on the North Side of Indianapolis.

"GUEST SHOT"

NICK HARBARUK

ONE OF THE first things Nick Harbaruk did after signing a three-year contract with the Indianapolis Racers in 1974 was to buy a house there.

The former right winger with the St. Louis Blues of the National Hockey League felt he had found a home in the Hoosier capital and he wanted to become totally involved in the community.

It was a typical move by the 31-year-old native of Drohiczyn, Poland, according to the man who signed him, Chuck Catto, former Racer director of player personnel.

"The city will enjoy Nick Harbaruk," said Catto.

"He's a class guy. Off the ice he's quiet and shy. On the ice he takes the game seriously and patrols his position everywhere he skates. He's just a silent leader."

That silent leadership came to the front just before the

"Nick has always been defense minded," said Catto. "It's always good to have a fellow like that when you're in a league with guys like Bobby Hull, Frank Mahvolich and Mike Walton."

Harbaruk admits his forte has been the checking of other teams' scoring stars, but one of the reasons he joined the Racers was to start scoring himself.

"I would like to do more offensive work, and I feel I'll get the chance with this club," he said. "I had no trouble scoring in the minors, but when I went to Pittsburgh, they told me they didn't care how many goals I scored, they wanted me to check.

"One game they used me for checking Bobby Hull the whole game and the next night I didn't even play. I asked to be traded and I played on a regular basis in St. Louis until I got hurt and couldn't get back in the lineup."

Although he scored only 45 goals in five NHL seasons, Harbaruk scored 20 last season, and is ahead of that pace this year.

"I'm still going to check in this league against guys like Hull and Mahvolich, but I think I can score 25 or 30 goals."

Harbaruk's enthusiasm for his family — he and his wife Nancy have two daughters, Kimberly, 5, and Debra, 2 — and his sport have become infectious to the players and Indiana fans.

"Sometimes you have doubts about an expansion team, but I have none here," he said. "In some ways this club is better run than anything I saw in the NHL. The fans here are enthusiastic and it has rubbed off this year on the players. We'll be all right."

Racers began their first World Hockey Association season when the players voted Harbaruk team captain.

"This is the first time I've been a captain since I was about 16 and still in the amateurs," said Harbaruk. "It means quite a bit to me because I was elected by the players."

After becoming unhappy with the amount of playing time he got at St. Louis, Harbaruk could have signed with the WHA Toronto Toros.

He opted for Indianapolis and upon hearing his reason it's obvious he's a realist and honest.

"I'm from Toronto and I thought it would be nice to be there," said Harbaruk, "but Toronto signed some stars like Frank Mahvolich and Paul Henderson, and I think I probably would have been just another girl in the chorus there. I think Indianapolis will be more exciting."

Harbaruk never had the reputation of being a chorus girl in his five-year NHL career.

McLeod gets his chance

The dictionary has a definition for "frustration," but followers of the Cougars have a better way to find out the meaning of that particular word.

All they have to do is ask goaltender Jimmy McLeod.

McLeod's entire career has been a series of frustrations, through a dozen seasons knocking around in the minor leagues to his present beleaguered status with the Cougars.

There have been, he admits, many times he thought about giving it all up and quitting, but this year curiously has not been one of those times even though the Cougars have not proven to be among the strongest of the WHA teams.

"I've got a chance to make some money, and I'm going to prove myself," he says.

Like so many of the WHA players, McLeod is one of those guys who repeatedly was bypassed for promotion to the National Hockey League while playing in the minors. That, too, he says was "frustrating," particularly when other players were being promoted.

"I've seen goalies go up whom I've played against and played with, and I know their capabilities, but they were up here and I was still down there," McLeod says.

To set the record straight, McLeod actually played nine full seasons in the Western Hockey League—with San Francisco, Los Angeles, Seattle and Portland—before finally getting his NHL shot with the St. Louis Blues last year at age 34. He led the WHL in shutouts in four of those nine seasons, had the best goals-against average twice, and set a league record for playoff shutouts.

It's not really a bad track record for a guy who was a defenseman in his teens and did not start playing goalie until he was 18 years old and realized he was too small to make it on defense.

Which is why McLeod says, "I'm pretty fortunate where I am right now," but he's not unwilling to discuss the past.

"I thought I was ready for the NHL the first year they had the expansion," he said. "But I was owned outright by Portland and didn't belong to any NHL club, and that was one of the big factors.

"If I would have belonged to an NHL club, they just wouldn't have protected me and someone else would have picked me up. But being owned outright, privately, I didn't have a choice; I just had to sit there and hope that somebody would come up with the bread to buy me from Portland—and they were asking for pretty good loot for the guys they owned, too.

"There could have been 10 or 15 times I might have had a chance for the NHL, but I'm the last guy to know about it. There might have been a lot of times that an NHL team phoned to ask about me, but I was never told that."

McLeod believes "politics" played a part in keeping him in the minors all those years, because he never played junior hockey in Canada like almost everyone else did. But the biggest frustration of all came last year with St. Louis.

"I think there's a lot of politics in the National Hockey League. Of course in every league there is, but up there I sat on the bench for 13 games and they tried two or three goalies they had, but that wasn't the answer.

"Then they tried me and we started to win. Then we changed coaches, and then they changed goalies. They made 50-some changes that year and it was just a matter of time who was gonna be next."

The end result was that the Blues went through three coaches last season—Sid Abel, Bill McCreary and Al Arbour—and finished third in the NHL West. They also used five

By Ira Miller

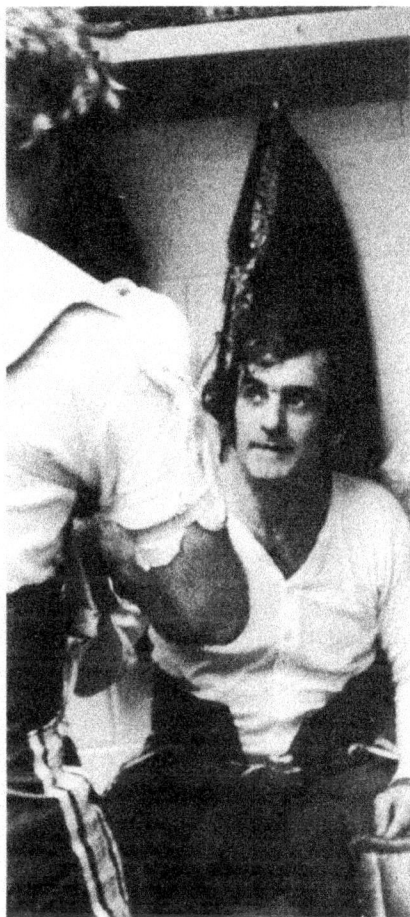

"I've got a chance to make some money, and I'm going to prove myself."

. . . he led the WHL in shutouts in four of those nine seasons, had the best goals-against average twice, and set a league record for playoff shutouts.

Jordon Kaiser, Cougar owner, congratulates McLeod after the game.

"He said, . . . 'Don't pass up the chance, you won't regret it,' and I haven't regretted it."

goaltenders during the year—McLeod, Jacques Caron, Wayne Stephanson, Peter McDuffe and Ernie Wakely—and had a .500-or-better record with only two of them, McLeod and Caron.

But after McLeod played 16 games with a 3.00 goals-against average and with the team posting a 6-6-4 record, he found himself back on the sidelines.

"When they let me go," he says, "I was probably their best goaltender out of the three who started the season. But it was the same old story, they said they had to make a change and since I was a little older than the other guys, they wanted to keep the other guys around.

"They said they'd put me on waivers and nobody picked me up. They didn't do it, but they tried to soft-pedal the idea as much as possible.

"It was very disappointing for a guy who spent so much time in the minors and came up and really appreciated it, to then get shot down like nothing." McLeod concedes he thought about retiring right then, but the WHA came along to change all that.

"The Cougars drafted me and I talked to Dennis Murphy (one of the WHA's founders) and he made it look kind of rosy," McLeod said.

"He said, 'You're their No. 1 goaltender, don't pass up the chance, you won't regret it,' and I haven't regretted it.

"I've gotten a lot of static from people in hockey generally, the established hockey people, and I said, 'Lookit, I think I've given you guys enough of my time'."

107

THAT'S KARLANDER — WITH A "K"

The reporters hunched around Al Karlander after a recent New England Whalers game.

"That's Karlander — with a K," yelled linemate John French across the room. Although the offhand comment did not receive a direct response, several of the writers later agreed the comment might have been more meaningful and perceptive than French originally intended.

For the quiet mustachioed Karlander has not received the kudos the left winger-centerman deserves. "Right now, John French and Al Karlander have been our most consistent forwards," said Whalers' coach Ron Ryan. "Al, particularly, has been terrific in recent games."

The statistics support the praise Ryan heaped on the 27 year-old former Michigan Tech star. A close look at the 12 goals 29 assists, 41 points scoring total rung up by Karlander reveals the kind of explosive bursts he has provided.

From October 22 to November 11, Karlander was hot, scoring 11 points in 7 games, but from December 22 to January 10, Al tallied but a scant two points. "I really can't explain my up-and-down scoring this year," said Karlander after a recent practice. "Lately I have been skating stronger because I'm finally getting into the kind of shape I want. That's the reason I have been scoring better of late, anyway."

As expected, Al started off very slowly for New England. "Missing the training

WHA

camp really hurt, because the players who signed from the NHL couldn't start playing exhibition games until after October 1, when our standard NHL contract expired. Hell, we started the season about a week and a half later (October 9). I haven't really been at tip-top shape until a month ago."

Karlander was signed by the Whalers from the Detroit Red Wings' organization in June, 1973. "Discontent in Detroit is the reason I left," Al said. "They were happy with my play but considered me only in terms of a utility player. They only used me as such—killing penalties and things. But like most players I wanted to play regularly. The Whalers offered me that chance." "So I accepted and I've no regrets at all."

Karlander played two full seasons with the Red Wings from 1971-73 and scored 15 goals in each of the two campaigns as a spot player. The Red Wings originally snared Al from Michigan Tech, after he broke the school's scoring record with 31 goals in his senior year in 1969. That year also brought about one of Karlander's bigger thrills as a player. " I scored all three of our goals against Cornell in the NCAA semi-finals although we lost 4-3 in over-time," remembered Al. "And the goal-tender was Ken Dryden." Karlander's performance that season earned him All-America status in his senior year.

Al Karlander is not the charismatic scorer with the flashy strides and the booming shot. But Al Karlander is a dedicated, hard-working forward who can dig the puck out of the corners on left wing or make the scoring pass at center ice. You won't find his name in too many headlines, but when you do, look for Karlander . . . with a K.

HARPOON
THE OFFICIAL MAGAZINE OF THE NEW ENGLAND WHALERS

ONE DOLLAR INCLUDES TAX

TED GREEN

HOUSTON'S

NO.9

By Bill Asnes

Houston, Texas — home of the wild west — cowboys, rodeos, oil wells. Hardly a place for a retired veteran of a sport played on ice to start anew. But I'm not talking about just any veteran. This man happens to be the Babe Ruth of hockey, Gordie Howe.

The man most responsible for filling the seats of Detroit's Olympia has decided to end retirement and resume his remarkable career in Houston with his sons.

Many athletes have retired and attempted comebacks, hoping that there was still a spark of natural talent left in those old bones. There is serious doubt, however, if any of those retired heroes could be placed in the same class as Mr. Howe.

For 25 years Gordie Howe was the staple on the Detroit Red Wings. His achievements may never be duplicated. When he retired the city and its hockey fans showered endless praise and affection on their favorite star.

The most probable question raised is "What can bring this super-star out of retirement and move him to another part of the country?"

For one thing, Gordie will be adding another first to a lengthy string of firsts. How many have seen a father and sons play professionally on the same team, at the same time? It may sound impossible, but that is exactly what the new hockey fans of Houston will be witnessing. Gordie, Mark, and Marty will be donning the blue and white of the

Houston Aeros for at least the 1973-'74 WHA season.

Skeptics will laugh and say, "Will the old man regain his form? Can he still keep up with the kids?" There were some questions in my mind, too — that is, until I met him for the first time in June. The only visual signs of "maturity" was the greying hair. Wife Coleen will tell you, however, that her husband's hair has been that way now for quite a while.

His body certainly reveals no hint of his actual age. "I'm in better shape for this coming season than I was in the last year I played for Detroit," Howe said. "My wrist was hurting me quite a bit two years ago and I've had plenty of time to rest it."

Doctors are also amazed at the almost perfect frame that has housed a quarter century of hockey greatness. There is not a single doubt among the Aeros

brass about Howe's physical ability to come back to active skating.

Whether or not the living legend substantially adds to his record number of career goals (786) is really immaterial. His presence alone is enough for Bill Dineen and crew. The Aeros need a leader. Despite their successful inaugural season in the WHA last year, the one ingredient lacking was a team leader...one man teammates could consistently look to for an emotional lift. Now they've got it.

Gordie Howe is something of a phenomenon to Houston sports. A traditional football city, Houston had only its first taste of major league hockey last season. There have been minor league clubs here in the past, but nothing that drew the crowds — hockey always played second fiddle to high school football. But as the years

110

went by, Houston's professional franchises started to make names for themselves as losers. Naturally, Houston became hungry for a winner.

Down from Dayton, Ohio came Paul Deneau and Jim Smith with their new hockey team. Smith, GM, hearing cries of "Give us a winner," loaded the club with seasoned veterans who played some good hockey. The Aeros came in second in the WHA's Western Division and made the playoffs. They weren't the league champions, but Houston was happy. But — pardon the repetition — there was no super-star. Somebody was needed.

Enter assistant coach and former great defenseman Doug Harvey.

He prompted coach Dineen and Smith to draft Gordie Howe's sons from the Canadian Junior Leagues. It was a move made amongst widespread criticism in the WHA and the NHL.

The NHL has a clause that prohibits its clubs from drafting "amateurs." The new WHA had no written law, but complied with this tradition. The Howes, however, are American citizens, born and raised in Michigan. When an American citizen gets paid for his work, he is designated as a professional. Thus, Mark and Marty were drafted, signed, and beckoned to bring their father with them.

As far as the eldest Howe, his eventual signing is equally, or even more important, than Bobby Hull's exit from Chicago. Howe is already a hockey Hall of Famer. He didn't "jump" leagues for more money. He was not in the middle of a lengthy contract, having to go to court for permission to play in another league. His decision to play again was made in order to fulfill a life-long ambition — to play pro hockey with his sons. Feuding with his

old league, trying to make a point, was not on his mind. What he did do was guarantee a secure future for his entire family, despite the problem of relocating.

The future of the Howes will indeed be secure, but so will that of the Aeros. In Mark, 18, the Aeros have a smooth skating, fancy stick-handling forward with unlimited potential. At his age, with the right coaching, he can be a super-star in his own right, even if his last name were not Howe.

In Marty, 19, the Aeros have signed a solid checking defenseman, also with star potential.

And in Houston, the Howes have found a young, growing city yearning for a champion.

The Howes and Houston — a combination that could spell trouble for WHA competition.

The league? Well, it now boasts hockey's top two all-time great scorers. Gordie Howe, 1, and Bobby Hull, 2.

Who can ask for more?

SERIES OF 20 — ©O.P.C.   13   PRINTED IN CANADA

GORDIE
HOWE
RIGHT WING • AILIER DROIT

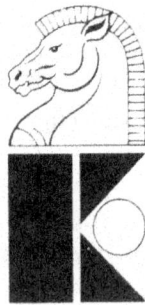

JERSEY KNIGHTS' RUGGED KEVIN MORRISON

Kevin "Killer" Morrison, as ferocious a defenseman as exists in hockey, was signed to a multi-year contract with the Jersey Knights of the World Hockey Association.

The 6 foot, 210 pounder has cooled his heels in penalty boxes for an average of 190 minutes in his four combat-filled seasons since graduated from the Quebec Junior League. His first two seasons were spent with the Eastern League New Haven Blades and then he stepped up to the AHL, skating last winter for the New Haven Nighthawks.

Morrison, 23, plays left defense and has also seen duty at left wing where he has equally applied his crunching style. The Knights plan to utilize Morrison exclusively on the backline and he will join newly-acquired Harry Howell as a new face on defense.

Two years ago "Sports Illustrated" romanticized Morrison's rough style in an article also depicting other bashers, John Ferguson, Johnny McKenzie, Jim Dorey, and Reggie Fleming. "Morrison is so feared that if a man is carrying the puck toward the New Haven goal and he senses Morrison bearing down on him from behind, he will leave the puck and skate elsewhere. In the 1970 EHL playoffs Morrison accumulated 44 penalty minutes and one match penalty, but not before he knocked the Johnstown goalie unconscious. The goalie thought he was protected because he was inside his net. In a game prior to the playoffs Morrison simultaneously broke the nose of one player and separated the shoulder of another.

Former Golden Blade Managing Director Jerry De-Lise said of the new acquisition, "Kevin Morrison is one of the toughest young hockey players I've seen perform. He'll hit you with his body or fist and he'll never stop to ask you which you prefer."

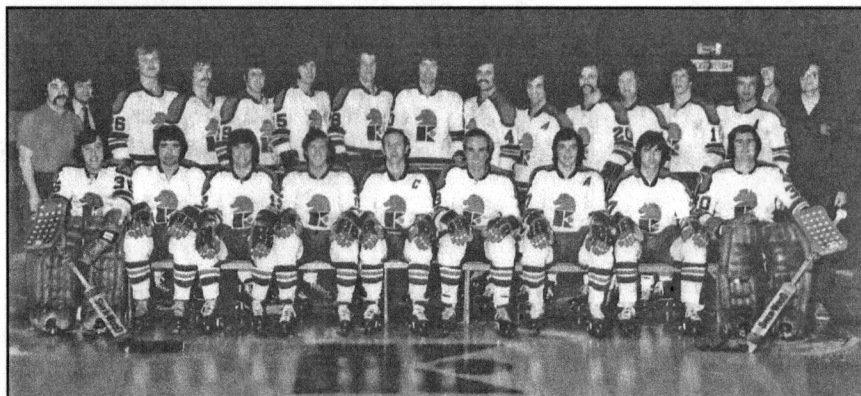

ONE HUNDRED AND TEN PERCENT

It almost makes you tired to watch him.

One moment New England Whaler defenseman Rick Ley is kicking at a puck and digging furiously in a corner against a winger who's often much bigger. The next moment he's recovered the puck and is now bringing it up ice only to shoot it into the zone and retreat to his spot at the point. In ensuing flashes of time he's blocking a shot, brilliantly breaking up a breakaway, or leaning on the opponent's roughest player. The action never stops when Ley is on the ice.

"One hundred and ten percent," is the most widely used phrase that describes Ley pronounced Lee). "It's kind of refreshing to see a kid with his ability who hustles constantly like he does. You realize that he plays the game not just for the money," says an unnamed rival coach, "I'd like to play for another 20 years," says the third team WHA All-Star defenseman, obviously not a take-the-money-and-run type.

Everything he does is that way. In a summer hockey camp he runs, in business, in personal appearance — Rick always devotes his all.

A native of Orillia, Ontario (Whaler winger John French also grew up there), Rick was tabbed as a "potential superstar" after graduating from the Niagara Falls Flyers Junior team where, as a defenseman, he scored the phenomenal total of 64 points in only 53 games. While on that team he played with Derek Sanderson, who was to introduce Rick to his wife. With the Flyers he did everything, once playing every position but goal in a game. Later with the Whalers this experience was to prove very handy as he practiced as a reserve forward when injuries decimated the Whalers' ranks during their march to the World Hockey Association championship in the playoffs last spring.

After graduation from the Juniors Ley stepped almost immediately into a defense position with the Toronto Maple Leafs. He, along with Jim Dorey and later Brad Selwood were tabbed the "Kiddie Korps" in those first few years. The Leafs were losing their share, but with this strong nucleus gaining experience, the winning seasons were on the way in bunches. During the opening round of the 1972 Stanley Cup Finals with the Bruins, the opposing player who drew the most raves was Ley. In less than six months, however, he was skating in Boston regularly with the Whalers at the Boston Garden.

Ley's decision to depart the Leafs for Jack Kelley and the New England Whalers gave the new team one of the finest defense corps in hockey. Along with Ted Green, old friends Dorey and Selwood, and Paul Hurley, they were a bunch that placed three defensemen in the three WHA All-Star teams. In every stop along the way when General Managers got to talking about the talent on the WHA rosters, the opinion "Gee, I'd like to have that Ley kid," always popped up.

At 5-9, 185 pounds, Rick is built more like a human fire plug than a top major league defenseman. The appearances are deceiving, however. Once at a Maple Leaf practice he and a slightly miffed Jim Dorey got into a spirited tussle that let the word out to everyone: Ley's not afraid to mix it up with anyone, even a teammate.

Rick has adapted his style of hockey to being the complete defenseman. His plus and minus total (ratio of goals scored while on ice to goals scored against while on ice), is one of the best in hockey. If he wanted to score goals he would — he just wants to play hockey.

COMING INTO FOCUS

by DENNIS FESER

In his second season after the high sticking incident which almost cost him his life and forced him to miss a year, the world of Ted Green was coming into focus.

The Boston Bruins had just won the Stanley Cup, so what could be wrong about that? Nothing, except Greenie was having trouble convincing himself he was part of it.

He sat, solitary figure in his dressing room cubicle as the Bruins rejoiced over winning the cup for the second time in three years.

But the other time had been the season Green sat our. And if he was having trouble climbing the heights of ecstasy, perhaps it was because the Zamboni man got on the ice more often than he did in the National Hockey League's final showdown.

"Am I sore?" he asked at the time. "Of course, I'm sore. But how can you be unhappy with seventeen-five? ($17,000 was each Bruin share for placing first and winning the cup).

"I've got to think beyond myself. It's not me any more, it's the team. I don't like the way I've been used — or not used. I've told them that, too. I've always told people right to their faces exactly how I feel."

But, he pointed out, "with this thing, the seventeen-five, I can't be sore. Not right now. What we've got to do is win it again next year, right?" Green who had spent some long losing seasons with the Bruins, turned out to be quite a prophet . . . he finally became a part of a cup winner, the Avco Cup, and he didn't have to leave Boston to help New England Whalers to the World Hockey Association title.

During the regular WHA schedule he played in every Whaler game, doubling his best ever goal production with the Bruins by scoring 16 times.

And then the rugged 5-11 defenceman followed that up by scoring a goal and five assists in the playoffs as Whalers defeated Winnipeg Jets in a five-game final.

The Whalers and the rest of the WHA was a new home, right at home, for Green.

"In the year I was hurt they (Bruins) made me feel a part of the team although I had no part in the Stanley Cup victory. That's the way I've felt about this (1972) series — sure I get the money and I wear the sweater, but if you're not out there bumping and sweating, then you don't feel a part — you feel kind of lonesome and left out of things."

And he was saying, around the time Bruins were winning their second cup, "If they move me one spot down on the bench, I'll have to buy a ticket."

The part that really hurt, he says of his last year with the Bruins (all 10 years of his NHL career were spent there), is that the fans must have felt that he was benched because of the head injury — one that requires him to wear a plastic plate to cover the damaged area of his skull.

"But I never felt better in my life, and I never wanted to play as badly," reflects Green.

With the Whalers, a season and change later — plus a cup — Green is back on top. And so are the Whalers.

"GUEST SHOT"
DAVE DRYDEN

By ART DUNN

"Don't bother me, I can't cope" is no longer the theme for Dave Dryden's life on the goal line. The last time the new Cougar masked man toiled for a Chicago hockey team, it was almost the case.

Dryden spent one of his three seasons with the Black Hawks as back-up for the incomparable Glenn Hall. He saw the mental anguish Hall went through — before, during and after each game.

"Hall was the best goalie I ever saw," says Dryden. "But I didn't think I could go through what he did." The young Hamilton, Ontario native admired Hall so much he tried to copy the veteran's leggy style of stopping pucks.

It didn't suit the lanky Dryden and in 1969 the Hawks drafted Tony Esposito and shipped Dryden to Dallas. So Dave became the first goalie in his family to "retire". He went off to teach math to grade school kids.

A year later, though, Dryden was back behind the mask with the Buffalo Sabres.

"Ken (his younger brother who also retired — and came back — after a contract dispute with the Montreal Canadiens) and I used to think hockey was a little boring," admits Dryden. "Maybe it took us longer to make a commitment to hockey. But we've both come to realize we're very lucky to be doing what we're doing."

What they're doing, of course, is performing with distinction in one of the most difficult tasks in sports — standing in a firing line of black rubber bullets.

Though the elder Dryden is noted for his calmness under fire, he knows full well how hazardous the duty is that he performs.

"It's got to be the most challenging, demanding position in hockey," he says, "but also the most rewarding. Every goal that goes in means the goalie screwed up — except in the empty net — and you can't redeem yourself or make up for your mistakes like a forward can. If the goalie doesn't come up big, the team loses. It's that simple."

But as with most subjects, there's another side to the puck. To wit: "When you make a big save or stop a breakaway you feel 10 feet tall."

Dryden — who has a degree in psychology and resembles actor Maximilian Schell — keeps his even keel with a realistic attitude about tending goal. "Sometimes, if you're sharp and alert you might get beat 10-1. But there's no point worrying — why me? You'd go crazy. There's too much luck involved. But still the goalie has to take the blame."

Dryden indicated that his normal placid exterior has changed as he looks forward to his first season in the World Hockey Association. "I'm psyched up more now than I was with the Hawks. I'm more serious, involved more. I do more

DAVE DRYDEN

yelling and pacing now."

The increased involvement made Dryden the team leader with the young Sabres, which he says is a natural situation for a goalie. "A goalie's total impact on the team is very important. Responsibility comes with the job."

Dryden is aware that his friend and former Black Hawk teammate, Pat Stapleton, is relying on him this year to shore up the back line of the Cougar defense.

"That's fine by me," says Dryden, who is coping very well these days, thank you.

ON THE COVER: No. 6, veteran defenseman Gerry Odrowski, still a classic skater at 36 ... one of smoothest penalty-killers in WHA, after learning the skill with such NHL clubs as Detroit, Oakland, St. Louis ... Runners' leading scorer for much of the yet-young season ... assistant captain. (Cover photo by Sue Levy)

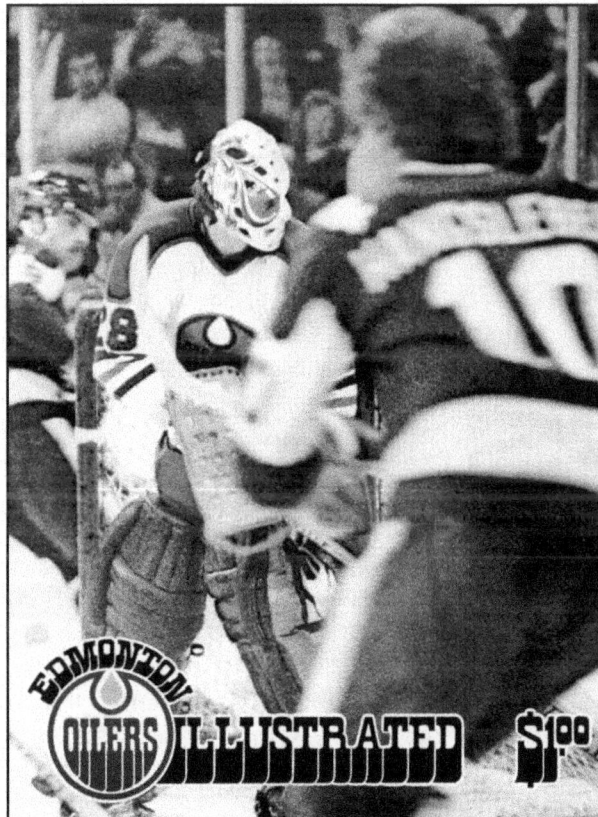

Dave Dryden as an Edmonton Oiler, 1976

NOT DRAGSTERS, DEGREES! ROADRUNNERS HOST EDMONTON OILERS FOR FIRST TIME

While their friends, fans and families are huddled around radios in cold Edmonton tonight, listening to the play-by-play, the Edmonton Oilers will be attempting to continue their successful record on the road. A week ago the Oilers, backed by the confidence of general manager Bill Hunter, had split their six road games and with five-of-six home ice victories sported one of the best won-loss percentages in the WHA.

More than a little of the success was being credited to one Jacques Plante, goaltender extraordinaire, who at the not-too-tender age of 45 (going-on-46 in January), had merely put together a 5-1-0 record in the early going while holding opponents to a skimpy 2.83 goals per game.

"It is my opinion," stated Hunter at a pre-season press conference in the McDonald Hotel in Edmonton, "that with our new players we have strengthened our club by as much as 30% and certainly our club has improved more than any team in the WHA. With Jacques Plante in the nets, together with new defensemen Barry Long and Ray McKay, we will be stronger defensively. Up front we have added excellent scoring power with talented performers like Bruce MacGregor, Mike Rogers and Don Herriman. With Bobby Sheehan and Tom Gilmore for a full season, and continued improvement from forwards Ron Climie, Blair McDonald and Eddie Joyal we have beefed up our scoring. Ken Baird will help considerably, too." Had Hunter but known then, he might also have added the name Ron Buchanan, definitely a plus since being acquired from Cleveland in a deal that sent disgruntled Jim Harrison to the Crusaders.

In signing Plante, the Oilers acquired one of the most daring and inventive goalers in the history of the game. Plante, six times winner of the NHL Vezina Trophy (plus sharing it once), painted 14 whitewashes in Stanley Cup play and also won the league's MVP honors once. Plante was the first goalie to wear a mask in NHL competition, a mask he himself designed and now manufactures.

In coming out of retirement, Plante himself stated that he prefers the work between the pipes to the headaches of coaching and managing, which he did last season with the Quebec Nordiques. The way he has played this year, it is understandable.

Offensively, in Bobby Sheehan the Oilers have a little speedster who potted 35 goals a couple of seasons ago while with the New York Raiders. Before that he'd scored 20 with the NHL California Seals before leaving for greener pastures. If "zero-to-70" applies to neither dragstrip racers nor temperature, it could be applied to the fleet Sheehan, a Yank from Weymouth, Mass.

Incidently, since their new Coliseum opened (belatedly) the Oilers have averaged over 12,800 fans per game at home. And, as an example of their drawing power on the road, they've played to crowds averaging 9,000.

Like the weather here in Phoenix, they're sure to get a warm welcome tonight.

Jacques Plante

Bobby Sheehan

WHA

RIGHTWINGER DAVE GORMAN: RESURRECTS THE WRIST SHOT

Predictions of success for a rookie player in professional hockey are a risky business: training camp flashes abound, and any amateur — no matter how glossy his record — is still an unknown quantity until proven in the pros. In hockey, many are called but few are chosen. However, one would seem to be on safe ground in forecasting a good inaugural season for Dave Gorman, rookie right winger for the Phoenix Roadrunners. Such a prediction would have the combined wisdom of the Runners' management and scouting staff behind it, because they all touted Gorman as a "can't miss" prospect upon signing him last summer and saw no reason to change their minds during training camp and on into the season.

Only 19 years old (he'll be 20 in April), Gorman entered the Roadrunner fold with one year of junior-hockey eligibility remaining under an agreement between pro and junior leagues which allows each professional team to draft and sign one under-age player by paying a $40,000 premium to the player's junior team. Looking back on his final year of amateur play last season, it would seem that Gorman's hockey education was, indeed, far enough advanced to permit an early graduation to the pros. Playing for St. Catherines, the Ontario Hockey Association champions, Gorman scored a whopping 53 goals and 76 assists for a total of 129 points. That made him the highest-scoring winger in the prestigious OHA and gave him a better scoring total at a comparable age than last year's WHA rookie-of-the-year, Mark Howe of Houston.

Gorman scores most of his goals from medium or short range using a hockey weapon that gets much lip service but little use in this slap-happy era: the wrist shot. Listen as Gorman tells how he adopted it: "I had a coach when I was starting out who taught me everything he knew, but he wouldn't allow his players to slap the puck.

And I think he was right in doing it. If you get a good quick wrist shot off, there's plenty of speed on it; not as fast as a slap shot, but it can really travel. And you can get it away quicker; the goalie doesn't have time to set himself. Accuracy is the big thing, though. You can tell where it's going all the time and shoot for a smaller opening."

A good all-around athlete, Dave might have had a future in professional baseball had he stuck to that sport. He might have, that is, if baseball had been willing to forego its prejudice against left-handed catchers, since young Gorman is a natural lefthander who does everything from the port side except shoot hockey pucks.

At the time of his signing, some concern was expressed about Gorman's size, or lack of it: it was felt that he might be a bit small for the pro ranks. Those fears were quickly allayed, though, the first time he stepped on the scales at training camp. The dark-haired youngster is deceptively big, packing 188 pounds on a solidly-muscled 5-foot 11-inch frame. That's certainly big enough to withstand the bumps and hard knocks of hockey while dealing out a few of his own to the opposition.

With all the high hopes and big bucks invested in Gorman by the Roadrunners, what are Dave's hopes and aspirations during his first season? "I just want to make the team," he says, "and make a contribution. I know I've got to work hard on the defensive part of the game. I was strictly an offensive player in junior hockey; a lot of kids are that way. Scoring goals is the big thing I've done best, and I know I can't do it in the same numbers in the big leagues, but I want to get my share. I'm making quite a bit of money playing hockey. Now it's up to me to go out and start earning it."

The Roadrunners are betting they'll have no regrets about handling young Mr. Gorman his paycheck for many years to come.

Dave Gorman

Making It in a Big Way

Little Andre Lacroix's businesslike approach to hockey is paying off. By Stan Fischler

Andre Lacroix takes a very pragmatic approach to contemporary hockey. Something like "it's a business to do pleasure with you." It's not that he likes money more than the next fellow, rather that he can smell a good business situation the way he senses a goal-scoring opportunity.

The records indicate he's been coming up green in both areas. Lacroix led the World Hockey Association in scoring two years ago (50-74-124) with the Philadelphia Blazers, finished second to Mike Walton last year (30-81-111) with the Jersey Knights, and has been right up

there scoring in the hockey business. A onetime member of the Philadelphia Flyers, Lacroix went into partnership a few years ago with his onetime Flyers' teammate Ed Van Impe, opening an ice rink in the Philadelphia suburb of Brookhaven, Pa. Business has boomed ever since the Lacroix-Van Impe Skateland opened during Christmas week 1972, even though the Flyers front office took a dim view of the enterprise.

The NHL club viewed the business marriage as something of an NHL-WHA merger made in hell. Rumors flew that the Flyers wanted to banish Van Impe to Oakland, or some such icy Hades, if he didn't divorce himself from his WHA partner. Van Impe called the bluff, remained a Flyer, and he and Lacroix have been coining rink money ever since.

"I knew I was going to go into some kind of business," says the French-Canadian Lacroix. "My theory is that you never know how long you're going to be able to play hockey, so if you get hurt on the ice you should have something worthwhile to fall back on. There were two choices for me—either distributing beer or running a skating rink. I figured it would take too much time to get into the beer business. Besides, I liked the possibilities of owning my own rink. I can run my own hockey school. I can scrimmage on it in the off-season. And, of course, my partner and I can make a buck."

In the United States these days, owning an ice rink is like having a license to print money, especially in the hockey-mad Philadelphia area. Lacroix's Skateland has more demands than it has time to supply leagues with ice. "I figure that we can pay for the rink in a few more years. Then it'll belong to us. Meanwhile, we want to build three more. The first one cost $650,000. A pre-fabricated building. We got a good loan—a steal at five-and-a-half per cent."

Lacroix the businessman got lucky when he landed with the Flyers. He became friendly with Howard Casper, an attorney who is Philadelphia's answer to Alan Eagleson. Casper has something of a golden touch, and Lacroix was on easy street long before he was traded two summers ago to Jersey (now the San Diego

Mariners).

"When I jumped to the WHA and signed with the Blazers," says Lacroix (who speaks fluent English), "I got myself a long-term contract with good money; five-years, no-trade. I had an agreement with the owner of the team that if I got 50 goals, we'd renegotiate my contract. When the Blazers moved out to Vancouver, the new management wouldn't renegotiate. So I talked to several other WHA clubs—Quebec, Houston—before getting the deal with Jersey. My contract was renegotiated—I signed a new five-year contract—and a trade was made."

The trade had second-leading WHA scorer Ron Ward and goaltender Pete Donnelly going to Vancouver for Lacroix and the rights to negotiate with former Blazers' goalie Bernie Parent. It was not a happy deal for eastern fans. They liked Ward. He meshed neatly with Brian Bradley and Wayne Rivers in 1972-73. And Ward was relatively big.

"Everyone says I'm small," Lacroix argues, "but I'm not *that* small. I'm 5-foot-8, 175 pounds. And what if I am small? Henri Richard is small and he's played 20 years in the NHL with no problems. Look at Yvan Cournoyer. He's small. The trick with us little guys is to use speed and avoid the checks. Camille Henry also managed pretty well in the majors for a skinny little guy."

Like Henry, Lacroix grew up in the hockey breeding ground in and around Quebec City. Henry followed Jean Beliveau's act at the Coliseum, then Lacroix stepped into the spotlight after Henry moved south to the Rangers. It was something like trying to follow Frank Sinatra's act at the Desert Palace. Lacroix skittered around the ice like a waterbug, however, and before long they loved him in Quebec as they loved "Le Gros Bill" and Camille "The Eel." And they still do love him. Remember the ovation he got from Quebec fans when he was introduced before the first Canada-USSR game?

He played a year of junior in Montreal, then moved to the Canadiens' junior team in Peterborough. In his two years with the Petes, he had a number of notable achievements: he won the OHA scoring championship, the Red Tilson Trophy (as most valuable player), the Max Kaminsky Trophy (for gentlemanly conduct), and a reputation as an exceptional scorer and playmaker. He counted 119 points his first year in Peterborough, and 120 the follow-

ing season. In short, he and linemates Danny Grant and Mickey Redmond were the terrors of the league.

He returned to Quebec for three years, playing with the Aces in the American League. He finally distinguished himself so noticeably (41 goals, 46 assists in 54 games) in 1967-68 that Philadelphia couldn't overlook him any longer. He finished out that season in the NHL, and spent three more with the Flyers (scoring at least 20 goals each year). Philadelphia, unfortunately, was suffering from an inferiority complex. Every time the Flyers played the St. Louis Blues, they'd get the tar beaten out of them. A scapegoat had to be found, and Lacroix was as likely a little guy as anyone. He was dealt to Chicago for huge Rick Foley.

Chicago was not precisely heaven. Coach Billy Reay wisecracked that Lacroix was the first French-Canadian he'd ever seen who couldn't skate. It soon became evident that the Hawks weren't ga-ga about Lacroix, and vice-versa. So when the WHA came along, Lacroix welcomed it with open arms—and open wallet.

"We play where the money is," he says. "It's not worth it to me and a lot of others, especially the kids, to sit on the bench in the NHL when we can get a lot of ice in the WHA. That's why it's a mistake to think the NHL is such a big thing with the younger players. They consider the money first. There isn't much difference between the leagues, except that the NHL defenses are more experienced."

This season, in San Diego, Lacroix's future has never looked brighter. His play on behalf of Team Canada has silenced the critics. He has yet another new five-year contract. Like all the Team Canada members, he suffered emotional decompression when the series ended; but all in all, he's in good shape. He has rented Ken Broderick's San Diego house—complete with swimming pool—and is developing a distinct fondness for southern California.

There is another Andre Lacroix already zigging and zagging—Andre Jr. He's four years old and, according to the old man, "has new tricks every day. This summer, I put him on skates." Then, to hockey school. And, maybe, by 1990 he'll have a five-year no-cut contract, or he'll be running one of Lacroix's rinks.

"Why not?" the pragmatist winked. "Hockey's been good to his father."

GUEST SHOT... Gordie "Machine Gun" Gallant

By MIKE LAMEY

Like the gunslinger in the old West who has the most notches on his Colt, Gord Gallant is a marked man.

Gallant earned the "bad guy" award in the World Hockey Association last season by leading the league in penalties. It is a title others will be seeking this season.

Gallant isn't out to necessarily lead the league in penalties. But having done so last year he knows that other tough guys will be trying to earn a reputation at his expense.

"I've heard of so many tough guys coming into the league this year," said Gallant, who picked up the name of Machine Gun during the season. The nickname developed because of the rapid fire punches Gallant would throw.

Gord Gallant

Gallant trained hard for the coming season knowing full well what might be in store for him. At 172 pounds, Gord knows, too, that he will be outweighed by most of his adversaries. He trained two hours a day for a month on the heavy bag, sparred with some of the top boxers in the area, and ran several miles each day.

Gallant was going to be ready.

The refreshing thing about Gallant is that he will admit he lost a fight. He's not an unbeaten champion. He had a black eye or eyes most of last season.

"I didn't go looking to lead the league in penalties," said Gallant of his 223 minutes last season. "That's just the way it went. But I think I got a little respect by leading the league."

Gallant had little respect when he joined the Saints in training camp a year ago. He had belonged to the Cleveland Crusaders, but they weren't going to use him so he got his outright release.

When he reported to camp his only thoughts were to get in shape to play in the minors. He had no contract, no guarantee that he would even make a minor league club.

But Gallant quickly established himself as a man to contend with at left wing. He dared anyone to take the puck from him. He dared anyone to try and take his job. He found no takers so he took the job himself.

When the regular season opened Gord found himself on the bench. In the first game he was in the penalty box despite not having stepped on the ice. He had to serve a penalty when the Saints were called for too many men on the ice.

Gallant wasn't around at the end of the game either. He got a game misconduct. He was involved in two fights and picked up 19 minutes in penalties.

Gallant didn't get another penalty until Game No. 9. But then he wasn't playing much. In fact, for the first half of the season he was lucky to get on a shift a game.

"There were eight games where I got on for one shift and eight more that I didn't play at all," said Gallant. "And even when I did get on a line with Shakey (Mike Walton) and Jimmy (Jim Johnson) I didn't see much ice time because they were killing penalties and playing the power play."

Nonetheless Gallant wound up with 223 minutes in the sin bin, including 16 majors for fighting.

"I thought I lost the one to Dave Hutchison of Vancouver and to Winnipeg's Kelly Pratt (now playing for Pittsburgh in the NHL)," said Gallant.

"Pratt was strong, but I was hurt. I couldn't close my hand. That Jim McCrimmon (Edmonton) was all muscle, 230 pounds, but he doesn't throw 'em too good."

Gallant rates Ted Scharf and Kevin Morrison as two of the toughest in the WHA.

During the playoffs Gallant had several other "engagements" with Edmonton and Houston. His main eventers were with Al Hamilton and Ted Taylor and he took unanimous decisions in both.

"All I want is my teammates to know is that I'll be there to help them," said Gallant, who had 22 stitches taken over his eyes last year. "At the beginning I started a few fights but at the end I was just protecting our guys."

ON THE COVER: No. 22, veteran forward Don Borgeson, who has the reputation among hockey people for being an outstanding corner man and defensive forward. Came to Runners during summer after last season in Ranger organization at Providence. Had big night vs. Aeros here, scoring pair of goals, including game winner in 6-4 victory.

fighting **minnesota saints**

Gerry Cheevers — One Of The Best

"If Cheevers had Tretiak's body, nobody in the world would ever beat him. If Tretiak had Cheevers mind, nobody in the world would beat him."

It's not nice to be overshadowed.

George Harrison was overshadowed by Lennon and McCartney. Harpo Marx by Groucho, Lou Gehrig was certainly overshadowed by Babe Ruth. Avis by Hertz.

But these injustices pale by comparison, when considering the recent Team Canada-Russia hockey series. For vastly overshadowed in the charges, countercharges, delays, accusations, counteraccusations of the series was the most magnificent goaltending ever witnessed on both ends of the rink.

Gerry Cheevers and Vladislav Tretiak staged the show. Solitary figures, a distance away from the high sticks and sharp elbows that marred much of the classic. But in their own distinct style, they symbolically walked off with the roses when the curtain finally fell on the hockey drama.

The styles of Cheevers and Tretiak are as diffuse as their political ideology. Think about their respective style. Think about their politics. From the free world comes the free goaler, Gerry Cheevers. Gerry is a roamer, skating from corner to corner, sometimes handling the puck like a Ralph Bachstrom, sometimes handling the stick like a Lou Fontinato. He's his own man and he guards his cage with the same reckless abandon.

Unlike Cheevers, Tretiak is chained to his net, much like the Communist rank and file is chained to their ideology. Tretiak is a machine, a robot programmed to keep pucks out of the Russian net. He is amazingly quick and uncommonly agile, a product of the rigorous Russian training program.

Take a look at Tretiak's mask. It's really a capsulized jail cell, steel bars running vertically and horizontally across his face. It's a mirror image of the Communist way of life.

But above and beyond the obvious differences of both common. They keep small, hard rubber discs known as hockey pucks out of their cage probably better than any other duo in the world.

Ask Al Smith.

The Whalers' all-star goalkeeper, brilliant in his own right, recently offered a goalie's eye view of the goaltending trade in general and Cheevers and Tretiak in particular.

"Cheesie (Gerry Cheevers and Bernie Parent) are the best around these parts," Smith said. "Parent is the tactician, the scientist. Cheesie is the George C. Scott. He's got the great mind and the great character.

"Tretiak is amazingly quick," Smitty added, "in fact, he's so fast he is unbelievable. They showed films of Tretiak working out before a game and it actually looked like they had speeded up the film. I couldn't believe it."

OK Smitty, who is the very best?

"Let's put it this way," Smith said. "You give Cheevers Tretiak's body, and nobody in the world would beat him. You give Tretiak Cheevers' mind, and nobody in the world would beat him."

The Abrahamsson brothers of Sweden have yet to test Cheevers, but they certainly know enough about Mr. Tretiak. Time and time again, the Russian netminder frustrated the Swedish National teams in world competition.

When I brought up Tretiak's name to defenseman Thommy, his eyes lit up like Christmas tree.

"Very, very good," Thommy said, "very quick with stick and glove."

Goaltender Christer Abrahamsson, a keen student of the art, also notes a big difference in the two styles.

"Cheevers skate much more," Christer said in broken but perfectly understandable English. "He uses stick in different way than Tretiak. Cheevers keeps puck and hits players in front of goal. Tretiak uses to stop and direct puck into corners. Both good, good."

Whether you're from Sweden, Toronto, Hartford, Springfield, or Walla Walla, Cheevers and Tretiak stand out above the crowd. Different in style and appearance, their performance belied their responsibility. And although the bickerings and controversies received much of the ink, Tretiak and Cheevers received and stopped most of the offensive shots. But they are overshadowed. And it's not nice to be overshadowed.

SHAKEY MIKE WALTON

Can he score 50 goals?

It was early in his hockey career that Michael Robert (Shakey) Walton got this feeling that someone up there didn't like him.

Up there. That was with the Toronto Maple Leaf organization, the National Hockey League franchise which owned Walton's rights.

Right from the start it was always a hassle with Leafs, said Walton, one of the Minnesota Fighting Saints' newest acquisition and a player expected to beef up Coach Harry Neale's attack.

"It just seemed Toronto was always on my back, demanding that I prove myself, even after I felt I had established that I was a National Leaguer.

"It was a very bad situation and in no way can be compared to the time I spent in Boston with Bruins. I really hated to leave Boston but it was simply a matter of finance."

High finance, really.

"I can't discuss any figures, but it was a very good contract and Boston's offer was also very respectable. But the Bruins' just didn't come close."

It was a summer, to say the least, that Walton really felt wanted. At Toronto he felt as welcome as a slap shot is to a goaltender.

In his 10 years in the Leafs system, Walton did so much proving of himself he began to feel like an equation.

Take 1963-64 for example, the last year he played junior A hockey for the Leaf-sponsored Toronto Marlboros of the Ont. Hockey Association.

In 53 games he scored 41 goals and 51 assists for 92 points and was one of the key players in leading the Marlies to the Memorial Cup title, the Super Bowl, World Cup and Stanley Cup championship of junior hockey in Canada.

Jim Gregory (now Leaf GM) was our manager at Marlies then and he felt sure I would get an invite to the big club's training camp even though I had a year left of junior eligibility. Lots of our players got invites to camp, but mine never came. Finally Gregory went to bat for me and convinced them to give me a look.

Walton gave them an eyefull. He had an outstanding training camp, impressing such longstanding Leaf veterans as Frank Mahovlich.

Toronto, then under the one-man rule of Punch Imlach, coach and GM, said nice going kid. Heckuva camp. You can score. You hustle. You hit. Got all the makings. How would you like to go to our Central Hockey League farm club in Tulsa, Oklahoma?

Undaunted, Walton went, passing up his last year of junior in which he surely would have to be one of the OHA's top two or three scorers.

At Tulsa he scored 40 goals and 44 assists in 68 games. It was enough to earn him rookie of year honors and of course he kept thinking about next fall when he would get another shot at making the Leafs big roster.

Although less impressive in his second shot at winning a job with Toronto than he had been the year before Walton still had a good camp. And, of course, it should have been considered the year that he had had at Tulsa.

But you knew they weren't going to keep him, said Red Burnett, a veteran Toronto hockey writer. From day one of camp there was talk about him needing more seasoning. Heck, he needed more seasoning like a Mexican dish needed more seasoning.

Walton heard the speech again. Nice going, heckuva camp, you can score,

hustle, hit. How would you like to go to our American League Club in Rochester?

It was kind of discouraging but I went, said Walton. I knew it was going to be tough to crack Leafs. It wasn't all that long ago but you can't forget that there were only six teams at the top in pro hockey so jobs were a bit limited.

With the Rochester Americans in 1965-66 he scored 35 goals and 51 assists and again was named rookie of the year. It was enough, Walton figured, to make the big club want to keep around fulltime in 1966-67. It wasn't.

He again started that season with Rochester and after scoring 19 goals and 33 assists in 36 games was finally summoned to Toronto. He played the last 31 games of the NHL—in spot duty only—and still managed seven goals and 10 assists.

In 1967-68 he started the hockey campaign with Toronto and in that year—if there were any doubts before—it became established in his mind that Toronto wasn't his niche.

I was leading the club in scoring in December when we went into a game in Chicago, Walton recalls. I was told not to dress. Since I wasn't hurt I knew something was wrong. After the game I was asked if I'd go back to the minors Walton paused, "get my confidence back?" The club's leading scorer needed a confidence builder?

He balked at going and missed five games before he and his attorney delivered an ultimatum to let him continue at Toronto. The Leafs did.

Walton finished that year with 30 goals and 29 assists which might have been good for rookie of the year honors had he not appeared in 31 games the year before. The Calder Cup, the NHL rookie award, went to Boston's Bobby Orr that season. He would have been a pretty tough guy to beat out even if I were eligible, said Walton.

By then it was just a matter of time before Walton knew he had to get away from the Leaf setup. He and Imlach had some run ins mainly because when asked by

123

Boston Bruins. Toronto got compensation from Philadelphia who received players from the Bruins. He finished the season with the Bruins so-so (3 goals, 5 assists in 22 games) and then in 1971-72 scored 28 goals and 28 assists on the beantowners Stanley Cup championship club. It was Walton's second Cup title. He had also played on '66-67 title team.

The only thing better than another Cup title would be his best career year and Walton figured he was going to accomplish that last January when the Bruins made a trip to St. Louis. He already had 21 goals and 16 assists in 37 games, putting a 40-goal definitely within reach and who knows, perhaps even more.

It was that night in St. Louis that he was thinking somebody up there must have liked him after all and it wasn't the Toronto hierarchy.

During some horseplay in the Bruins St. Louis hotel, Walton fell through a glass window and was cut up so badly they almost called for a zig-zag machine. He took more than 150 stitches.

It was just an example of what can happen when people fool around. I was guilty; too. We had arrived and some of our bags were lost. We were all in one of the rooms borrowing some clothes from the guys who got their luggage so we could go out. There was some teasing about who had the best clothes. Somebody—it is not important who—started to throw some water on me. I jumped back tripped and went through the glass.

Coincidentally, and then again maybe not, the Bruins lost the game the next night as Walton lay in the hospital checking the stitchwork. In fact, they lost five of their next seven games which in the tough NHL East was enough to sink them from first place to fourth.

In total, Walton missed 22 games. Boston continued to struggle.

Walton tries to explain what happened to the Bruins last year when the club went from Stanley Cup champs to second in the

reporters, Walton told them what he thought. Since it wasn't always what Imlach thought, there was a clash.

I was always being put down. The situation went from bad to worse to worser, said Walton. I was unhappy.

The issue festered in 1970 when Walton played in only 23 games and then left the team for good. The end result had a Toronto psychiatrist stating that the stresses on Walton playing in Toronto were too great and he should be allowed to play elsewhere.

Walton felt the issue was blown somewhat out of proportion. Despite his nickname of Shakey, strictly inherited from his father who was called that when he played pro hockey, there wasn't anything wrong with his head that a change of scenery wouldn't correct.

In a three-corner deal he moved to the

East and were knocked out of playoffs on the first round.

We missed Gerry Cheevers some (the goalie who left for the WHA team in Cleveland,) said Walton. But you really couldn't fault the goaltenders. The goaltending was bad in the playoffs, but during the season it was good enough.

I think it was just one of those situations where everyone went sour at the same time. Usually two or three or four players might go into a tailspin. But the rest will pick up the slack. That sort of thing goes on during a hockey year because you just can't play a season where its full speed all the way.

There was also some turmoil about Sandy (Derek Sanderson) coming back to Boston from the Philadelphia Blazers and maybe everyone wasn't concentrating like they had the year before. There was always conversations about switching leagues and contracts and then when the

stories started about the Storey Broadcasting Corps buying the team that gave everyone something else to think about.

These aren't excuses. The biggest thing I think was still everyone playing poorly at the same time. The team put on a helluva rush and finished second but just didn't have anymore to give in the playoffs.

Walton is looking forward to playing with younger brother Bob who also came to the Saints this summer. "We've never played on the same club before (the Waltons were the first WHA brother combination although the Howes in Houston signed later). I believe he'll be one of the top three centers in the league.

Personally Shakey has some very solid goals for 1973-74. About 50 of them to be exact. That sounds like a lot, I know, but I think I can score that many. The Saints have made me a great contract and everything. Now its up to me to show that I'm worth it all. I want to help this team be a first place club which I believe it can be.

fighting minnesota saints

HUGH HARRIS:
"SERIOUS WHEN IT COUNTS"

Following a recent plane trip, the Roadrunners were disembarking from their flight at Detroit when a fellow passenger on the plane, a prosperous-looking businessman, asked his traveling companion who were the group of young men on the aircraft — apparently a sports team of some kind — had been. "They're the Arizona Sun Dogs hockey team," was the reply. "They're on their way to Windsor, Ontario to play the Chicago Typhoons. That big guy over there told me. He's one of their players."

"That big guy" who supplied the mis-information was Phoenix leftwinger Hugh Harris. Had the rest of the Roadrunners known from whom the traveler was seeking information they might have warned him not to expect a straight answer. For by that point in the season (mid-November) Harris already had a solid reputation as the Runners' funny man and one of the genuinely humorous people in the game anywhere.

Harris' role as the man who keeps the team loose was quickly established on the first road trip of the year when he ensconced himself in a seat at the back of the team bus from hotels to airports and practices and delivered himself in a loud voice of opinions, comments and one-liners on virtually everything from hockey to politics to the private lives of his team-mates, launching occasionally into humorous monologues like a rambling sketch in Quebec in which his roommate, Gerry Odrowski, was cast as Count Odrowski, a vampire haunting Quebec's looming hotel, the Chateau Frontenac. When he's in top form, a Las Vegas standup comic might be envious.

Every team, an old hockey adage has it, needs a player like Harris who can bring a little humor into the locker room and help keep things in perspective. Levity, though, can't carry over into the game, and Harris has a sure instinct about where to draw the line. Once the puck is dropped, he's all business . . . and perhaps the prime offensive threat on this year's Phoenix team.

Harris, a 26-year-old native of Toronto, has taken a while to blossom into the star status that's been predicted for him by many observers. Following four years with Muskegon in the International League (during one of which he led the IHL in goals scored), he spent a year in Cincinnati of the American League, then put in a season with the Buffalo Sabres in the National Hockey League. Despite a paucity of time on the ice, he still managed to score 12 goals.

Last year Harris — following a promise that he'd get a lot more playing time — defected to the New England Whalers of the World Hockey Association, but still found himself cast somewhat into the shadows on a club which had nine players who scored 20 or more goals. Harris collected 24 goals and added 28 assists for the Whalers and was picked as a member of the Eastern Division all-star team for the WHA's mid-season classic in Minnesota. Still, despite his considerable success with the Whalers, it came as no disappointment to him to learn he'd been traded to the new Phoenix Roadrunners in one of those deals involving "future considerations".

Harris' stock in trade is one of the hardest and most accurate shots in all of hockey, delivered as a rule from medium range; say 30 or 35 feet. He's right on target most of the time and gets his shots away quickly, not affording the opposing team's defense and goaltender much time to get themselves set. And for a big man, strong on his skates, he's surprisingly agile, possessed of a variety of clever moves which allow him to slip a check in the attacking zone and deliver his shot. His old teammates from New England have been a favorite target so far this year: Harris scored the winning goal in both of Phoenix' early-season wins over the powerful Whalers.

For an expansion team like the Roadrunners, there are bound to be a lot of bad times mixed with the good. Thus, the 'Runners can count themselves fortunate to have happy-go-lucky Hugh Harris around to help them revel in the good moments and take some of the edge off the bad ones. But more importantly, Phoenix can look forward to having him as an offensive mainstay of the club for a long time to come. He's a fellow who forgets the funny stuff and turns deadly serious when it counts.

Hugh Harris

"GUEST SHOT"

ANDERS HEDBERG

By PAT YANKOSKI

ANDERS HEDBERG is a young Swede with a lot of guts. He's done things that not many others have done.

First, he decided to leave his native Sweden to play professional hockey in another country; that is a feat in itself since North American pro leagues have been revered in Europe for many years and were thought to be the best. Then he comes over to Winnipeg and gets Bobby Hull — one of the game's most prolific scorers for his linemate. And in spite of the pressures that were obviously on him, he performs superbly. In his rookie season, he scored 53 goals — a record for a rookie in pro hockey.

What surprised a lot of stalwart hockey fans was the fact that this Swedish hockey player could play and keep up with the Canadian boys. Even though, he was not taught to fight, he proved himself in that department by not backing away.

In 1957, the Montreal Canadiens, at the height of their glory, were on their way to another Stanley Cup. That was also the year six-year-old Hedberg began skating. His first pair of skates were single blades which he fastened onto his ski boots. He didn't begin skating on a hockey rink either, but rather on a canal which went by the village.

When he was seven, Hedberg started school in his village. In that same year, a rink was built in his village, and Hedberg remembers it quite well. "I was every day there after school . . . three guys most interested in hockey went down, and I played against the two others myself; that was every day."

In 1972, Hedberg was selected to the Swedish National team. He was in the line-up for the Swedish Nationals when Team Canada '72 faced them in Stockholm before going to Russia for the last four games of their Russian series.

During the time Hedberg spent on the Swedish Nationals, he played about 20 games against the Russians. The Russians, Hedberg maintains, are not dirty hockey players. They are just so good that you can't really stop them. When asked what he thought of Valery Kharlamov, a Russian forward, Hedberg shook his head and said, "I've never seen anything like him."

The speedy Hedberg made a name for himself at the last world championship he played in. He led the Swedes in scoring by firing in seven goals and assisting on three others. When an all-star team was selected at the end of the tournament, Hedberg rated fourth overall.

The three preceding him were Maltsev and Yakishev, both Russians, and the Czech player Nedomansky, now with the Toronto Toros. Hedberg was followed by another Russian — Kharlamov.

The Winnipeg Jets don't have scouts in Europe, but they did have a valuable connection in Dr. Gerry Wilson. Dr. Wilson was in the same university class as Hedberg in Stockholm. Hedberg asked him if he would like to come to some of their hockey games.

Dr. Wilson was impressed with their play, and when Hedberg and Nilsson (Ulf) talked with him about turning pro, Dr. Wilson promised he would contact the Winnipeg Jets. On May 4, 1974, both Hedberg and Nilsson signed two-year contracts with the Winnipeg Jets.

Anders is the first to admit there was some adjustments for him to make when he started playing hockey professionally. The fighting aspect of the game has bothered him a lot. To Hedberg, this has been the hardest adjustment he has had to make. "I think I couldn't really, and I still can't understand why that sort of thing has to be included in hockey," he said, "I still don't enjoy it."

Hedberg isn't sure if anybody really likes the fights. "I know most of the guys, even Canadians that never fight, and they don't like it . . . maybe the best fighter in the league likes it because he can fight anybody."

Fighting is not Hedberg's cup of tea, but playing hockey is. His 53 goals last season were not luck, but a combination of work and talent. Hedberg claims his shooting has improved since coming to the Winnipeg Jets. He credits Bobby Hull with teaching him how to use the curve to his advantage.

A factor which has helped the Europeans is their excellent conditioning. In Europe, hockey players practice all year round — including the summer. Hedberg firmly believes in staying in shape, and coming to training camp fit — not coming to training camp to get into shape.

"If you're not in shape when you come to training camp, you're never going to be during the season," maintains Hedberg. "I tell you, you're in best physical shape after training camp, when the season begins, then you keep that level . . . I'm honest if I say that I'm in better condition and less tired than most of the players."

THE HOT LINE

The Winnipeg Jets number one line, consisting of Bobby Hull, Ulf Nilsson and Anders Hedberg, has been labelled the "Hot Line". For some months, the media people toyed with various labels which they thought would be most descriptive for this exciting addition to the Winnipeg Jets Hockey Club.

This line has received so many accolades since it started in the 1974-75 WHA season, primarily because of the European players. The European influence has made the Winnipeg Jets one of the most novel teams in North America. The fast skating, quick shooting, precision passing and hard work by the fastest line in major league hockey makes this line the biggest threat to opposing teams. The Hot Line has been broken up on several occasions during this short season due to injuries suffered by members of the line or as strategy moves by the coaching staff. However, the effectiveness of the line suffers and when back intact again, the reason for Hull, Nilsson and Hedberg is best revealed on the score board.

At present time, the Hot Line is leading all WHA teams in total production. Hull has 43 goals; 35 assists; for a total of 78 points: Hedberg has 22 goals; 20 assists; for a total of 42 points: Nilsson has 14 goals; 48 assists; for a total of 62 points: for a total of 79 goals; 103 assists and 182 points for the season.

This line has already achieved many scoring records—most points per game, most points per season — you name it, they've done it. It is not unusual for the hot line to rack up 12-15 points per night. No wonder opposing goalies have a great amount of respect for the Hot Line as opposition goalie averages tend to suffer each time the Winnipeg Jets play them.

The Swedes were suspect at the beginning of the season as rookies to the WHA. Everybody was concerned as to what would happen when they were under pressure. They were treated like rookies and it is a natural thing in professional hockey that rookies are tackled to see what they are made of. Bobby Hull, the third member of the line has never known to be a crushing checker or fighter.

All three members of the line get the job done by using their outstanding skills rather than bar-room tactics. This in itself has often been disadvantageous to the Hot Line on that opposing teams have defenced them physically but what the Hot Line has proved is that they can take the lumps of opposing players and what they hand out mostly is goals and assists, which is the most important thing when you want to win the game on the score board.

The home opener in 1974 resulted in a final score of Jets 4, Edmonton 0. The game

WHA

was only 41 seconds old and many of the 7,700 fans were still filing into the Winnipeg Arena, getting a box of popcorn and casually moving to their seats. Perhaps they expected to see the usual humdrum type of hockey game they had been accustomed to. From the opening face-off, it was Hull to Hornung—to Hedberg—back to Hornung to Nilsson—shot—score! An unbelievable exposition of hockey finesse and skill. From that point on, Winnipeg fans became accustomed to sheer excitement when the Hot Line hit the ice. Anything is possible. The Hot Line gives the Winnipeg Jets the mobility it needs and it really is rubbing off on the other lines.

The individual members of the Hot Line is each a specially talented hockey player. Reports throughout the league include every known superlative.

Anders Hedberg: "Will be a star before Christmas." "Can skate like the wind."

"His wrist shot has the velocity of a bullet." "Has tenacity to work in the corners." "Has the guts to take physical rebuttal and come back for more." "A gazelle on skates." "The Jets swiftest Swede." "The phantom Jet."

Ulf Nilsson: "Will o' the Wisp—leaves them gasping." "A dirty player—because he makes the opposition look bad." "Best straight line man on the team." "The unsung hero for the Winnipeg Jets." "The quarterback of the Hot Line." "A witty little bugger and something of a joker too." "A gangly athlete who may not have received his fair share of body muscle."

Bobby Hull: Everything that possibly could have been said about Bobby Hull has probably already been said. His speed and precision and hard slap shot, plus his outstanding P.R. have truly earned Bobby the accolade of being the best buy that that Winnipeg ever made. Bobby has been described as: "hasn't got a lazy bone in his body." "Work is a better tonic than rest." Hull in his unassuming manner tends to give credit rather than take it. He has stated that Nillson and Hedberg are holy sinners the way they steal pucks and score.

"It's a real pleasure to be playing with two such talented athletes." One opposition goalie when asked to single out the one factor that lost them the game that night, simply replied, "too much No. 9."

Hull, Nilsson and Hedberg are probably the hardest working line in major league hockey. To them work is fun. The sense of humour of the three players endears them to other members of the hockey club and to the general public. Ulf Nilsson normally comes up with the best straight lines of the group. When asked what it is like playing beside Bobby Hull he replied, doubling up with laughter, "awful, just awful. He can't skate, can't shoot and he never gives me the puck."

Ulf Nilsson is the hub of the wheel that keeps the hot line rolling along. Ulf doesn't have the hardest shot. For that matter, he rarely shoots that much. He is persistent;

he is dedicated to the cause and is doing more than was expected of him when he arrived from Sweden. Ulf has possession of the puck more often than any of his teammates. He makes the play happen. He sets up the plays more often than he scores them. When he skates, he does it meticulously, not with frantic leg motion or dramatic colour.

Hull and Hedberg are the two that the fans relate to more often. Hull, the super-star, the Golden Jet and probably the most celebrated hockey player, and the player who has been the game's most prolific scorer. Hedberg, the blonde Swede who skates like the wind and who can leave defencemen gasping in his wake. Nilsson handles the puck like a veteran centreman. He has the quickness to spring Hull or Hedberg loose at any moment. His assist total, highest in the WHA underscores his outstanding ability as a play-maker.

Rudy Pilous has been quoted many times on the Hot Line as a delight and a pleasure to coach. In fact, Rudy has been known to say that this is the best line that he has ever coached in 35 years of professional hockey.

The Hot Line is hot and remains hot regardless of the performance of the rest of the team. They are the most consistent, hard-working line and that probably accounts for their outstanding performance to date. Opposition teams have attempted every kind of defence to stop this production line. Most recently, the strategy seems to be that if you can't skate with them or check them, maybe you can injure them and keep them out of the line-up. All three members of the Hot Line have received their share of stitches, bruises and outright physical abuse from frustrated opposition defencemen. But they keep coming back for more. While there has never been any question about Bobby Hull's professional stature, his ability to stand up under strain and his consistent 110% effort each and every game, there have been questions raised about the Swedes ability to endure a whole season at the torrid pace they have been setting. The answers to these questions are becoming more evident and disbelief is turning into amazement at the continuing top class performances of the two Swedish stars.

By the end of the season everybody will know that in addition to Bobby Hull Nilsson and Hedberg are here to stay. Their performance both on and off the ice, their total points, and their exciting play will probably put them down in the hockey history books as the most exciting line in professional hockey in the 1970's.

ULF NILSSON

By SUSAN NICOL

It's Ulf Nilsson's third season as a Winnipeg Jet. He is so much of an institution as the play-making centre for the Hot Line that his name is mentioned in the same breath with Bobby's and Ander's. That breath has become a bit of a hiccup recently since he has changed position with another stellar centreman, Peter Sullivan.

"We play a lot the same . . . all the players from Sweden," Ulf says. "So we know a little how to criss-cross. It didn't take Bobby, Anders and I very long to get used to one another. Sometimes he (Kromm) puts me back, depending on how the game is going. If we keep winning though, I don't think he'll change it."

The advantage to the change, according to Ulf, is more balance in the lines.

"Now he have three lines going," he says, "because Velo's playing really well too."

He added, "Maybe my production is going to go down a little bit because Bobby and Anders were scoring goals and they gave me a lot of assists. I think Danny and Willy are playing well, too. We've had a lot of chances and as long as you get them, you don't have to worry because you'll get your share of goals."

It seems odd that someone who collected as many points as Ulf did last year would be worried about his shot. But Ulf is.

"I'd like to improve my shot a little so I stay after sometimes and do something extra on it," he explains. "I think the guy in the best position should shoot it so it really doesn't matter who is there. But when I am in the best position I want to be able to shoot it. I haven't that good of a shot so if I see a guy in position who I know is going to score I'll pass to him rather than gamble myself."

One thing that Ulf seems to be doing regularly, besides getting assists, is breaking his nose. The first game in the new year saw him rearrange it again.

"I broke it once last year and a couple of times in Sweden . . . and now again," he adds with a wince. "It couldn't be any worse . . . and I'm married. I think it was accidental, because Willy was breaking in on the right side and I had pretty good speed on the left. Gordie Howe heard me so he tried to stop me. He stuck his stick out on the left side and hit me over the nose."

After spending two seasons in Winnipeg, Ulf has settled into living here, although he says there was never much of an adjustment to make in the first place.

"It's really similar to Sweden," he says. "I didn't find it hard to come and live here.

In fact, Ulf is one Swede who is considering making Canada a permanent home.

"I don't know if I'll ever go back to Sweden. I like to visit there every once in awhile. I know a lot of Swedish companies that are exporting goods to the United States and Canada. I get requests every summer from companies that ask me if a certain line of goods will sell here. I can always find a job with them. But I don't think of that too much right now . . . the main thing is hockey."

He says that the Jets have to concentrate on playing more defensively if they want to keep the AVCO Cup.

"We've had some problems with our defensive play, but I think we've straightened those out," he says. "We've been thinking too much about scoring goals instead of stopping them. Then it's enough if we score one or two."

He adds, "It's tough with so many defencemen injured. Hexi has a cracked foot . . . Barry Long's shoulder isn't right . . . Shoe's out. We've got really good talent on this team, we just have to put it together and give 100%."

Whenever Ulf gets the time, he indulges in a little woodworking.

"I've been doing some work in wood," he says, "like making a couple of beds and things. I'm not really good at it, but I like to fool around. I've found a shop where the owner lets me use his equipment. I'm going to make my own dining table next."

It's only natural that Ulf is looking forward to winning another championship. But he has a special reason for his optimism. He kind of missed out on it the first time.

"It was nice to win it," he says, "but I couldn't be that happy because I was in the hospital with my eye injury. It's not the best way to celebrate those things, but we'll win it this year and hopefully, I'll be there."

A Guy Playing In His Own Native Land
(REAL "BUDDY" CLOUTIER)

Most managers and directors of the World Hockey Association have acclaimed with much publicity the signings of Pat Price, Ron Chipperfield, Dennis Sobchuk and all of those junior players that signed multi-years contracts with WHA's teams.

Right near us, the Nordiques have made a good bid when they invested a lot of money to obtain an underage player by the name of Réal "Buddy" Cloutier. "Buddy" did not get all of the publicity that occured with the signings of Sobchuk, Price

and others, but without an inch of a doubt, he is an exceptional talent that will be a great centre of attraction in Quebec and all the WHA's Cities. In all levels of hockey, he has always shown an unlimited potential, and he was always at the source of great success for teams for which he played.

The hockey fans in Quebec remember him from his Pee-Wee days at the fabulous International Pee-Wee Hockey Tournament in Quebec. During his midget career, he established and broke all the records. Cloutier began his junior career at the age of 15 and his ascension with the Remparts was one to see as he made revive the Guy Lafleur's glorious years, along with another new WHA's member, Jacques Locas. With a great season of 93 goals and 123 assists, he broke Guy Lafleur's record with

the Remparts of 209 points, with a top mark of 216 points in his last junior season.

Cloutier is anxious to get his name along those WHA's Stars. For the Nordiques, it marks a first great win, after losing such brilliant names as Lafleur, Richard and Savard that opted for the NHL after their junior careers in Quebec. This gives the Nordiques an opportunity to build around him a strong and very impressive team, as mentioned earlier, he always brought success to the teams that he played for. For those that were sceptical, let us mention that Cloutier was voted on the All-Star Squad in the Last Memorial Cup series in Calgary, along with Dennis Sobchuk. In learning that Cloutier was only 17, Scotty Monroe, coach of the Calgary Centennials, could not believe his eyes. To his knowledge, Cloutier has as much value in the hockey's market as Dennis Sobchuk, Pat Price and others. Having not deceived himself with the National Hockey League, he chose to remain in his own native land to pursue his professional hockey career, playing for the Quebec Nordiques in the WHA.

The Buffalo Sabres were to claim him as their first round choice at the National Hockey League draft, but they changed their mind when they learned of his multi-year contract with the Nordiques. Let us remember that Punch Imlach, Buffalo Sabres' G.M., has a great eye to claim top picks and Cloutier could have been one of them along with Perreault, Martin and others. What he could have been for the Sabres, he will be for the Nordiques and the WHA.

Good stickhandler, he knows how to prepare good plays for his team-mates and he has the natural instinct of a great scorer, which gives him the extra punch for being a potential super-star, as he is acclaimed to be the Nordique's lifetime insurance for years to come.

If the fans can be patient with an 18-yr. old kid, they will find back the idol that he personally wishes to be, to make the fans forget the loss of earlier promising players that opted for the NHL in the Nordique's difficult years.

"Buddy" a guy playing in his own native land for the Nordiques and the WHA. Watch him closely and you'll see that he is a real potential SUPERSTAR.

ALL STAR THREATS

By GEORGE BILYCH

It should not come as any surprise that Danny Lawson and Smokey McLeod are the only members of the current Cowboys entourage to be selected to the official WHA All-Star team through the first four years of competition. The teams, particularly the first team, have been dominated by a very select few.

Considering the consistency in which the same names kept popping up year after year it's clearly evident there's been a wide variance in the talents of the performers. The class is clearly at the top.

Consider the names. J.C. Tremblay, Bobby Hull, Andre Lacroix, Paul Shmyr. Not to mention Gordie Howe.

J.C. and Winnipeg's Golden Jet have hogged most of the laurels in the early going, each being picked to the first team on three occasions and to the second on the other. Shmyr and Lacroix are also three-time first team members. Howe twice was named to the first team at right wing.

Which easily explains what sort of competition Lawson has been up against. He claimed the laurels first year out of the gate, before Papa Gord made his appearance. Then last year along came Anders Hedberg and it may be a long time before somebody else gets a shot at right wing again. Even with Buddy Cloutier waiting in the wings.

About the only position that has been up for grabs has been that of goal. There have been four different winners in as many years, starting with Cleveland's Gerry Cheevers and going on to McLeod (then with Houston), Ron Grahame (Houston) and Joe Daley (Winnipeg).

This backs up a popular theory that goaltending has been the real strength of the WHA through the league's formative years. There have been some outstanding netmen in the league, not the least of which was Bernie Parent.

There, however, appears to be a definite change on the horizon. Especially in the front line ranks where a whole new line of snipers are starting to assert themselves.

It actually began to happen last season when Ulf Nilsson, Marc Tardif and Hedberg supplanted all the former heroes on the first team. Robbie Ftorek and Cloutier were named to the second team, leaving Hull as the lone member of the old guard to gain any recognition.

The dye has been cast and the trend is almost certain to continue. The youngsters are bidding for recognition

and they're at the point where they've earned their spurs.

Take centre ice. Nilsson and Ftorek are having outstanding seasons again. Cincinnati's Rich Leduc is suddenly looming as a big threat. The Stingers' Dennis Sobchuk is also coming of age. Quebec's Chris Bordeleau has been there all along but he may some day get the recognition he deserves. Lacroix and Bernier are still around but they shouldn't make it against this crowd.

Right wing is where the action's at. Nobody's going to dispute Hedberg's scoring exploits and he may well become the WHA player of the year. It's of little consolation, though, to Cloutier or Mark Napier who some day may surpass them all. It must be disheartening to a fellow like San Diego's Norm Ferguson that his outstanding season doesn't even get a mention in the light of the accomplishments of the above threesome.

The one area where the competition is thinned out is left wing where Marc Tardif once again appears to have an easy path to the throne room. The Racers' Hugh Harris got off to an excellent start but was sidelined by injury in mid-season. Houston's Mark Howe has seen as much action on defence as he has up front this year. The Roadrunners' Del Hall is still scoring at a prodigious clip but his contribution ends there. The Whalers' rookie George Lyle may have as good a chance as anybody to make it the second team.

Look for Houston's Paul Popiel to get a lot of votes on defence. He and Shmyr have once again enjoyed outstanding seasons but the popularity pollsters will make another bold bid in trying to sneak J.C. in there. Cincinnati's Ron Plumb will also get a lot of attention but the forgotten man may well be the Racers' Darryl Maggs. The former Centennial junior is enjoying an outstanding season and his contribution to the Racers takes on added dimension considering that injuries to Ken Block and Byron Baltimore have put giant holes in the Indy defence this season.

The point being made, though, is that the old guard is finally giving way to the new. The new cast, by and large, is not a batch of rethreads but rather a group of athletes who have developed within the league.

The proof of the pudding is in the number of NHL scouts who have been closely following WHA teams all season. While the Cowboys have not been an active part of it, the WHA in its fifth season is beginning to produce some outstanding individual talent of its own.

The future of the league may well depend on it.

DANNY LAWSON

By SUSAN NICOL

The Winnipeg Jets, as the name denotes, is one hockey club that is known to be high-flying and fast. Danny Lawson, who was acquired in a recent trade with the Calgary Cowboys, fits right in the speed department.

"When you have a certain skating ability and you're associating with other players who have the same ability, then things naturally start to happen," he says.

"Even if you're not a natural goal-scorer, you can skate your way around the defence and make a play that's going to result in a goal. It's a matter of going up and down until something happens eventually."

Danny attributes his speed to the coaching he received in the junior leagues.

"I started playing with the Hamilton Red Wings about 15 years ago," he says. "The final two years there probably were instrumental in making me a conditioned athlete for professional hockey. The coach whipped me into shape. I was kind of bitter about it at the time, but I think in the long run it payed off. I've had a very successful career."

One of the coaches Danny had while he was playing with Hamilton was Rudy Pilous, the Winnipeg Jets general manager.

"It was kind of rewarding when we had Rudy Pilous coaching," he says. "I learned a lot from him. He was an exuberant individual who expressed his emotions rather erratically, but he got his point across. I enjoyed him."

Danny says he doesn't know whether the previous association was a factor in his arrival in Winnipeg.

"In junior hockey you meet a lot of coaches and scouts along the way. Rudy knew me. He knew I could skate, I had the legs which means a lot. I don't know whether he kept his eye on me or what.

"I would imagine the people in Calgary were the ones who wanted Ketola so bad that they had to give up me in return."

He adds that his first reaction was one of surprise until he gave the situation more thought.

"My first reaction was one of uncertainty when I first heard about the trade. Mr. Pilous must have been let down when he called me after talking to Mike Ford. Mike was elated about the whole thing. The first thing Rudy said to me was, 'You don't sound too happy,' and actually I wasn't."

He added, "I had been with the Calgary franchise for five years. I was the pioneer, the only one left. I felt like the father of the team. But when I had a chance to get my breath and analyze the situation, I decided I was better off in Winnipeg."

He says he has an idea about how he will have to adjust now that he is a Jet.

"I'll have to adjust to the offensive, puck-controlling style of hockey the Winnipeg Jets play. The Cowboys play a very physical, hard-hitting type of game."

"Each of the players associated with Calgary aren't what you'd call stars. They are hard-working individuals who have to give 100% all the time, which is hard to do. The Winnipeg Jets are natural, fluid hockey players. Things just seem to happen as they quickly skate up the ice."

He adds that after a few games, things should start to fall into place.

"I'm not too familiar with their style of play as far as back-checking is concerned. Mr. Kromm went over most of the details. It's a matter of putting into practise."

As it turned out the first game Danny played in a Jet uniform was against Calgary.

"That's something that couldn't be helped," he says. "I'm sure that Crozier or Mr. Pilous didn't want to clash right away, but because of the deadline they had to make the trade. It just so happened that the first game was a make-up game with Calgary filling in."

He says his interests basically fall into the categories of business and sport.

"I have three corporations that deal mostly in land. I've just put together another one that will help out athletes. I can't go into details now but we hope to go world-wide. We will assist all athletes, not just hockey players.

"I like tennis and all phases of sport . . . running, squash, golf. I don't play anything else at a professional level except for tennis. I think I could go into a professional category in that field."

"GUEST SHOT"

DAVE DRYDEN
By TERRY JONES

LAST SPRING people kept coming up to Dave Dryden and telling him he probably really regretted leaving Buffalo Sabres because they were in the Stanley Cup playoffs.

The "little" brother of Montreal Canadiens Ken Dryden, smiled.

"I wouldn't trade my experience last year," he said of being goaltender, part-owner and publicity director of Chicago Cougars, a team that doesn't even exist any more.

"It was a super experience.

"Mind you, it was hectic as heck. But man, did I ever learn a lot. Like how expensive it is to run a hockey team. I mean when you withdraw $3,000 from your personal bank account for meal money for the team, you think 'holy cow'."

For Dryden, who came to Chicago from Punch Imlach's Sabres, the running of the Cougars with teammates Pat Stapleton and Ralph Backstrom wasn't a big risk deal like a lot of fans would have figured.

"On Dec. 26 we found out that the owners didn't have the money to pay anybody," he said.

"Financially it didn't make much difference. We had the league over a barrel. If we didn't get investors, the bill would have to be paid by the league. The only thing we lost was our time and, while there was a lot of it, I look at it as a totally worthwhile experience.

"We'd all just moved to Chicago and we didn't want to have to pack up in the middle of the season and move somewhere else. My job was in public relations and promotion and I've never been involved in that before. You try to solve the problem of why people don't come out to games. Some things we tried worked. Others didn't."

But Dave Dryden comes to Edmonton Oilers this year with a whole new perspective on the game that's his business.

"My knowledge of hockey is greater than ever. With our team last year we were all, in effect, coaches. And from a business point of view it was so fascinating that I'd like to get involved in that area when my playing days are over."

He is, at the same time, rather delighted to be coming to Edmonton where his total responsibilities will be to keep the puck out of the net.

Dryden, who is six years older than his more famous brother, wasn't a total hit in his first year in the World Hockey Association. He finished with a 3.87 goals against average, almost a goal a game worse than his best National Hockey League season.

"I had a strange season," he admits. "In Chicago I didn't feel like part of the team until we took over ownership. At that point I started to play better and feel that I was contributing. That's the funny thing. I really do believe I played better after I was involved in management. As a team I think we were really quite lost. As a team, I doubt if we played any better. I think it was more unsettling to most of the other players.

"I didn't feel any pressure in Chicago. Normally I like to feel some pressure. I did more experimenting last season than I've ever done. I tried a lot of things. Because of that I'm probably a better goaltender today. Before I could never experiment because I didn't want to give up bad goals because of the pressure.

"One thing I do know, it will be nice to get back to playing in Canada where you have a hockey atmosphere. Edmonton is really a heck of a sports town and the people are hockey oriented. From being with the Cougars' management, I discovered the Edmonton management is first class and I'm looking forward to a season of being 100 per cent a goaltender again."

Last season, Dryden didn't notice any major change in lifestyle from going from the absolute big top of the NHL to "the other league" as the NHL keeps referring to the large elephant in their backyard.

"I played with the Black Hawks in Chicago and I played with the Cougars. As far as I was concerned there was no difference in the way the fans, press and everybody reacted to you. Absolutely no difference.

" Mind you, it wasn't the same as Buffalo. The way Buffalo treats a team — and Edmonton is the same kind of place — is entirely different. The team was part of the city and everybody was behind the team."

As for Buffalo going great guns last year and in the Stanley Cup playoffs . . .

"I knew before I left that they had a heck of a shot at doing it. The team has been building and I assumed they'd have a great shot at the Stanley Cup."

There's one other thing Dryden is looking forward to in Edmonton.

"Never in all my years have I met Jacques Plante," he said of the ancient goaltender who was with Oilers last year and who planned to play his final year with the team this year.

"He is acknowledged to be the smartest and most knowledgeable goaltender in hockey. I consider myself to be really lucky to be on the same team as him. Look at the history of some of the goaltenders who have played with him. Everybody who has played with Plante has learned something from him. Last year I thought he had a heck of an influence on Chris Worthy and Ken Brown in Edmonton."

DEFENSEMAN AL McLEOD
(Team Captain)

By JOE DAGGETT

SOME TIME, say ten or a dozen years from now when his playing days are over, one of hockey's general managers might be well advised to talk to Al McLeod about a front office job. Now, McLeod might not be interested, but it would certainly be worth a try. With the education he's got (a B.A. in Business and Marketing from Michigan Tech) and is continuing to get (graduate courses at Arizona State), plus an appealing personality, a demonstrated capacity for dedicated hard work and a good knowledge of the game, he'd undoubtedly be an asset in anybody's hockey organization. And if he related to the front office work as he does to the team as a player, he'd be a heckuva company man.

In an age of rampant athletic egocentrism, McLeod is sadly out of step with today's trend in pronouns: to him, in matters relating to the Runners, it's always "we", not "I". Extremely cooperative with reporters, he yet poses a problem for them. You ask him questions about his play and the answer nearly always comes out as a statement about how his play relates to the team or how the team in general is doing.

McLeod and Phoenix Coach Sandy Hucul may have been made for each other. McLeod's not flashy or colorful or inclined to brawl. His satisfaction in the game comes from contributing to his team's success with workmanlike positional play and an exceptional ability to handle the puck and move it out of his defensive zone. And that's exactly what Hucul wants.

As McLeod puts it, "The key word for Sandy is discipline. He gets the maximum out of a group of players by insisting they stick to their positions and all follow his system. And it works. I've seen it happen time and time again that a disciplined team can defeat another club that may have superior personnel, but doesn't play together. We had a great season last year because this team's management did a good job of getting the players and then Sandy molded them all into the system."

The Hucul system, among other things, calls for defensemen to refrain from rushing the puck into the other team's end, a stricture McLeod has no trouble complying with. It isn't that he's not capable of approaching the other team's net: he was forward in college, in fact. But in general, McLeod feels, with Hucul, that a defenseman's job is to defend. This he did well last year, ending up a plus-12 in goals for and against and being voted the Roadrunners' Most Valuable Defenseman and Unsung Hero by his teammates at season's end. His three goals last season were one fewer than his professional career high recorded at Tidewater of the AHL in 1972-73.

McLeod actually came into his own as a professional the year before last. Called up by Detroit of the NHL at mid-season, he played regularly and well for the Red Wings the rest of the year and was told that he figured in their future plans, a continuing and perpetual rebuilding program. But while he was not unhappy with the Red Wings, Detroit as a place to live and

spend his career had little appeal. So an early-summer conversation with Roadrunner Coach Sandy Hucul and President Bill MacFarland led to his signing on the new Phoenix entry in the WHA.

McLeod and his wife, Ruth — whom he met while both were students at Michigan Tech — are now year 'round Valley residents. Al passed last summer in a post-graduate marketing research project at ASU . . . and spent a lot of time in a local gymnasium in an exercise program that helped him add some muscle to an already-sturdy 5-foot 11-inch frame. "I'm going to be playing heavier than I did last year," says McLeod, "but I feel good at the new weight. I'm a lot stronger in the upper body than I was, and I think that'll help me."

Roadrunner officials agree, both as to this season and the future. They don't feel McLeod will be ready for a job in their — or anybody's — front office for a long time to come.

DEFENSEMAN AL McLEOD: BRINGS WINNING ATTITUDE TO RUNNERS

Roadrunner defenseman Al McLeod doesn't particularly dig country and western music, but he can certainly sympathize strongly with the lyrics of a C&W number from a few years back called *Detroit City*. Remember it? It's about a young man from the South who bemoans life in the Michigan metropolis and ends up pleading, "Lord, how I wanna go home."

McLeod spent last winter in Detroit as a member of the NHL Red Wings, and his impressions of the Motor City are much the same as those of the sad Southerner in the song. "I didn't have anything against the Red Wings' organization," says McLeod. "I enjoyed playing for them and being in the NHL, but the city itself is awful. It's dirty and it's dangerous. You're afraid to step out the front door there. You really felt your wife might be in danger when you went on the road."

Given McLeod's views on Detroit, the city's Chamber of Commerce could hardly lament his departure. But the Red Wings certainly did. After his stint with them last winter — a 26-game span in which he played a steady defensive game while scoring two goals and a pair of assists — the Wings saw enough promise in the young blueliner's play to place him on their protected list going into the June draft. "I thought I played well in Detroit," McLeod asserts. "And they told me at the end of the season that I figured in their plans for the future."

But an early-summer visit with Roadrunner President Bill MacFarland and Coach Sandy Hucul changed all that and induced the 26-year-old defenseman to sign on with the new Phoenix entry in the WHA. "The money was roughly comparable with the two teams," says Al. "But I didn't relish the idea of going back to Detroit, and I came away from the meeting very impressed with MacFarland and Hucul."

"They seem to be taking a very intelligent approach to building a winning

Al McLeod

hockey club here," McLeod goes on. "The whole idea, after all, is for the team to win as many hockey games as it can. And you do it by playing together as a team, not by going out there as a grab-bag of individuals. That's their attitude towards it, and it's the way I think the game ought to be played, too."

McLeod's strong point as a player is his ability to handle the puck well and move it smartly out of his own defensive zone, an ability deriving at least in part from two seasons he spent on left wing as a collegian at Michigan Tech. Besides earning a degree in Business and Marketing at Michigan Tech, McLeod got a healthy taste of the experience of winning. The Huskies won their conference (WCHA) title all three of his varsity seasons and, his senior year, went all the way to the final game of the NCAA tournament, losing the national title in a 4-3 overtime decision to Cornell. "We outshot them by about two-to-one," McLeod recalls, "But they had Ken Dryden in goal and he was absolutely unbeatable."

More study lies ahead for McLeod this coming summer when, according to present plans, he'll enter Arizona State University to start work on a Master's Degree in Business Administration. Al and his wife, Ruth — whom he met while they were both students at Michigan Tech — are buying a home in Phoenix and plan to take up year-round residence in the Valley.

As for this season, McLeod says, "I think Sandy Hucul can help me improve a lot mechanically. Sandy's known as one of hockey's finest defensemen as a good teacher, too. I'm going to set out this year to pick up everything he can tell me about the fine points of playing defense. It should be a real good season."

And on the 'Runners' three trips to Michigan, a few choruses of "Lord, how I wanna go home" should sustain him just fine until he's outward bound from Detroit City.

137

RON CHIPPERFIELD

BY JOHN SHORT

It was fascinating last season to watch Ron Chipperfield.

He grew up, right in front of Joe Crozier and Calgary's growing number of hockey fans. And it happened almost overnight.

One day, Chipper was a promising young man with one foot still in junior hockey where he developed an immense reputation as a scorer. He indulged in junior-type habits. He held the puck too long sometimes and he made one move too many sometimes and he stopped skating on defence many times.

Then came the change. Nobody knows why and Chipper, if he knows, isn't talking.

The puck started to go in the net. He became the focal point of the Calgary Cowboy attack, especially with a man advantage. He became a professional, willing to take a bump to make a play.

He became all the things -- or almost -- that he was expected to be when Crozier prevailed upon owner Jim Pattison to part with big wads of thousand-dollar bills.

That's only part of the story, maybe even the smallest part.

Where does Ron Chipperfield go from here? How good can he be?

There is no limit, because Chipperfield, among other things, has learned to compensate for his shortcoming. His skating is good enough. His checking continues to improve. He is just possibly the most valuable property in the WHA. Remember he's only in his third pro year. He has time to repay almost any investment.

The clever young centre, entering his third professional season, will never be six-foot-two and he will never weigh 200 pounds, unless he develops an unwanted glandular condition. He will remain a stocky five-foot-eight or nine and weigh about 175.

He will never be a blazing skater like Danny Lawson or Lynn Powis. He will never be an accomplished checker like Peter Driscoll, who has the added advantage of being a team policeman.

What Chipperfield has instead is a God-given ability to score goals and fill seats with people willing and anxious to pay to watch him use his gifts. He is exciting.

Watch him closely, tonight and again soon. He handles the puck cleanly and shoots it quickly. He is improving as a faceoff artist. He has the capacity to become a team leader, if he isn't already. Despite his development, when you come back, you will note improvement.

There's another side of Ron Chipperfield, which bears describing. He is a gentleman. That isn't important when he steps on the ice, I suppose, but it's at least a pleasant change from the attitude of some -- make that many -- professional athletes.

COUGARS TRACK ROADRUNNERS TO NEST SEEKING WIN

The season is still young as far as the Chicago Cougars are concerned, and yet it has been extremely frustrating already. Picked by many to cop the Eastern action last season, the Cougars have played in fits and starts. The only consistency they have shown to date has been lack of consistency.

Last season the Cougars finished in fourth place during regular season play, but then, behind the magnificent leadership of player-coach Pat Stapleton and the outstanding playmaking and

WHITEY STAPLETON
One of great attacking defensemen, pulls double duty as Cougar coach.

penalty killing of longtime ace Ralph Backstrom, the Chicagoans upset the first-place — and then defending WHA champion — New England Whalers in a seven-game quarter-final series.

The semi-final set matched them against the powerful Toronto Toros,.and again the Windy City crew prevailed against the odds, setting the Toros to an early summer after another full set, four games to three.

The WHA championship series against the Gordie Howe-led Houston Aeros was somewhat anti-climatic. Forced to play their "home" games in a tiny suburban rink, and drained physically and emotionally after their pair of playoff triumphs against the Whalers and Toros, the Cougars went down in four straight games to the well-rested Aeros. But their showing forced the odds-makers to take a good look at the club going into this season.

"Jimmy the Greek" made the Cougars the odds-on favorite to dethrone the Whalers, and others followed suit. But the New England club, after one road defeat, rolled up six straight home ice victories before being stopped by the Roadrunners, and that splurge lifted them to the top of the East and there they remain. The Cougars, meanwhile, have occasionally shown brilliant play but it has been inconsistent to date.

Somewhat disconcerting is the fact that the promised new arena they were to play in has not been built ... nor even begun. Which is a shame, because the Cougars undeniably have talent to burn.

Stapleton remains one of the foremost rushing defensemen, a superb playmaking defenseman. He was the outstanding blueliner in this most recent Team Canada-Russia series. Backstrom is the clever maker of plays among the forwards, and he also had an outstanding series against the U.S.S.R. squad. His penalty killing alone made him an invaluable member of that Team Canada unit.

In goalies Dave Dryden and Cam Newton, the Cougars have a talented pair. Defenseman Darryl Maggs is on the verge of shedding the incumbering mail of "great potential" and donning the mantle of greatness that was predicted for him several years ago when he played with the Black Hawks and Golden Seals. Twenty-year-old Gary MacGregor is one of the outstanding amateurs to sign with the WHA last summer.

The Roadrunners found out against Cleveland a couple of weeks ago that they could not count on "home ice" — as much as they've been on the road, it's foreign to them — for a victory. Against the Cougars they'll have to scrap and bear down all the way.

Remembrance of Things Past

Paul Henderson intends to give his family what he, as a child, never had. By John Gault

During the final few minutes of the first game of the 1974 Canada-USSR series, I remember Howie Meeker fantasizing about how maybe Paul Henderson would score the goal to break the 3-3 tie. Seconds earlier Henderson had been open to the right of the Russian goaltender, Tretiak, but Bruce MacGregor, Henderson's linemate and former Detroit teammate, couldn't control the bouncing puck. Perhaps it's just as well; the fates may have given Henderson immortality in the fall of 1972, but they exacted their fee over the next two years. They clipped his bones, tore at his tendons, sent parasites into his bowels to eat away his energy—all this after a prolonged and heavy dose of post-victory depression.

In the two seasons before the 1972 hockey summit, Henderson had scored 68 goals for an essentially defense-minded and generally mediocre Toronto Maple Leaf team. In the two seasons following, his final two as a Leaf, Henderson scored a relatively meagre 42 goals; in 1972-73 he played in only 40 games because of injuries. To the credit of the Toronto fans and the sports press (with a couple of exceptions) there were no attacks, no derision, no cheap shots. Perhaps it was because he'd already given us memories we'd carry to our graves, or maybe that's just our way. Maybe both.

But over that period, there was a growing disenchantment—a mutual one—between Paul Henderson and the Maple Leafs. It began when Alan Eagleson, Henderson's lawyer, attempted to use Henderson's Team Canada heroics to get Leaf management to tear up a two-year, $75,000 per (estimated) no-trade contract that had just been signed and write a new, more lucrative, longer-term agreement. The Leafs, not really surprisingly, refused.

The next step followed the publication of *The Fans Go Wild*, a book I wrote in collaboration with Henderson, in which he took some shots at Leaf management—especially for allowing a number of good young players to defect to the then new WHA—and complained mildly that the Leaf style of conservative, defensive play hampered his goal output. The day after the press conference which launched

the book, Jim Gregory, the Leaf general manager, called him in and asked him if he would like to be traded to the Boston Bruins. Apparently a deal had been arranged, and it was just a matter of Henderson's approval.

Now think about this: the Bruins were a Stanley Cup contender and no doubt would be for many years to come; they played an offensive game, the kind Henderson loved and thrived upon. He said no. And that provides a real insight into the character of Paul Henderson and the reason he joined the Toronto Toros this year.

Hockey is a priority with Henderson: it has, after all, given him just about everything he has, and access to just about anything his decidedly non-exotic tastes might desire. But it isn't his number one priority. That spot is reserved for his family—his lithe, pretty wife Eleanor and their three daughters, Heather, Jennifer and Jill (and perhaps to some degree, his slightly nutty pug, Sam.) He made a decision, when they'd moved into his big but unprepossessing home in Mississauga (after he'd joined the Leafs from Detroit), that Toronto was where he was staying. He was going to give his family stability and safety and security, and by 1972 I believe he'd have quit hockey, rather than be traded away from Toronto. He was about to turn 30 then, giving serious thought and taking definite steps to get his life firmly in order.

He'd never known that comfortable feeling in his own childhood. Born on a horse-drawn sleigh near Kincardine, in western Ontario, on January 27, 1943, he wouldn't meet his war-veteran father until three years later. Most of the early years were spent moving from town to town as the CNR shifted Garnet Henderson at whim. The family eventually settled in Lucknow, where Henderson senior began to drive his precociously talented son toward the NHL. Garnet Henderson was an overnight telegraph operator; the money was bad; the family was poor. When he died in 1968 at the age of 48, from arterial sclerosis derived from a severe diabetic condition, he left the family nothing. Paul swore that would not happen to his family; security became an obsession for him. So did dying young, for a short while—there is diabetes on both sides of his family—but he overcome that fear.

The Toros represented for Henderson

an ideal solution, for a number of reasons. First, they wanted him: John F. Bassett had been making that clear for some time; they liked one another and respected one another. It was an ill-disguised secret that Henderson and the Leaf management (except for John McLellan) were antagonistic, and in fact a number of Leaf players were heard to mutter privately and sarcastically about "Captain Canada" in reference to Henderson. Also, the Leafs were not prepared to meet his contract demands in 1974, which included a four-year, no-trade agreement. The Toros were willing to go for a five-year, no-trade contract (at an estimated $150,000 a year) with the additional provision that if the team ever moved more than 50 miles from Toronto, Henderson would—if he so desired—become a free agent.

And, of course, the Toros and most of the other teams in the WHA play wide-open type hockey, which suits the Henderson style. Watching him in the 1974 USSR-Canada series reminded me—and everyone who appreciates seeing a marvellously gifted athlete at work—just how incredibly fast the man is on the ice.

At one point he came back on his own wing, from a good ten feet behind, to overtake Boris Mikhailov (who was in full and unimpeded stride at the time), came part way around the Russian player and hooked the puck away. Another thing I noticed was that Henderson was handing out clean, crisp bodychecks and was battling in the corners. I recalled something he'd told me over the summer: that he'd been lifting weights for the first time in his career and feeling very much stronger than ever before. The new Russian series wasn't the reason, he said: he was simply tired of being pushed around by the ever-bigger, ever-stronger kids coming into the game.

His body and his physical skills, translated into hockey performance, are the means to an end for Paul Henderson—a means of satisfying his deeply ingrained, number one priority. "Money gives you peace of mind," he once told me. "I don't ever want to be really wealthy, but I don't ever want to go to bed at night wondering if I can pay for this or that. It's a hell of a lot easier to live in this world if you don't have financial problems."

Paul Henderson — Mr. Dependable

By JIMMY BRYAN

As long as ponds freeze in Canada so little boys can grow into Hockey players, Paul Henderson's place in the game's history is secure.

Just as Bobby Thompson will be remembered forever by baseball fans for his dramatic homerun against the Brooklyn Dodgers in the 1951 National League playoffs, third game, bottom of the ninth, Paul Henderson will be remembered in Canada for THE GOAL that beat the Russians.

It was September 28, 1972, and the first ever Canada Cup Series between the best hockey players in Canada and the best hockey players in the Soviet Union had wound down to the eighth and deciding game. Henderson had won games six and seven to deadlock the series 3-3-1 but the Soviets lead in goal scored.

The odds were a million-to-one that the star left winger, then of the National Hockey League's Toronto Maple Leafs, would do it again in the crucial final game on Russian ice. The first four games were in Canada, the final four in Russia. In fact, Team Canada appeared beaten as the Russians nursed a 5-5 tie into the final minutes of the final game. A tie would have given Russia the series win on total goals scored along with invaluable propaganda ammunition. Canda had to win . . .

With just 34 seconds remaining, Henderson took a pass in front of the Russian net and fired the puck past Soviet netminder Vladislav Tretiak for as dramatic a hockey goal as has ever been scored. Team Canada won the game 6-5 and the series 4-3-1.

Henderson had pulled the incredible feat of scoring Canada's winning goal in three straight games. He was mobbed by teammates and became an instant national hero. Anybody who was six years or older in Canada at the time remembers Paul Henderson.

It's a long way from Maple Leaf Gardens to Birmingham's beautiful Civic Center Coliseum but that's where we find Paul Henderson today, citizen of Birmingham, Alabama and a member of the World Hockey Association's Birmingham Bulls.

Henny, as the 34 year old winger is known to his teammates, doesn't talk a great deal about his 1972 heroics which toppled the Russians, but it's naturally a proud moment in his life. His teammates might occasionally kid him about his achivements but they too are proud of him.

Hockey began for Henny at 11 years old in his home town of Lucknow in Canada. Of course he had been skating since he was a toddler, but says, "I started organized hockey rather late. A little place like Lucknow had no artificial ice and it was difficult. There were about 1,000 people in the town then, and not many more now. The most games I had played in any one season was 16 until I got to Junior hockey."

"I started Juniors with the Hamilton Red Wings in 1959," Henny says, "and played there for three years. As the name suggests, Hamilton was a Detroit farm team. Following my Junior days, I spent five years in the NHL with the Detroit Red Wings followed by six additional NHL seasons with the Toronto Maple Leafs." The totals were impressive . . . 229 goals and 235 assists during his National Hockey League career.

With the advent of the WHA's Toronto Toros, Henny joined the John Bassett owned organization and was with the team when stories began circulating about the team's imminent move to Birmingham. Like most of his teammates, Henny viewed the move with apprehension. Things he'd heard about Alabama hadn't been exactly lattering.

"I approached the move with an open mind, as best I could," Henny recalls.

"Hockey in the south was just something you never imagined, even though the Atlanta Flames had already joined the NHL. I didn't know a thing about Birmingham but agreed to come down and take a look.

"It was quite an experience for Eleanor (Mrs. Henderson) and me. A crowd of people met us at the airport, we had police escorts into town and I have never been treated nicer. We were sold.

"Now we truly love it here and are ready to make Birmingham our home. We could not be happier."

"We" includes three pretty Henderson daughters, Heather, Jennifer and Jill, along with Paul and Ellie.

For the Henderson's Birmingham is truly "SWEET HOME ALBAMA" . . .

Goalie Gary Kurt:

"What A Difference A Year Makes"

"I go on a fishing trip into northern Ontario every spring. We fly up into the woods, and it's very isolated, so I was actually out of touch with the world when the expansion draft was held. But on the way back I stopped at the first telephone I could find and called my wife. She told me I'd been drafted by Phoenix, and I let out a whoop that nearly broke her eardrum."

Thus does goaltender Gary Kurt recall his acquisition—he was the number-one pick—by the newly-formed Phoenix Roadrunners in last year's expansion draft. For many players, it might have been a comedown to go from an established team to an expansion outfit. But for Kurt, it was welcome news, indeed. You see, the team he played for last year was far from established.

Kurt last season was a member of the peregrinating New York-New Jersey franchise now ensconced in San Diego as the Mariners. He became an original member of the club, in fact, when he and Norm Ferguson defected from the NHL California Seals three years ago to join the New York Raiders, who went through a melancholy two seasons in which they became known as the New York Golden Blades, and then fetched up at mid-season a year ago in Cherry Hills, New Jersey where they campaigned under the banner of the Jersey Knights.

"We all lived in northern New Jersey, just across the river from New York," Kurt says, looking back on last year. "But when they moved the team to Cherry Hills

every game became a road trip; it was about a 2-3 hour ride down there. They used to have one bus for the players and another for the wives and we'd leave about the middle of the afternoon."

"There wasn't any fan interest to speak of; that was depressing, and you never got home from the game until about 1:00 in the morning. One of the pleasant things about playing hockey is for everybody to get together after the game and socialize a bit, but there was none of that, obviously. They were a good bunch of guys, and management treated me well, too, but the closeness that a team needs to be a winner never developed."

"I can tell you how much better my situation is now. Anybody needs stability to do his best, and I think that's a big reason why things are going better for me this year." Better, in Kurt's case, is a goals-against average that's gone steadily down to the low 3's, a shutout to his credit, and, as of mid-December, a string of five straight games without a loss.

The 27-year old Kurt, a big (6-3 and 205 pounds), pleasant person with a mild disposition, is a prototypical standup goaltender, an attribute that endeared him to the Runners' Director of Player Personnel, Al Rollins, a former goaltending great himself.

Gary is also quick to give credit for his success this year to his fellow Phoenix goalie, Jack Norris. "There's absolutely no substitute for informed criticism," Kurt claims, "and Jack has really helped by analyzing my play. This is the

first time I've ever been on a team where I wasn't the senior goalie. You can't go asking somebody for advice who has less experience than you do. You'd think the two goalies on a team might be cutting each other's throats, but Jack is a very unselfish person. There's competition between us, sure, but it's friendly competition. What Jack and I want is for both of us to do well so the team will benefit when either of us is in goal."

A native of Kitchener, Ontario, Kurt played junior hockey in his home town back in the days before the player draft, when amateur players were already chattels of a pro club. He went on to play in the Ranger chain with Omaha of the CHL, then was taken by Cleveland in the reverse draft in 1969. With Cleveland he was the American League's leading goalie in 1971. That led to a promotion the following year to the NHL's California Seals, where the defense had the goaltenders—when they weren't in utter shock—singing choruses of "Oh, Lonesome Me."

From California, Kurt decamped with Norm Ferguson to become a WHA original with New York-New Jersey and thence moved to Phoenix, of which he says: "It's a real pleasure to play here. The organization has treated us well, the fans are good, and Sandy Hucul is great to play for. He has a great way of inspiring people to want to do their best for him."

It's amazing, isn't it, what a difference a year—and a new team in a new city with a helpful colleague, a congenial coach and a little added confidence—can make.

RIGHTWINGER CAM CONNOR: "GIVE 'EM THEIR MONEY'S WORTH"

Unless you're a student of geography, Flin Flon, Manitoba is a tough place to draw a bead on. People who hear the name for the first time are mildly amused, as they might be over Beanblossom, Indiana, for example, or Tuba City, Arizona. Hockey fans, for the most part, are aware that it exists, but are satisfied with second-hand accounts of it, and few have taken the trouble to find a map that goes far enough north to show where it actually lies.

Flin Flon is in the mining country of northern Manitoba. It's remote and isolated, with a forbidding climate and people with tough, hard-rock types. It's biggest civic asset, outside of its mineral deposits, is the local junior-hockey team, the Bombers, a club whose personality has traditionally reflected its rigorous setting. Any number of good hockey players have been developed in Flin Flon, and the Phoenix Roadrunners think they have the latest in Bomber alumnus Cam Connor, a rookie rightwinger with the 'Runners this year.

Connor's a big, strapping kid, 6-feet 2-inches and 205 pounds, and his instincts impel him to play an aggressive, physical style. That's been both a blessing and a curse. In this era when the Philadelphia Flyers' brawling approach to the game is both successful and celebrated, hockey coaches and managers are ever on the lookout for tough types: "scrappers," if you will, or "policemen," or "enforcers." And the quest extends all the way down to the game's amateur strata. Listen as Connor tells how his junior career started in his hometown of Winnipeg. "I was already big for my age when I started out my first season there, but I wasn't playing much. The only time I got on the ice was when the game started getting rough, and they wanted me to fight someone. It go so bad I asked to be traded." Finally, through a complicated deal with a third team, Victoria, Connor ended up last season in Flin Flon.

Now, a transfer from Winnipeg to Flin Flon might not be welcomed by some, but to Connor it was good news. The change of scene resulted in a fine season of 47 goals and 376 minutes in penalties. "I did a lot of penalty time in Flin Flon," Connor recalls, "but the coach never once told me to go out and get somebody. I felt I was a leader on the team and not just a guided missile."

"Flin Flon was quite an experience," Connor goes on. "All the hockey players had jobs in the mines. My first day there I was 3,700 feet underground. They're mostly iron mines, but they pull out some gold, too. We didn't actually have to work that hard. The hockey team was the biggest thing in town, and they didn't want us overdoing the work at the expense of our play."

Following last season Connor was drafted in the first round by the Montreal Canadiens at the National Hockey League, and the new Phoenix entry in the WHA but was turned off by a visit to Montreal. "They wined me and dined me," he says, "but I picked up a French newspaper while I was there and noticed a picture of me alongside of (John) Ferguson and (Dave) Schultz. I put two and two together and figured out I was being billed as the new tough guy of the Canadiens. That's when I started talking seriously with Phoenix."

"There's nothing wrong with being a tough hockey player, but I'm not going to be an out-and-out goon. I feel my abilities are more like those of (Ken) Hodge or a (Wayne)Cashman. You know, tough but respected, not a wild man."

Phoenix had to bid high to snare Connor away from the Canadiens, and that, says Connor, adds a lot of pressure to what is already a difficult situation for a youngster: being a highly-touted rookie in hockey's big leagues. "I expected the WHA to be a big step up, and it is," says Connor. "Everything is speeded up; you don't have as much time to think. There's

Cam Connor

somebody right on you all the time. And the money aspect of it gnaws at me, too. I have a five-year contract and I know Phoenix drafted me for future potential. Still, you feel there's pressure to produce right away. I'm my own worst critic and when I'm not playing well I'm certainly aware of it. What I need most is time and experience. The big leagues are a big adjustment, but I think things will work out all right. All I really want to do is to earn my salary and be worth the money I'm getting." The Phoenix management is quite certain that their investment in Connor is a sound one and that, with his attitude and ability, they'll be well repaid.

LEFTWINGER BARRY DEAN

By JOE DAGGETT

MOST AMERICANS without a degree in geography would have a tough time pinpointing Medicine Hat, Alberta for you. In a conversation this side of the border the mention of Medicine Hat would probably evoke the same sort of amused chuckle called forth by other Canadian place names such as Moose Jaw, Saskatchewan or Flin Flon, Manitoba. Most hockey fans, though, while perhaps not able to give you an exact bearing on where it *is*, could certainly attest to the fact that Medicine Hat exists, because its junior hockey team has produced a string of good hockey players over the past few years.

The latest Medicine Hat alumnus to enter the pros with great promise is leftwinger Barry Dean of the Phoenix Roadrunners. A 20-year-old native of Maple Creek, Saskatchewan (good for a wry smile but not in a class with Medicine Hat, *et al*), Dean made his way to the Roadrunners late this summer under remarkable circumstances.

Roadrunner scouts had rated young Dean the top winger in Canadian junior hockey last year off a season of 40 goals and 75 assists in his final amateur campaign. But Edmonton, picking ahead of Phoenix in the WHA draft, selected Dean, a 6-foot, 195-pounder. He was also chosen in the first round of the NHL draft by Kansas City, making him the second player chosen overall in the older league.

So the Roadrunners had no chance of ever getting him. Or did they? Kansas City dropped out of the bidding early on and it appeared that Dean would go to Edmonton. But by midsummer there were indications that Dean, despite a generous monetary offer, was not entranced by the idea of signing with the Oilers.

The explanation — a credible one — given out in quotes from Dean and his agent was that the youngster was fed up with the cold Canadian climate and didn't want to spend his winters in Edmonton. There were also hints, later confirmed, that Dean and his advisor had some misgivings about the people who'd have been employing him in Edmonton.

Whatever the real reason, a valuable property with a stated desire to play in warm surroundings was up for grabs and the Roadrunners moved fast. A deal was negotiated with Edmonton for Dean in exchange for Phoenix' first- and third-round draft picks next year, and Barry signed on as a member of the Runners.

Fans tend to forget the tremendous pressures put upon a highly-touted young player trying to make the adjustment from amateur to major-league professional. With all of the fanfare attendant upon the signing of one of these highly-paid young men and all of the talk about his talents, fans can easily feel that he should deliver immediately.

The obvious fact is, it's a big jump. As Dean puts it, "You're playing the same game, sure, but it's different. The company's a lot faster. You go from number-one to just another rookie. You're playing in strange buildings before big crowds. And the teams are all good; there aren't any breathers on the schedule. It's tough."

There seems, however, to be little doubt that Dean will make the accommodation rapidly. He is a pleasant, earnest young man, given the early locker-room sobriquets of "Dizzy" and "Dino" by his teammates. Both the image of the screwy baseball pitcher and the singer with a reputation for hard drinking are wildly inapplicable to Dean, but imagination is seldom shown in hockey nicknames, anyway.

He is surprisingly disciplined for a rookie, Dean is, with good sense about coming back and checking his opposite number. He has good speed for a big man, is aggressive and willing to hit people. His shot is excellent; hard, accurate and triggered quickly.

It seems only a matter of time before he gets his feet under him and gets to know the league and his new job and makes himself a Phoenix fixture. U.S. hockey fans may continue to chuckle at Medicine Hat, but they're apt to be taking the name Barry Dean seriously for a long while to come.

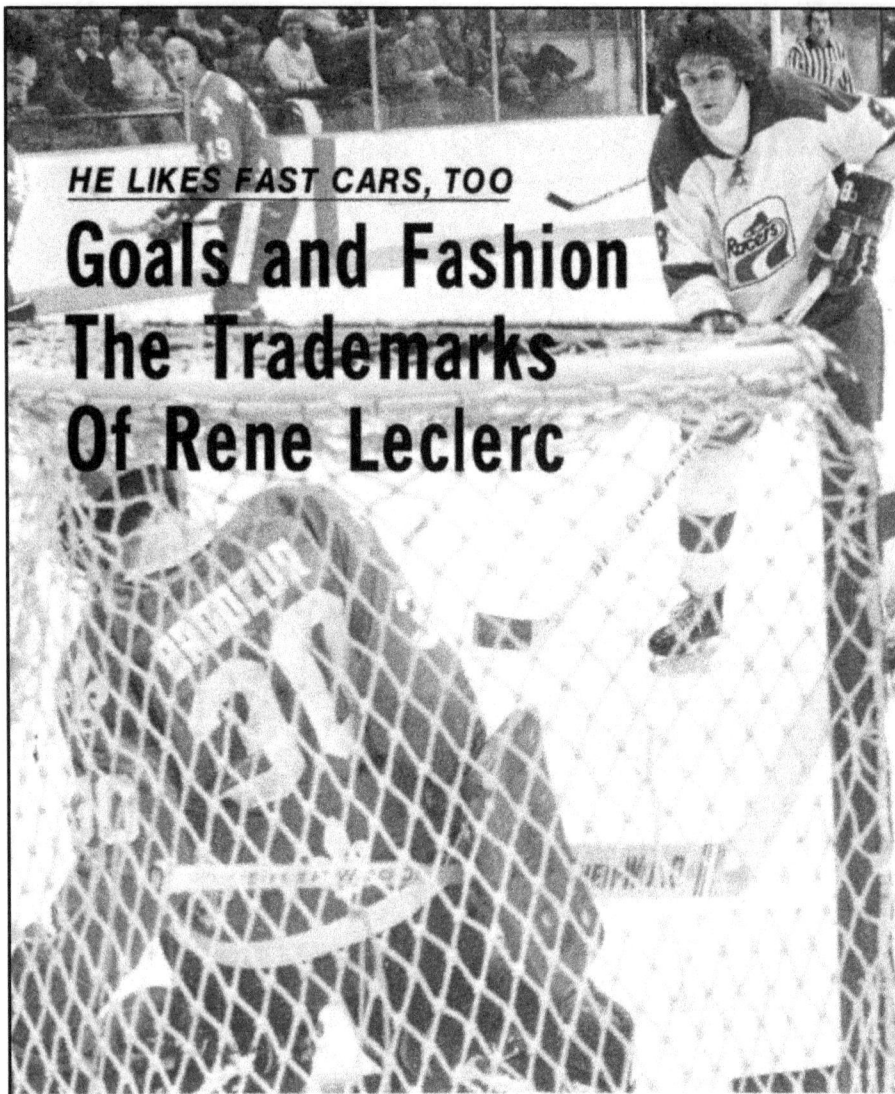

HE LIKES FAST CARS, TOO

Goals and Fashion The Trademarks Of Rene Leclerc

LECLERC FIRES ON FORMER TEAMMATE RICHARD BRODEUR

Indianapolis Racers' right wing Renald Leclerc has a problem that a lot of his athletic counterparts wouldn't mind sharing.

No matter how much spaghetti, potatoes or other fattening foods Rene piles onto his plate he still cannot gain weight. Not quite 6 feet tall, the slender Leclerc weighs only 160.

"There are many heavier guys in this league and I really have to skate," he explains. "I work at it, too. If you are skating well you have more chances to score."

Leclerc's inability to gain weight also poses some problems for the 28-year old, former Quebec Nordique who joined the Racers back in January in a trade for Bill Prentice.

"If we play two or three games in a row I find myself getting tired and I don't feel as strong," he says. "I can't afford to lose any weight. After a game I try to eat and gain back the poundage I might have lost."

Rene's Canadian friends suggested that he try the age-old formula for restoring lost body liquid -- a few post-game beers. But Leclerc has found that all brew does for him is make him ill.

Loss of weight to the contrary, Leclerc ranks among the most prolific point producers in the WHA. His input to the Racers' attack has been a vital force in the club's drive for a playoff berth, particularly since the arrival of former Quebec teammate Michel Parizeau.

Leclerc considers his wrist shot his most effective scoring weapon.

"A wrist shot is very good maybe 15 or 20 feet out from the goal," he stresses. "You can get it off quickly, where with a slapshot the goalie has time to see what you are going to do.

"I haven't been using my wrist shot lately and I think that's a mistake. But I'm working on it."

Leclerc is a soft-spoken man with a thick French accent. He likes to assume a contemplative attitude before a game and usually sits quietly in the dressing room.

"I get as much rest as I can the day of a game," he explains, "but it is not so easy to sleep then. It's not that I'm nervous . . . . it's just that I get bugs in my stomach. Of course those bugs usually mean I'm going to play good, that I'm really up for it."

A native of Ville de Vanier in Quebec province, Leclerc -- like many Canadian youngsters -- began skating at age 4, and by 15 was playing junior hockey for the Hamilton Red Wings, at that time an affiliate of the Detroit Red Wings.

Leclerc, having been raised in French Canada, knew no English when he reported to Hamilton. But, by his own admission, he learned quickly -- out of necessity.

The parent Red Wings turned him professional in 1967 with Fort Worth in the Central League, ultimately bringing him up for a total of 87 games.

With the berth of the WHA, Leclerc seized on the opportunity to return to Quebec where he played three plus seasons before his acquisition by the Racers for Bill Prentice.

Along with his regular uniform Rene always wears a turtleneck sweater.

"I didn't know if I would wear it here or not," he recalled. "I was afraid they would call me Flashy Leclerc.

"But I don't wear it to show off," he protests. "I don't like my shoulder pads rubbing my neck and the turtleneck protects me from getting scratched. I do think, however, that everyone should wear one. It looks a lot cleaner, a lot nicer than just the front where you see the underwear and the padding."

Leclerc is somewhat of an expert on fashion outside of hockey. He and his wife, Therese, own two boutiques in Quebec, one for women and one for children.

"I don't know what other hockey players do with their money but we thought we should get into some business," he says. "Since both of us like clothes a boutique seemed good."

Therese Leclerc does all the buying from Paris. Rene brings in the customers.

Leclerc is looking for a home for next season in Indianapolis. It has to be one that will not only accommodate his wife and young son but two extra members of the family -- an Old English Sheepdog and a St. Bernard.

If Rene does not find a house this spring he'll have plenty of time to look for one this summer when he comes to Indianapolis for the "500" and the National Drag Racing Championships.

Rene used to own a Chevelle Supersport and is a devoted racing fan.

"When I come back for the races I'll be bringing my wife and good friend Pierre Guite," he says with a grin.

Guite, as Racers fans know, is a member of the Cincinnati Stingers and has been the other half of many celebrated fights with Racer Kim Clackson, whom Rene also likes.

"The problem is what to do when Kim and Pierre get into a fight," asks Rene. "Well, I play for the Racers and I must be on Kim's side. And if Pierre gets beat up by Clackson, then too bad for Pierre."

Hugh Harris Man With A Mission

By D.R. O'Laughlin

Hugh Harris considers himself quite a talker.

Off the ice the Indianapolis Racers left wing-center is, in fact, a glib, out-going individual who gets along well with his fellow players and likes things lively in the locker room.

During a game, Harris -- who came to Indianapolis from Calgary in January -- also produces a constant chatter, "shouting and carrying on" to keep his adrenalin surging.

But the most important talking the 6-1 athlete does is with his hockey stick and his booming shot.

He's a perennial scoring threat, keeping the pressure on with deft stick handling from the red line in.

Last year with the Vancouver Blazers (since moved to Calgary) the curly-haired Harris scored 23 goals and 34 assists, making him the club's leading scorer.

This season Harris -- who missed seven weeks of action before being traded to the Racers -- has targeted himself a minimum of 20 goals.

"In order to score you have to think goal everytime you get the puck," he explains. "I may go several games and not get a goal. Then I think about it and I realize that I haven't been telling myself I'm going to score."

Harris, 27, started playing hockey much later than the average Canadian youngster.

"I was born in the inner city in Toronto and there was no organized hockey," he says. "None of my three brothers had much interest in the game and my mother, from Scotland, didn't understand it."

Harris was about 12 when he moved from the center city and started skating. He caught onto it quickly and within 3-1/2 years he was playing Junior B hockey, a feat that seemed to him like playing in the National League at the time.

"One thing that I quickly learned," he recalls, "is that to play hockey you have to be coordinated. You have to shoot while you're going at different angles, while you're getting hit and while you're traveling maybe 20 miles an hour on 1/16th of an inch of steel. If your skate is properly rockered you're only skating on about four inches of it.

"To the average fan the game doesn't look that difficult," he adds.

Harris skated in the International League four seasons and then the American League 2-1/2 seasons, including a stint with the Cincinnati Swords. He played 60 games for the NHL Buffalo Sabres before coming over to the WHA in 1973.

If it hadn't been for the deal between the Calgary Cowboys and the Racers, though, Harris' hockey career might have ended this Christmas.

The problem started when Harris and Calgary management couldn't agree on a contract.

"They kept telling me I would be rewarded for my good year at Vancouver, but they never fulfilled their part. I was getting down on myself, too, and wouldn't play anymore.

"I used to go to practice and the coach was so mad at me that I would sit there for an hour and a half without doing anything," he explains. "I got to the point, around Christmas, where I had had it. At home I was a bad guy -- a regular Ebenezer Scrooge.

"My feelings have changed drastically since I came to Indianapolis," he adds with a smile.

Because of his problems Harris joined the Racers playing less than his normal 210 pounds and feeling weak from lack of activity.

But one bright thing was apparent to the new Racer.

"When we came in last year if we got one or two goals against the Racers we could score 9. But this team has really changed around -- their attitude is much better. Now they give up one or two goals and still come back," he says.

Hugh Harris Out-Maneuvers Quebec's Serge Bernier

He also found the Racers' fans were morale builders.

"This is a good crowd," he says. "You have your basic fans and then an open-minded group that comes in -- they all want to have a good time. But the majority of the Canadian and NHL crowds come just to see a win. They turn on the team or individual players if they don't win every night.

"I've even had fans come up and say they didn't like me on the ice just because they didn't like the way I looked -- not so much how I played," he says.

Harris, his wife and two daughters started looking for a new home in Carmel shortly after he joined the Racers.

They'll stay in Indianapolis during the summer, a time that often proves a trying one for the amiable Harris.

"If I have one bad fault it's that I don't keep myself in the greatest shape in the summer," he says. "I putter around the house and play some golf. I can relax for only so long then I have to get out of my wife's hair!"

To keep from getting too lazy in the off-season the Harrises head West -- to Los Angeles, San Diego and Las Vegas or for their summer home on Lake Michigan. The couple also are movie buffs.

One goal Harris and his wife are looking forward to before the end of the season is the birth of a new member of the family.

"We're expecting a boy in March," a proud Harris reveals, grinning broadly.

BOB SICINSKI

"He never quits in a game regardless of the score . . . he has great desire!" That is the way Chuck Catto, Racers Player Personnel Director, described Bob Sicinski following completion of the World Hockey Association Expansion Draft last May 30th in Toronto, Ontario. Bob was made available for the draft by the Chicago Cougars and selected by the Racers in the fifth round.

The rugged 5-foot-11, 181-pound centerman was born in Toronto, Ontario, but played his junior hockey with the St. Catharines Black Hawks in the Ontario Hockey Association. From there he graduated to the stiffer competition offered in the Eastern Hockey League where he strung together three super years as a member of the Greensboro Generals . . . scoring 227 points in 213 games, including 107 goals. His 115 points —40 goals and 75 assists—were tops in the league for the 1969-70 campaign.

In addition to leading the EHL in scoring that season, Bob was also No. 1 on the assist parade, named to the league All-Star team and voted Greensboro's Most Popular Player by local fans.

His performance record with the Generals earned him a promotion to Dallas, the Chicago Black Hawks farm club in the Central Hockey League, the following year. Misfortune struck early in the 1970-71 season when he suffered an injury to his left knee which required surgery and kept him out of the lineup for all but 20 games of the season.

Fully recovered from his knee surgery, Bob picked up his outstanding performance pace where it left off prior to his injury. In his first full season in the CHL he notched 84 points to finish fifth in the league's scoring race, gained a berth on the CHL All-Star squad and helped the Dallas club capture the league championship that year . . . not bad for a rookie! But Bob did not stop there. He assisted on 10 goals in post season action, which turned out to be the high mark for the 1972 CHL Playoffs. When added to his 61 assists for the regular season, it gave him an overall total of 71.

Coupled with the 75 assists he garnered at Greensboro in his last full season of action he had helped out on the scoring of 146 goals— prompting the hockey scouts to stamp him as a talented playmaker and a good bet to make it up to the Chicago Black Hawks and the National Hockey League the next year.

However Bob chose another path to the big leagues when he signed as a free agent with the WHA Chicago Cougars in August, 1972. While with the Cougars, he centered their top line with Jan Popiel and Rosaire Paiement on his left and right sides respectively. Once again he turned in a commendable performance and added to his reputation as a top-rated pivot man. He led the Cougars in assists (63) and total points (88) that first season in the WHA.

Since coming to Indianapolis, Bob, his wife Pat and their son John, are now living on the Northeast side but make their off-season home in Mississauga, Ontario, Canada.

STEADY ON DEFENSE

Bob Woytowich

Bob Woytowich is 33 years old and is in his 13th season as a pro. The 5-foot-11, 197 pound defensive specialist is a product of the New York Rangers system and turned pro in 1962 with Sudbury of the old Eastern Pro League. After a little more than a couple of years in the minors, Bob moved into the big time to stay—he played eight straight seasons in the National Hockey League with four different clubs ... three with the Boston Bruins, one with the Minnesota North Stars, where he also served as team Captain during his stay, three-plus at Pittsburgh and the remainder with the Los Angeles Kings. He was named to the Sporting News NHL—West Division All-Star team for the 1969-70 season, and also played for the West in the NHL All-Star game of 1970.

The much travelled Woytowich headed for the World Hockey Association in 1972 when the Winnipeg Jets picked him in the league's first Player Selection Draft held in February of that year. His decision to leave the NHL in favor of the Jets was not too difficult considering that Winnipeg is not only his off-season home, but the place of his birth and the scene of his early triumphs as a member of the Winnipeg Rangers in the Manitoba Junior Hockey League.

Held out of action during the first few weeks of that first World Hockey Association season, pending the settlement of litigation, Bob got off to a shaky start but then settled his play down and assumed his intended role as leader of the Jets defensive brigade. Bob was the Jets top defenseman last year. In addition to anchoring their blueline corps, he contributed 34 points to their offensive effort on 6 goals and 28 assists. It was his most productive year as a major leaguer, and second-best of his pro career—he had 44 points on 17 goals and 27 assists in his rookie pro season with Sudbury.

Bob joined the Racers early in December, 1974. At the time of his acquisition, Jim Browitt, President-General Manager of the Racers stated, "Bob Woytowich will provide us with a lot of experience at the blueline, he's a steady performer and that won't hurt us a bit back there. In fact, his know-how will add stability to our play on defense, and cut those goals-against down."

MIKE FORD HOME AGAIN

By SUSAN NICOL

When he talks about the Jets, he switches from first person to third person and back again. But that's exactly how this season has gone for Mike Ford.

Ten games into the season Mike traded his Jet sweater for a Cowboy shirt. On the last day before the trade deadline he was back in a Jet uniform. You can't blame him for getting confused.

"Winnipeg is my home," he says. "I was very disappointed to leave and I'm happy to be back."

He says both trades came as a surprise to him.

"I really didn't expect to get traded at the beginning of the year," he says. "I tried to make the best of it, because I knew if I wanted a second chance I'd have to play well. I did my best hoping Winnipeg would keep me in mind."

He adds, "I must have kept my head just above water long enough for Winnipeg to throw me a lifeline."

Mike says he never really adjusted to Calgary's style of hockey.

"The play was very different," he says. "Winnipeg is a finesse club. They try to hang on to the puck and work it. Calgary just dumps it in, chases it and tries to rile the other team.

"I didn't enjoy much ice time and that's the name of the game. If you're not playing, you're not happy. That made it doubly worse, because I felt displaced being in a strange town."

He says he feels comfortable in Winnipeg, even though he hasn't been back very long.

"I'm starting to play a bit more," he says. "Bobby (Kromm) is still experimenting. He's using me a little more sparingly than he did last year, but I'm just glad to be back. All I want to do is contribute in a small way."

He adds, "When you're happy you play better. I'm much happier and I feel that with a few more games I can get myself back to my full potential."

Mike started his hockey career with the Winnipeg Junior Jets. Half-way through the season he was traded to the Brandon Wheat Kings where Rudy Pilous was coaching.

In the following two years, Mike played for Detroit's Port Huron club in the minor leagues. In that time he made the all-star team and travelled to the play-offs twice.

"After those two years my contract was up," he says. "So I called Rudy and he gave me a try-out with the Jets. I was able to hang on for the first year playing with Sjoberg and behind Bobby, Anders and Ulf. I seemed to enjoy a reasonable amount of success. Last year we played together again and we won the cup, so it was a pretty good year that way."

Mike is notorious for his shot from the point. The first game he played in familiar surroundings saw spectators ducking rubber in the greys.

"I think my role is to move the puck, get it up to the forwards and get them moving," he says. "We've got the fastest forwards in the league, I think, so if we can get the puck to them we'll be successful. Maybe if I can get a few good shots on the net I may get a couple of goals. But that's gravy."

Being part of the opposition for a time gave Mike an opportunity to assess the Jets from a different point of view.

"Calgary only beat us two games out of seven so it is difficult to say the Jets had a weakness," he says. "The smaller ice surface in Calgary cramps the style of a team like the Jets. We need the big ice for our 'wheelers and dealers.'

"Other teams try to run at the Jets and intimidate us, but we just keep coming. They try to get chippy and haul us down, but we're pretty good at getting power play goals. That makes the other teams shy away from taking stupid penalties."

He says team morale and fan support is lacking in Calgary.

"Calgary right now is fighting to hang on to their franchise," he says. "They're getting very poor crowds. The team, of course, can feel this and it affects the Cowboys knowing they're on shaky ground. Winnipeg, on the other hand, seems to enjoy a reasonable amount of support. The team is doing well and the players are happy so why rock the boat?"

POSITIVE WAVES!!!

To: The Racer Family

Back in February '76 in our 2nd season, things looked bleak as far as Racers getting a play-off spot. Many had given up, but not the Racers. After analyzing their situation and seeing what had to be done, they began to get it together.

About this time while in Hartford, some of the players watched a war movie on TV. In "Kelly's Hero's" Donald Sutherland played a character named Moriarity who's outfit couldn't seem to do anything right and believed they couldn't. He decided to reverse this negative thinking so formed the Moriarity's Theory of Positive Waves. It worked.

Those watching the movie decided to put Moriarity's Theory to use. It worked for us too! (Just ask Hollarin' Hughie!) The Racers won twelve of their last nineteen games, tied three, and lost only four. Thus, the last place Racers became the Eastern Division Champions for 1975-1976.

As a fan appreciation gesture that spring, Mike did a sketch of what the spirit of Moriarity meant to him. This showed him with red hair, blue eyes, and pointed ears — the Irish name suggesting a leprechan and good luck.

Over the summer Booster Club members began to wonder if the club couldn't develop an on-ice mascot for our team.

We got together and plans began, even though an experienced commercial artist, building this costume head presented many new problems to Mike. Annette had been sewing for years but had never before made hockey pants or a monster-sized shirt. Dave had learned to ice skate but never dreamed he'd be asked to balance that 46 pound head while on skates. After much work and lots of "positive waves" the big fellow was ready by early November 1976.

Moriarity is full of good luck — literally! While building the head of corregated board and paper mache, Mike used lots of Racer pictures and clippings. (If the wearer gets bored, he can always read!)

Various props were built for him to use — a gun with sign "pop it to 'em", an oil drill bit "ream 'em", a rocket "blast 'em", a limply inflated jet "crunch the jets", giant sized match "scorch 'em", a huge oar "wallop the Whalers" and the most frequently used rabbits foot. The latter was hurriedly done last December to help us defeat the Mariners (finally!) (Sorry 'bout that you ex-Mariners, but now you're on OUR team! The rabbit's foot'll bring good luck to you now!) If you are so inclined, give the foot a whack as you come on the ice next game.

Moriarity also has hidden pockets for "lucky stuff". He carries pennies, pictures, clippings, a tiny black and gold bee, a whaler pen, etc. If you wish to give the big guy any item to carry — feel free! His laundress is used to emptying pockets!

We just wanted to fill you in on a bit of Racer and Booster Club history. But mostly, we wanted to say we're glad you're here!

From: "The Moriarity Family"
Dave and Patty Caldwell
Jon and Annette Gilman
Mike and Karen Kennedy

FOR PIZZAZ, CHEEVERS IS NO.1

By BOB SCHLESINGER

There may be better quarterbacks than Joe Namath, better basketball players than Pete Maravich.

And yes, there may be, and then again there may not be, better goaltenders than Gerry Cheevers.

But whether or not Cheevers is number one in the world at the profession of keeping red lights turned off (vice squad super cops are not considered part of this discussion), or whether he's rated way down there as third or fourth best, he shares something with Broadway Joe and Pistol Pete.

Politicians call it charisma. *Variety* Magazine might term it pizzaz.

You'll see Gerry play many great games, some good ones, and yes, a few not so good ones, if you watch him work a lot. But you'll never see him turn in a dull performance.

He makes things happen instead of letting them happen. Action instead of reaction.

If there's a more exciting play in hockey than Cheevers coming 20 feet out of the nets to throw a flying tackle at the puck, which is on the stick of an enemy forward coming in alone, this writer hasn't seen it yet.

To do that sort of thing requires two characteristics:

A: You have to be very brave because a fellow can get hurt trying something like that.

B: You have to be prepared emotionally to hear a lot of not very nice things from the fans if the maneuver doesn't work.

In games I have seen over the past three seasons, Cheevers' percentage

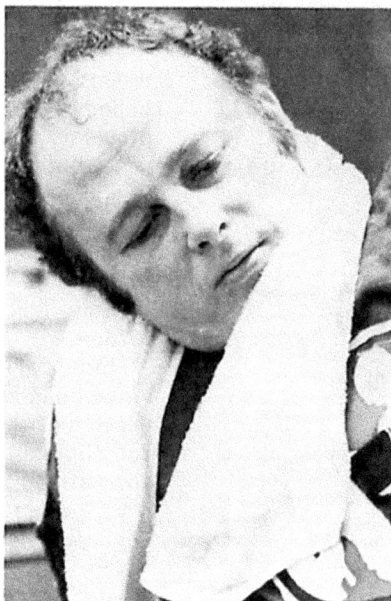

of stopping breakaway opportunities has been phenomenal.

A one-on-one (attacker on goalie) situation is supposed to be almost even money according to most hockey texts (some say 6 to 5 in the goalie's favor). Yet through the years, I'd estimate that Dr. No has stopped a half dozen breakaways for every time he was beaten on one.

Only twice can I recall that he looked really silly getting caught far from his cage. And neither was actually a bad play.

That his setbacks are so rare that they are memorable should tell you something.

One time he came far out to confront Bobby Hull, who was walking in all alone. Alas, the Golden Jet put on the breaks, avoided Cheevers, and coasted in to tap the puck into the deserted cage.

Still, Cheesy has used the same maneuver on Hull a couple more times, and it has worked.

What makes it a good play? If you sit back in the cage and give Hull (whose shot is as deadly accurate as it is unbelievably rapid) all the time he wants, the odds are great that he's going to score anyhow.

If you do it that way, you don't look as silly as Cheevers did, but a goal against is a goal against is a goal against.

The other play which comes to mind came in the last 20 seconds of a game against Minnesota with the Crusaders trailing by a goal.

Cheevers came out nearly to the blue line, to meet an enemy forward who was coming in alone. He tried to steal the puck with a poke check, repeatedly, until both players wound up in the corner.

Alas, the attacker was able to pass the puck to a teammate and an empty net goal resulted.

Still, if you accept that the object of the game is to win and not just to keep the score down, it was a great percentage play.

If Cheevers had sat back and allowed the Saints to play with the puck, the clock would have run out. Only by stealing the puck quickly and making the outlet pass for a breakaway in the other direction did he have a prayer of giving his teammates a chance to tie the score.

After the first Russia-Team Canada series, which saw Ken Dryden and Tony Esposito share the netminding chores (not very successfully) for Canada, the conventional wisdom was that the only way not to get sucked out of position by the smooth

passing Russians was to stay in the cage and stand up.

When Cheevers was selected for Canada-Russia II last fall, it was suggested that he would be the wrong man for the job unless he greatly modified his ramblin' man, gamblin' man style.

Instead, Gerry changed his style not a bit, unless it was to play with even more calculated recklessness than usual.

The result is now history. Cheevers was spectacularly successful, shutting off the Soviets to a far greater degree than either Dryden or Esposito had managed. Although Russia won the series, Cheevers became a Canadian national hero in the process.

It's possible to debate the number one goalie in the world issue eternal-ly without convincing each of the top netminder's advocates that their man is not the best.

Still, it's not too hard to make a case for the stitched-masked Crusader.

Against the Russians, Cheevers was superior to both Esposito and Dryden. That was in the most pressure-filled circumstances imaginable.

And in that series last fall, he seemed slightly superior, at the very least equal, to Tretiak, the Soviet netminder who has to be considered in the number one competition.

Finally, there is Bernie Parent, the new Golden Boy of those scribes who worship at the shrine of Clarence Campbell and the National Hockey League.

Playing behind the Philadelphia Flyers, whose checking is awesome, Parent has fared spectacularly well.

But let's not forget that Parent, in the World Hockey Association's first season, was playing behind the Philly Blazers, who recognized only one kind of a check, the type you put in the bank.

Cleveland met Philadelphia, its "natural rival" many times that season. Indeed it seemed we were looking at those ugly orange uniforms every week.

And in a vast majority of those head-to-head confrontations, Cheevers was the superior netminder.

Number one in the world?

It just could be.

And Gerry is best when the chips are down.

Watch him closely.

You may never see another one like him.

The Stoughter Comes Up Big

He claims that he never works up a sweat when playing and furthermore he says that he never will. He has gone on record saying that before this year, hockey had always been a big aggravation for him, and that he was only in it for the money. He has asked Captain Rick Dudley to see if 'Duds' can get the last sixty-five games of the regular season cancelled so "we can move right into the play-offs right now." And, on top of all this, he has developed an off ice saying of "Harrr, Harr, Harrr" that has caught on so well that he now has everyone on the team saying it day in and day out. If you can believe it, he even went so far as to give teammate Richie Leduc a "Harrrrrr" on the ice last Saturday night when he was looking for a pass from Leduc. Richie was so befuddled by hearing it that "I didn't know what to do, I just stood there and their defenseman took the puck from me."

He also scores goals. Boy, does he score goals.

His name is Blaine Stoughton and he plays right wing on the Stingers L.S.D. Line, along with Rick Dudley and Richie Leduc. It is one of the most explosive lines in the WHA.

He is a character, to say the least, but he is the type of character who is welcome on a hockey team because he keeps the rest of the guys loose. He's not serious about sweating on the ice, or about cancelling that last sixty-five games, and even though he owns up to giving Leduc a big "Harrrrrr" on the ice, he wasn't serious about that either.

"I had to do something . . . we were up by seven goals (9-2 vs Phoenix) at the time, and I was just having some fun," recalls 'The Stoughter.' As a matter of fact, its tough to find Stoughton in a serious mood, off the ice, that is.

The line "Did you hear what 'The Stoughter' said today" is a daily occurrence in the Stinger dressing room. His dry sense of humor has brought the entire team closer; it has made them one big happy family.

"It's not my humor that has brought us closer" protests Stoughton. "It's because they made the dressing room smaller this year."

On the ice, it's a different story, he's always serious and "comes to play" according to Terry Slater.

* * *

'The Stoughter' came to the Stingers this past summer, by way of the Toronto Maple Leafs of the NHL. He had been with the Leafs for two years and prior to that, he spent his rookie campaign in Pittsburgh with the Penguins. He is now on a long term contract with the Stingers.

Before the Penguins made Blaine their Number 1 draft choice in 1973, he had played his junior career in Flin Flon with the Bombers of the WCHL (Western Canadian Hockey League). At that time, curiously enough, Stoughton was touted as a hockey player with the same amount of talent as another Stinger, that being Dennis Sobchuk. They were being compared regularly, because they were playing against each other.

Although Blaine was a year older than Dennis, they did play against each other for two years, which is long enough for each of them to form a pretty accurate opinion of each other's play.

Sobchuk recalls now that "Stoughton was a tremendous junior, he always was around the puck. I looked forward to playing against Flin Flon when he was with them because it was always a challenge to try and get more points than he did against us.

"Looking back, I'd have to say that I hold a lot of admiration for Blaine for

the way he played in his junior career" continued Dennis "simply because of the travel schedule. Stoughter played FIVE years with Flin Flon, which is two more years than the average player plays. Blaine was so good in his middle teens that he graduated to the junior ranks earlier than most guys. I only played three years in that league myself, and I can tell you travelling on that 'Iron Lung' (nickname for bus) for that long was just brutal. On top of that, you are always aware that there are scouts in the stands looking for pro material and so you know that you have to put out if you want to be drafted. I don't know how he managed to play so good under those conditions for five years."

"Dennis was a helluva player in junior" remarked Stoughton the other day. "I think that the only year that I beat him in scoring was his rookie season, and that was only by three points (126 to 123). I'm glad that I'm playing on the same team as he is now. He's played the same way this year as I remember him in junior.

* * *

Earlier it was mentioned that the Stoughter had a dry sense of humor, and that he doesn't play to work up a sweat. These are jokes that Stoughton has spread throughout the dressing room so far this season. It should be pointed out

In the first 13 games, Stoughton has scored 11 goals.

154

that yes, indeed, the Stoughter does sweat when he plays hockey, and the proof is in the pudding. After the Indianapolis game in Cincinnati Nov. 3rd, he led the team in goals with ten (10) and was the 9th leading scorer in the WHA. At twenty-three, his future is bright.

"This is the closest knit team that I have ever played on, or for that matter ever seen," said Stoughton. "I guess it is because we are all so very young and we just get along so well. Sure, part of it is because we are playing so well, but there is more. All other teams that I've ever been on there has been a sort of rift between the English and the French. Not here. Everyone gets along very well with each other, and that goes a long way.

"I'm sure that personally, I'm really happy here because I'm on a real good line and it makes you want to give it all you've got. Duds gets the puck to me a lot, and Richie (Leduc) is an ideal player to work with.

"In the past, hockey was an aggravation to me. Now it is fun, and what a difference that makes in your attitude. You want to give it everything. It's great here."

*   *   *

In the summer months Stoughton generally takes it easy; he plays a lot of tennis, and according to the Voice of the Stingers Andy MacWilliams, "he's tough out on the courts. We played three different days when we were in Hartford for a week, and he was the best player out there."

Not bad for a guy who has only played for two years.

*   *   *

This year the Stingers are a much improved club over last season. The apple cart was upset in the last two months of the season, and players who didn't live up to their expectations are no longer on the roster. They are calling Cincinnati one of the best teams of the future in all of Major League Hockey . . . or at least they were. Now people are starting to look up to the Stingers and say "hey, they may just be one of the best teams right now. What'll they be like in two years?" Beyond a doubt the Stingers are going to be a team to contend with this year, and for years to come. It's no secret that one of the main reasons is a guy who keeps the team loose off the ice with a dry sense of humor and at the same time has the uncanny ability to continuously 'come up big' for Slater in a game that this year has become 'a lot of fun.' "Harrrrrr!" ℂ

155

Tonight's game showcases the old (Gordie Howe, Dave Keon, J.C. Tremblay) and the new (Gordie Roberts, George Lyle, Mark Napier); the borrowed (Thommie Bergman, Ulf Nilsson, Anders Hedberg) and the blue (John Garrett, Del Hall). But amidst all these players either voted or named to this year's All-Star Game is a young man with perhaps the most remarkable story of them all.

Robbie Ftorek.

Scandinavian of face, Henry Winkler of body, Robbie Ftorek has overcome many obstacles to reach his particular pinnacle. First, Ftorek is an American, reared in the affluent Boston suburb of Needham, Mass., known primarily for pretty girls, ten-speed bicycles, and well-to-do Route 128 industrial businessmen. Although Needham produces its share of teachers, engineers, and mothers, this pretty town is not exactly Kirkland Lake, Ontario when it comes to producing hockey players. While his WHA hockey peers were engaging in war after war in Canadian junior hockey, the wispy Ftorek trucked off to Needham High with a hockey stick in one hand and an algebra book in the other.

But even more significant than this early environment is his size, or lack of it. In street clothes, Ftorek looks like he just worked as the altar boy for Father O'Hurley at the ten o' clock high mass. Or maybe he just got through working the all-night shift at the local flower shop. Maybe his next class starts in 15 minutes.

Whatever, at about 150 pounds, Robbie Ftorek is a Willie Shoemaker in a world of Willie Mays'. Scout after scout would watch Ftorek in high school wind his way around and under enemy defensemen, shattering records and cheerleaders' hearts, only to sit back and say, "he's just too damn small." But this did not stop Ftorek. Nothing Stops Robbie Ftorek.

Cap Raeder, the sensational second-year goalie with the New England Whalers, knows Ftorek best. While a senior at Needham High, Raeder was the sophomore goaltender.

"My favorite Ftorek story occurred late in the year after we won 16 straight and looked like we were on our way to another state championship," remembered Raeder. "Walpole High broke our undefeated string the year before and they were the last team we had to beat to go undefeated this next year. I'll never forget that game. They were leading 3-1 with a minute and a half to play. Then Ftorek stops the game, skates down to our goal and says to me, 'Rades, how many do you want?' I say, 'Enough to win.' So do you know what the guy does? Ftorek scores two goals, sets up two more and we win, 5-3. It was the most unbelievable thing I've ever seen in hockey."

Raeder has followed Ftorek's exploits very closely, through the Detroit Red Wings and through his early days with Phoenix.

"I have patterned my attitude after Robbie, Raeder said. "He is always working, always digging, always on the go. And then Boom, he's in bed by eleven o'clock. I mean every night. We go fishing in the summer and he'll get me up at some ridiculous hour like six o'clock and he won't quit until supper. He is the most dedicated guy I've ever met. But with all the success he's met with Phoenix, he is the same Robbie Ftorek I knew in high school. He'd cut off his right arm for a friend."

Raeder also recalled Team USA incident.

"We were in practice one day in Providence and I was going through the motions. All of a sudden, Ftorek stops, throws down his stick, and starts yelling at me to get to work, that he was sick and tired of watching me loaf through the practice. Don't forget, we've been friends since grade school. I couldn't believe it, but then I remember, this was Robbie Ftorek yelling at me, my friend, my buddy, and I worked my butt of the rest of the camp. I love this guy, he's just the greatest."

His busy-as-a-bee style filled the cavernous Boston Garden to capacity during those high school days, the only schoolboy *drawing card* in scholastic history. But his work with the Phoenix Roadrunners, his leadership, and his play under adversity makes Ftorek a very special breed.

While the Roadrunner organization trimmed the budget by dispatching such stalwarts as Cam Connor and Barry Dean elsewhere, Ftorek was left to carry the load on his 150-pound shoulders. At the end of December, his 24 goals and 30 assists ranked fourth behind Buddy Cloutier, Anders Hedberg, and Serge Bernier in WHA scoring. While the Roadrunners allowed about 40 more goals then they themselves have scored, Ftorek stood at plus-10, the only plus player on the Phoenix roster, a statistic belying the club's poor overall p-m mark.

Robbie is well on his way to another 100-point, 100 penalty-minute season, proving that true grit is not just exclusively part and parcel of burly wingers and defensemen. His hit-and-run style angers the opposition but as Robbie says, "I don't mind big guys trying to run me, but by the time the defenseman gets where I am, most of the time I'm gone."

So to the Wily Coyote's of the hockey world, Ftorek just scores his goals, sets up plays, and bugs the hell out of his opponents.

Beep-Beep. Robbie Ftorek is the ultimate Roadrunner.

And tonight, the smallest star.

156

LEST STAR ★ ★ ★

Ftorek jaws with referee Ron Ego in recent game against the New England Whalers.

While serving time in the penalty box, Ftorek contemplates his infraction.

One of the top scorers in the WHA, Ftorek speeds down the ice in recent Roadrunners game.

SOBCHUKS GIVE STING TO

DENNIS SOBCHUK

Stingers Cincinnati

GENE SOBCHUK

In late May, Dennis and Gene Sobchuk arrived in Cincinnati, having driven for 24 straight hours from their parents home in Lang, Saskatchewan. At the time, they came to the Queen City mainly to find a home to live in when they moved permanently in September. When asked why they drove for a day and night without stopping, they glanced at each other and sheepish grins spread over both their faces. It was then suggested that maybe they left Lang for a reason, perhaps because it was seeding time for farmers, and indeed their father is a farmer.

"To tell you the truth," said Gene, "there really isn't that much work to do. Actually, the farmer's busiest season is in the fall, just about the time the Stinger training camp opened here."

"Gene is right," said Dennis. "We grew up working on the farm, and we've always helped our father when we could. Of course, when we started playing junior hockey, that naturally put a damper on our farm chores, although we always helped when we could. Camp did not open until the last week of September, so we were able to help Dad out quite a bit."

Now that they are here in Cincinnati to "finally play hockey for the Stingers" they both are happy and content, with good reason to be so. You see, Dennis and Gene have belonged to the Cincinnati Hockey Club Corporation for so long, they even beat the team nickname by *nine months*. They signed hours apart in June of 1973.

"I signed with Cincinnati when I was 19," relates Dennis. "So after I signed, I knew that I still had one more season of hockey in Regina, and as things turned out, it was a great year 'cause we ended up winning the Memorial Cup."

"I was in the same situation," said Gene, "and I was aware that the Stingers wouldn't begin play until the new Riverfront Coliseum was completed, and that turned out to be this year."

Last season both Dennis and Gene were loaned by the Stingers to the Phoenix Roadrunners, and although Gene subsequently ended up playing the majority of the season in Tulsa of the A.H.L., Dennis scored 32 goals and added 45 assists in helping the Roadrunners to a play-off berth.

While talking with the two brothers, it's not hard for one's mind to drift back to the days when the Mahavolich Brothers played together for the Montreal Canadians. Both Frank and Pete were very at ease, laughing, joking, and fielding every question with a sly grin, especially Peter. This is true also of this Brother act, and honestly, it isn't hard to tell why. They both love hockey, and seem to sense the potential of being great in their profession. Dennis pointed out that "it has always been my dream to play with Gene, and it appears that this dream will become a reality here in Cincinnati."

They both concur that "now it is up to us to stay together. We have been given the opportunity to fulfill an ambition of ours, and now we have to produce. It's as simple as that."

There have been very few successful brother acts in hockey — most recently would be the Howes with Houston, but it seems that there is an intangible quality about situations such as this, a quality that is tough to put your finger on, and yet, it is an admirable quality. They are on the same team, they are brothers, but also, they are friends, sincere friends and this commands respect.

As Dennis looked back for a moment to Lang, Saskatchewan, he spoke of a town with a population of 120 people, and as he did, Gene smiled. "You know," said Dennis, "everyone in Lang said that we'd have trouble adjusting to a big city, but it's been no problem at all. And another thing, everybody, and I mean everybody, asks us about the Stingers, the new Coliseum, and the city in general. I think they are really interested, you know. Ever since I can remember our family has been friends with everyone else in Lang and now they are all Stinger followers."

Judging from not only the companionship and the humbleness exhibited by the two Sobchuks, but also their sincerity, it is not too difficult to understand why the people in Lang have adopted the Stingers as their team.

CENTER DENNIS SOBCHUK: "HOW YA GONNA KEEP HIM DOWN ON THE FARM?"

The Phoenix Roadrunners can thank Gene Sobchuk — and the dilatory pace of building construction in Cincinnati — for the fact that they have the services of Dennis Sobchuk, one of the most promising young players in the game. The story goes like this: In a celebrated case, the Cincinnati Stingers, a WHA expansion team, drafted and signed Dennis while he still had a year of junior eligibility remaining. But the slow pace of construction on Cincinnati's new Coliseum forced the Stingers to postpone their advent in the league until 1975-76, and Sobchuk was told to pick a team on which to play this season. His brother Gene, a frequent visitor to Phoenix last year while playing with Seattle in the Western League, asserted there was no better place to spend a winter than Arizona, and Dennis forthwith declared for the Roadrunners.

Dennis' debut in the major leagues of hockey represents about as radical a change of environment as could be possible for a youngster. He hails from Lang, Saskatchewan, a town of 200 souls set in the vast prairies of western Canada. The Sobchuk family owns a wheat farm there and, outside of the farm work, Dennis recalls, there wasn't much to do besides play hockey.

A late bloomer, Dennis didn't make much of a splash until he was about 17 years old. He had college scholarship offers from Notre Dame and North Dakota, but went instead to a training camp for the Regina Pats, the junior team representing the capital city of Saskatchewan, about 40 miles north of Lang. "My brother, Gene, was doing real well for Regina," Dennis remembers, "and I think they invited me just to keep the family happy. But I surprised them by making the team and they never did get rid

of me." Rid of him, indeed! With Dennis developing rapidly and setting the pace last year, the Pats captured the Memorial Cup, emblematic of Canadian junior-hockey supremacy.

Dennis is a talkative youngster, easy-going and friendly. A lean 175 pounds, he feels he will add more weight to his 6-2 frame as time goes on, feeling that he can go as high as 190 pounds. For the nonce, he's a thin, wiry type, deceptively strong, extraordinarily fast, and resistant to injuries despite his slender build.

Has the money he got for signing with Cincinnati (an estimated $1.75 million over ten years) changed life for him and his family? Not really, says Dennis. "I bought them a car, and I suppose we're all secure for life now, but you don't all of a sudden go out and start throwing money around like a member of the Jet Set. My Dad is doing some scouting for Cincinnati, but it's a job he deserves and can do very well at. You really can never do enough for your parents, especially mine. My Dad used to drive Gene and me 60 miles three times a week to play hockey in Weyburn. He and my Mom are great parents in every way."

Dennis has already settled into the Arizona life style and professes to enjoy it. He spends his spare time swimming, playing tennis and golf, and relaxing to stereo music. As to the ladies, there are many of them who'd like to put their brand on him, but he claims there's nothing real serious at the moment. The problems of a rookie in hockey's major leagues demand his full attention at the moment.

"When you're breaking in," Sobchuk says, "you've got a lot on your mind. And when you've gotten a big contract to sign, people expect fabulous accomplishment from you right off the bat, unfair as that may be. I've taken the attitude that you

just have to do the best you can. And believe me, it doesn't make any difference to me that I'm not in Cincinnati yet. You should always try your hardest, no matter where you are, and I want to produce for the Roadrunners. The people and the management there have been great to me, and I don't want to let them down. And I have a feeling I'm going to miss Phoenix next year when I have to leave."

There is little question that Phoenix is going to miss him too.

Dennis Sobchuk

A MID-SEASON REWARD THAT IS RICHLY DESERVED

By JOHN HEWIG

This year the Annual WHA All-Star game will be held in Hartford's Civic Center, home of the New England Whalers. Representing the Stingers will be no less than five players, two defensemen and three forwards.

I think that it is fitting that we have a closer look at the five Stingers that will compete in the All-Star Classic this year.

DEFENSEMAN RON PLUMB. Plumb has been a steady blueliner for Coach Slater since the beginning of the franchise a year and half ago. He was overlooked last year, not only in the nominations, but also in the selections made by the Aeros Coach, Bill Dineen. It was an oversight that really was not understandable. Coaches and players throughout the league would tell you that "Plumber" is one of the best around, in any league, period.

This year Plumb received more votes than any other defensemen in the entire league, which seems to indicate that writers and media are beginning to see the value of Ron as a defenseman.

"Let's face it" commented Stinger Director of Player Personnel Jerry Rafter, "He's not flashy. Some guys are very flambouyant, and they are noticed more than others.

"Plumb hasn't done anything different this year than he did last, but I think last season, it was kinda an after the fact realization. In the second part of the year, the writers who had not voted for Ron were saying to themselves 'hey, why didn't I vote for him?'

"This year they made sure that they did.

"It's great to see him recognized as an All-Star" continued Rafter, and as an after thought, he also offered that "I'm just glad that he's on our side when it counts."

CENTER RICH LEDUC, Leduc, to date has been the most productive player on the Stingers scoring parade. In thirty-four games, Richie has 18 goals and 30 assists, for 48 points and fifth in league scoring. He was selected on the second team by the media, behind Quebec's Serge Bernier.

The day before the selections were announced, I sat with Richie in the Bee-hive Club, and over lunch we discussed the selections, or at least we discussed who we thought would be selected.

"There are some really good centers in the WHA," Leduc had said, "and I'd like to be considered one of them."

"No, I don't think that I'd be disappointed if I didn't make it, but I'd consider it an honor if I was."

Consider yourself honored, Richie.

"He deserves being picked" commented captain Rick Dudley when he was told of the appointment. "When I played with him, it was good because I knew if I threw him the puck from the corner, something would happen. He makes things happen. I also like a center who back-checks, who is willing to come back and try and take it away from the other team. Richie does that well. He's an honest hockey player, one with desire and the willingness to sacrifice."

Leduc is second highest on the Stingers with a +18 rating. Highest is Ron Plumb at +24. This statistic, though not generally released to the public, is a very vital one. It indicates how many more goals, a player is on the ice when his team scores, as opposed to when the other team scores, when both sides are at equal strength.

Leduc joined the Stingers this year after playing with Cleveland for the last two seasons. There he had 34 and 36 goals respectively, but he was somehow overlooked in the All-Star selections.

This year both he and Plumb probably have the same feeling. It's nice to know that you are appreciated.

Although these two were the only Stingers actually selected by the media, the two Coaches who guide the players in the Annual Classic also pick other players to compete. Because only the first two teams are selected, other players are needed to fill out both squads.

Racer Coach Jacques Demers had six spots to complete the 18 man roster and THREE of them are from the Stingers.

That totals to five out of the 18 spots, which is very complimentary to Rafter, Head Scout Flo Potvin, and Western Scouting supervisor Jim Bazdell. Here they are.

DEFENSEMAN JOHN HUGHES, Nicknamed "Captain Crunch" by the Voice of the Stingers Andy MacWilliams, Hughes is now in his third season of Major League Hockey, having spent the first year in Phoenix because the Stingers weren't ready to step on the ice yet.

Last year John had been hampered by a series of injuries, including a slow recovery from a knee operation that was

Dennis Sobchuk was selected by Racer Coach Jacques Demers to play in the All-Star Classic, January 18th in Hartford.

KEN BLOCK

DEFENSIVE DEFENSEMAN

The Racers acquired 30-year-old defenseman Ken Block from the San Diego Mariners in exchange for Jim Hargreaves.

Block, who is 5-foot-10 and weighs 185 pounds, has been a pro for 9½ years and a WHA performer for the past 2½. In fact he has missed only four games of WHA action since joining the New York Raiders (now the San Diego Mariners) in 1972 for that inaugural season—all four absences from the lineup occurred during the 1973-74 campaign.

Highly regarded as a "defensive defenseman," Ken also has acceptable offensive credentials to offer as evidenced by the 58 and 46 points credited to his record in the previous two seasons. This year in 61 outings he has helped set up 23 goals and chipped in a power play goal of his own for 24 points. He was named to the WHA All-Star squad two years ago.

"I am very familiar with Ken Block's ability as a hockey player and know he can be a big help to us," stated Browitt. "Ken has a great shot and he can shoot on net. A lot of players can shoot, but not all of them can put it where it counts. Kenny is a good point man and will add to our power play. His presence on the ice will also tighten up our play in the defensive zone."

Born in Steinbach, Manitoba, Block played his amateur hockey in the Manitoba Junior League with the Flin Flon Bombers before becoming a member of the New York Rangers (NHL) organization in 1964. He spent that first season in the Rangers system playing for the New York Rovers of the Eastern Hockey League and the suc- ceeding two seasons with minor league affiliates in the Central, American and Western Hockey Leagues as a pro.

In June, 1967 Ken was drafted from the Rangers by the Los Angeles Kings in the NHL Expan- sion Draft and immediately traded to the Toronto Maple Leafs for Leonard "Red" Kelly veteran NHL star. He remained in the Leafs system until signing with the New York Raiders of the newly-formed World Hockey Association in 1972.

50 Goal Scorers

Bobby Hull

Mike Walton

Danny Lawson

For the seventh time Robert Marvin Hull surpassed the magic 50 goal mark in regular season play. Despite a mild case of ulcers and the added duties of playing coach, the Golden Jet scored 53 goals while appearing in 75 games. It seems like only yesterday when Bobby first scored 50 in the 1961/62 season while a member of the Chicago Black Hawks. In the 1968/69 season with Chicago in 74 games Bobby scored a then league record 58 goals. Everyone expects that Bobby Hull will naturally score goals and also exceed the 50 goal mark each season. After the first 50-goal season and six more to boot, you would have to say that Hull is "doing what comes naturally."

Mike Walton had what one would describe as a sensational debut in the W.H.A. Appearing in all 78 league games with the Minnesota Fighting Saints, Mike scored a league high 57 goals and 60 assists to win the W.H.A. individual scoring title over runner-up Andre Lacroix with a comfortable six point margin. Mike failed to reach the established league record of 61 goals in one season held by Vancouver Blazer Danny Lawson and set in the 1972/73 season. Mike Walton is now firmly established as one of the top centre icemen in the W.H.A. and with his free-wheeling skating style no one will be surprised if he surpasses last season's 57 goals.

We waited and waited for Danny Lawson last season to reach the 50 goal mark. Maybe you can remember it was the last Blazers' regular season home game when Danny finally hit the 50 goal mark. But hockey fans sometimes have short memories for it was in the inaugural season of the W.H.A. when the same Mr. Lawson set the league record of 61 goals, and as of the close of last season not one player in the league, in fact the two other players listed on this page, could reach Lawson's record either with a tie or a tie breaker. So with two consecutive 50 goal seasons under his belt, Danny Lawson has five more to go to catch the illustrious Mr. Hull.

WHA HALL OF FAME

The Masked Crusader

Gerry Cheevers is a man of many talents—not least among them, stopping pucks. By Stan McAlister

Some athletes are doomed to notoriety, the bastard brother of fame. Remember Roberto de Vincenzo? If you do, it's probably not as a fine golfer (which he was), but as the man who signed an erroneous scorecard, thereby defaulting the Masters. Garo Yepremian is the man whose first passing attempt almost cost Miami the Super Bowl two years ago. In the 1941 World Series, Dodgers catcher Mickey Owens dropped a third strike—and cost his team the series. Jim Marshall, a former Minnesota Vikings player, Fred Merkle of the old New York Giants, Harvey Wyley of the Calgary Stampeders: all are remembered because of incidents or circumstances that have overshadowed otherwise admirable careers.

There's a little of that aura about Gerry Cheevers. Many people know of him, and recall him, for reasons that have little to do with what he does best—play goal, presently for the Cleveland Crusaders. Example: I ask a secretary if she knows who Gerry Cheevers is. Answer: the goalie who wears that ugly, marked-up mask.

The white fibreglass of Cheevers' mask is emblazoned with black Magic Marker stitches, a dramatization of what would have happened to his face had it been unprotected. "That started in practice one day," says Cheevers, who, by his own admission, is not the most diligent or effective practice goalie. "I was stopping shots and not looking too hot. The puck hit me in the mask and Frosty Forristall, our assistant trainer at the time, had to carry me off." The mask had only a tiny nick in it. Cheevers felt almost embarrassed by the apparent innocuity of the shot, so he had Forristall mark 10 stitches on the mask. Over the next few years the mask was embellished each time Cheevers was hit in the face; there are now well over 100 stitches on it.

Some people remember Cheevers for the less fortunate incidents in his goaltending career. You may have heard the story of Boston's loss to Chicago in 1966, Cheevers' rookie year in the NHL. The loss fell on the day after the 25th anniversary of Pearl Harbour, with which the game shared certain characteristics. The Bruins also got bombed, 10-2. After the

game, Boston general manager Hap Emms demanded of Cheevers: "What happened out there?" The reply was instant: "Roses are red, violets are blue, they got 10 goals, we only got two."

Which brings us to Cheevers' sense of humour—another of his memorable attributes. Where to begin? Perhaps at Bobby Orr's restaurant, The Branding Iron, on New Year's Eve a few years back. Cheevers suddenly disappeared through a revolving door into the kitchen—and appeared a moment later dressed as a busboy. He vanished again, and reappeared dressed as a waitress. Presto: he whipped into the kitchen once more, and returned dressed as the chef.

The stories about Cheevers and Mike Walton have reached the stature of legend. The two were roommates while with the Bruins, and about as compatible as Felix and Oscar on The Odd Couple. Walton is compulsively neat, and Cheevers quite the opposite. Says Phil Esposito, "Gerry used to drive Mike nuts." Once, Cheevers had Walton lie down on the floor of an airplane while he, Cheevers, asked him

about his childhood and took notes. This was shortly after Walton's move from Toronto to Boston, and his well-publicized visits to a psychiatrist. All the passengers were stunned—all except the other Bruins, that is: they roared.

Another of Cheevers' distinctions is his mania for useless information. He's a trivia freak, a devoted watcher of quiz and game shows, and he has an extensive repertoire of questions whose answers don't matter much. Examples: When General Motors took the Indian head trademark off its Pontiacs, what was the last part of the car it was removed from? (the high beam indicator). What actress has won the most Academy Awards? (Katharine Hepburn). Which players were involved in the seven-player trade between Los Angeles and Philadelphia two years ago? (Jean Potvin, Ed Joyal, Serge Bernier, Jim Johnson, Bill Flett, Bill Lesuk, Ross Lonsberry). Incidentally, Cheevers' all-time favorite quiz show is Jeopardy.

Yet another well-known point about him is that he negotiated his own seven-year contract with Cleveland. Bob Woolf, the Boston lawyer, had handled previous contract dealings, but, says Cheevers, "This time I didn't think I needed anyone with me. At first I thought of 999 reasons why I should stay in Boston, then I thought of 999 reasons why I should jump." The deciding factor, no doubt, was his success as a negotiator; his contract calls for roughly $1 million over the seven years. That's about twice as much as the Bruins were willing to spend to keep him in a Boston uniform.

He took a chance on the new league and doesn't regret having done so. He, his wife Elizabeth and their three children (two boys and a girl) bought a house in Rocky River, a residential area in the west end of Cleveland. The kids have made the adjustment without difficulty, and everyone's happy. Cheevers doesn't mind the differences between the two leagues ("There's bad things here, but the good outweighs the bad").

During the summer, Cheevers indulges a passion he's had for years: horses. His stable consists of seven thoroughbreds; they race mostly in Maryland. Cheevers

started going to the track when he was 17, and worked (at jobs ranging from mutuels clerk to public relations man) for the Ontario Jockey Club for eight years. He is, it seems, anything but a dilettante. He usually has *The Racing Form* with him, and he knows how to read it. "You nearly always make money when you go to the track with him," says Derek Sanderson. When his playing days are over, Cheevers hopes to pursue his interest in horses fulltime. The prospect of working at the coaching or executive level of hockey holds no appeal.

There are, in short, many facets to the man. But to dwell too long on the periph-eral ones is to risk overlooking the central one. Gerry Cheevers, first and foremost, is a goaltender—and a very good one. Many hockey men consider him among the finest clutch players in the game, and his record supports that view. Cheevers is one of the few major league goalies whose playoff average is better than his regular season mark. When Boston won the Stanley Cup three years ago (his last season in the NHL), he posted two shut-outs in eight playoff matches—the same number he recorded in 41 league games. In the 1969 playoffs he had a remarkable 1.68 average for nine games, with three shutouts. His last season with the Bruins was his best; his record for the year was 27-5-8, by far the best in the NHL. He set a record by appearing in 32 straight games without a loss.

Statistics, however, don't tell the whole story. Cheevers is an intensely competitive goaltender. The goals-against average isn't the important thing: winning is. "He didn't care if we won 9-7," says Phil Esposito, "as long as we won. He insisted an average didn't matter. I found out he was one of the all-time greats when it came down to the money." Sanderson concurs: "He'll win 1-0 or 10-9, but he'll win."

He's carried on in the WHA where he

left off with Boston. In his first year with Cleveland he logged a wearying 3,144 minutes during the regular season and, despite a defense that wasn't exactly impenetrable, had a goal-against average of 2.83—lowest in the WHA. He led the league in shutouts, with five. Without question he was the one man most responsible for Cleveland's strong second-place finish in the East Division. During the playoffs, he led the Crusaders to a four-game sweep over Philadelphia; he played in all four games and allowed a total of six goals. Cleveland was finally knocked out by WHA champion New England, but the team fell despite a fine performance in goal.

Last year he maintained his form, playing 3,562 minutes, finishing with a 3.03 goals-against average and four shut-outs. Only Don McLeod had a better average. The Toros knocked off the Crusaders in the first round of the playoffs, but again, Cheevers was all that stood between a loss and a rout. When Team Canada coach Billy Harris was picking his club, Cheevers was the logical choice in goal. And against the Russians, of course, he played brilliantly.

Of the Toros, he says, "They're good. They can play a tight, defensive, checking game. With the players they've got this year, they have to be very strong. They're obviously well coached, and they have a lot of outstanding young players."

But let's not get started on Gerry Cheevers the hockey analyst, even if he is a perceptive one. There are already enough sides to him, enough angles and slants. Call him what you like—clown, trivia freak, horse fan, financial success—but don't forget one basic fact. Cheevers is now among the very finest goaltenders in hockey. If you overlook that, if you fail to appreciate the physical skills and competitive attitude that combine so superbly in him, you're doing the man an injustice.

Penalty Killing

Lesuk and Guindon Two of the Best

By SUSAN NICOL

Penalty killing is a pressure situation. The players who make up a penalty killing unit can respond when the odds are against them. The Winnipeg Jets, who have vaulted into first place in the WHA, aren't known for racking up penalties, but they certainly can handle them when the need arises.

Coach Larry Hillman of the Jets is an ex-defenceman. He thinks defensively and picks the players for his penalty-killing units accordingly.

"Penalty-killing requires very good positional players," he says. "Naturally, on this hockey club, Ulf and Anders are two of the best in the business. They're puck-control artists and good positional players.

"After them, I go with Bill Lesuk and Bobby Guindon. They're two wingers who play exceptionally well together and they have the hustle to go into the other end. They also have the determination to get back into play.

"They play their positions well in their own end. I count on them because they're gung-ho type individuals."

There are two styles of penalty-killing. One way is to artfully control the puck so that the opposition can not gain possession of it. The other is to consistently dump it down the ice.

Coach Hillman doesn't have preference as long as both styles are performed well.

"If it's Ulf Nilsson and Anders Hedberg who are out there, you'll see them control the puck a lot more than anyone else. I don't mind Lesuk and Guindon trying to

hang on to it, as long as they've cleaned up their own end. If they're out at centre ice and the puck is taken off them, the defencemen can back them up.

"If they're trying to stickhandle it in our end, I'd rather see Lesuk or Guindon shoot it down the ice, then hustle up and stop the opposition coming out of their end."

When the penalty is about to expire, the third man of the forward line joins his mates until the play is stopped and the whole unit is relieved.

The Jets penalty killing units are so aggressive, they've chalked up a number of short-handed goals.

The next consideration, of course is picking the right defencemen.

"I usually go with Teddy Green and Barry Long or Thommie Bergman," Larry explains. "I use Green on the right side when the face-off is in our corner. If the centreman draws the puck to Teddy, he has the opportunity to use his forehand to ice the puck if he has to."

"Sometimes I use Lars-Erik Sjoberg and

continued on next page

166

"GUEST SHOT"

Shmyr Tactics

By RICK BOULTON

He has sold no razor blades on TV, does not appear in ads with a Stanley Surform planer to smooth the handle of his hockey stick, is not the man in the Riviera slacks, owns no hockey schools and does not relieve his aches and pains with Antiphlogistine Rub A-535. He is, however, a first-team all-star, and has captained his team to the playoffs for two consecutive seasons. The biggest accolade he received before the Canada-USSR series came from a Cleveland Crusaders' publicity man: "He leads by quiet example."

Paul Shmyr's problem is both geographical and personal: he plays in Cleveland, a fairly anonymous place as hockey cities go, and he has a genuine talent for remaining inconspicuous. When I asked for some background stories on Shmyr, the PR man replied, "There aren't any. The papers didn't do any stories on him last year." Adds Shmyr: "I don't go around trying to impress the newspaper guys."

Yet Shmyr is a very capable, aggressive and colorful player. He had 169 penalty minutes two seasons ago and another 165 last year, and though he doesn't intimidate, he does believe in "clearing all opponents from in front of the net." With his blonde Beatle haircut, ski-jump nose and leonine appearance, he roams the ice head up — a solid 5-foot-11, 185-pound package of endless arms and legs.

On offense, he bangs down the ice with elan, determination and skill; he barrels into the corners without fear and sometimes gets a chance to swat at the puck from in close. In 1973-74, Shmyr (pronounced "smear") scored 13 goals (a career high) and added 31 assists to lead the Cleveland defensemen in scoring.

Perhaps his most valuable contribution in his consistency; he does his job very well, game after game. He is, a teammate says, "very steady." Shmyr, at age 28, has 2½ seasons of NHL experience behind him, with Chicago and California, as well as pro stops in Fort Wayne, Dallas and pre-expansion Vancouver. He has been team captain since his arrival in Cleveland, and is one of only two Crusaders to have played in all 78 regular-season games last year (the other was Grant Erickson). Last year, in balloting for the Dennis A. Murphy Trophy (as the WHA's best defenseman), he was second to Pat Stapleton; the season before he was runnerup to J. C. Tremblay. Yet Shmyr's fortunes, and those of the Crusaders, could never be described as spectacular.

Last year, Cleveland wound up 37-32-9 and, like the Toros, did not clinch a playoff spot until the last weekend of the season. Two years ago the Crusaders were 43-32-3. Shmyr's poise and quiet leadership all season undoubtedly had a lot to do with the team's success, but mostly he is as invisible as a poltergeist. While others complain loud and long about contracts, Shmyr, at last season's half-way point, quietly signed a five-year deal "that is not spectacular," he says, "but appreciates the fact that I'm around. I'd hate to think that my salary depended on my press clippings. Sure, I read the papers, and sometimes I wonder if I was at the game at all. But the point is, that doesn't bother me. I have security and this club appreciates me. All I want really is the respect of my teammates."

He has that, and he has a nice, easy, not-too-serious outlook on his life. "I don't know what I do wrong, what it is that makes me invisible," he says, tongue firmly in cheek. "I keep reading about all these other young guys who haven't made all-star yet. Maybe it's because I have one gray hair. I'll tell you this. I do remember one write-up I had years ago and it was pretty good. I enjoyed it."

Shmyr has discovered that sportswriters are usually in search of an angle. The Young Lion is a good angle: Cleveland defenseman Tom Edur is a young lion. He signed a large contract to turn professional before last season, at 18, is good-looking and well-spoken and, according to one writer, "has the world as his oyster." Another good angle is The Old Lion. Larry ("The Coach Wants to See You") Hillman is an old lion. He has been traded more times than anybody, knows the ropes and speaks from experience.

Shmyr, fortunately or unfortunately, misses on both counts. His efforts on behalf of Team Canada have made his name considerably better known than it used to be, but he still doesn't have the problems of, say, Bobby Hull. No media men dogging his steps. No autographs to sign. No crowds to fight. Just a nice long-term contract and unanimous appreciation from his teammates.

Paul Shmyr

Lesuk and Guindon continued

Dave Dunn as defence partners or Dunn and Thommie Bergman . . . depending on whether Green or Long have had their shifts. But my two best, I'd have to say, are Long and Green."

Face-offs are critical during a penalty. A coach has to pick his players and their positions carefully.

"Face-offs are very important in your end. In those cases I won't use Lesuk or Guindon because they're not natural centremen. I'll throw Peter Sullivan out to take the face-off if it's in the right-hand side of the goalie.

"If it's on the left-hand side, I'll use Lynn Powis. Again, this is only if Ulf and Anders are not available because they have just finished killing the penalty or have just finished a shift."

"Bobby Guindon has a few short-handed goals to his credit," Larry explains, "as well as Anders. It's just because of their determination to go both ways as hard as they can."

How important are penalty-killing units to a hockey club?

"I think it's a proven fact that if you're adequate at killing penalties and have a good power play, then you're going to win games come play-off time."

167

THE CINCINNATI KIDS

(Left to right) Claude "The Rocket" Larose, Blaine Stoughton and Dennis Sobchuk are 3 of Slater's Cincinnati Kids. They are shown here discussing strategy after a recent Stinger practice.

The Cincinnati Kids. That's what they are becoming known as in circles around the Queen City these days. It seems to be a very appropriate name for these high-flying, free-wheeling 'bandits' that call beautiful Riverfront Coliseum their home. The Coliseum sits magestically on the banks of the legendary Ohio River, and this also fits into the story quite well.

If you were to check with the WHA League Offices in Hartford they would tell you that the official name of this team is the Cincinnati Stingers Hockey Club Corporation, and that it came into being in March of 1973. That's officially.

Unofficially they are indeed the Cincinnati Kids. The team has an average age of just over 23; the youngest in Major League Hockey. On the Ice, they are led by firery, flambouyant, supersitious Head Coach Terry Slater, a man who loves his mother dearly, but when she left after a two week visit, he openly admitted that he was happy that she "got back to Canada safely." The reason? Let Slater explain it.

"She is a dear lady, and it's nothing personal, but the day she arrived, we lost to Birmingham here 6-2. She stayed for two weeks and we ended up losing seven straight. The day of the Birmingham game, we had quite a bit of snow and I wasn't sure that she'd be able to get her flight out. It scared me. But by four o'clock that afternoon she was safe in Canada, so everything was alright. We

won 7-1."

Slater's Kids have brought a new dimension into the city of Cincinnati, a dimension that has been lacking in sports teams for some time now in the Queen City. They are anything but conservative, both on and off the ice. As a unit, they thrill in the sensational, witnessed by individual celebrations after scoring a goal.

Take for example rookie right winger Dennis Abgrall. Upon scoring he immediately faces the net, reverses his stick and 'shoots the net' machine-gun style, reminicent of the old days of the roaring twenties and the day-light attacks that were so very common of that decade.

Twenty year old Rookie Peter Marsh has by-passed the traditional arm raising in favor of immitating 'The Fonz's "aayyyy" when he scores, and former Toronto Maple Leaf Blaine Stoughton simply twirls his stick like a baton and places both his hands on his hips and skates back to center ice.

Collectively, they applaud each other. Fifty years ago a mob was thought of as a group of hoods that broke the law. Nowadays, a mob on Coliseum Ice occurs everytime a Stinger scores, with players leaving the bench to congratulate the goal scorer. It is a peaceful mob, one that exemplifies the unity of the team.

"We are a young team" stated Dennis Sobchuk, who by the way, signed with the Stingers in '73, even before Cincin-

nati had decided upon the team nickname, "and our youth reflects the enthusiasm that we show on the ice."

"They say we gamble a lot (on the ice) and I guess that we do. We aren't yet to the point of realizing that we sometimes should sit on a one or two goal lead in the third period, instead of trying to make it a three goal lead. Sometimes our gambling pays off, sometimes it doesn't."

"Terry doesn't like it too much when it doesn't pay off," he added with a smile, "but we're learning."

This year Slater has used former Michigan Tech star Billy Steele mainly as a penalty killer, although in certain games Steele has a regular shift.

"He's definitely an asset to our club" remarked Slater recently.

"If one of my regulars is going a little flat, I'm not hesitant at all to throw Billy in. Mainly, though, I like to keep him fresh so he can give it all he's got when we are short-handed."

Steele is a member of Terry's 'Killer Bees', along with Dennis Sobchuk. These two, as forwards, almost exclusively take the responsibility of thwarting the opposition when they have a Power Play, and to date they have been very successful.

"One of the weak points we had last year was killing penalties," continued Slater, "but this year we have done much better. I think right now we are one of the better teams in the league at holding off the other team when we are a man short. San Diego does an excellent job, but after them, I'd say we are as good as anyone else."

Rookie goaltender Norm LaPointe also figures into the rambunctious theme of the Cincinnati Kids. He's the one who has been doing the stealing, more accurately, the down right robbing. His goals against average is one of the best in the league, and Slater attributes the teams success in wins over Winnipeg and Quebec to the outstanding job that Norm LaPointe has done for him in the early going of those games.

"No question about it," explained the coach, "If Normie hadn't come up big in the early going against Winnipeg up there, we'd have been out of it by the time we started going."

LaPointe turned aside 35 Jets shots in that game (13 in the first period) and Cincinnati went on to win 4-2.

In Quebec on Oct. 17th, Cincinnati scored three unanswered goals in the last two periods to win 5-2 over the Nordiques.

"Norm stopped two breakaways in the middle period when we were tied with them, and that was the turning point," said Slater.

LaPointe also stopped 11 more shots in that period, and a total of 25 in the game.

Then, in mid December, the rookie netminder who finished his junior career with Three Rivers of the QMJHL, put together back to back shutouts on Coliseum Ice to match a league record. He stopped Phoenix 8-0 on December 12th and then three days later he whitewashed Minnesota 5-0.

Team Captain Rick Dudley is one of the youngest captains in Major League hockey, but it is an honor that he has earned hardly.

At twenty-seven, Dudley has gone from being a 'goon' on a minor league team to an inspirational leader with the '74-'75 Stanley Cup Finalists, the Buffalo Sabres. After that year he signed with the Stingers and led all team-mates in scoring last year, with 43 goals and 38 assists for 81 points.

He's been around, and his experience is rubbing off on the younger kids.

"If you want to learn by example" smiled Stinger 21 year old left winger Claude Larose, "then you watch Duds. His desire and determination is unbelievable.

Twenty-five year old center Richie Leduc echoed Larose's feelings not long ago.

"Last year when I was with Cleveland, I held an awful lot of admiration for Dudley," he says.

"Rick reinforced my thinking about what a big factor determination can play in this game.

Rounding out these Gambling Kids from the Queen City, you can't overlook guys like steady defenseman Ron Plumb, (who received more votes for the mid-season All-Star Classic than any other blueliner in the league) John 'Captain Crunch' Hughes (given the nicknamed by Andy MacWilliams, the talented Voice of the Stingers, because of Hughes devastating body checks that he delivers just about as often as bartender 'Bago' serves a drink in the luxurious Beehive Club after another Stinger home ice win) rookies Greg Carroll, (another top draft choice signed by Cincinnati, Carroll had 111 assists and 60 goals for Medicine Hat last year.) Jamie Hislop (recently recalled from Hampton of the Southern League, Hislop scored three goals and added four assists in his first two games he played with Cincinnati on a regular shift . . . former All-American at the University of New Hampshire) and defenseman Barry Melrose, who is richly ladden with talent and after spending time in the AHL with Springfield, he seems ready to step in and perform steadily for Slater.

Finally, there is the spacious Coliseum. Within a hard slapshot of the Ohio River, this $20,000,000 structure that was completed in August of '75 is the last piece that fits ever so neatly into Cincinnati Kids' puzzle.

It is very fitting that the Coliseum sits on the banks of the Ohio, because it is these same river banks that in the mid 1800's saw so much Riverboat Gambling that delivering machinery, textiles and other goods to Cincinnati became secondary in the minds of the Riverboat captains and their crews. It was gambling first, and if you had time, or had lost all your money, you helped with the loading and unloading.

Perhaps when the Stingers come onto Coliseum Ice, the organist should be playing 'Rambling, Gambling Man' instead of 'The Sting.' ✐

Rookie Dennis Abgrall "guns down" the opposition.

Dennis Abgrall: Looking To The Future

As the phone in Indianapolis was ringing, I hoped in my mind that I wasn't going to wake him up. "Dennis, did I wake you up?"

"Yeah, but it's O.K. What can I do for you?"

"Well, I'd like to talk with you a bit because I'm writing a story for the program next Wednesday."

"Sure, what would you like to know?"

At twenty three, Abgrall is a Rookie with the Cincinnati Stingers, having joined them in the off season after spending three years in the Los Angeles Kings organization.

As a right winger who was primarily brought to the Queen City to shore up a lack of defensive hockey that was found on the right side last year, Dennis has proven to be more than just a fine back-checker, which he certainly is. He has come up with some big goals for Slater in the early going this year. Overall, as of November 15th, Dennis had totalled 14 points on 8 goals and 6 assists. Of these fourteen points, 12 of them are listed in the weekly league release as "Important Points." An important point is one that is critical in a game. The first goal of a game is an important point, as is the tying goal, the winning goal, or an insurance goal. In baseball Abgrall would be the fiesty shortstop that hits .240 for an average but he always seems to be the one to get a hit with men on base. Because of his average, you don't notice him that much, that is, until he knocks another run in. In hockey, more specifically with the Stingers, it is Dennis Abgrall.

Take for example the third game of the season in San Diego. With little over three minutes left in regulation time, Abgrall fired a shot past Mariner goaltender Ken Lockett to tie the contest 7-7. The overtime period was scoreless. Two games later, in Indianapolis, Abgrall pounced on an rebound in front of the Racer net and rammed it home to even the score at five apiece. There were three minutes and thirty three seconds left in regulation time.

Two nights later in Minnesota Abgrall was at it again. With a little over five minutes left in the first period Dennis Sobchuk fed Abgrall a pass just inside the Fighting Saint blueline and the rookie right winger fired it home to give Cincinnati a 2-1 lead. Mid-way through the second period, Abgrall notched the Stingers' third goal of the evening, and the eventual winner, with assists going to Peter Marsh and Jacques Locas. It's goals like these that have helped Cincinnati to a share of first place in the Eastern Division of the tough WHA. It is goals

like these that will help keep them there.

* * * *

When Abgrall joined the Stingers in the summer of '76 he was actually in Flagstaff Arizona attending summer school to, as he puts it, "prepare myself for the future." He has been doing this for the past five summers, after the hockey season is over. The four previous summers he had been attending the University of Saskatchewan, and next year he plans to attend San Diego State. He is majoring in Secondary Education.

"In this game you know that you can't go on forever" explains Abgrall "and I want to be ready to step into the business world with a concrete education."

"There is so very much going on outside of hockey that, in a way, I feel I'm cheating myself if I don't explore things while I have a chance" continued Dennis.

"It's funny you know, I appreciate what hockey has done for me, and hopefully will do in the future, but it is a profession that requires odd hours and a different time schedule. I try to take advantage of that as much as possible by doing things during the day that maybe a person like you can't do." I didn't quite understand.

"Well, let me put it this way. As a hockey player, you are just dropped in a city, and you aren't really a resident of that city. I didn't know much about Cincinnati before I got here in September and so I've taken the time to get

to know it a little. Have you ever been to the Playhouse In The Park? I'm going tomorrow night when I get back home. I don't know, maybe it is just an escape from hockey, but I think I'll find it interesting."

When I first met Abgrall, I thought of him as a shy person. After having gotten to know him a little, I now think of him as a very pensive intelligent person. His views on life are interesting, 'food for thought' type views.

"Playing hockey in a city is kinda like taking picutres. I could be here for ten years or I could be traded tomorrow. That is one of the gambles of playing professional sports. Whenever it is that I leave Cincinnati, I want to be able to remember the city. It's only natural. That's why I say it is like taking pictures. I can recall a lot of things that I saw in Los Angeles when I was with the Kings, but now that I'm with Cincinnati, we don't go in there to play, so I can only remember those things mentally."

* * * * *

During the pre-season, the Stingers went into Quebec City to play the Nordiques. On the flight back, Abgrall was sitting by himself reading Oedipus Rex. Oedipus Rex? That's right, the play.

As I sat down next to him, he had just finished the book. I can remember in High School I was supposed to read it as an assignment, but somehow the thought bored me and I never really did get around to reading it. At the time it

Right winger Dennis Abgrall has a lot of "Important Points" for the Stingers this year.

170

intrigued me, because here was a guy that was reading a play for enjoyment. I had never thought of it that way. Asking Abgrall about it, he smiled jnd said that "I found that it isn't as good as I had heard it would be." He had hoped for more.

On the phone, I asked him about the book again. This time he laughed. "My sister gave it to me a while ago and it was on the top of the stack when we left for Quebec, so I took it with me. I just finished one that you might like. It's called "Murder In The Cathedral" by T. S. Elliot. If you get a chance to read it, you should, you'll like it." I promised him I would.

✵ ✵ ✵ ✵ ✵

The Dennis Abgrall that you see out on the ice tonight is Dennis Abgrall the hockey player. He skates up and down his wing, playing a close-checking game and waiting to spring on a mistake that an opponent might make. If it happens, chances are pretty good that he'll capitalize. Basically, Dennis is one of these hockey players that is 'unsung' if you will; he doesn't get as much publicity as a Rick Dudley or a Dennis Sobchuk because in truth, he's not as flashy. BUT, day in and day out, he'll perform steadily for Coach Slater, and he should be applauded for that.

Off the ice, Dennis is an individual that

Abgrall attends university in the off-season.

is pensive and aware, very aware. His interests are diversified and his mind is one that is preparing for the future, whether it comes in ten years or ten days, he'll be ready for it, because he feels that he has to be ready for it. As he puts it "I want to capitalize on the time that I have here." ℮

faceoff
official publication of the stingers

GORDIE HOWE, AEROS HERE IN FINAL REGULAR SEASON VISIT

The Houston Aeros just keep rolling along. Perhaps they're taking their cue from the acknowledged leader of the group, Gordie Howe, who himself has set new standards for continuity of quality, and longevity, and performance, etc.

The Aeros need just one more victory to break their own WHA record for most victories in a season (48) with plenty of time to accomplish that feat. And, with 96 points, they're within six of setting a new record in that department, a mark that they already own.

The Roadrunners, of course, will be trying their utmost to delay the Aeros' assault on the record book tonight. Not that they have anything personal against Bill Dineen's sextet; it's just that each home win is so important at this stage, with both Minnesota and San Diego breathing heatedly down their tail feathers.

Last time the Aeros came to the Coliseum they skated off with a lopsided 7-2 victory, thus edging into the series lead, three games to two. (The Runners had copped the first meeting here, 6-4, while the Aeros had won twice times on their home ice, 8-2 and 6-4, sandwiched around a 6-4 Phoenix triumph.)

Here's a great photo of hockey's greatest player, Gordie Howe. Howe is within striking distance tonight of reaching a plateau never before attained by a pro hockey player. He needs just three more points to reach 2000 regular season major league points. Howe plans to retire following this campaign (except for making an appearance at Houston's first home game next year, inaugurating their new arena). There will never be another like him.

Spunky former Roadrunner Andre Hinse gives and receives equally. Above left, Andy is wrapped up by Phoenix defenseman John Hughes. At right, Hinse administers a solid crosscheck, lifting Bobby Mowat off his skates and over on goalie Wayne Rutledge.

No. 9

Photo By Fred Anderson

Your mind windmills back to the last night of the 1975 schedule. As one old pro to another, 21-year old Marty Howe skated over to the gray, grizzled fellow in the Number 9 jersey and gave him a rough hug. "Helluva season, Gord," he said.

The fact that Number 9 had once claimed him as a tax deduction made the words no less touching. Not fresh or flip, just touching. He was really saying, what a swell way to go out, to end a career. It was as if Prince Charles had said to his mother, "Nice reign, Liz."

Then, Mark Howe arrived. For just an instant, Number 9 thought he detected a tear in the eye of his younger son. Naw. It was probably the reflection of the lights off the ice. "Great," he said. "Just great." And he laid his head on the shoulder of his dad.

An alert photographer snapped them like that, a fine moment frozen in time. A few feet away, Captain Ted Taylor was accepting an enormous bucket called the Avco World Trophy, living proof that the Houston Aeros had won the championship of at least half the hockey world.

Ted Taylor had been thinking about that trophy even before the final game against Quebec. In the locker room he approached Gordie Howe and said, "If we win that thing tonight, it'll be your last chance. Do you want to receive it?"

Gordie shook his head. "No," he said, "you're the captain."

That was characteristic of the Aeros, their success and their class. But trophies are like memories. You only have room for so many. If you treat it right, a photograph, like a good woman, is forever.

A week later, Gordie was telling a friend: "When I saw it in the papers the next day, it just choked me up. It seemed to sum up everything. Mark had his head on my shoulder, and I was looking at something straight ahead."

Back then, we all thought we knew what Gordie was looking at: retirement, and the presidency of the Aeros, under George Bolin's new ownership. It happened, but not quite the way we expected. Gordie didn't retire to that great swivel chair in the sky.

In fact, no club president in the history of professional sports ever made a move more certain to help his team, than Gordie Howe did when he put himself back in the uniform of the Houston Aeros for one more year.

And that is part of the greatness of Gordie Howe. He goes on. Now, a lot of men stay at their jobs for 27 years, and all they ever have to show for it is a watch presented by the plant foreman. But it's a nice quality, nonetheless. Gordie has entertained our fathers, and us, and now our sons. He is as close to a perpetual flame as the sport of ice hockey has ever seen.

At 48, Gordie can only be described as a golden oldie, still the star attraction and gray eminence of the only championship team this city has produced since the dark ages. As the first father-sons act in pro sports history, the Howes are still one of the best stories around.

By his presence, Gordie has taught us all a good deal about hockey, and about winning by intimidation (to lift the title of a current best seller.)

I am reminded of a story told by Smokey McLeod, the former Houston goalie, of a time when he was a rookie with the Detroit Red Wings, and Gordie Howe was in the sunset of his long National League career.

"We were playing Toronto," recalled Smokey, "and a rookie, Jim Dorey, took him into the boards, took him in heavy, gave him an elbow and all that. Hurt him a bit, knocked the wind out of him, but he never showed it. He came to the bench later and sat beside me. Gordie has a funny habit, if you've ever watched him. He never uses his glove to wipe off the sweat like the other fellows. He just leans over and wipes his forehead on the shoulder of whoever is sitting next to him. He did it to me, and I'm thinking to myself, 'what's this?'

"But Gordie's mind was still out on the ice. He said, 'You know, Smokey, these rookies never learn.' Oh, boy. The next shift he went into the corner with Dorey and I'm watching like a hawk, see, because I *knew* Gordie was going to show him he was the boss.

"The next thing I knew Gordie was skating away and Dorey is coming off the ice, and his forehead is cut and bleeding. I was watching and I never even saw it."

It is a tough school, pro hockey, but you learn in it, eventually.

But that's Gordie. He has had 27 years of bruises, of banging into bodies and boards that didn't give, of playing the game as well as anyone who ever played it. Yet it isn't easy to part with. He tried twice and couldn't. Now he says that this is the last one, for sure, cross his heart. And when the bruises are gone forever, the goals and the good times—and the photographs—will be there still.

HOWE A PLAYING PRESIDENT

That's what the World Hockey Association unveiled as it entered a historic fourth season on the major league sports scene. Pruning, it has been said, is the kindest thing you can do for a growing thing — and no one can deny that refinements have played an integral role in the WHA's young but spectacular existence.

New dynamic leadership, solidification, new arenas and an emerging crop of blossoming super stars, not to mention two new franchises — Cincinnati Stingers and Denver Spurs — offer irrefutable evidence of the league's ongoing progress.

It is with pardonable pride that Chairman of the Board and Chief Executive Officer Ben Hatskin points to an accelerated growth pattern of which he has been an instrumental force since the league's founding.

> **It was Hatskin, of course, who, as the original owner of the Winnipeg Jets, engineered the sports coup of the decade with his electrified signing of the incomparable Bobby Hull June 27, 1972.**

It was also Hatskin who put the wheels in motion for the momentous WHA Team Canada-Sovet Union series a year ago. Clearly, when the historians get around to updating the history of major league hockey, Gentle Ben — as he is affectionately known — commands something more than casual mention.

He is not a man who relates to small talk and appeasement. His philosophy is to accomplish much in a minimal amount of time with equally minimal verbalizing.

The Hatskin style is to define problems and expedite decisions rapidly.

And when the WHA lifted the curtain on its fourth season, it was with startling change keyed to the stabilization of 14 franchises employing sound business practices.

It's Hatskin's unvarnished view that the WHA is the most successful of all the new leagues, a fact that not even the most argumentative of detractors can dispute.

The WHA's emergence as a dominant force can be measured in ever increasing attendance figures of 2,479,679 in the inaugural season, 2,764,506 the second season followed by 4,095,911 last season. The increase is a startling 70 per cent.

Houston, Phoenix, San Diego, Minnesota and Denver comprise the Western Division while Cincinnati is paired with New England, Indianapolis and Cleveland in the East. The Canadian Division was streamlined with Edmonton, Winnipeg, Quebec and Toronto, and Vancouver moving to Calgary.

There's new ownership along with a new arena in Houston, and Cincinnati came in with a new building and an exciting team.

All the ingredients, to be sure, are now present for all clubs to be successful — not the least of which an 80-game schedule which calls for teams to play more games within their own division and fewer with the other divisions which should result in greater rivalries.

The extreme west-based San Diego Mariners offer a case in point.

Their schedule calls for at least five home and away games within their own division (Houston, Minnesota, Denver and Phoenix), and two each home and away with the four Eastern Division clubs and with the five Canadian Division teams.

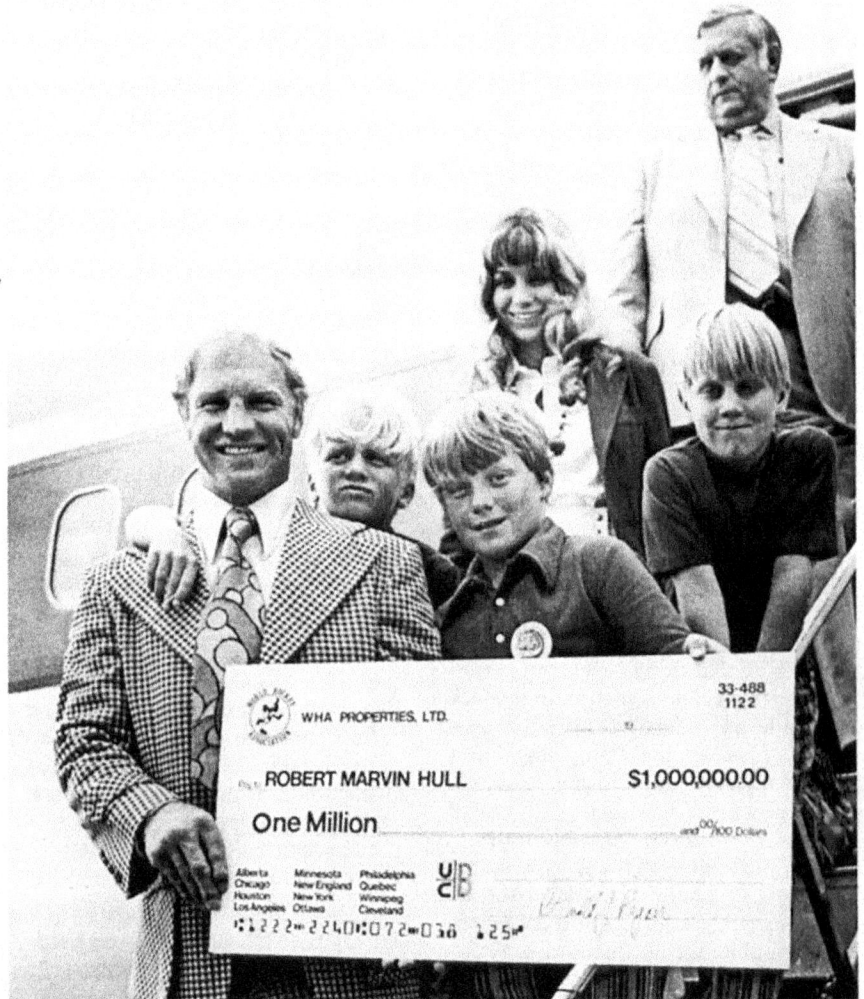

Participants on that historic hockey day in Winnipeg, June 27, 1972: The Bobby Hulls and Ben Hatskin.

"Ownership changes in the course of building a league represent positive steps." Clearly a positive step this season, not to mention a unique one, is the involvement of legendary Gordie Howe in the purchase and operation of the Avco World Trophy champion Houston Aeros.

Howe is the club president, marking the first time in the history of major league hockey that a player has ascended to a management role of such stature.

There is also uniqueness in the fact that Howe's two sons, Marty and Mark, play for the Aeros.

The Howe situation is a throwback to the NHL's Lester Patrick era, when the latter managed the New York Rangers, and his two sons — Muzz and Lynn — performed in starring roles. And the younger Howes, like their father, are destined for super stardom.

It is the young player, of course, that is the life-blood of the WHA or any league.

In the beginning, the object of the WHA's affection was established players offering instant identity with the fans. With the emergence of the Howes in Year II the league has stressed youth — and the cast of young lions that are on display this season offers irrefutable evidence that a new crop of hockey heroes has been harvested.

The new breed, besides the Howes, includes the likes of Kevin Morrison in San Diego, Anders Hedberg, Ulf Nilsson, Lars-Erik Sjoberg (Winnipeg), Mike Rogers (Edmonton), Ron Grahame, Terry Ruskowski and Don Larway (Houston), Gary MacGregor and Francois Rochon (Denver), John A. Stewart and Tom Edur (Cleveland), Vaclav Nedomansky, Richard Farda and Peter Marrin (Toronto), Robbie Ftorek, John Gray, Michel Cormier and Cam Connor (Phoenix), Nick Fotiu, Garry Swain and Thommy Abrahamsson (New England), Dennis Sobchuk (Cincinnati), Real Cloutier and Jean Bernier (Quebec), Brian Coates and Kim Clackson (Indianapolis), Ron Chipperfield (Calgary) and Jack Carlson (Minnesota).

Not to be dismissed is this year's rookie crop of Brian Maxwell in Cleveland, Mark Napier and Mario Vien in Toronto, Peter Morris in Edmonton, John Tonelli in Houston, Danny Arndt in New England, Barry Dean and Pekka Rautakallio in Phoenix, Claude LaRose and Norm LaPointe in Cincinnati while Denver has Nick Sanza and Ron Delorme.

And, naturally, there's another influx of Europeans.

Further evidence of the WHA world-wide image lies in the fact that two teams — the Toronto Toros and Winnipeg Jets — held their pre-season camps in Sweden and Finland, re-

spectively — representing another first for major league hockey.

The league, to be sure, has not directed efforts solely to the acquisition of promising talent.

Accomplished major leaguers making WHA debuts this season included Brent Hughes (San Diego from Kansas City), Rick Dudley (Cincinnati from Buffalo), Bill Lesuk (Winnipeg from Washington), Lyle Moffat (Cleveland from Toronto Leafs), John A. Stewart (Cleveland from California), Henry Boucha (Minnesota Fighting Saints from North Stars), Norm Ullman (Edmonton from Toronto Leafs), and highly-talented Davey Keon, now a Saint after 15 brilliant seasons at Maple Leaf Gardens, also the home of the Toros.

Keon, of course, represents one of several genuine super-stars to join the WHA — having been preceded by Winnipeg's Hull, Houston's Howe, Toronto's Mahovlich, Cleveland's Gerry Cheevers and Indianapolis' Pat Stapleton.

Coaching, without dispute, is an important factor in any league. And major league coaching, it follows, is a pre-requisite to major league performance. The WHA has it in abundance.

Making their WHA debuts this season are Bobby Kromm in Winnipeg, Jean-Guy Talbot in Denver, Clare Drake in Edmonton, Bobby Baun in Toronto, Ron Ingram in San Diego, who shared bench duties last season with player-coach Harry Howell, and Jacques Demers in Indianapolis.

Baun, a standout defenseman for 17 years in the NHL until his retirement two winters ago, looks to the day when the best of North America will compete against European teams for a true world championship. "Hockey is no longer a parochial game," he says.

Drake, in taking over the helm of the Edmonton Oilers, stepped out of the collegiate ranks where, in 17 years with the University of Alberta, he never missed the playoffs and led the Golden Bears to three national championships.

Winnipeg's hiring of Kromm, 46, ended eight years of grooming in the Chicago organization for a man who was beginning to wonder if he'd ever see the majors.

But then, the WHA has answered that same question for a lot of deserving hockey people.

Gordie, Marty and Mark Howe

175

GUEST SHOT . . .
Gilles Gratton

By MARK TILDEN

Gilles Gratton, the Toros goalie, is one of those rare people who elicits a whole spectrum of emotions from the people who know him. To some, he's totally admirable: an independent, very bright, outspoken, capable athlete; and a *bon vivant*, which my dictionary defines as "a person who enjoys the good things in life." To others he's a flake, a guy who wastes his time reading occult books and playing the piano, a goaltender who's as liable to blame a bad game on astrology as to admit that he wasn't sharp.

Of course, there are things about him that everyone agrees on — most notably, that is among the most brilliant, talented young goaltenders in professional hockey. His selection as a backup member of Team Canada 1974 indicates that his peers and his coach, Billy Harris, think so. And the Toros' second-place finish in the Eastern Division of the WHA last year confirms that assessment: Gratton was superb in the critical final games of the 1973-74 season, just as he was in the closing games of the previous season, when the Ottawa Nationals (the name of the team before the franchise was shifted to Toronto), on a late-season surge, made the playoffs.

If you want further evidence of his ability, it's to be found in the Buffalo Sabres' wooing of the 22-year-old goalie. The Buffalo management negotiated with Gratton at the end of last season, believing that he might be the solution to the Sabres' defensive woes. As it turned out, Ken Dryden returned to the Canadiens — instead of signing with the Toros, as many people believed he would — and the Toros were forced to come up with a multi-year, multi-dollar contract to keep Gratton in a Toros uniform.

As for the charges of flakiness, of inconsistency, that's simply Gratton's way. He's a young man whose personality and upbringing have established his lifestyle, and that lifestyle shows in his attitude on the ice. Hockey is a psychological battle for him; he has to work to get himself into a competitive frame of mind. Away from the rink, he meditates to calm himself down. "Meditation purifies your nervous system," he says. "There's so much stress, so much nervous pressure packed in there that it takes years and years to get it out." He doesn't meditate on game days, because it gives him what he calls "a floating attitude". To play well he has to be mentally right. "It's hard to tell myself I've got to go in there, we've got to win, we can't afford to lose, I can't let any goals in. I sweat my brains out."

Gratton was born in LaSalle, Quebec, a working-class suburb of Montreal; his father works for Fleishmann's. He fills the English-Canadian's stereotype of the Quebecois: animated, musical (he's a self-taught and surprisingly accomplished pianist and guitarist), independent. He's a modern-day gypsy, in his words, "a specialist of nowhere".

He quickly endeared himself to Toros fans with his fine play, particularly when injuries to Les Binkley forced him into action. ("It's funny about Gratton," says Billy Harris, "but he always seemed to play best when Bink was hurt. It was as though he didn't really think he should have been playing when Bink was healthy.") Gratton not only gained fame, he earned a

measure of notoriety, too. When streaking was in vogue last spring, he took a quick spin around the ice at practice one day — dressed only in facemask and skates. And during a telvision interview between periods, he bitterly criticized his defensemen for their sloppy play. In hockey cicles, of course, public criticism of a teammate is a no-no.

"Remember, though," says Dryden, "he was scored on at 19:59 or something like that, and he went on television right after. Like any good goalie, Gilles despises letting in a goal. It's a personal affront."

A firm believer in astrology, Gratton points to the stars to explain his competitive streak. "Leo is the competitive sign — *sportif*, in French — and, although Cancer is my ascendant, which means I'm sensitive and not physically big, I've got my Sun, Venus, Mercury and Pluto all in Leo. I've also got Mars in Scorpio. That means war or sadism. When I want something, I get it. I'm tough in the head." Says a teammate: "He's tough period. He's not afraid of anyone — he's fearless — and he only weighs about 160. But unlike a lot of fearless guys, he's not really a high liver. I think he pretends to like having a good time more than he really does."

Indeed, Gratton is unlike many pro athletes. He enjoys solitude. It's instructive, perhaps, that when Team Canada 1974 went to Russia, each player was allowed to take one companion, free of charge. Most players took wives or girl-friends; Gratton took his mother. So much for Gilles Gratton, *bon vivant*.

ON THE COVER: No. 23, hard-working defenseman Mike Stevens. Originally the property of the St. Louis Blues, Stevens played the last couple of seasons in Denver, earning the team's Most Valuable Defenseman award. Signed with the Runners just before training camp. Defensive oriented, he's extremely strong and possesses excellent hip check.

GILLES GRATTON

CHICAGO COUGARS vs OTTAWA NATIONALS

"GUEST SHOT"

FRANK MAHOVLICH

IMAGINE. HE'S ONE of the biggest stars in pro hockey, a guy who's been a phenomenon since he turned pro at 18, now the third highest scorer in the history of the game. So what was Frank Mahovlich's comment when he was appointed captain of the Toros just before the start of last season? "I was pretty nervous going down to the Gardens on the subway."

Mahovlich still gets nervous? And he takes the tube to his job, like any other working stiff? It's hard to believe that the man who plays left wing so effortlessly that fans accuse him of dogging it actually gets nervous. But at the same time, the subway comment synthesizes much of the man. He's nothing if not pragmatic — about hockey, business and the business of hockey, which in Mahovlich's view, are not necessarily the same things.

"Why not use the subway?" shrugs Mahovlich. "It's comfortable, fast and handy to my home." Besides, he adds, "It's nice to have people sit down beside me for a minute and talk." Can this be the same reticent, hyper-tense Mahovlich? He admits he's changed since he left St. Mikes at 18. He wasn't into art, leisure travel and frequenting good restaurants back then.

But he also says his image has always been somewhat misleading. "Look," he emphasizes, "I'm a simple guy. Sure, I've heard most of the questions I'm asked before. But I answer them. And still, most of the things that have been written about me have been based on what the writer has read about incidents involving me. Not many judge me for myself."

He has a point. A cavalier attitude towards checking is frequently mentioned as his main hockey weakness. He's been depicted as an emotional, unapproachable, moody prodigy. Yet it's hard to imagine a more approachable, casual star off the ice. Indeed, this worry at having been misrepresented is about the closest he comes to criticizing either the press or hockey management.

In fact, Mahovlich is a player whose style on the ice closely parallels his manner off it. He tends to stroll, not walk. He makes his point in conversation quietly, slipping easily between the jargon of the dressing room and a discussion of art, finance or an intimate restaurant in Montreal. He's the sort of individual who commands respect not only from teammates and rivals at the rink, but from well-heeled hockey executives and team owners, even former employers. "The other night my wife and I flew to Montreal as guests of David Molson to attend the gallery opening of an artist we know," he says.

So he's an owners' boy? Hardly. He explains: "We just got to know the Molsons when I was playing there. We remain in touch socially." Besides, social contact doesn't interfere with business. He left Montreal, didn't he? And he is more likely than most players to come into contact with the front office. He does his own contract negotiating. "I get advice from some businessmen friends and my lawyer," he says. "But I like to be in control, to make the final decision."

The toughest one recently was to leave Montreal, "a city our whole family enjoyed. But in the end, having a house here and my travel agency business, it made sense to move to Toronto." And the treatment he received from the Toros, he says, has been first class. He looks at this attitude in the executive offices as the best foundation for a good team. "The owners' attitude filters down through a team, instead of the other way around," he says. After stints with the Leafs and Detroit Red Wings, he knows whereof he speaks.

Mahovlich claims hockey expansion and the formation of the WHA has taken some of the pressure off playing the game, which isn't welcome news to the other WHA teams. "I feel like I'm 18 again as far as hockey is concerned," he says.

Actually, he doesn't see his change in teams as a defection so much as a good business decision. Typically, he describes it in those terms. "The WHA has given hockey players the opportunity to change jobs and go to work for the highest bidder, just as any other businessman can."

The new lease on his career has put off going full time into his travel agency business, but he still keeps active in the business that he started with an eye to the years when his hockey career will be a memory. Although he himself was not especially interested in travel at first, his wife got him to tour Europe one summer and presto — he was hooked. "We've been back three times since then," he says. "I particularly love France."

Even though he has built up his business interests he admits "an aching to try coaching," even with some reservations. "Johnny Bower told me once that when a guy becomes a coach, he changes. I also get a little nervous when I look at the average time a guy lasts as coach in hockey. But I still watch the good coaches closely and try to learn something from each one of them."

In the meantime, he's trying out his teaching techniques and at the same time helping himself. "I like working with the younger guys on the Toros. Sometimes I can show them something that would normally take them five years to learn. It's a shortcut that might help them and me too, if they can help the team."

Intermittent jeers — from fans and sportswriters — to the contrary, it's unlikely that the Toros could have selected a more professional player to be team captain. And Mahovlich clearly has risen to the task so far. If he's going to have problems with any part of the job, it's sure to be complaining to referees on the Toros' behalf. It's frankly not in the man's nature to bitch and whine.

But his arms are certainly strong enough to hoist the Avco Trophy, and if he performs to his potential, it may not be long before he's called upon to do just that. ●

A Night To Remember
Connelly nets 5 goals

Twas truly a night to remember — one Wayne Connelly will never forget.

It was Thanksgiving Night, Nov. 27, 1975.

Wayne Connelly just scored all five of the Saint goals in a 5-3 victory over the Cincinnati Stingers at the Civic Center. The five goals tied Connelly with four other WHA players who accomplished the same feat.

Those three are Ron Ward, Ron Climie, Andre Hinse and Valcav Nedomansky.

An oddity is that just three days after Connelly netted his five goals, Ward came back and duplicated the record he first set on Jan. 4, 1973 while playing with the New York Raiders.

Climie got his five goals on Nov. 6, 1974 while playing with Edmonton (he now is with New England and got the three-goal hat trick on Nov. 29). Hinse popped in his five Jan. 15, 1975 for Houston against Edmonton. Nedomansky got five for Toronto against Denver this year on Nov. 13.

Another inch and Connelly would have had the record all to himself.

Just after he collected goal No. 5, Mike Antonovich dropped a neat pass to Connelly at the right side of the net. Wayne tipped the shot goalward, but it just missed the right post by an inch.

Wayne had only six shots on goal in the game. Not a bad percentage. And the one shot he missed caught goalie Rich Coutu high on the shoulder.

Connelly was asked to explain each of the five goals for historical reasons if nothing else.

No. 1 — "I got a pass from Fran (Huck) inside the blueline. I cut in toward center and fired from 30 to 40 feet out. The defenseman was backing up and screened the goalie. It was a wrist shot."

No. 2 — "I took another pass from Fran and was going down the right side. I have been working on a play where I moved my left hand to the lower part of the stick as I'm leaning toward the defenseman then I move my right hand high on the stick and shoot it like a backhand. I've been fooling around with it in practice, but this is the first time I've scored on it. The puck went in off Coutu's glove in the near corner."

No. 3 — "Fran and Mike (Antonovich) dug the puck out from back of the net and got a pass out in front to me. I was all alone. I deked the goalie once and had plenty of time and just shot it by him."

No. 4 — "This goal came on a power play. Pie (John McKenzie) came off the ice and Keon was way up front on the play. He saw me coming in behind and drop me a pass. I tried to get the puck up high, but Coutu got a piece of it, but it just got over him and in by a couple of inches."

No. 5 — "I started the play in our zone and passed up to Anton and Anton passed to Fran. I came down Anton's side and got a pass from Fran and shot it right away. The goalie was facing Fran and I fired the puck along the ice. When they're going in, they're going in.

"Ten seconds later I tipped Anton's pass an inch wide. If it had gone in I don't know what I would have done."

The Saints tried to set up Connelly for the remainder of the game, but because of the closeness of the contest, the club had to stick to a close checking game instead of opening up.

ONE OF FIVE FOR CONNELLY
Congrats from Busnuik, Antonovich

"I had one other good chance," Connelly continued. "Coutu had come way out of his net and Anton was set to feed me a pass. But the puck hit the toe of one of the defensemen and went behind me. Otherwise I would have had the whole net to shoot at.

"It was unbelievable," Connelly added after the game. "After two periods I sat in the dressing room with four goals and said to myself that I must have been dreaming. Imagine, four goals and still 20 minutes to play. I kept thinking that I might fluke another in.

"The rest of the guys were as startled as I was. Henry (Boucha) came over with his stick and rubbed it against mine, must be some Indian trick or something."

Up until that point Connelly's line of Huck and Antonovich had been shooting in bad luck. They had only 14 goals between team and only three in the past six games.

"It is strange how things work out," said Connelly. "I remember the last time we played Cincinnati in here, I had better chances than I did tonight. I had seven shots that night and came up empty and tonight I had six and five went in."

It was a night to remember and a night to be thankful for, too.

178

RACER NEMESIS

Whaler Pleau No Stranger

LARRY PLEAU a Whaler from start

Larry Pleau and the World Hockey Association aren't exactly strangers.

They've been together five years, and Pleau---going into this season---has been no friend to the Indianapolis Racers. He's victimized Racer goaltending for 14 regular season goals.

From the beginning, when he was lured from the talent-rich Montreal Canadiens in 1971, his adventures with New England have read like the travels of Gulliver, from Boston to Springfield to Hartford, from a league championship to a recent eight-game losing streak.

While time, in addition to graying our temples and softening our stomachs, tends to tinge many of our attitudes about people and life, Larry Pleau is the same gentleman, the same professional, who gambled and crossed into the land known as the World Hockey Association.

Why does General Manager Ron Ryan sign this man to a long-term contract, when these pacts have been the contributing germ to the basic diseases in which professional hockey now suffers?

Why?

The answer is simple.

Take your basic hockey coach, ask him to comb through his attic and dig up the old erector set Santa dropped off a few years back. Ask him to build the model hockey player.

Chances are the coach would build his pieces into a form over six-feet tall and weigh his robot to about 200 pounds. He would then wave his magic wand and give his little monster a strong torso and an ability to skate circles around others.

But robots need personality and temperament, so our Picasso would undoubtedly inject shots of leadership, humility, and industry into our young Hockeystein.. Then, as the coach laced the blades onto the feet of our paragon of hockey virtue, he would instruct the model to forget to alibi when things turned sour and to carry himself in a manner his organization would be proud of.

Coach Harry Neale would say, "If there were more Larry Pleau's in hockey, they wouldn't need coaches." And that's the reason why Ron Ryan tells rival general managers, "If you're calling to make a deal for Larry Pleau, forget it and save the long distance toll for somebody else."

Lest you confuse these preceding paragraphs as foolish idolatry, let it be perfectly clear that Larry Pleau is not the perfect hockey player (if one actually exists). He is a more mortal, unable to score 50 goals per year, unable to vent fear into the hearts of his opponents through physical intimidation. But yet, for his given ability, Larry Pleau is a coach's idea of Shangra La.

What is Larry Pleau's idea of Larry Pleau?

"Well, I think I'm a bit of a gambler," said Pleau recently. "I gambled when I left the Canadiens to join the WHA, I gambled when I invested in my marina in New Hampshire, and I'm gambling about the long-range success of the WHA when I signed my recent (long-term) contract. I love the New England area and I'm pleased and proud to be a Whaler."

Like most of his contemporaries, Pleau keeps a highly-tuned ear on the sport of hockey itself. He maintains close relationships with player and management personnel in both leagues and his thoughts echo both a concern and a hope for the future.

"Let's face it, professional hockey is in trouble in a number of cities. Attendances are way down in places that you'd least expect. For the player, jobs will be harder and harder to get and maintain. So when I had my chance to sign this most recent contract, I sacrificed a good deal of cash for the short term, for long-range security. Because hockey is in such a state of flux, I have to believe some kind of agreement or merger is in the offing between the two leagues. Sure, maybe players' associations might fight that idea, but if it comes down to an agreement or a death notice, I think they'll take the agreement. The fat-cat days are over."

In reference to this season, Pleau again speaks from the heart.

"I know that the veterans of this club are going to have to come with big performances and solid leadership if the Whalers are going to have a good year," analyzed Larry. "We are very young and the young always tend to follow the older, more experienced guys. To win, we must all work together and work very hard because we just don't have the kind of club that can blow a team off the map by six or seven goals a game. I feel that responsibility and hope everybody else does, too."

Larry Pleau.

Honest, sincere, and willing.

179

GOALTENDER GARY KURT

By JOE DAGGETT

ROGER CROZIER'S bleeding ulcers — Glenn Hall's mental anguish ... Terry Sawchuck's nervous breakdowns. The pressures of goaltending — and the physical toll they exact — have been well reported over the years.

We all just *know* that goalies up-chuck in the dressing room. That they're miles away mentally on the day of a game. That they yell at their wife and kids. That their nerve ganglia are virtually thrusting through their skins in anticipation of another night in front of a four-by-six-foot cage with hostile people propelling hard-rubber discs at them. Now aren't they?

Well, yes and no. To one degree or another every player suffers some anxiety and nervousness, some of the goaltenders — as noted above — to a truly excruciating extent. But there's a lower end to the goaltending nervousness scale, too, a bunch of goalies who are able to take the job pretty much in stride. Like Gary Kurt of the Roadrunners, who says, "Nah, I've never been one for that sort of stuff. I get a little bit tense in the dressing room before a game sometimes. But once we get out on the ice, it's all gone."

Now, don't get the idea that Kurt's languorous about his job. No, indeed, the competitive fires burn brightly within him. But they're banked well below the surface and his genial and easy-going exterior camouflages an intense desire to win.

Winning is something that Kurt did last year with a regularity surprising even to those who expected most from him. He had known his ups and downs in a seven-year pro career that included three minor-league stops, a stint with the California Seals, and two melancholy years with the New York-New Jersey (now San Diego) franchise in its various manifestations. In none of his big-league hitches had he shown the consistency he demonstrated last year when, after being picked by Phoenix in the expansion draft, he turned into one of hockey's best puck-stoppers.

Just to touch last season's high spots, Kurt (1) was the Roadrunners' MVP, (2) made the Hockey News' second all-star team, (3) recorded a pair of shutouts, and (4) established a WHA record by going without a loss for 12 consecutive games, the whole month of December and more.

Now that is consistency, indeed, part of it attributable, says Kurt, simply to the fact that he's older and more experienced. "The place you improve is in the head," he claims. "There's no way my reflexes are as quick as they used to be, but I'm a much better goaltender. You learn to shade the shooters and do a lot of other little tricks. And you build up your 'book' on the other teams."

Kurt openly avowed last year that the advice and guidance of Jack Norris played an important part in his success. "I used to go into a game thinking it'd be 'hard' or 'easy' depending on what team we were playing, where it was in the standings and so on," Kurt recalls. "Jack's figuring is that every time you step into that goal crease you're in for a tough time and you've got the same job to do. So what I now do is to review the individuals

on the other team, the playing styles of each line, to try to figure what to expect."

The Kurt-Norris Seminars in Advanced Netminding continue this year, Gary reports. "We still talk it over all the time, Jack and I. He's a great analyst. We always get together the day after a game and discuss the goals. And we make mental notes about who's playing well on the other teams and file them away for future reference." Their data bank is a formidable one, a Rand Corporation of Hockey.

One of the WHA's biggest goalies (at 6-3 and 205 pounds), Kurt says he hopes for continued improvement in consistency and concentration. "It's really amazing," he asserts, "how it can pick up a team when the goalie makes a big save. And on the other hand when you let one in that you shouldn't, you can see the spirit go down."

Gary Kurt has raised Roadrunner spirits far, far more than he's let them down. And, though nobody knows what's in a goalie's heart of hearts, he's done it all without any overt signs of that nervousness, tension, worry and anxiety that goaltenders are supposed to have.

He's easy-going, all right. Except when you're trying to put pucks past him.

GUEST SHOT ... MARC TARDIF

Hockey fans throughout the world have always loved to identify themselves with their super-star idols. Quebec fans are the same way and the deal that brought Marc Tardif to Quebec last December 7 gave the fans the chance to applaud another hero.

For many months there were talks about the possible deal that would bring Tardif to Quebec; for many it was a dream that was impossible to realize. Quebec fans had always admired his talents since his days with the Montreal Canadiens, as they could watch him twice a week on TV.

They also applauded his 40 goals last season with a last place team, the Los Angeles Sharks. When he joined the Nordiques this season after long negotiations between Quebec and the Michigan Stags, he had only 12 goals and he still ended this season with 50. Before putting on his Nordiques' uniform, he said quite often that he would be subjected to a lot of pressure, and he did not know at the time if he could respond to all the fans' aspirations. His 38 goals since December 8 are his answer to all his doubts. His 49th goal in the last minute of play recently in Minnesota brought a Canadian Division championship to Quebec City.

After two seasons out of the playoffs, the Nordiques are now in. "It feels good to count on players like Marc to bring us into it with a lot of confidence," says coach Jean-Guy Gendron.

Before joining the Nordiques, Marc was considered by many as being a solitary type of player, joyful, and most of all a team player. His talents have proven to all that he has worked to bring the Nordiques and his talented teammates a playoff spot. Marc is now a hero in Quebec; he knows that he will have to live with his super star reputation and along with his buddy Rejean Houle, with whom he played his junior years and later on with the Montreal Canadiens, he will earn more acclaim in Quebec.

When he brought him to Quebec, General Manager Maurice Filion told the press that the Nordiques had acquired

Marc Tardif

"one of the best, if not the best, left winger in all hockey." Those that were skeptical are now opening their eyes and seeing that the Quebec GM was right. Tardif, at 25 years of age, is still young and his enormous talents will bring hockey fans of all cities to recognize the Nordiques as one of the great franchises in the World Hockey Association.

ON THE COVER: Seeming to draw attention wherever he goes on the ice is Robbie Ftorek, who blistered the opposition during the second half of the season when he returned from Tulsa and a nagging injury. During his last 31 regular season games, Ftorek scored 26 goals, 31 assists. (Photographic Illustrators)

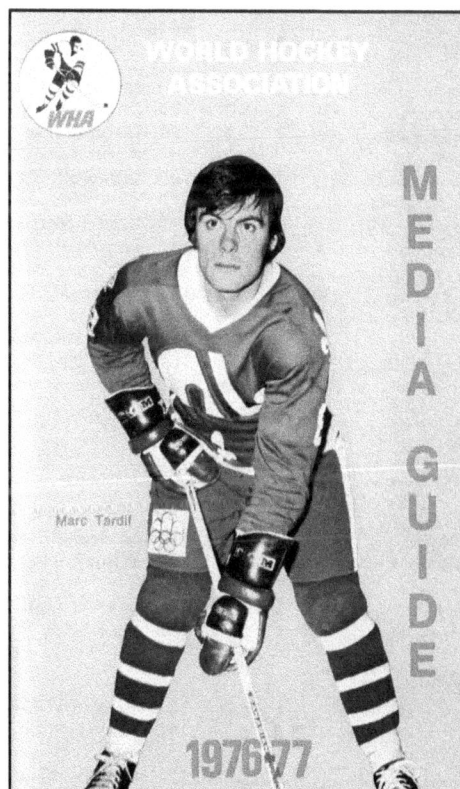

WORLD HOCKEY ASSOCIATION

MEDIA GUIDE

1976-77

Dion's Handy With a Wrench

Look for Indianapolis Racers' goalie Michel Dion off the ice and you'll likely find him under the body of a 1965 Corvette.

"Everything on the car is the original except for the engine," Michel proudly explains. He handles a wrench almost as well as a goaltender's stick.

Dion, winner of the WHA's best goaltender award last season, purchased the car at Mohawk Valley when he was toiling for the minor league team Comets.

"A friend of mine was the Chevy dealer and gave me a real good deal," said Dion. "I replaced a lot of the mechanical parts — you won't believe how super that car looks."

Dion has resisted any temptation to race his car, although he admits that he occasionally tests out the engine on a nice stretch of road.

"It's 352 horses so it can go about 150 miles an hour," he says, grinning.

If the curly-haired goalie is somewhat apprehensive about the dangers of fast driving, not so about goaltending.

Early in the season Dion's head and the puck had some serious, unfriendly confrontations. But the 22-year-old shook off both hits and continued playing.

"You go back to the old cliche," says Dion. "You don't have to be crazy to be a goalie but it helps."

INDIANAPOLIS RACERS 1976-77 ROSTER

FORWARDS

NO.	NAME	POS	S	HT	WT	PLACE & DATE OF BIRTH		1975-76 CLUB	GP	G	A	PTS	PIM
7	Hugh Harris	LW	L	6-0	190	Toronto, Ont.	6-7-48	Calgary (WHA)	29	5	9	14	19
								Indianapolis (WHA)	41	12	28	40	23
8	Renald Leclerc	RW	R	5-11	170	Ville de Vanier, Que.	12-12-47	Quebec (WHA)	42	15	17	32	35
								Indianapolis (WHA)	40	18	21	39	52
9	Reg Thomas	C	L	5-10	180	Lambeth, Que.	4-21-53	Indianapolis (WHA)	80	23	17	40	23
10	Nick Harbaruk	RW	R	6-0	195	Drohiczyn, Pol.	8-16-43	Indianapolis (WHA)	75	23	19	42	26
11	Brian McDonald	RW	R	5-11	190	Toronto, Ont.	3-23-45	Mohawk Valley (NAHL)	10	5	9	14	17
								Indianapolis (WHA)	63	16	17	33	58
14	Blair MacDonald	RW	R	5-10	180	Cornwall, Ont.	11-17-53	Edmonton (WHA)	29	7	5	12	8
								Indianapolis (WHA)	56	19	11	30	14
15	Al Karlander	C	L	5-8	175	Lac La Hache, B.C.	11-5-46	Indianapolis (WHA)	79	16	28	44	36
16	Michel Parizeau	C	L	5-10	165	Montreal, Que.	4-9-48	Quebec (WHA)	52	12	27	39	24
								Indianapolis (WHA)	23	13	15	28	20
19	Francois Rochon	LW	L	5-11	181	Montreal, Que.	4-18-53	Denver (WHA)	41	11	10	21	10
								Indianapolis (WHA)	18	6	2	8	31
22	Gene Peacosh	LW	L	5-9	170	Sheridan, Man.	9-28-48	San Diego (WHA)	79	37	33	70	35
23	Mike Zuke	C	R	6-0	180	Sault Ste. Marie, Ont.	4-16-54	Michigan Tech (WCHA)	43	47	57	104	42
25	Mark Lomenda	RW	R	6-0	186	Esterhazy, Sask.	4-14-54	Indianapolis (WHA)	2	0	0	0	0
								Denver (WHA)	37	6	17	23	11

DEFENSEMEN

NO.	NAME	POS	S	HT	WT	PLACE & DATE OF BIRTH		1975-76 CLUB	GP	G	A	PTS	PIM
2	Darryl Maggs	RD	R	6-1	195	Victoria, B.C.	4-6-49	Denver (WHA)	42	4	23	27	42
								Indianapolis (WHA)	36	5	16	21	40
3	Dick Proceviat	LD	L	6-0	180	Whitemouth, B.C.	6-25-46	Indianapolis (WHA)	72	7	13	20	31
4	Kim Clackson	RD	R	5-11	195	Saskatoon, Sask.	2-13-55	Indianapolis (WHA)	77	1	12	13	351
5	Bryon Baltimore	RD	L	6-2	190	Whitehorse, Yukon	8-26-52	Denver (WHA)	41	1	8	9	32
								Indianapolis (WHA)	37	1	10	11	30
12	Pat Stapleton	LD	L	5-8	180	Sarnia, Ont.	7-4-40	Indianapolis (WHA)	80	5	40	45	48
24	Ken Block	LD	L	5-10	185	Steinbach, Man.	3-18-44	Indianapolis (WHA)	79	1	25	26	28

GOALTENDERS

NO.	NAME		S	HT	WT	PLACE & DATE OF BIRTH		1975-76 CLUB	GP	MP	GA	SO	AVG
1	Andy Brown		L	6-0	185	Hamilton, Ont.	2-15-44	Indianapolis (WHA)	24	1368	82	1	3.60
28	Jim Park		R	6-1	190	Toronto, Ont.	6-22-52	Mohawk Valley (NAHL)	37	2208	168	0	4.48
								Indianapolis (WHA)	11	572	23	0	2.41
31	Michel Dion		L	5-10	170	Granby, Que.	2-11-54	Mohawk Valley (NAHL)	22	1294	83	0	3.84
								Indianapolis (WHA)	31	1860	85	0	2.7

MICHEL DION
At last count
he had won
seven in a row.

Michel started out as a high scoring centerman in his young hockey days.

"I figured that since it was so easy to score goals it would be more challenging to figure out how to stop other guys from getting them," he recalls.

He donned goaltending equipment when he was 10 and hasn't taken it off since.

Dion played for the Montreal Red, White and Blue (junior league) for two years, moved to Mohawk in 1974 and joined the Racers last year.

Ironically, there was a time when he considered becoming a professional baseball player instead of going into hockey.

"I was a catcher for two years in the Florida State League," he says. "I had signed with the Montreal Expos and was playing for West Palm Beach in 1972. But I thought about it and decided it would be easier for me to make it in professional hockey.

"I don't know . . . you're a Canadian and it's your sport and you've been playing hockey since you were a kid," he adds. "Canadian baseball doesn't have that much competition, so I figured it would be pretty tough for me to make it in the majors."

Michel credits his baseball experience with improving his glove hand in hockey, however.

Coach Jacques Demers usually lets his goalies know a couple of days in advance if they'll be playing on a particular night. Dion uses this time to prepare himself for the contest.

"You say to yourself, this particular team has guys that skate fast or shoot fast and it's going to be tough," he explains. "Being physically ready helps you to be mentally prepared, too."

Dion doesn't like to miss too many games, either.

"If I'm hot then I want to keep going, play every game. If I have a bad night, well then it's good to get a rest once in awhile," he says.

Watch Dion during a practice session and it's easy to see that behind those soft, blue eyes is a disciplined competitor.

Not long ago winger Rene Leclerc was teasing Dion after a hard go-round at the Fairgrounds Coliseum.

"Hey, you didn't look so tough to me today," chided Rene in fun.

Michel glared intensely at his countryman and repeated a few unprintables, which were greeted by laughter from fellow Racers. Being beten, even in practice, was no joke to young Dion.

"There's a lot of pressure on a goaltender and most of the time you don't get all the credit you deserve," he claims. "Of course if you're really outstanding they give you your due. But some goals won't be your fault and people start booing you because they don't understand this.

"Most of the time when you win the fans say it's the team that won," he adds. "But when you lose they blame it on the goalie."

Dion admires goalies Jacques Plante and Bernie Parent but claims he has never patterned his style after any one person.

"They're two of my favorites and have identical styles," he explains. "I'm different from them, though. On low shots I'll go down on the ice and on high shots, I'll stay up. They tend to stay high on all of them."

Will success spoil the goaltender who had an award-winning 2.74 goals against average his rookie season in the major leagues?

So far it hasn't.

"I guess I'm really shy," he says with a boyish grin. "People come up to me on the street and ask for my autograph and I'm kind of embarrassed. At my age it's kind of strange to have people say that you are their idol."

JOHN GRAY: "THE RUNNERS' 'THIRD ASSIST' MAN"

Edmonton goaltender Jacques Plante recently announced he is working out an esoteric new statistical system which he hopes will supplant the old categories of wins, losses, goals-against, and saves, and render the true picture of goaltending effectiveness which he believes has been missing. The story roused hopes that somebody would devise some kind of a new system for forwards which, instead of just goals and assists, would reflect such things as solid body checks dealt out, confusion sown in the enemy zone, goaltenders screened, pucks dug out of corners, and all-around hustle and conscientiousness; that is to say, exactly the commodities John Gray is supplying the Phoenix Roadrunners this year.

Gray's the Runners' original "third assist" man: he does the heavy work on numerous Phoenix goals but frequently ends up without credit for it in the points column. The find out how valuable he is to the team, don't look at the scoring totals — even though Gray's are respectable enough. Go to coach Sandy Hucul and his teammates, who unanimously acclaim Gray as one of the team's unsung heroes.

The one statistic that *does* reflect the caliber of Gray's play — and it's a figure the public doesn't see — is the plus-minus record; i.e. the ratio between goals a man's team scores while he's on the ice versus goals against. Last year at Oklahoma City on the Central League's champion Blazers, Gray was a whopping plus-44, best in the CHL. And he's remained consistently on the plus side of the ledger this year, too.

Gray's father, John reports, never urged him to participate in sports in general or hockey in particular. In fact, he nearly took an entirely different tack: music. He was once a promising tuba player in the Cobourg, Ontario high school band. "It was a glamour activity, actually," Gray laughs. "The band

traveled a lot. You had to take an elective, and it was either that or typing. The drums were already taken so I went for the tuba. I figured it has a big mouthpiece and only three valves, so I wouldn't need as much coordination as in typing. Diane (his wife) and I still go to German-type biergartens once in a while, and I really have the urge to get up there with the band and oompah a little bit."

The statistics after John's name in sports record books might well have been passes completed and touchdowns scored instead of goals and assists. As his interest in the band waned, he took to football and became an outstanding quarterback and middle linebacker at Cobourg and, upon graduating, was offered a football scholarship at McGill University in Montreal. But hockey, which he played during the winter at the Junior B level, interested him more and he sorted through several scholarship offers in that sport before settling on the University of New Hampshire.

The football experience, says Gray, has been of considerable value to him in hockey. Not a big man at 5-10 and 180 pounds, he's yet one of the most effective body-checkers on the Roadrunners. "I was an aggressive football player," Gray recalls, "and I liked the contact in the game. They go to a lot of pains to teach you *how* to hit in football, and the same techniques carry over into hockey. A smaller man can do a good job of body-checking if he knows how."

At New Hampsire, Gray was the Wildcats' top gunner his senior year when, playing center, he scored 29 goals and 33 assists for 62 points in a 29-game schedule. A serious student who got good grades in his Geography major, John thought he might like to go into teaching after college, and even went so far as to apply — and be accepted — into a Master's program at the University of Toronto.

JOHN GRAY

But hockey was still tugging at him . . . from two directions. He was picked by New England in the original WHA draft and also got an offer from the NHL's Maple Leafs. He accepted the latter and spent the past two seasons with Leaf farm teams in the CHL, going from 15 goals to 25 and from 40 points to 60 in two seasons, while recording roughly 150 penalty minutes both years. Last season he was the league's 2nd all-star right wing as Oklahoma City won the CHL flag only to lose out to Dallas in the playoffs.

He was signed by the Roadrunners last summer and Phoenix management — keeping that phantom third assist column in mind — sees him as a fixture on the Birds' right flank for a long time to come. Music's . . . and football's . . . and pedagogy's loss is the Roadrunner's gain in rightwinger John Gray.

LEFTWINGER DEL HALL

By JOE DAGGETT

EVEN THOUGH IT happened just a few days ago, one can say with assurance that it will go down as one of the most memorable moments of the 1975-76 hockey season. To relive it, return with us now to Saturday, December 6, 1975. The previous game, Roadrunner coach Sandy Hucul, looking for scoring punch, had put Del Hall on a line with Robbie Ftorek and John Gray, and the threesome had responded with three tallies, two of them by Hall, in a 5-4 win.

Now it's overtime of the Saturday night contest against Houston. Ftorek has three goals and Hall one in a tense, 5-to-5 game. On the first shift of the extra period, a Ftorek pass catches Hall in full flight at center ice. He slows slightly to receive the puck and stay onside, bursts into full gallop, fights off a frantic Aero defender, and backhands the puck into a narrow gap at the top of the Houston net for a Phoenix victory.

The result? Pandemonium in the crowd, exultation on the Bird's bench, and even a bit of mild jubilation — a whoop and a smile — on the part of Del Hall. Nothing excessive, though, mind you.

To paraphrase the telephone company slogan ("Let your fingers do the walking.") Del Hall prefers to let his performance do the talking. He's friendly enough, you know, but as a talker he'll never be confused with effusive types like Hubert Humphrey, Prof. Irwin Corey or Robbie Ftorek.

He's a coach's delight, Hall is. That overtime game-winner illustrates some of his best hockey attributes: explosive acceleration, excellent skating speed, and a hard, accurate shot. He works diligently, skates up and down his wing, and effectively checks his opposite number. And he doesn't give the coach any back talk.

Hall's spent the greater part of his time the past three years as a California Seals chattel in Salt Lake City of the Western and Central Leagues. He averaged 32 goals a season for the three campaigns and ended up a solid "plus" — on the ice for more goals for than against — in all of them. He led Salt Lake's CHL titleists in scoring during the playoffs last season.

With all of California's notable lack of success the past few years, it's tough to figure why Hall got to play only 8 games with the parent club in three years. But they kept him languishing in the minors and he ended up getting his first real major league opportunity this fall with Phoenix following one of the oddest sports trades since the Detroit Tigers and Cleveland Indians swapped managers.

To refresh your memory, the Roadrunners got two players in a trade for one player they did not have. Here's how it worked: Last year the Runners signed up Gary Holt, a youngster at Salt Lake with major league potential. California then signed Holt to another contract. The Runners, with an earlier date on *their* contract with Holt, expressed a willingness to take the matter to court to get him. California offered a 2-for-1 counter-deal . . . lay off Holt and get the rights to Hall — a youngster of exceptional promise — and Ron Huston, a veteran with NHL credentials. It was another California move difficult to fathom, but Phoenix management wasn't asking questions and speedily got both Hall and Huston under contract.

A left-handed shot who's most comfortable on left wing, Hall can also play center with skill. A bachelor, he spends his free time off the ice engaging in outdoor sports of all kinds: golf, tennis, hunting and fishing, water skiing and the like. He's an inveterate card player, one of the regular pasteboard aficionados on Roadrunner plane flights. And he has a year of business studies at St. Clair College in Ontario behind him.

So, keep your eye on this young man. They may not all be so explosively dramatic as the one in that game against Houston, but Del Hall figures to be involved in a lot more memorable moments for the Phoenix Roadrunners.

AND HOWE

To find out what lies ahead for Gordie, the game, and the Aeros,
AEROS Magazine contributing editor Dale Robertson conducted the following
interview with Gordie on the Aeros first road trip of the season.

They call him Mr. Hockey. He has played more games, scored more points and earned more respect from his peers than any other man in the history of the sport.

Gordie Howe. After 27 seasons, the name has become synonymous with the best that hockey has to offer.

But Gordie Howe the man is bigger than Gordie Howe the legend. He is real people, a face in the crowd that would be recognized on any street in Canada.

The statistics, laurels and lines in the record books are the window dressing. His heart is bigger than his massive forearms; his boyish love for hockey greater than the 2,000-plus points he has scored.

He'll skate with kids and he'll golf with heads of state. That's Gordie. He's always got time for kids—and Presidents.

When Gordie visits hockey's Hall of Fame, he sees himself on almost every wall, yet he stands a little bit in awe, almost as if he cannot see himself as part of all the dusty greatness.

Despite little formal education, he is a shrewd businessman with a good eye for a person's character. He reads people well and is easily read himself. He is honest, open and a simple man to understand.

His family means a lot to him. So does hockey. Combine the two and you can figure why, at age 47, he is still playing for the Houston Aeros alongside sons Mark and Marty.

The sport is Gordie's past and, when he steps in as the Aeros' full-time president after this season, it will be his future, too.

What lies ahead, for him and the game? He talks candidly about his life in hockey.

Robertson: The World Hockey Association has survived through four seasons, Gordie, but is it making real, tangible progress? Has it come in from the cold, so to speak?

Howe: I think it's gained a lot of credibility. One of the big things that has helped the WHA was the success our Team Canada enjoyed last year against the Russians, who had learned quite a lot from playing the NHL team two years prior to that. The Russians lost by a close margin, but they had outscored the NHL. If it wasn't for the heroics of a young fellow we have in our league right now, Paul Henderson of Toronto, NHL Team Canada would have been in a lot of trouble. Pat Stapleton, who's now playing for Indianapolis, had a big role in that series, too. I think we are respected, even if the NHL might hesitate to admit it.

Robertson: How about financial stability? The WHA has played in more cities than "Jaws." Is the league ready to stabilize?

Howe: From the standpoint of financial strength, I don't think there is any comparison now with the first two seasons, when most of the moving of franchises occurred. We have improved ourselves a great deal in this respect. Look at the new rinks in Houston, Cleveland, Indianapolis, Cincinnati, Denver and Edmonton. The old Cleveland and Edmonton buildings were bad little rinks. But look what we did in Edmonton last year. Houston went in there on three occasions and sold over 45,000 tickets. The WHA is making tremendous strides. It looks very healthy.

Robertson: How healthy? Financially strong enough to prevent the sort of power play move Denver and New York made in the ABA? Would a strong franchise, say the Aeros, attempt

a jump to the NHL?

Howe: No, I don't see that happening. I don't know what kind of system they have in the ABA, but in the WHA the owners are all partners. If one of the brothers is having a little trouble, the others will all jump in and help.

Robertson: OK, but let's assume the Aeros could and would do so. Could they compete? Are the WHA champions, after just three years, ready to challenge the best the NHL has to offer? If anybody can answer that question, you're the one.

Howe: I definitely believe we could participate with the best teams in the NHL. No, we couldn't win them all, but we would win our share. I have played with and against many of their better players and I can see as much potential talent on our club right now as those NHL teams have on theirs. It's a question of depth, period. Going back some 20 years in the NHL, we had, maybe, two lines that could put the puck in the net and only one checking line, which, when it got a goal, was a bonus. The checking line was just in there to break even against the top guns. But in Houston, the balance of our scoring is unbelievable. The first year, Lund's line and the line I play on tied in the total amount of goals scored and (Ted) Taylor's line was right behind us. The second year we went to four lines and goal production dropped off a bit, but it was brought up by the Kid Line. When you talk about balance like that, you talk about the future. There are a lot of good, young legs on this club. You have to give coach Dineen credit for putting young and old legs together, producing lines which have matched in mind and thinking. This is a very together outfit. I like that.

Robertson: Forgetting the

league rivalry a moment, what about the future of hockey in general? Is the sport, NHL and WHA alike, facing a crisis situation because of the inflationary spiral, not the least of which is caused by ballooning player salaries?

Howe: The demand for salaries is unbelievably high. I mean, it's hard for me to believe, in cases quoted, that players are worth as much money as you once paid for a franchise. It kind of scares you, but at the same time it's like a pendulum that's swung too far in one direction. I find it hard to go against high salaries because so many hockey players have dedicated so many years to the game and come up crippled with little to put them through the rest of their lives. A lot of us joined the league

Gordie Howe captured in an unnatural pose: sitting down.

when we were 17 or 18 years old and it's understandable the education we needed for a future out of hockey was not there. You didn't have time to prepare yourself for the future, especially if you were married and had to work summers like I did. You didn't talk much about money then because, in most cases, you weren't that proud of it. The owners were taking in quite a bit of money and the boys were not sharing in it, despite devoting themselves entirely to the earnings of the club.

Robertson: In other words, the situation has gone from one bad extreme to another?

Howe: That's right. Then the pendulum was way up on the left side. Now, with the great demand for talent, it has gone down through the middle and is way over on the right side.

Robertson: The question is, what can bring about a change for the better? As an executive what solution might you offer? Or, since you are still playing, do you view the problem from an executive vantage point?

Howe: Hey, that's not an easy question. As President, I've got a leg on each side of the line. But, if I'm still in uniform, I'm about 90 per cent player. If I've got to be thinking, I've got to be thinking 'hockey player' too. As for solutions, a common draft would definitely help. It would give only one team the rights to speak to an individual, which, of course, would cause the player to lose his bargaining position. A merger would do the same thing.

Robertson: Would you sup-port such measures?

Howe: I would push for a common draft with a little common sense involved. Again, like I've said, I would not want to see the hockey player hurt. I don't want to see the so-called good old days come back. I'm tied to a lot of things right now, which require quite a bit of running around, because I got started in them to make ends meet. But I don't have any regrets. Anytime you tie yourself up to winning people, you're that much ahead. Changes probably have to be made in the salary structure, though. I'd hate to see the game of hockey go belly up. It offers too many things to too many people.

Robertson: Assuming that it doesn't, will the game continue to improve itself? For that matter, has it improved in recent years, with the

Russian influence and the influx of Scandinavian players into the WHA and NHL? What, if anything, has changed?

Howe: I'm going against our league now, but I was very much against dropping the rule that kept you from icing the puck when you were a man short. That, I thought, was a tremendous innovation. I put quite a bit of stress on the talent you put out there to kill penalties. But, other than that one rule, hockey has changed very little, except for maybe the equipment—the curved sticks, better pads, things like that. It has always been a pretty good game. There's been a little bit of brutality, yet there's a lot of finesse and talent out there. When you can skate, handle the puck and dodge people at the same time, as well as keep your head up and see what's going on around you, that's where the real beauty of the sport shows up.

Robertson: Yes, but recently the brutality seems to be getting most of the attention. Why? Is the game getting rougher? Are teams, quick to note the brawling success of the Philadelphia Flyers, looking for the so-called "hit men" to make them instant winners?

Howe: We've always had strong players who are good for their club. I don't think anybody is hired only to go out on the ice and swing at people, or they wouldn't take a stick with them. Most of the guys who have this reputation today are strong, young men who like to fisticuff. But, they are also in a position to be top hockey players. Take Nick Fotiu of New England. He's got talent. He's improved unbelievably for a guy who was, literally, taken off roller skates and put on ice skates. There is nothing wrong with a hard-nosed hockey player. I would like to think that's what teams are looking for, not brawlers. There is too much demand for talent, for people who can back check as well as score goals, to waste your money on a guy who just likes to fight.

Robertson: It goes without saying then that you were opposed to the Boucha-Forbes incident ending up in court?

Howe: No question about it. This is our game and it's played on the ice. I've been hit in the eye, too, and put in the hospital. I know how hockey fights develop. Somewhere along the line Boucha might have given him a good whack to irritate him. But that's a rare situation anyway. Only once in a long, long time do these sort of things come about. I would think the league

(Continued on next page)

has adequate men to take care of the problem. I don't know how it was handled, but I do know it should never have gone to court. Hockey should wash its own laundry. Otherwise, every time you hit a guy you'd end up in court. Games would be won and lost in the courtroom.

Robertson: But, isn't the fighting often excessive? Can't something be done to clear out the constant sparring in the corners? Forbes might have had second thoughts about raising his stick if the deterrent were more positive.

Howe: The Russians have come up with a pretty good idea to get rid of individual fighting. I think they thought it up after we were over there last year. That series was rough, darn rough. Anyway, they figure the fellow who initiates the fight should get 10 minutes and, if you retaliate, you get five, which leaves someone shorthanded for five minutes. What you're doing there is jeopardizing your team for a little self-satisfaction.

Robertson: Would you support such a rule?

Howe: I think so, if maybe for not that long a period. We'd have to test it out thoroughly.

Robertson: Getting back to the original question, what about the foreign influence on hockey? Other than the non-violence thing, what can be expected from the Russians and the Swedes?

Howe: A lot of people don't understand—I know I didn't—how much progress the Russians have made. It is almost unbelievable. They used to come over to Canada and absorb tremendous beatings, but all the time they did they were taking films back, learning and adding little things of their own to improve the game of hockey. Hockey offers so much as incentive over there, things like better homes and public recognition. There is nothing better for the ego than a little recognition. The Swedes? They have adjusted nicely with Winnipeg. Their shooting has improved greatly, complementing their natural skating and passing ability. If anything, they still have trouble with the rough aspects of hockey over here. But the Swedes are tremendous physical skaters.

Robertson: That's enough on hockey in general. Let's hear about Houston hockey and the Howe family. Is the game making strides in the great Southwest?

Howe: Listen, there is a lot of know-how in Houston. So many Northerners have transferred down here

and the local people are picking it up rapidly. Compared to football, hockey is a very easy game to get used to. I don't understand football and I've watched Marty play it over the years. I just get caught up with the finesse of the individuals, their strength and maneuverability. All that is hockey. One thing we've got going for us is, when we say 60 minutes of hockey, that's what you get. In football, the ball can be laying dead on the field and time will be ticking off, which hurts the fan—yet people cheering for the winning side are happy. I don't understand it.

Robertson: Granted, you love hockey as much as any man alive, but it's no secret that you wouldn't be here if it hadn't been for the chance to play alongside Mark and Marty? After two seasons and part of a third, do you still get that gut twinge when the kids get a cheap shot? Where does teammate Gordie stop and father Gordie start?

Howe: You've seen the togetherness on the Aeros. If one takes a shot, we'll—given the opportunity—do a little banging in return. We don't hold grudges, but we don't forget. When someone gets a cheap shot, I feel that way about all the fellows, not just my boys. Although, naturally, I tend to jump in when they're involved. If I didn't do that, I wouldn't be much of a father. I would say it's harder on my wife, Colleen, sitting in the stands. She has no way to fight back.

Robertson: What about Mark? Is he a young Gordie Howe?

Howe: I would like to think I had that much potential when I was his age. I can't believe I had his quickness. But, Mark's game is not like mine was when I was his age. I had a little of the Ruskowski-type in me. My first 10 games or so I had about 15 fights. Then they told me you can't score goals in the penalty box and scoring goals was what I was getting paid for. It didn't take long for the message to sink in. Mark is strictly hockey. If somebody takes a cheap shot at him, it's not out of the question that he might use his body or a little timber if he gets the chance, but he'll never go out of his way to get the guy. He'll bide his time.

Robertson: You wouldn't have, right?

Howe: I would have run over to the bench to get someone who took a cheap shot at me.

Robertson: What can we expect from Mark, if not any all-time penalty records? And how is Marty coming along? He seems to be a much

more polished hockey player than he was as a rookie.

Howe: I really don't know what Mark's got, but, even as an old-timer, he's pretty to watch. He's unselfish and that grabs my attention right off the bat. He has the same capabilities that might make me say about a kid on another team, 'Jeez, if he's only 20 now, I'd hate like heck to see him when he's 24.' Marty? This might sound funny, but the improvement Mark might make can't match what Marty's already done. He has come along incredibly fast. He'll try things in practice sometimes that leave him way out in left field, but he is learning through the process of testing. At one time he could take the puck from a guy, but he'd have trouble getting rid of it in the proper manner. He'd stop skating at center ice and wonder what to do. Now I think he's proven he has the capability to take it all the way. He's made a 200-foot improvement there as far as I'm concerned.

Robertson: After this season, Mark and Marty have one year remaining on their Aero contracts. What happens when the NHL comes a-calling?

Howe: I've talked with the boys about it. They have convinced me their interests are here with Houston and the WHA. But, basically, I have very little to do with that end of it. Colleen acts as their agent. However, I assure you we'll never sit down at a table, me as president and her as agent, and argue about salaries. It won't happen.

Robertson: Last, but certainly not least, how about the old man himself? What does Gordie Howe, age 47, hope to accomplish in this, his 28th and, presumably, last season?

Howe: Well, three Avco World Trophies would be nice. Individually, I'll tell you what I've always done to keep from getting myself excited. I'd count on one goal for every three games, which guaranteed me 20 right there. If I get lucky and score a couple one night, I'm that much ahead. That's how I'll play it this year. If I don't get hurt I'll be about where I was the last two, between 80 and 100 points.

Robertson: Next summer?

Howe: I'll start learning how to retire—for good.

High-Scoring Mike Walton
Leads Fighting Saints
Against Roadrunners

At the start of this week, the Minnesota Fighting Saints were well ahead of their record setting goal-scoring pace of last year ... at least according to their publicist, Mike Lamey. Lamey also pointed out the Saints were allowing almost one goal more per game than they did last year, and consequently, the Minnesota sextet was lagging somewhat on home ice, which bodes trouble for Saints' opponents in their own rinks.

As a matter of fact, the visiting clubs this season have almost made a myth of the once reliable home-ice advantage. Another statistician, Frank Polnaszek of WHA headquarters, pointed out that this season visiting clubs were winning right around 40-percent of the games. In "normal" times (is there such a thing?) the visitors figured to win perhaps one-third of their matches. But this obviously is not a typical season. Last week, as an example, visitors copped four of five games played one night.

For that matter, the Roadrunners themselves have been involved in 10 games in which the home team lost. Six times the Runners have won on the road (while losing eight), while losing four games on home ice as well.

Just last Tuesday the Roadrunners outplayed and outscored the Cougars in their Chicago lair, and things looked promising for picking up a couple of points in the standings ahead of the Saints, who were playing the Toros in Toronto. What happened? The Minnesotans stayed right on the Roadrunners' heels with a 4-2 victory over the Toros, who were going down to their sixth straight home ice defeat. The old cliche that sports spawned, "any team can beat any other team on any given night", never seemed more true than this season in the WHA.

Getting back to the Fighting Saints, as mentioned earlier, they have a high-scoring, explosive team, that can score goals in bunches. The first time the Roadrunners faced the Saints this season, at the tail-end of that early 18-day, eight game road trip, the Saints mauled the Runners, 10-4. Weary or whatever, the Runners made a battle of it for two periods before a four-goal Minnesota final period caved in the roof. In that game the Saints burst through for three goals in a 46-second span in the opening period, with fleet Mike Walton accounting for a pair of those within eight seconds.

The most recent meeting between the clubs took place up there earlier this month, and despite the fact that again they surged to a quick 3-0 opening period lead, the Fighting Saints were forced to go down to the wire before Danny O'Shea's late

MIKE WALTON

Last year's WHA scoring champion is again among the league's leaders this season. In earlier game vs. Roadrunners, Walton had big five-point night, with hat trick and pair of assists. An explosive player, Walton potted a pair within an eight-second span.

steal and goal gave them a narrow 4-3 triumph. The Runners had again gamely battled back to knot the score, three-all on a pair of goals by John Gray and the tying one by Bobby Mowat.

It could be the classic confrontation tonight of "slugger" (Minnesota) against "boxer" (Phoenix). And if that comes to pass, we should have a dandy game.

SMALL IN SIZE
BUT BIG IN SCORING

Ice hockey may not be a game for giants, like, say, basketball, but when you stand only five feet, eight inches—and that's stretching a point—a guy can have his problems.

However, that hasn't scared Gary Veneruzzo of the Michigan Stags off the ice. Nor will it ever.

"Sure, the bigger guys take advantage of me," says Veneruzzo, who moved east during the recent off season when the Stags came to the Motor City after two years in Los Angeles.

"They try to push me around as much as they can and knock me down, but I've learned how to hold my own and even enjoy the upper hand against these fellows."

What are Gary's tactics?

"It's simple," he says. "For one thing I've learned to keep my head up. A guy my size can't take a chance of skating around with my eyes and head down.

"I've got to keep looking where those big guys are and by doing so, I don't do badly against them."

And?

"Well, for another thing, a guy my size has to learn to skate fast . . . the faster the better. When you're really moving on the ice, the bigger guys find it a lot tougher to catch up to you.

"I refuse to be a standard target for anybody. And to avoid that, well, I just have to keep skating and skating."

The 31-year-old Veneruzzo, a native of Fort Williams, Ontario, figures to become the "darling" of the Detroit fans in short order. He's fresh from two big seasons with the Los Angeles Sharks in the WHA. Two years ago he flipped in 43 goals for the Sharks. Last season he came back with 39 goals along with 29 assists for 68 points.

The arrival of the WHA on the hockey scene turned things around quickly for Veneruzzo. For six seasons prior to the WHA's debut in 1972-73 Veneruzzo belonged to the St. Louis Blues of the National Hockey League.

"They'd have me up and send me down. I'd spend more time in the minors than in the big league. But, they did use me in the play-offs and I got a thrill—my biggest thrill—play for the Stanley Cup."

When the WHA downed, Veneruzzo switched leagues.

"The money made a difference," he admits. "But, more important, it's provided me with a chance to show that I belong in the majors on a regular basis.

"I think I have proved it now beyond any doubt."

Veneruzzo now makes his home in Thunder Bay, Ontario. Thus, the shifting of the Los Angeles franchise to Detroit suits him since he's now closer to home.

"My family won't enjoy that nice warm California weather any more. . . . no more swimming in the winter for them. . . . and they'll again be seeing the snow and ice. But that's the way we grew up and it was all sort of unnatural for us out in California the last couple of winters."

Veneruzzo and his wife have two youngsters, Liza 9 and David 5.

During the season they'll reside in Farmington, a suburb of Detroit.

RIGHT WINGER GARY VENERUZZO

By JOE DAGGETT

"WHEN YOU'RE MY SIZE and you have a record as a goal scorer, you can count on it; guys are going to be running at you all the time. You know those defensemen are gonna try to carve you up in front of the net. It's nothing personal; they just have a job to do. One thing's for sure, you can't let it intimidate you. You just have to respond the best way you can. You stand in there and take it and wait for your chance to retaliate . . . or better yet score a goal on them."

Thus does Garry Veneruzzo of the Roadrunners describe one of the occupational hazards of hockey as he's played it in the pro ranks for the past ten years; namely, as a small man skilled at scoring goals, particularly on rebounds and scrambles out of the heavy going in the slot area. If the opposition has taken its toll in any other way than a few bits of scar tissue around his face and a lot of bruises and welts on his body, it doesn't show. He's still hanging in there in hockey's violent vortex in front of the cage. And he's recorded 115 goals in three WHA seasons, an average of 38 goals per year.

Those consistent scoring totals were what made the Roadrunners go after Veneruzzo when it was learned that Cincinnati wasn't playing him much early this season. Acquired in a trade for defenseman Ron Serafini at Thanksgiving time, Veneruzzo came to the Runners at a juncture when goals were about as frequent in Phoenix as rainstorms.

Gary's initial reaction to the deal was to hump his back for a time and consider saying no. "But it wasn't because I didn't want to play in Phoenix or anything," he says. "I was just tired of moving. I liked Cincinnati and last year I'd gone through the Michigan-Baltimore thing. I'd had a lot of aggravation; a lot of expense. I dreaded facing my wife (Evelyn) and my kids (Lisa, 10; David, 7) and telling them we had to move again and they had to change schools. Now that we're settled here, though, I guess it's all been for the good. We really like Phoenix now. I'm just anxious to start making a bigger contribution to the team."

A 32-year-old native of Fort William, Ontario, Veneruzzo broke into pro hockey with Tulsa of the Central League in 1964, then was claimed by St. Louis in the NHL's first expansion draft in 1967. Roadrunner fans who go back a few years may remember him as a key member of one of the Western League's latterday powerhouses, the Denver club of 1972. In addition to Veneruzzo — who led the league with 4 goals — that Denver outfit claimed Fran Huck, Don Borgeson, Curt Bennett, Ron Buchanan and Jacques Caron. It was a team that "would hold its own against a lot of the major-league competition around nowadays, I think," says Veneruzzo.

The following year he became a WHA original with the Los Angeles Sharks, where current Roadrunner Jim Niekamp was among his teammates. When the Sharks moved to Detroit as the Michigan Stags, Veneruzzo went with them and suffered all the vicissitudes of a melancholy year that saw the franchise falter financially in the Motor City, decamp to Baltimore where many of the players spent a third of the season living in a hotel, and finally limp through to a dreary conclusion in last place.

It's easy to see why one more move was almost one too many.

Happily, that's all behind him now as he takes to the ice with linemates Jim Boyd and Michel Cormier, of whom he says, "they're great to play with; two hard workers. We're playing a little defensively right now, but I think we're gonna score a bundle before it's over."

Most observers would agree the Boyd-Cormier-Veneruzzo line has great offensive potential that'll bear dividends over the latter half of the campaign. There probably isn't time enough left for Veneruzzo to match his 30-plus average. But you can bet he'll be hanging in there, taking his lumps from those enemy defensemen . . . and scoring more than his share.

PROUD WHALERS ATTEMPT TO EVEN SERIES

The New England Whalers, currently operating out of hockey-historic Springfield, Mass., will soon depart for their sparkling new palace in Hartford, Conn. where they will atttempt to write more history about their successes in' the WHA. As far as they're concerned, what more suitable place is there for the historic, the heroic, the extraordinary.

The Whalers, of course, are the first-ever champions of the WHA, copping the title in a series that went five games against Bobby Hull's Winnipeg Jets in the Spring of 1973. Preceding that, they had earned

Wayne Carleton

series triumphs over Ottawa and Cleveland, also by four-games-to-one margins.

Last season the Whalers sped to the Eastern Division title, winning by four points over Toronto, but in a reverberating upset, they were unceremoniously dumped from further playoff action by the Chicago Cougars in a quarter-final series that

carried to seven games. The Whalers don't plan on letting that happen again. Installed as pre-season favorites to cop the Eastern title, Ron Ryan's club rebounded from an opening night loss this season to spin off seven straight victories.

They were looking to stretch that to eight last Saturday against the Roadrunners. They didn't make it.

Phoenix, in the next-to-last game of their lengthiest road trip of the season, tripped the Whalers, 4-2, in the Springfield arena. For the Runners a most important victory. For the Whalers, not all that important except in the pride department.

The game showed the Phoenix "Kid Line" — Dennis Sobchuk centering Dave Gorman and Cam Connor — to excellent advantage. Sobby scored the Runners first goal that tied the score at 1-1 in the opening period. Gorman scored a power-play goal early in the middle stanza that tied the count at 2-all, then connected for the insurance in the final period after ex-Whaler Hugh Harris nailed the game-winner in what had to be a gratifying effort. Cam Connor assisted on all three goals scored by the kids.

All in all, the Runners played a sound game, with the forwards backchecking well and the defensemen sweeping the slot clean in front of goalie Jack Norris.

Tonight Roadrunner fans will see a former Phoenix hero, Wayne Carleton, opposing them. Carleton, loaned to the Runners during the 1968-69 season, scored a pair of goals in his first outing to account for a 2-0 victory over Vancouver, and he went on to pot 16 goals in 32 games here. Two years ago with the Toros he scored 42 goals and last year 37 and then he was suddenly traded to New England midway through this past September.

It's also likely that the Whalers will have goalie Al Smith working tonight.

Al Smith

Smith, who posted a fine 3.08 average through 55 games last year, entered this week of play in the runnerup spot among WHA netminders with a 2.24 goals-against average.

All the ingredients are present for what could be a classic battle tonight.

MIKE HOBIN

THE FIRST IMPRESSION one gets upon meeting a civies-dressed Mike Hobin is here's a clean-cut kid, perhaps an undergrad at ASU, majoring in history or accounting, or some other non-violent field of endeavor. His off-ice demeanor and soft conversational tones only reinforce that impression.

The awakening comes when you see him glide smoothly onto the resident rink and once the disc is dropped, watch him tirelessly pursue the puck into the corners, around the unyielding iron of the net, along with the ungiving boards and hounding his opponents constantly, attempting to force them to give up the black disc that attracts so much attention. It is then that you realize how wrong your first impression was.

Well, maybe not all wrong. Hobin is an off-season college student at McMaster University in Toronto, studying business management. His quiet nature belies a pair of laughing blue eyes that seem to recognize the incongruity of his seemingly docile, passive nature with the tough profession he has chosen to master. Twenty-three years old on February 21, "Hobie" has long since given every indication that he knows what the game is all about.

After playing his junior hockey with Hamilton (OHA), the red-haired native of Sarnia, Ont., was drafted in a high round by the Montreal Canadiens, but chose instead to sign with the WHA Vancouver Blazers where he was tabbed in the 7th round during the May 1974 ivory hunt. He was assigned to Charlotte where he promptly turned the Southern League on its ear, averaging almost two points per game: in 37 contests with Charlotte, Hobie scored 21 goals, added 52 assists for a total of 73 points practically before the season was half over.

And after being purchased by the Roadrunners in mid-January 1975, Hobin still left impressive enough credentials to be voted that circuit's Rookie of Year honors even though he was in another league, the CHL with Tulsa, the second half of the season.

What led to this massive point production? "It wasn't all that unusual," Hobin decried modestly. "It was just one of those things where we had a line that complimented each other well. I centered a couple of pretty good players, Steve Hull and Andy Deschamps, both of whom are now with Calgary. I also made up my hind that this, playing hockey professionally, was what I really wanted to do. I just decided to bear down harder."

Mike finished his rookie campaign with Tulsa, adding another 28 points (for a season total of 101), then scored at a point-per-game clip (66 in 66) last year with Tucson, leading the club in scoring.

Hobie started this season slowly. Seeing only spot duty, he admits to losing his confidence. "I tried always to be ready to play, tried not to get down in the dumps when I didn't play. I think most players go through this when they're not playing regularly. In my case though, I knew I had the ability to play, I had trouble shooting the puck and lost confidence in my shooting, couldn't put it where I wanted, missed the net and worried a lot. Lately, however, I've started scoring again and I'm playing more. Sometimes it takes just a single goal scored to turn it around. 'Hey', you say to yourself, 'I can score', and then sometimes you wonder, 'well, why not all the time?' "

At the start of January, Hobie had managed just one goal and two assists in 25 games. The January output was four more goals and seven set-ups in 13 games, almost another point-per-game pace.

Mike recognizes the need for improvement in certain areas. "I've always played for offensive teams," he smiled, "so now I have to think defense more, concentrate on stopping the other guys. Just like offense, I think that will improve with regular play. And thinking DEFENSE all the time."

College student that he is, Mike should pass with flying colors next exam time.

MURRAY KEOGAN:
MR. CONSISTENCY AT CENTER ICE

Enter, if you will, the executive offices of the Phoenix Roadrunners Hockey Club. The player under discussion is center Murray Keogan; the speaker, one of the Roadrunners' top officials, whose comments went something like this:

"He figured in our plans right from the start when we were putting the team together. He's not the kind of guy you notice particularly, but when you look at the scoresheet at the end of the game you notice that he's gotten a couple of important points. The results are what counts.

"His record has improved every year he's played professionally. He was second in the Western League in scoring last year and he could play regularly for almost any team in hockey.

"He's very steady and smart. He's strong on his skates. He has a good ability to get open in front of the net. Doesn't have an overpowering shot but he's extremely accurate. And he's got a good attitude about checking, too. So what else is there?"

When one of your bosses speaks about you that way, you might tend to become complacent and apathetic, even if you only hear about it second hand. Nothing, though, could be more antithetical to the personality of the hardworking 24-year-old Roadrunner centerman than an attitude of complacency. He's a plugger, Keogan is, one of those never-say-die types who never quit trying even though the issue, to all other eyes, has long since been decided.

Not that Murray would ever be caught talking about himself that way. No, indeed. In fact, the soft-spoken youngster never has a great deal to say about anything, preferring instead to do his job, keep his peace and stay to himself. But he inspires eloquence in others . . . when they're talking about him. Like a former teammate, for example, to wit: "Murray has great anticipation for the game. He's usually thinking a couple of jumps ahead

of the opposition and engineering things they're not ready for. He's a very intelligent player. I think he's going to get even better as time goes on."

These tributes — and the development in Keogan they reflect — might come as something of an embarrassment to the St. Louis Blues organization. The Blues originally had the playing rights to Keogan after drafting him out of college. And they almost assuredly could use him these days, considering their lowly estate in the NHL.

The Blues sold Keogan outright to the then-minor league Roadrunners a year ago just before training camp . . . close on the heels of two minor league campaigns in which he'd gone from 22 goals to 34 and from 49 points to 69. Last year his play bore out the acumen of the Phoenix

management as he recorded 31 goals and 56 assists, good for 87 points and second place in the Western League scoring derby. And thus far this season . . . even after a big step up in the class of his competition . . . he's continued to click at better than a point-a-game pace and leads the Roadrunners in scoring through the first third of their initial season in the World Hockey Association.

"I felt bad about it at the time," Murray says, recalling his sale by the Blues, "But I figured if they didn't want me it was better to be someplace else. Looking back on it, things really worked out for the best. Last year gave me a lot of confidence. I used to score in bunches but I'm a lot steadier now."

Keogan was born in the Saskatchewan town of Biggar, a settlement of 3,000 souls in the west-central part of the province whose name, to Canadians, is a celebrated homonym. A sign on the outskirts of the village greets visitors thus, correctly to the eye but not the ear: NEW YORK IS BIG, BUT THIS IS BIGGAR. The Keogan family — it's a Irish moniker — moved from Biggar to Edmonton, Alberta when Murray was 16.

By that time he was already showing considerable promise as a hockey player and, after a year of junior competition at Weyburn, went off to play collegiate hockey at the University of Minnesota-Duluth where he earned a degree in Business.

Keogan — a bachelor — still spends the off-season in Duluth where he has a summer cottage and teaches in a hockey school. If he continues the consistent play he's shown so far this year — and all the signs indicate he will — he should really enjoy next summer in Minnesota's North Country. He'll have another good scoring season under his belt, the applause of the fans and the praise of his teammates echoing in his ears . . . and maybe even a playoff check to stick in his hip pocket.

J. C. MIGNEAULT: HARD-WORKING HUSTLER IS COACH'S DELIGHT

"He's one of those guys who does his job so well you don't notice him; he's always in position, always helping out the defense. He's good in the corners, gets his share of scoring chances. He set himself back with that injury or he'd probably have a lot more goals than he does. And there isn't a harder worker on the Phoenix team."

Thus did the chief scout for one World Hockey Association team recently size up John Migneault of the Phoenix Roadrunners. Migneault, a 26-year-old leftwinger, was acquired from the Vancouver Blazers with Peter McNamee and Serge Beaudoin in an early-December trade that sent Hugh Harris to the Blazers.

Sizing up the transaction on a strictly statistical basis, it looks like a coup for Vancouver, since Harris has gone on to take the Blazers' scoring lead. However, no less an interested party than Vancouver General Manager Joe Crozier says to look deeper at the swap. "Let's face it," Crozier points out, "Harris is an offensive hockey player who couldn't adapt well to the defensive style of play that Phoenix emphasizes. Migneault, the way he checks, may not get as many points as Harris, but he fits right into the Phoenix system, the whole attitude that Sandy Hucul is trying to build. And when you consider the other two players, I think Vancouver gave up a lot."

The scout's comment about Migneault's injury and the effect it's had on his season is a pertinent one. He aggravated a chronic left ankle in mid-January, sat out nine games, and still is not entirely recovered from the problem. He continues however — with the help of ice baths, bandages and liniment — to play and make a consistent contribution to the Roadrunners as they battle down the stretch towards a hoped-for playoff spot in their first season in the WHA.

And as if the ankle injury weren't enough, Migneault — his teammates call him J.C., not John — suffered through a slump once he returned to action that saw

him go 14 games without a goal. Part of it was the injury and part of it was the mental funk that any slumping player seems to work himself into.

"You know you have to relax and play loose," says J.C., looking back on the drought, but your whole impulse is to tighten up and press too hard. You get so uptight you try to do more than you're capable of. The worst thing for me was the feeling that I wasn't contributing. It hurt my pride because I feel that I'm a good team player. I'm happy that things seem to be coming together for me now."

Migneault is a native of Tompkins, Saskatchewan, a farming community of roughly 500 people. If the town's not populous, the Migneault family is: J.C. is one of a family of nine children, the first eight of them boys. And he's not the only hockey player in the family: his brother, Kevin, is an outstanding senior goaltender at the University of Saskatchewan whose playing rights are held by the Vancouver Canucks of the NHL.

J.C.'s advent in the World Hockey Association is edifying as to his play-anywhere-I-can-help attitude towards the game. After playing junior hockey in Vancouver, Regina and Swift Current, he languished three years in the Montreal Canadiens organization. When the WHA was being formed three years ago he got word that the then-Philadelphia Blazers were in need of defensemen. Migneault went to camp, tried out as a blueliner, and made the team. As the season wore on he became a swing man, then exclusively a forward. Last year, playing strictly on left wing in Vancouver he scored a career high of 21 goals.

Migneault and his wife, Val, have three children and have bought a house in Phoenix. Off-season plans call for them to spend most of the summer here with occasional trips up North. "I have some Charolais cattle up in Saskatchewan and I'll go tend to them," J.C. reports, "but I have to keep busy in the summer. You can

J. C. Migneault

only loaf around and go fishing for so long. I may even take some time and go work for my brothers in Vancouver." His brothers have a plumbing concern in Vancouver, specializing in construction and installation.

But don't get the idea that he's anxious for the season to end. "Actually," Migneault smiles, "I'd like to see the season go on for another month or so." — meaning well into the World Hockey Association playoffs.

Now, in that desire the Phoenix fans can concur with J.C. Migneault one hundred percent.

Kim Clackson Adds A Touch . . . A Crunch Along The Boards

By SUSAN NICOL

The Winnipeg Jets have been together as a winning unit for some time now with few changes in personnel. Usually, a newcomer is spotted easily on the ice because of "Jet Lag" if he isn't as fast as the others or because of defensive lapses that come with playing for an offensive club.

If a rookie doesn't stand out immediately, it's usually a credit to him, and number 5 is one such newcomer. The fans in the Winnipeg Arena have scrambled for their programs only when a resounding crunch has been heard along the boards. They have nodded with approval when they have discovered the hard-hitting new defenseman in Kim Clackson.

Kim admits his ability to hit is one of the reasons the Jets signed him.

"I play an aggressive brand of hockey," he says. "The Jets are expecting me to be an aggressive, as well as a defensive, defenseman."

Playing strictly defensive is not always easy, especially when the rest of the team isn't. But Kim hasn't found the adjustment a difficult one to make.

"The Jets play more of a European style than I'm used to, especially the way they come out of their own end," he says. "But hockey is hockey."

Since Kim has played against the Jets for two years as an Indianapolis Racer, he feels he knows the club and its style fairly well.

"I had a pretty good idea of the team before I came. They're a high-scoring, very aggressive club." He quickly adds, "Not that they're physically aggressive. They're a goal-hungry aggressive hockey team."

He says there are advantages and disadvantage to the Jets' style, especially where defensemen are concerned.

"Their skating style is one of the best. When you're on such a high-scoring team, it's nice to have that advantage. You've got the forwards who are going to get you the goals."

However, he adds, "I think Larry Hillman is making the team a lot more defensive than the previous coach did. That's good, because if you look at other teams, like the Montreal Canadians, they're checking teams. They've got the forwards and the defensemen to move the puck quickly. They can break for the openings and score goals when the occasions arise."

As far as Kim is concerned, the change is for the better.

"I would like our team to be a little more defensive . . . being a defensman. It helps my job a lot. But we've forwards here who are very offensive-minded," he says. "I think Larry is doing a little bit here and there to change things."

Much has been said about the training camp this year, although Coach Hillman believes it was a success. Kim has mixed feelings about it.

continued on next page

"GUEST SHOT" Pat Price

By Tony Gallagher

It's really hard to say which was tougher on Pat Price: Joe Crozier's quote saying that he was another Bobby Orr or the fact that he cracked up the brand new Ferrari he bought with his signing bonus.

Both have had their effect on the splendid 20-year-old defenseman from the Saskatoon Blades of the Western Canada Hockey League. Neither one helped.

First there was this murky road just outside Trail. It was good for a scare, a big bill for the Insurance Corporation of B.C.

PAT PRICE

and as much adverse publicity as any rookie could handle.

"I came over this hill, and it was raining hard," explained Price. "When I got over the crest, the road was washed out on the other side. If I'd been in any other car but the one I was in, I might not be here today."

So the talented defender had to be content with a lease U-drive until the body shop had finished his car.

Then there was Crozier's quote, which probably was blown somewhat out of proportion. Nonetheless, the expecting public took it to heart and it's placed Price in a position similar to the position of Dale Tallon when he came to the Vancouver Canucks in their first year in the National Hockey League. Tallon was expected to be the greatest thing since the wheel. But if you'll pardon the weak pun, he couldn't get rolling. The same thing could happen to Price if he lets all the pressure get to him.

Price, Crozier, Andy Bathgate and just about everyone else in hockey knows that it's going to take him at least half a season to get his full confidence in pro hockey. It's plain to see he has all the tools, but if he

gets down on himself, he may never reach the fantastic potential he possesses.

"Pat's getting better every game," said Crozier of his 1.3 million dollar bonus signing. "It's the same with this team as it is with Pat. It's going to take time for them to jell."

One thing did help Price — his association with Team Canada. Although he didn't get much playing time and not even much practice time in Moscow, the experience of being under the gun like the Canadians were had the effect of making other pressure to win small by comparison.

"Moscow was a great experience for me," said Price. "I never want to go back there, although I suppose if I was ever asked to play for Canada again I'd say yes. Just to be with those guys like Howe and Hull was great."

But even Team Canada created problems for Price.

"He wasn't in the best of shape when he came back from Moscow," said Crozier. "When you're not on the ice every day, it's a lost day. And he lost a few days with Team Canada."

But all this has the effect of making excuses for the rookie. People say he's making all that money, let him go out and earn it. The same goes for the Blazer organization. That's quite a normal reaction from fans and management.

But there will come a time when there will be no need for any suggestion of excuse for the rookie. There won't be time in between the extensive praise for his moves and hockey sense.

Sure there's been pressures. Playing the right side point on the power play has made it tough. The excuses, or explanations, could go on forever. But theyr're not necessary. All that is required is to sit back and watch the Blazers' number three develop. Chances are he won't be a million dollar flop. He'll earn his money and probably pay dividends to both the club and the Vancouver fans. Predictions are hazardous. But prediction of success for Pat Price minimizes the risk.

He'll be a good one!

ON THE COVER: No. 19, defenseman Wendell Bennett. Converted from right wing to defense midway through last season, a move that complemented Bennett's size, strength and stick-handling abilities. Started this season with Tulsa Oilers but was recalled in early November.

Clackson continued

"I think we should have practised a little more," he says. "But that's pretty hard when you have to play that many games. It was good to get over there and see Sweden. I appreciated the chance."

Larry Hillman had said he was pleased with the condition of most of the players in training camp. Kim doesn't believe he was part of that group.

"I could have showed up in better shape than I did," he says, "but I wasn't expecting to come to camp that early. I was expecting to come two or three weeks later than the time it actually started."

His former club, the Indianapolis Racers, had the distinction in the WHA of having the most enthusiastic fans and the best-attended games. For this reason, he hasn't noticed any great change in fan

support since he's joined the Jets. If anything, Winnipeg fans are more subdued.

"Indianapolis has really rabid fans. They were good for two goals a game at home. But I think that's an exception where American hockey cities are concerned."

He's looking forward to the pending trip to Japan in December, although it may prove as costly as the trip to Izvestia last year.

"I'd like to see Japan like everyone else on this team," he says. "I don't think it's actually going to help us, but that remains to be seen. The last trip didn't bother me that much. It does bother some guys, some it doesn't."

So far, Kim Clackson enjoys being a Jet.

"They've got good morale here. It's a winning hockey club and it's great to be a part of it."

Dave Dunn

Born: Wapella, Saskatchewan, Aug. 19, 1948. Height: 6-3 - Weight 200 lbs. Position: Defence - Shoots Right. Wife: Sandra. Children: Angela, Greg. First Season as a Jet. Graduate of the University of Sask.

Considered a tough customer in contact circles . . . Takes an abundance of penalties exerting his authority . . . Most adept working in close quarters, such as in front of nets and in corners . . . Born Aug. 19, 1948, the son of a farmer . . . Elected to go to the University of Saskatchewan and play in collegiate ranks rather than junior . . . Set the Western Hockey League scoring record for defencemen with 19 goals and 56 assists for 75 points with Seattle Totems in 1972-73 season . . . Not a good skater but he gets there . . . Owns a small contracting firm in Vancouver . . . Resented his role in Toronto where, he said, the Maple Leafs asked him to pick fights and be a goon . . . Became a free agent in the summer of '76, opting for the Jets over a couple of NHL clubs . . . A good team man.

Bill Lesuk: Plays Anywhere, Anytime

By SUSAN NICOL

Billy Lesuk is one of those rare hockey players a team can count on in any situation. He plays offence and defence well. He can check or score goals. And he always gives 100 per cent in any role he plays.

"I believe that, through experience, you gain more knowledge of the game," he says. "I've always had a desire to learn how to play all over. It means a lot to me to be able to move into any position."

It means a lot to the Winnipeg Jets, as well. They've utilized his abilities in just about every capacity, especially on the checking line.

"There isn't any secret to checking well. It's just something I've had to do over quite a number of years to keep a job," he says. "At times I don't do all that well, either. I try to learn from my mistakes. I just hope that when the situation comes up again, I will remember what I did and I won't wind up giving away the puck."

Bill started his junior hockey career with the Weyburn Red Wings. Six years later, he attended a Boston Bruin training camp. He spent three years in the minors — two with Oklahoma City and one in the American League in Hershey, Pennsylvania.

He was picked up by Boston in time to win the Stanley Cup. From there he went to the Philadelphia Flyers in an intra-league draft. Two years later he was in Los Angeles.

"I felt I wasn't contributing there," he says. "I kind of like ice time, so I wanted to make a move. I went to the Washington Capitols, but if I had to do it again, I think I would have stayed in Los Angeles."

Through most of his NHL career, Bill learned to play defensively.

"I've checked a lot of high-scoring wingers and you can't let these people get a step on you . . . even half a step. You're always aware of where your man is and you're not so concerned about the puck.

"When you're in the position of preventing your check from getting a shot on goal, you find yourself in an intimidating role. I really don't care for that. Everybody likes to score goals. Everybody likes to contribute to winning. I've missed out on a lot of that."

199

BIRMINGHAM BULLS

Birmingham may sound like an unlike spawning spot for a major league hockey franchise but it appears to have rejuvenated what was a sorry Toro aggregation.

Coach Gilles Leger, who replaced Bobby Baun in the Toros' Coaching Box during the course of last season, has his own theories about the surprising emergence of the Bulls as a legitimate contender.

"Training in Europe was an interesting experience for the players last year but it gave them a false sense of security playing against competition that wasn't as strong as teams in the WHA," commented Leger. "On their return to Toronto the Toros began filling training room and hospital beds. By the time the season was over they had played only seven games out of 81 with the full starting lineup."

In Leger's words, there were other factors contributing to the Toros' decline.

"Our goalkeeping most season long ended up in the hands of rookies and while they gave their best they just didn't have the experience or the stamina to play full-time in major league competition."

If you listen to him enough, Leger starts to make sense. Late last season the Toros plugged the gap in their netminding ranks through the acquisitions of John Garrett from the ill-fated Minnesota Fighting Saints and Wayne Wood from the Cowboys. During the off-season they required Gavin Kirk from the Cowboys, thereby reuniting their top offensive threat that has Mahovlich and Napier on the wings. And by adding Hoganson and Lagace, a couple of veteran pros, they settled down what had been a rookie studded defence.

It may not look like much on the surface but upon giving it careful scrutiny one suddenly comes to the realization that the Bulls have filled the holes that were so evident last year.

"The Addition of Garrett, Wood, Hoganson and Lagace should cut down our goals against average by over a goal a game," added Leger. "When you consider that we lost 23 games by one goal last year it's easy to see what difference these men can make to our club.

Those are the physical facts. But there are others that don't necessarily show on the surface.

In Toronto, the Toros were made to feel like second-class citizens who in the eyes of the public could see only the Maple Leafs. It had to have an effect on the team morale.

In Birmingham the Bulls are No. 1. They are, in fact, the only game in town. They're the major tenant in a spanking new Coliseum that seats 16,750, beautiful-appointed throughout. And while hockey may yet be a completely foreign sport to the citizens of Birmingham, they've been warmly received by the city's sporting gentry.

While the signs at the Coliseum say that "Birmingham is Bullish on the Bulls," there is no guarantee that the WHA will succeed in Dixie. Owner John Bassett has sold 40% of the team to Birmingham business interests in an attempt to inject a feeling of local participation but it's a matter of fact that pro hockey has yet to gain total acceptance in most southern U.S. centres.

Only time will tell whether Birmingham changes the pattern. Certainly the Bulls appear to have.

OUR PLAYER

by **JIM FINKS, JR.**

JOHN C. STEWART

Young John Christopher Stewart appears to be making the most of the opportunity to play center ice for the Birmingham Bulls, since his arrival in early December of 1976. John C. scored a goal in his first appearance with the Bulls last December 2nd against Edmonton, after being secured from Syracuse of the North American Hockey League.

Since that time, the Toronto native and former Bowling Green State University star has been a big plus in the drive to catch the New England Whalers for a playoff birth in the W.H.A. Eastern Division.

Just for the record, John C. Stewart is no relation to John A. Stewart who appeared in one game for the Bulls earlier in the year, and has since been waived. Both Stewarts played together with the Cleveland Crusaders last year.

With a hockey oriented family of 3 brothers and 5 sisters vying for starting positions, "Stewie" fled for the rink at the tender age of 4. He's been going strong ever since. The combination of a patient Father and instruction from

older brother Tom, (who played pro with Detroit) started young John in the right direction for a career in pro hockey.

Quite often you'll find the aspiring young hockey player who makes the mistake of trying out for goal early in their career. The budding center iceman was one of those victims. Fortunately, the outdoor conditions of an Ontario winter put a halt to Stewart's netminding. "It was too cold standing around in goal, so I went to center," he said.

From there it was up the ladder to Junior hockey, and eventually a scholarship offer to play both hockey and golf at Bowling Green. "I was very much interested in furthering my education," says Stewart. "It was the best of three worlds at Bowling Green with School, Hockey, and Golf. Golf has been a big part of my life." He has a 2 handicap to justify that statement.

After a second year at Bowling Green, Stewart decided to turn pro, and was expecting to be drafted by the Detroit Red Wings. Instead, he was the second pick of the Cleveland Crusaders in the W.H.A. amateur draft in May of 1974. The General Manager of the Crusaders at that time was Stewie's College Coach at Bowling Green for a year, Jack Vivian.

The 59 games spent in his first year and 42 the next year with Cleveland, were at best a lesson in patience and perseverance. Three different coaches guided the fortunes of the Crusaders in those first two years. "It was hard to establish credibility without a coach being there for any length of time. And it was tough to crack the lineup at center behind Jim Harrison, Rich Leduc, and Ron Ward." Leduc is a leading scorer with the Cincinnati Stingers, Ward was recently acquired by the injury-riddled Winnipeg Jets.

With the Cleveland Crusaders moving to Minnesota for the 1976-77 season, Stewart was looking forward to starting a new season with the Fighting Saints.

Especially since there would be a better opportunity to earn a spot at center, then there was the previous two seasons. As things turned out, patience and perseverance were summoned once again. The season would start in Syracuse. Little did Stewie know it would end up in Birmingham, Alabama — Hockey Capital of the South.

"The hospitality here is just beautiful," he says. "Management has been really fair with me, and the big crowd against Quebec is definitely inspiring for hockey in Birmingham."

PHOTOS by Doug Redd

The play of Stewart's line has also been quite inspiring as of late. Scrappy Gord Gallant keeps everybody honest on left wing, Mark Napier keeps rolling along in pursuit of 50 or more goals at right wing and center Stewart is helping to jell it altogether by scoring 6 goals in the last 8 games.

As for off-season activity, the summertime means lots of Golf and instructing youngsters at Bob Whidden's Hockey School in Cleveland. The 23-year-old bachelor can be seen frequently teeing it up at the pretigious Firestone Country Club in Akron, Ohio. No doubt many hours of patience and perseverance went into perfecting his golf game, just like his hockey game.

NEW LEASE ON LIFE
Harbaruk's Shingle Will Have to Wait

BY D. R. O'LAUGHLIN

NICK HARBARUK

Indianapolis Racers right wing Nick Harbaruk has always thought about entering law school when he finishes his career in hockey.

Last season it looked as though Nick, unhappily, would get his wish much earlier than planned.

Appointed the team captain at the beginning of the season by then coach Gerry Moore, Nick lost the honor when he and Moore "did not see eye to eye."

And although he ended up scoring 20 goals and 23 assists, it seemed to Harbaruk that his first unpleasant year in the World Hockey Association would never end.

"It looked like this year was going to be the same," says Nick, drearily recalling training camp and the early days of the season when he was not playing.

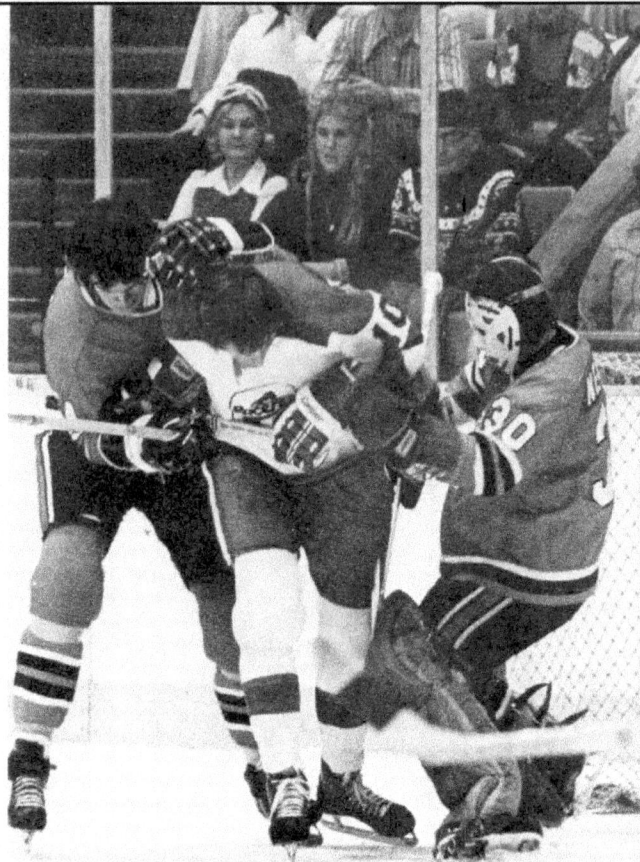

LOOKING FOR THAT LOOSE PUCK
photo by Ed Moss

But when Nick's future began to look the bleakest, two things happened that changed his attitude and put that law shingle far in the future.

The first was Jacques Demers.

"Gerry wasn't using me. When Jacques became coach we had a talk and he said I would be playing," Nick recalls.

The second was the return of his confidence.

"When I knew I would be playing the good feeling came back," he admits. So did the goals. And Harbaruk found himself in the enviable slot of Racer's top scorer.

"I don't think I've gotten that much better," the 32-year-old athlete claims. "My improvement is due to our great team. There is unity off the ice and on. That's been winning us hockey games."

Nick also credits line mates Bob Sincinski and Bob Fitchner.

"Sinker and I have played together for two years and we tend to anticipate what each other is going to do," he says.

Coach Demers has designated the trio as his strong checking line. And their success in holding down such scoring greats as Winnipeg's Bobby Hull has been phenomenal.

"Hull was my responsibility when I played with the Pittsburgh Penguins in the NHL," Harbaruk points out. "I get psyched up when I know I will be facing him because if I give him the slightest opportunity he will turn it against me.

"I leave Hull alone, basically. I don't bodily abuse him, run him in the corner or stick him. But I don't get far enough away from him that he can get a shot on net, either."

Born in Poland during World War II, Nick and his family fled to Germany and immigrated to Canada when he was 5.

"I don't remember the war years, I was too young," he says. "But when my family gets together they talk about it and I enjoy hearing their stories."

Most hockey players put on their first pair of skates when they are 3. Harbaruk's initiation into hockey didn't come until he was 10.

While Nick's father encouraged his son to play the winter sport, he also wanted the boy to get an education.

" 'Go to school,' he was always saying to me," recalls the slender athlete. Nick took his father's advice and earned a B.S. degree in economics from Tulsa University while he was playing for the Tulsa Oilers of the Central Pro Hockey League from 1965 to 1968.

From Tulsa he went to the Western Hockey League and the Vancouver Canucks. Pittsburgh obtained him in an interleague draft in 1969 and he played for them until coming to the Racers last year.

Harbaruk and his wife, Nancy, and their two daughters, Kim, 6, and Deborah, 3, live in a home they bought on Indianapolis' Northside.

Nick has found family activities help him relax between games. "I take my girls to the zoo or wherever and we all go skating at the Coliseum," he says.

In the summer the Harbaruks return to their home near Toronto where Nick and his father operate a sod farm.

"Farm work helps you keep in shape because it is tough," he points out. "A lot of our guys — Pat Stapleton, Reggie Thomas, Andy Brown — say they really enjoy working on their farms."

Looking to April, Nick has nothing but positive thoughts about the remainder of the season.

"Our team has gained a lot of respect from other teams this year," he says. "But there are those who expect us to fall apart. I don't think we will, but I'd like for them to go ahead and think of us as an underdog. We'll prove them wrong at the end of the year."

Maggs Top Choice for MVP

Referee Ron Ego and Darryl Maggs take a stroll — to the penalty box

Selection of the Most Valuable Player, more often than not, is an exercise in false evaluation.

A 50-goal scorer, regardless of his overall talents and leadership qualities, is a perennial candidate. The stance is taken that the team couldn't win without him, when, in actuality, said player is complemented by so many fine players his accomplishments come with relative ease.

In other words, give centerman Michel Parizeau two 50-goal wingers, and he'll generate 100 assists---and immediately be regarded as the premier centerman in the league.

That's not to imply that he's not already a fine centerman. It's just that he would be a better one with that kind of carbonation to work with.

When the WHA's fifth season winds down, the strong MVP candidates, doubtless, will be the likes of Marc Tardif and Real Cloutier of Quebec, Anders Hedberg of Winnipeg, Blaine Stoughton and Rich Leduc of Cincinnati, and, perhaps, ageless Gordie Howe in Houston.

All, indeed, are worthy candidates---but no more so than the Racers' Darryl Maggs, who, in the unvarnished view of Coach Jacques Demers, ranks as the best defenseman in the WHA today.

Maggs, at 27 and a six-year veteran of the pro ranks, is experiencing a vintage year. Chances are good he'll finish as the top scoring defenseman in the league---but his contribution to a team decimated much of the season with injuries far exceeds his point totals, already in excess of his career high of 50.

"There have been nights when **Maggs has played upwards of 45 minutes,"** advised Demers. "He just goes out and does a consistently good job. . .the kind that keeps you in the game. . .the fact that we are in second place, still challenging the Nordiques for first can be attributed to the kind of year he's having.

Certainly, Maggs---who served two seasons in the National League with the Chicago Black Hawks and California Seals---is among the best puck-carrying rearguards in the game. And no one can deny his pure defensive talents.

"This is the kind of team that to succeed every man works his butt off night after night," says Demers. "We don't have any of those big gunners that can break a game open. We do it with hard work, earning every goal we get. Without a Maggs, a Pat Stapleton or a Dick Proceviat, I prefer not to think where we'd be in the standings."

It's Demers' view that the MVP award is for the man who represents the most value to a given team that, minus his presence, would take a colossal pratfall. Since the injuries to Bryon Baltimore (20 games

ago) and Kenny Block (10 games ago) Maggs has logged more ice time than those guys up on the **Alaskan pipeline.**

When Maggs was unjustifiably overlooked for the mid-season All-Star team, he declined an invitation from Demers to participate as a coach's selection.

It was with the thought, of course, that since the media hadn't selected him, they wouldn't miss him. And what the hell, he needed the rest anyway.

Danny Labraaten — Better This Year

By SUSAN NICOL

Danny Labraaten is in the midst of his second season as a Winnipeg Jet. His English has improved considerably and he no longer shies away from interviews. He is more poised on the ice and his contributions to the team are improving as well.

He had a good rookie year, but he says it did have its low points.

"I came over here (to Canada) and right off I had a problem with my knee," he says, referring to an injury he sustained during the Canada Cup series.

"I had it in a cast and for a month all I could do was come to practise and watch."

The injury kept him from starting the regular season with his new team mates.

"It was tough to get over that, but I did and I started to play not bad, but not great either."

Just as he started to adjust to professional hockey, he separated a shoulder and spent more time on the sidelines. He recovered from that setback and went on to score 24 goals and to collect 27 assists.

"I think the whole year was pretty good. I don't think I could have done much better in my rookie year. Now that I'm starting a new season, things are going even better."

Danny was chosen "Rookie of the Year" for the club, but he says the title meant nothing to him.

"Not that I wasn't glad to be chosen," he adds quickly, "but it wasn't really fair. There were only two of us . . . Kent Rhunke and myself and Kent was sick (with mononucleosis) for most of the year. I had a pretty good chance to be chosen."

He smiles when asked about living in Winnipeg.

"That wasn't much of a problem," he says. "I have lots of Swedish people around me. And Winnipeg has really nice people . . . friendly people."

This season Danny has been playing with Kent Nilsson, another Swedish import.

"Kent and Peter Sullivan play much the same. Peter plays like any other European centre. I like playing with both of them. Their styles aren't much different. Kent had a really good start, but now he's a little down. The whole line is down right now . . . maybe the whole team."

Although the Jets have sagged a bit after their tremendous start, Danny believes it is mainly due to the rest of the league catching up.

"I think the other teams are playing a lot better now," he says. "It took them a little longer to get into the season. We came from Sweden and a good training camp at the beginning. We skated a lot there so we were ahead of them — in better condition."

An ailing Kim Clackson, who played defence behind the Lindstrom-Labraaten-Nilsson line, has left a gap that isn't readily filled.

"Kim Clackson is good for the whole team," Danny says, "and especially good for us. He was behind us the whole time."

Looking ahead to the Czech/Russian games, Danny is predicting an exciting series.

"I know the Czech team this year," he explains. "They are good skaters and it's going to be tough to beat them. The fans can look forward to more skating than they're used to, more passing and a faster game. The Europeans haven't changed much, except that they may be tougher.

"In the first games, they'll be at a disadvantage. We'll be working on the rebounds. We have a good chance to take them here in Canada. But we'll have to skate with them."

As far as the games against the Russians in Japan go, Danny says the Jets can count them as true away games. Not only will the travelling affect the team, but the style of game will be European.

"I've heard about their rinks. They are the same size as those in Europe so the game will be the same as played there."

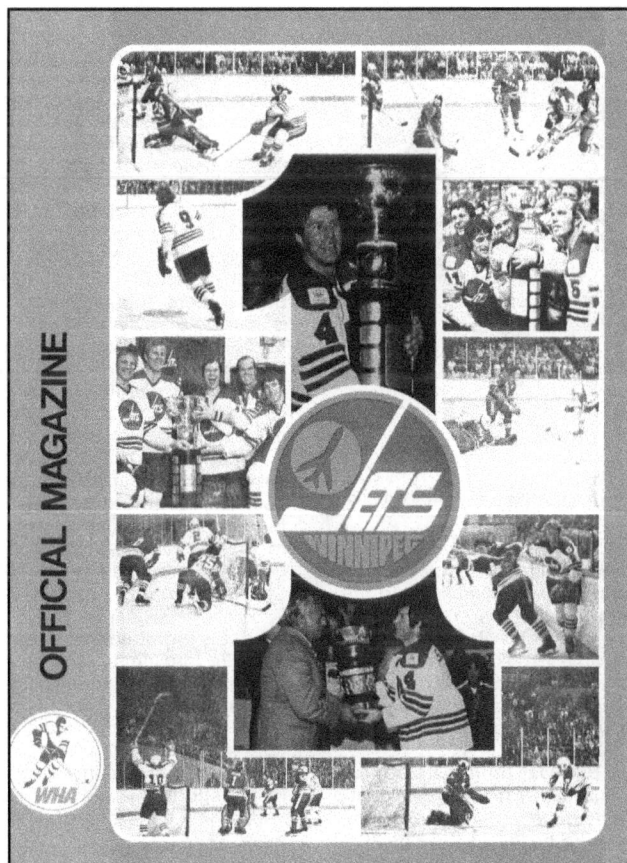

OFFICIAL MAGAZINE

You've Come A Long Way Baby

BY JOHN HEWIG

Billy Steele came to training camp this fall with a little different attitude than he had had last year, and with good reason. You see, at the first day of camp, it is photo day when all contracted players have their photos taken for newspapers and various publications. Last year Steele wasn't under contract (he had come to camp as a free agent, on the recommendation of his former Michigan Tech coach John MacInnes and his agent Art Kaminski) and so he was excluded when it came time for the other players to smile for the birdie.

"It's no big deal really," said Steele recently, "but it does kinda make you wonder. At first I thought to myself that 'hey, this team is already picked,' but I just made up my mind to have the best possible camp that I could, and go from there."

As it turned out, Steele was sent to the Stingers farm club in Hampton, Va. and he was told down there that there really wasn't any room for him. Coach John Brophy had pretty much the same team that he had the year before, and he was going to go with the same guys because he was gunning for the league championship and he felt that it was within his grasp if he had players who had played together and knew each other's style of play.

"Broph told me that he was going to trade me so I could play somewhere, and it turned out that I was sent across the river to play for the Tidewater Sharks. I was just finally happy to have a place

out, it was the best thing for me."

There seems to be quite a bit of truth to this, because all Steele did was get named to the second All-Star team in the league, as well as win the Rookie of the Year Award at the end of the season.

With the year over for the Tidewater Sharks and Steele, the Stinger management was impressed enough with his play that they called him up for the last three regular season games here in Cincinnati. All Billy did was score two goals in three games, even though he managed only three shots on net during these games. A month later the Stingers signed steele to a contract for the '76-'77 season, and all was well. He came to camp knowing that he'd been in line to have his photo taken with the other guys. He was happy, and so was coach Slater.

"Billy really deserved to be signed after the way he played for us those last three games at the end of the year" recalls Terry.

"He always hustles for me, and that's the type of guy any coach would want on his team. It's not really how big you are when it comes down to measuring a player's heart, and Steele has one of the biggest hearts in the league."

Slater has been promoting Steele since the opening game, and it has gotten contagious. In the beginning portion of the schedule Steele was a member of Slater's 'Killer Bees' (along with Dennis Sobchuk) and he performed so well that when members of Slater's regular lines needed a rest for a game or

to play, so I didn't mind it all. As it turned two, Terry started using Billy in a regular role along with killing penalties. Now Steele is entrenched on a regular line, for most games, and he is very deserving of it. His hustle and desire seem to have rubbed off on the rest of the guys, and the team is better for it.

"He's a little fireball that seems to get some of the guys going when we are flat" remarked Slater, "and he'll continue to play on a regular shift until he plays himself out of the line-up. His value serves to pick guys up when they are flat, and he seems to ignite them. I'm very pleased" Slater concluded.

Steele is thankful for the chance to play regularly, but if he does have to go back to serving as a 'Killer Bee' exclusively, he'll do it happily.

"I'm glad that I'm here and I'll perform any duty that the coach wants me to. If I do my very best every time that I'm out there, the rest will come with time. I'll tell you this, it is nice to know they have enough confidence in your hustle to put you on the penalty killing team.

Billy's size has been much publicized because he is considered small as a Major League hockey player. It doesn't bother him that much, although he does feel that it takes away from his efforts to stay in front of the net a little bit.

"I do have a tough time staying in the slot, because those big defensemen can

Steele has earned a regular shift with Stingers this year.
Steele is one of Coach Slater's "Killer Bees".

push me away, but I do think it serves to my advantage sometimes going into the corners. My size there makes me more aggressive, plus they don't think that I'll be able to take the puck from them so I think that they let up a little. Then they are pretty surprised when I come out with the puck."

* * * * *

Although Billy was born in Edinburgh, Scotland, his family moved to Canada when he was quite young, and this obviously is where he learned the game of

hockey. His Aurora (junior hockey) coach knew the coach at Michigan Tech (mentioned earlier — his name is John MacInnes) and so he was contacted and all of a sudden Billy had a scholarship to play college hockey.

"In college they really condition you, really get you in shape. I think that I put on 20 lbs. my first year up there, and it really helped me."

Steele played with another former Stinger, defenseman Bruce Abbey (who is currently playing hockey over in Europe) and he also was a team-mate of New England's George Lyle. He recalls what it was like playing with Lyle, and is kind of surprised that George is off to such a quick start.

"Lyle was always a slow starter when I played with him at school," recalls Billy, "but I'm not saying he doesn't deserve the points that he is getting. It's good to see him doing so well but I hope he gets his points when he's not playing us" Steele added with a grin.

* * * * *

So it is that Steele has found a home here in Cincinnati, and he is rapidly becoming a well rounded player that coach Slater can count on when the going gets tough, especially in the corners. To him, he is happy to be here and he'll readily admit it. But what is more important is the fact that Slater is happy he's here, and after all, he's the boss. 🖾

An Unfair Assumption ...

By Bob Neumeier

"If I can't make it in pro hockey by my skating, then I don't deserve to be here." Alan Hangsleben

When Nick Fotiu left Hartford for fame, fortune, and a few extra shifts on ice in New York City, some Whaler fans immediately concluded that Alan Hangsleben would assume Fotiu's role as enforcer. These fans gazed at his muscular frame and John Bunyon-sized fists and unfairly assumed Hangsleben would be spending most of his working hours in the penalty box. But unfortunately, they forgot to ask Alan his opinion on the subject.

"I don't want to be a goon, I don't want to go around starting fights or causing trouble, I wan't to be a hockey player," admitted Hangsleben recently. "Sure, Harry Neale would like me to be aggressive in forechecking and I think that's the strongest part of my game. If I can't make it by my skating, then I don't deserve to be here."

Asking Hangsleben to goon is like asking Joni Mitchell to sing at the Metropolitan Opera. Asking Julia Child to whip up a peanut butter and jam sandwich. Asking Howard Cosell to play Rhett Butler in Gone With the Wind.

In short, asking Alan Hangsleben to play enforcer is a bit unfair and presumptuous. He's not cut from that mold.

"I don't think there is anything wrong with a clean body-checking or even a good toe-to-toe fight," Alan said. "I'm not against that type of play and I think nobody else is, either. But the cheap stuff, the elbows and sticks, and the running around is for the birds. When I played college hockey, hell, they threw you out for two games if you dropped your gloves."

As for this farm boy's present contribution to New England, we asked his coach, Harry Neale.

"For Hank to be truly effective on left wing, he must use his size to his advantage. He must be aggressive, he absolutely must throw his weight around in the corners. He is truly at his best when I can *hear* him forechecking."

At the beginning of the year, Harry Neale could not hear Alan forechecking, in fact, he could not see him accomplishing that end. For after a sound stint with Team USA, when the Warroad, Minnesota native hit everything that moved in that international series, he settled back with the Whalers into strictly a finesse style, thereby not taking advantage of his assets.

"I was upset when Harry benched me earlier in the year," concluded Hank. "I think every athlete is super-egotistical and I'm no exception. I know I can play regularly in this league and I wondered what was wrong. Then, we had a few talks and he told me some things that I wasn't doing very well. But now everything appears to be fine. Sitting on the bench has a way of awakening you to the true facts of life. I'm probably better off from that benching, now that I look back."

If goals are truly a barometer of excellent play, Hangsleben is certainly better suited for success after his initial troubles. After 24 games, the left-winger accounted for eight goals, exceeded only by Tom Webster and George Lyle. If Alan can sustain this torrid pace, he would end the season around the 25-goal mark, which if he continues his forechecking aggressiveness, would be a fine season.

This success would be even more remarkable considering his unfamilarity with the position of left wing. As a high school Jack Armstrong in Minnesota and a collegiate Jim Thorpe at North Dakota, Hangsleben solely played defense. But with Rick Ley, Brad Selwood, Thommy Abrahamsson, and the Roberts boys in town, a change was necessary for the Whalers to take advantage of Hangsleben's abilities.

Hangsleben amplifies.

"I played a little wing in college, but most of the time I played at defense. Playing the wing is tougher for me, because you have to adjust to so many of Harry's systems. Some nights we forecheck with one man or two, and our individual responsibilities are always changing. The physical part of the change is not that tough, but the task of knowing exactly what to do in each style of play is the toughest for me. But I have received a lot of help from many of the older wingers, for which I am grateful.

It seems unlikely that this soft-spoken winger will ever develop into a big goal scorer. But in this dump-the-puck era, the need for big, tough wingers is obvious and can not be underestimated. Let us hope that goal scoring success does not give Hank illusions of Guy Lafleur, but rather serves as a tasty dessert to the main course of tough forechecking and spirited play.

Lyle Moffat — An All-Round Athlete

By SUSAN NICOL

Lyle Moffat of the Winnipeg Jets has played consistently well through the season thus far, although the club has had its ups and downs. He has had numerous scoring opportunities during the Winnipeg wins in the first twelve games of the schedule and during the drought that followed.

However, he and his checking linemates would rather exchange those chances for points.

"We've had a lot of breaks as far as chances are concerned," he explains, "but as far as putting the puck away, we've had a lot of bad breaks. We get the opportunities, but we've hit goal posts, the goalies have been hot or we've just missed the net. If we could have scored with the opportunities we've had, we'd all be doing pretty well."

The so-called third line has undergone a few changes recently especially with the appearance of a fourth line on occasion. Lyle, Bobby Guindon and Peter Sullivan were together for most of the games and he says they play the same style.

"We go hard into the corners and try to work the play from behind their net," he says. "We try to create havoc in their end, because if you can put pressure on their defencemen, you make opportunities for yourself. Most of our chances have been attributable to hard work."

He says his line has played well, even when the other two lines were having problems.

"We worked together when the other two lines weren't putting the puck in the net. The team has had dry spells as far as goals go, because we were only scoring two or three when we're capable of scoring five or six, on the average, in a game. Even during the time when the team was having trouble, our line was playing reasonably well, getting the chances to score

goals, as well as keeping the other teams from scoring."

Lyle is not worried about the drought that placed the Jets in third place.

"The season's still young," he says. "We're only a quarter of the way through the schedule. We have something like 50 games left. That's lots of time to get back on track. Most of the games we lost by one goal and a lot of those in overtime. It's not that we were doing anything drastically wrong. We just have to correct the mental lapses that come late in a game."

He says the Winnipeg Jets don't handle the European teams any differently than any other opposition club.

"I'm sure most of the guys on this team believe that they (the Europeans) should start preparing for us. We have a pretty good hockey club. Before the games, we go over how they come out of their own end and whether or not they favour coming up the middle. But if we work and skate, I think they will have to try and look after us, instead of us checking them.''

Winnipeg has been humming of late with talk of new arena plans. It appears that the city fathers favour the idea of expanding the present facility, but Lyle says the talk has not affected the players directly.

''It's all happening on the outside. It's important to management of course, but we have enough trouble trying to win hockey games, never mind worrying about arena we're going to play in. It would be nice to have a new facility, but this building has a lot of atmosphere. It would be great if it could be renovated the way

the Montreal Forum has been renovated. They've really updated it. It looks super and it's a great building to play in.

''The players don't really care as long as the people come out and get behind us and we can win our games.''

Lyle Moffat is an all-round athlete who had a chance to play pro baseball as well as hockey. He says the choice was an easy one to make.

''I did have an opportunity to go to the Expos training camp when they were first inaugerated, but I was already committed to Michigan Tech on a hockey scholarship. Besides, there are only a couple of Canadians playing pro ball and fielders are a dime a dozen in the States. I had a chance to get an education and play in a super league at the same time. It wasn't tough to choose.''

Stapleton: No

Patrick James Stapleton, by normal measurement, hardly fits the Super Star mold.

He drives an ordinary car, his wardrobe is somewhat less than devastating --- and you'll rarely find him frequenting a night club.

He's more at home at a farm implement store or watching his daughter play kick ball.

The Pat Stapleton you see on the ice, however, is another person. At 5-8 and a stocky 180, he's a giant at his trade. He's one Racer whose name you'll find in the Hall of Fame in years to come.

Stapleton's been among the top defensemen in the game for a mere 16 years. He comes from the school of offensive defenseman---but it has been long since established that he plays a better grade of pure defense than most of his counterparts.

And at age 36, he shows no signs of letting up. Whatever he has lost in quickness has been compensated for with experience. Rarely is he caught with his rompers out of adjustment.

INDIANAPOLIS RACERS 1976-77 ROSTER

FORWARDS

NO.	NAME	POS	S	HT	WT	PLACE & DATE OF BIRTH		1975-76 CLUB	GP	G	A	PTS	PIM
6	Rosaire Paiement	C	R	5-11	170	Earlton, Ont.	8-12-45	New England (WHA)	80	28	43	71	89
7	Hugh Harris	LW	L	6-0	190	Toronto, Ont.	6-7-48	Calgary (WHA)	29	5	9	14	19
								Indianapolis (WHA)	41	12	28	40	23
8	Renald Leclerc	RW	R	5-11	170	Ville de Vanier, Que.	12-12-47	Quebec (WHA)	42	15	17	32	35
								Indianapolis (WHA)	40	18	21	39	52
9	Reg Thomas	C	L	5-10	180	Lambeth, Ont.	4-21-53	Indianapolis (WHA)	80	23	17	40	23
10	Nick Harbaruk	RW	R	6-0	195	Drohiczyn, Pol.	8-16-43	Indianapolis (WHA)	75	23	19	42	26
11	Brian McDonald	RW	R	5-11	190	Toronto, Ont.	3-23-45	Mohawk Valley (NAHL)	10	5	9	14	17
								Indianapolis (WHA)	63	16	17	33	58
14	Blair MacDonald	RW	R	5-10	180	Cornwall, Ont.	11-17-53	Edmonton (WHA)	29	7	5	12	8
								Indianapolis (WHA)	56	19	11	30	14
15	Al Karlander	C	L	5-8	175	Lac La Hache, B.C.	11-5-46	Indianapolis (WHA)	79	16	28	44	36
16	Michel Parizeau	C	L	5-10	165	Montreal, Que.	4-9-48	Quebec (WHA)	52	12	27	39	24
								Indianapolis (WHA)	23	13	15	28	20
17	Bob Sicinski	C	L	5-11	175	Toronto, Ont.	11-13-46	Indianapolis (WHA)	70	9	34	43	4
19	Francois Rochon	LW	L	5-11	181	Montreal, Que.	4-18-53	Denver (WHA)	41	11	10	21	10
								Indianapolis (WHA)	18	6	2	8	31
22	Gene Peacosh	LW	L	5-9	170	Sheridan, Man.	9-28-48	San Diego (WHA)	79	37	33	70	35
23	Mike Zuke	C	R	6-0	180	Sault Ste. Marie, Ont.	4-16-54	Michigan Tech (WCHA)	43	47	57	104	42
25	Mark Lomenda	RW	R	6-0	186	Esterhazy, Sask.	4-14-54	Indianapolis (WHA)	2	0	0	0	0
								Denver (WHA)	37	6	17	23	11

DEFENSEMEN

NO.	NAME	POS	S	HT	WT	PLACE & DATE OF BIRTH		1975-76 CLUB	GP	G	A	PTS	PIM
2	Darryl Maggs	RD	R	6-1	195	Victoria, B.C.	4-6-49	Denver (WHA)	42	4	23	27	42
								Indianapolis (WHA)	36	5	16	21	40
3	Dick Proceviat	LD	L	6-0	180	Whitemouth, B.C.	6-25-46	Indianapolis (WHA)	72	7	13	20	31
4	Kim Clackson	RD	R	5-11	195	Saskatoon, Sask.	2-13-55	Indianapolis (WHA)	77	1	12	13	351
5	Bryon Baltimore	RD	L	6-2	190	Whitehorse, Yukon	8-26-52	Denver (WHA)	41	1	8	9	32
								Indianapolis (WHA)	37	1	10	11	30
12	Pat Stapleton	LD	L	5-8	180	Sarnia, Ont.	7-4-40	Indianapolis (WHA)	80	5	40	45	48
24	Ken Block	LD	L	5-10	185	Steinbach, Man.	3-18-44	Indianapolis (WHA)	79	1	25	26	28

GOALTENDERS

NO.	NAME		S	HT	WT	PLACE & DATE OF BIRTH		1975-76 CLUB	GP	MP	GA	SO	AVG
1	Andy Brown		L	6-0	185	Hamilton, Ont.	2-15-44	Indianapolis (WHA)	24	1368	82	1	3.60
28	Jim Park		R	6-1	190	Toronto, Ont.	6-22-52	Mohawk Valley (NAHL)	37	2208	168	0	4.48
								Indianapolis (WHA)	11	572	23	0	2.41
31	Michel Dion		L	5-10	170	Granby, Que.	2-11-54	Mohawk Valley (NAHL)	22	1294	83	0	3.84
								Indianapolis (WHA)	31	1860	85	0	2.74

WHA

thing Fancy, Just Talent

The trail that led Stapleton to Indianapolis started in Chicago in 1966, where he was a standout with the Black Hawks for eight seasons. He bolted to the WHA Cougars in '73, led them to the Avco Trophy finals and later wound up with a sizeable piece of the team before it expired following the '74-75 season. He then joined the Racers---and emerged a dominating force in the club's march the Eastern Division championship last season.

In 1971 Stapleton set a NHL record for assists by a defenseman (14) in the Stanley Cup playoffs. Two years later, with 15 assists to his credit, he tied another NHL playoff record.

His first year in the WHA he was named the league's outstanding defenseman.

"I think my biggest plus is that I can anticipate well," says Stapleton, whose thick blond hair is as much of a trademark as his hockey ability.

"I can always see what's going to happen," he adds. "It's like a gift, not something you can work to perfect. You see a situation develop the way you have so many times and you know instinctively which way to go. Sometimes you get burned, but overall you do all right."

Stapleton's anticipatory power was one of the key factors in the Racers rise from bottom place in the WHA East Division to first place last year.

He averaged at least 40 minutes a game playing time last year.

"Once you get into a game, minutes don't mean anything. I actually feel better the longer I play," Stapleton confesses.

This year minor injuries have limited his playing time somewhat but the muscular Stapleton has not lost any of his enthusiasm for the game.

"I have another year's commitment to the WHA after this one and then I'll see what happens. But even after I finish my playing career I don't doubt that I'll be involved in hockey someplace," he says. "It gets in your blood."

Stapleton, whose fair hair has earned him the nickname Whitey, expresses concern for the future of the WHA, however.

"I thought we were really on the right track at the start," he admits. "Now, I honestly believe we have stepped back and a lot of good young hockey players have gotten away from us the last year or two.

"It takes good young rookies to build a strong league," he adds. "I don't know if agents are playing a big part or not--directing the guys the other way

because of teams folding and not living up to contracts. There are a lot of factors involved and we must work hard to overcome them."

It's not unusual to see Pat encouraging his own young sons on the hockey rink. Although he doesn't push them toward the game, they express the same enthusiasm of most Canadian youngsters to the sport. And the two oldest boys seem to have inherited some of the father's ability.

"I say very little about it to them, but I'll help if they need me," he says. "I enjoy watching them perform. They've been involved in track and field and football. And my girls (three) play kick ball."

Stapleton and his wife, Jackie, relegate their brood of six to a farm in Ontario in the summer.

Farmer Stapleton has about 500 head of cattle, 250 acres in one area and 290 in another.

"My people were farmers and I imagine I'll end up there when I retire," he says, admitting that the farm routine in the summer is a good way for him to stay in shape.

"One thing about the farm is — you never have to hunt for work — you're surrounded by it," he adds, grinning.

Stapleton has other business interests as well - - - remnants of his many years in Chicago.

In 1971 he and his associates built an ice rink (there were only 11 artificial surfaces in the city then and now there are 56). Although the ice is down in the summer, Stapleton sees that the building is used for other activities, such as concerts.

But, he admits, sometimes outside interests can be detrimental even to the dedicated athlete.

"When you're young you think only of the game," he points out. "Then when you develop outside interests it takes some of the edge off hockey."

"You've got to work on keeping that mental attitude. It's easy to get off the beaten path -- you have to learn to bear down and keep with it."

Aside from his ability, the thing that sets superstar Pat Stapleton apart from other hockey players and other athletes, as well, is his attitude.

There is rarely a time when Stapleton doesn't have a friendly word or an autograph for an interested fan.

Once, as he watched his daughter playing kickball at an inter-school contest, he was beseiged by scores of young autographer seekers. Patiently, and with that familiar grin that Racer fans have come to love, he satisfied the demands of all the youthful fans --- much to their parents' delight.

ROBBIE FTOREK:

"It Isn't The Size Of The Dog In The Fight..."

Part of the appeal of professional hockey may lie in the fact that the players are actually rather average in size. You can identify with them. Who can truly picture himself as a 6-10 basketball player dunking the ball? Or as a 275-pound defensive lineman storming through to sack the quarterback? Although you might not be able to see yourself flying down the ice at 30 miles an hour to score a goal, the fact remains that hockey players aren't all that much bigger than the average fan.

There does seem to be a minimum, though, say somewhere around 165-170 pounds, or roughly 10-15 pounds heavier than Robbie Ftorek of the Phoenix Roadrunners. The program lists him at 160, but don't believe it. He only hits the upper middleweight limit fully dressed, soaking wet and with a brick in each pocket.

The whole business of size must become a bore to Ftorek, who is invariably quizzed about it by writers and broadcasters in interviews. A reporter's impulse is to remark that Ftorek's accomplishments are amazing in light of the fact that he's the smallest player in the World Hockey Association. Robbie himself though, to judge by the way he plays, doesn't seem to realize that he's any smaller than Gordie Howe, Andre Lacroix or Bobby Hull.

Now no brief will be made here that Ftorek is in a class with the aforementioned superstars. Not yet, anyway. The opinion is vigorously advanced, however, that he is one of the brightest young skaters to appear on the hockey scene in some time. There is little question that if he were playing in New York, Chicago or Toronto he would be the toast of the town. Playing in Phoenix has limited his impact on the national media but they're starting to catch on, and with good reason.

During the just completed WHA campaign, Ftorek utterly smashed the record for most points in a single season by a player born in the United States. The old standard was 87, set by New England's Larry Pleau (like Ftorek, a native of Massachusetts) during the league's first term of operation in 1972-73. Against vastly improved competition, Robbie has eclipsed Pleau's mark by 25 points while performing for a Roadrunner club that is known more for its tenacious defense rather than offensive prowess.

Though he is an obvious target for intimidation by larger opponents, there is no record of their ever having succeeded. Ftorek is dead game. He fights back, and his self-preservation tactics have brought him over 100 minutes in penalties this season, making him the first player in the WHA ever to break the century mark in both points and penalty minutes in one year.

Since you're here tonight watching him, be on the lookout for his skating ability. It can be traced in part back to figure skating lessons he took as a youngster in Needham, Mass., before he got into kids' hockey.

He is a passer and playmaker of remarkable cunning, continually engineering good scoring opportunities for his wingers and usually operating several steps ahead of his opponents. He's

particularly dangerous from behind the net, a spot from which he is gifted at threading the needle with passes out to open teammates or even scoring himself. At least a half dozen of his tallies this season have been tuck-ins from behind the goal, a move he works on assiduously in practice sessions.

Robbie seems an unlikely candidate to work the corners and the boards against defensemen who can outweigh him from thirty to fifty pounds but his appearance is deceptive. An intensive program of working with weights to develop strength in his arms and upper body has made him a pesky, unrelenting attacker, clever at hemming in opponents along the boards, dislodging the puck with his stick and then darting away to cause further havoc with his passes.

Will success spoil Robbie Ftorek? Not a chance. He is an extremely dedicated competitor, his own severest critic, and seems unlikely to relax the demanding, self-imposed standards that have put him where he is, well advanced towards the top of his profession.

Robbie Ftorek

ROBBIE FTOREK: Soccer Star

Stinger center talented athlete during career

Robbie Ftorek, one of the premier hockey players in the World Hockey Association, was an outstanding high school soccer player, although his start was anything but auspicious.

"I played in high school because I couldn't make the football team," explained Robbie, the WHA's Most Valuable Player in 1976-77. "My science teacher saw I was disappointed and said, 'Why don't you come out for soccer?' A couple of weeks later, we were playing.'

"I said what are the rules? They told me 'How far can you go?' He said, 'As far as you want.' So he mentioned I had to dribble the ball every third step. I did it, then I dropkicked the ball into the net. I turned around, and the coach was on the ground laughing!

"What's so funny? I asked. Then he said I couldn't pick up the ball. So the next time, I kicked the ball down the field and into the net. This time, they're not laughing."

Robbie played soccer for four years at Needham and was named all-state in his junior year. In his first year, the team was unbeaten in ten games, and the team went on to enjoy considerable success while Robbie played.

Just what attracted Robbie to the sport?

"I like the flow of the game," he explained. "It's much like hockey. It's give and go. You create openings just like hockey. In soccer, it's stopping and going. It really sharpens your legs."

When he was a student at Needham High School, Robbie played soccer in the fall, then hockey in the winter and baseball in the spring, and despite the rapid transition from one sport to another, it never bothered him or affected his play.

Ironically, Robbie's greatest thrill in soccer was also his saddest moment. It occurred in the state finals during his junior year, and he talked about his ambivalence.

'We were in the finals, and our captain had a tremendous game," said Robbie. "I was watching him, and when they went to announce the most valuable player, I congratulated him, but when they said my name, I really got upset.

"I accepted it, but I didn't feel I deserved it. Afterward, my dad talked to me. He said Billy had a great game, but you had a great season and a great game. It could have gone either way. You have to accept it. If they voted for you, you won it."

When he played baseball, Robbie played a variety of positions — catcher, second base, shortstop and pitcher. He especially remembers a particular incident as a catcher, trying to handle a fireballing pitcher.

Robbie said he threw so hard, the ball burned his hand because there was no padding in the glove. To insure against such unneeded pain, Robbie put a handkerchief in the glove. That wasn't quite good enough, so Robbie sent one of the kids to the store to get some sponges, and only then did he get relief from this pitcher's overpowering fastball.

Like many hockey players, Robbie Ftorek began skating at an early age, five. Strangely enough, he started out as a figure skater, taking lessons from the late Marabelle Vincent Owen. He figure skated until he was eight, by which time he had developed a strong interest in hockey.

The impression was solidified when his father took him to a Boston Bruins game and he got a puck autographed by the players.

Robbie rapidly developed his skills, and he skated on the U.S. Olympic team in 1972. He played briefly with the Detroit Red Wings of the National Hockey League twice, then solidified his reputation during three years with the Phoenix Roadrunners.

He won the league's MVP award in 1976-77, scoring 46 goals and racking up 71 assists for 117 points, fourth best in the league.

For Robbie Ftorek, hockey is a way of life, and one which he especially likes, but he downplays his own accomplishments.

"I really enjoy it," he said. "Whatever I attain in hockey, it's not obtained by myself because it's a team sport. The objective is to win and I do everything in my power to win. It's the accumulative thing — winning.

"It doesn't mean anything when you don't win.

As Cincinnati Stingers fans readily know, that is the way Robbie Ftorek plays the game.

"GUEST SHOT"

RICHIE LEDUC

SO MAKE WAY now for another product who sharpened his hockey skills in Three Rivers, Quebec, that noted spawning ground for feisty, swift and agile pushers and propellers of the puck.

This one is one of the hardest working young centers in the World Hockey Association, Richard Henri "Richie" Leduc, who, along with Phoenix' Michel Cormier and Serge Beaudoin and Houston's Andre Hinse, along with many other outstanding players were either brought up or played some of their Junior years in that hockey hotbed.

Leduc, just 24 years old, is now in his second WHA campaign with the Crusaders, and is still impressing fans and players alike with his skating and stick-handling abilities as well as his quick Gallic temper which last year amassed 122 penalty minutes for a guy who is not built like your normal slugging hockey heavyweights. As a matter of fact, Richie is a rather slender 5-11, 170 pounds, but the intensity with which he plays every game won't let him back off from what he considers to be *gaucheries* toward him by his opponents.

The flashy Frenchman saw more playing time last season than in any previous pro season dating back to 1971 when he divided time between Boston and Cleveland, both in the AHL. Even moving about between those two cities, he still produced a 58-point season, including 27 goals, not bad at all for a first year pro.

The following two campaigns found Richie splitting between the Boston Bruins (NHL) and their AHL farm team, and again he displayed both scoring ability and aggressiveness. In the '72-73 season Leduc totaled 75 points, including 32 goals; the year following, he suffered a broken wrist that handicapped him and limited him to spot duty in just 57 games.

Then came the move to the WHA last season, and Leduc had his most productive totals logging more ice time than ever before. And Cleveland fans responded by voting him "Player of the Year" honors for his efforts.

All the lefthanded shooter did during his 77 games, plus a disappointingly short five-game playoff series against Houston, was score 35 goals, add 31 assists and soar well past the century mark in penalty minutes as noted above.

Was he happy with the results? Uh-uh, according to Richie. "You can never be satisfied with what you do," Richie was quoted once, "not unless you score 10 goals a game and shutout the opposition. I've never yet seen a player play a perfect game."

Cleveland fans, incidentally, aren't the only ones appreciative of Leduc's talents. Knowledgeable hockey people around the league are aware of his puck lugging ability and playmaking skills. The Crusaders undoubtedly are aware that having Leduc in the lineup, on the roster, is like having money in the bank.

Leduc, incidentally, is in a current streak, so watch out for him tonight. He's scored nine goals in his last eight games, which could mean trouble for the Runners. ●

THE SWEDISH EXPRESS
51 Goals in 47 Games

Anders Hedberg has become the first player in the history of major league hockey to score fifty goals in fewer than fifty games.

The Swedish right winger of the Winnipeg Jets scored goals 49, 50, and 51 Sunday night in the Jets 6-4 win over the Calgary Cowboys. The game was the Jets' 49th of the season, and it was only the 47th that Hedberg has played in.

Hedberg broke the record established 22 seasons ago by the immortal Maurice 'Rocket' Richard. That record was matched just two seasons ago by the equally immortal Bobby Hull. In 1944-45, Richard became the first player ever to score fifty goals in a season by scoring his 50th in the last game of what was then a 50- game NHL season. In 1974-75, Hull scored a dramatic hat trick for goals number 48, 49, and 50 in the Jets' 50th game of the season. Hull went on to score a record 77 goals that season.

Neither of their performances was more dramatic than the 25 year old Hedberg's the other night. Hedberg, already playing with a cracked rib, and having scored eight goals in his last two games to literally come from nowhere in his bid for immortality, overcame a second period knee injury to score two third period goals and collect his record.

Two weeks ago, after 43 games, Hedberg had 40 goals and a rib injury that was supposed to sideline him indefinitely. He missed but two games. When he returned to action, on Jan. 30 against Phoenix, he was 'held' to one assist. Then the onslaught began.

On Tuesday at Edmonton, Hedberg scored four times to bring his season goal total to 44. Returning home against San Diego on Friday, he scored four more, numbers 45, 46, 47, and 48.

Entering Sunday night's game, the man who was the WHA'S rookie of the year two seasons ago had a chance to do what no one had ever done before --- not even the great Richard. He knew it, and so did the crowd.

As he was to say later, 'I got a very special feeling from the fans tonight from the moment we stepped on the ice. I knew they expected something special from me tonight. It helped me concentrate more and I know it helped me get the record.'

In the second period, with the score tied 2-2, and with Calgary defenseman John Miszuk serving a double minor, Hedberg started working on the 'something special'. At 13:42 Hedberg carried the puck down the right boards, behind the net, and jammed it home between the post and goaltender Gary Bromley's stick side. Goal number 49.

Less than 40 seconds later, however, it appeared that the dream might be over. Still skating on the power play, Hedberg attempted to vault the Calgary defense, but instead fell heavily to the ice.

He was removed to the Jets' dressing room where he was examined by the team doctor. The doctor's verdict: stretched knee ligaments.

The Jets went to the dressing room for the second intermission with a 4-2 lead. When they returned to the ice for period three, Hedberg did not return with them.

While the crowd may have thought that all hope for the record had vanished, Hedberg refused to surrender. His knee heavily taped, he returned to the Jets' bench shortly into the period.

Even Hedberg, though, doubted his own chances. After the game he recalled, 'after I was hurt I did not think I could get the record, I knew I couldn't skate as well as I should.'

But get the record he did, and it happened just that quickly. Midway in the period, Hedberg took the ice on a line change. Just seconds after

ANDERS HEDBERG

he went over the boards, he gathered in a pass from Bill Lesuk, fired towards Bromley, and scored number 50. At 11:21 of period three, the third year pro had completed a feat that no major league player had ever before accomplished.

He added lustre to his mark by scoring still another goal, an empty-netter with one second remaining on an unselfish pass from linemate and countryman Ulf Nilsson.

After the game, Hedberg attempted to brush off his achievement by saying, 'I consider our Avco Cup championship of last season a bigger thrill than my record tonight.'

But moments later he belied his pride, and at the same time added a touch of humor, by saying, 'now when they look in the record books they will see Rocket Richard and they will see Bobby Hull, and they will wonder 'who is Anders Hedberg? '.

The answer to that is not so difficult. Anders Hedberg is the player who currently leads the WHA in scoring with 92 points. He is the player who has scored 11 goals in his last three games, a record. He is the player who has now had three separate four goal games already this season, a record. He is the player who has scored 50 goals in each of his first three major league seasons, a record. And he is the player who scored 51 goals in 49 or 47 games, pick the one you like. They are both records.

ROOKIE ON THE LINE

A glimpse at Morris Lukowich's chances with the Aeros.

By Chuck Myers

For a while, at least, Bill Dineen is determined not to permit Morris Lukowich to become a victim of circumstance. In this case "circumstance" means the new WHA ruling that clubs suit out no more than 18 players for each game.

It's a reduction of two from last year and the problem, of course, was that, by opening day, Dineen found himself faced with having to cut two more players than in times past.

He did not want it to be Lukowich. The 20-year-old rookie and top pick by the Aeros in the amateur draft, had made a strong impression on Dineen throughout training camp and the exhibition series.

More than a few times Dineen has talked of Lukowich's speed and quickness and puck control and skills as a shooter.

"One of the biggest things he's got going for him, though," Dineen says, "is aggressiveness. It's one of the things coaches look for first. It can't be taught. With Morris it's a completely natural ability."

Dineen's plan is to carry 19 players through the first few weeks of the season, which means someone will have to sit out each game. Dineen said he will determine who on a day-to-day basis.

"He's earned a chance to play," Dineen explains. "The only way to see what he can do is put him in games. If it weren't for the new limit, there is no question he'd stay on the roster. Even as it is now, I don't think it will be long before he makes an impression on the rest of the league."

Actually, Lukowich became aware he was being watched by an opposing team for the first time during an exhibition game with the NHL's Atlanta Flames a few weeks ago.

The precise moment is unimportant. Lukowich couldn't even remember the period.

"We were in their end of the ice and I crossed very close to their goalie," he said. "Anyway, one of their defensemen skated past me a few seconds later and said, 'Watch your step, rookie.'"

Thus it came to pass that Morris Lukowich, officially, was no longer anonymous in professional hockey.

The question that immediately occurred was, why the warning? Hockey, after all, is not played across a table. Other players, even rookies, have been known to sweep in close to an opponent's goal.

"I guess it was because I let him have it on the hand with my stick as I went by," Lukowich continued with a grin. "Their defenseman must have thought I hammered it a little too hard or something, and wanted to let me know he had seen it.

"I didn't let it bother me."

Lukowich, of course, was not really anonymous to begin with. In 72 games for the Medicine Hat Tigers of the Western Canada junior hockey league last year, he scored 65 goals and was credited with 77 assists.

But it's quite a step from junior hockey to the WHA, and winning a spot the first year is the exception. John Tonelli made the step successfully for Houston last year.

"I know just how Morris felt the first day he practiced with the Aeros," Tonelli said. "You just can't help thinking where you are. That it's going to be a lot different. Now, it's the Howes and Hulls who will be on the ice with you.

"When you are a rookie, you are in awe of all this the first few weeks. Then you discover you can compete, but you realize you are still a rookie and you will have to work hard, harder than you ever worked before.

"Also, a lot of how long you last in

the pros is how fast you learn. It seems like I got two or three new lessons every game. Some the hard way. Morris has looked pretty good to me so far, but I'm really in no position to evaluate."

Dineen feels Lukowich's learning process is on schedule.

"I overheard him talking to some of the players one day after practice," Dineen said. "He'd missed a couple of faceoffs, and was saying if he did this a little different, he'd have a better chance.

"I can tell he's thinking about other things, too, because he just has not made any glaring mistakes since the first exhibition game."

Lukowich says the first thing he learned was to keep his head up.

"You can get away with keeping your eye on the puck a lot in junior hockey because the defensemen move back more, all the way to the net, in fact, most of the time.

"Up here, though, you find out very quickly that, if you skate with your head down too much, one of them will be waiting for you at the blue line. It's a good way to get your head knocked off.

"And I can tell there are a lot of little tricks you have to pick up to stay around, too," he continued. "Ways to slow someone down, for instance. How to make sure you keep the guy with the puck between you and the wall. You just don't realize how much you don't know until you're thrown in with the pros. Most of them, especially the ones who have been around for a while, are just very smart hockey players."

Whether Lukowich is still in an Aeros uniform in a month, then, depends upon his performance in the next few weeks. Otherwise, Dineen will place him with Oklahoma City, Houston's Central Hockey League affiliate.

Dineen says that wouldn't be the worst thing that could happen either.

"If nothing else, it would assure him ice time in every game. And he'd probably be back with us before the end of the season anyway."

Lukowich dismissed the possibilities with no more than a shrug.

"Sure, I want to stay here," he says, "but I work for the Aeros. I'm under contract. Whatever Bill feels is necessary is okay with me."

Dineen has used the 5-8, 165-pound Lukowich at wing and center, and usually in the same line with Ted Taylor and Cam Connor. Connor joined the Aeros in time for the league opener after being traded from Phoenix. •

"GUEST SHOT"

GOALIE JOHN GARRETT

LAST SEASON and this, John Garrett has been in the nets every time his team has played the Roadrunners. He is the only WHA goalie to have played every minute against Phoenix and his record overall is (entering this series) 5-4-1 with an excellent 3.04 goals-against average. In the two-game series here last month, Garrett was voted top honors in each game, even though the clubs split. Let's hear, then, from young, talented, articulate and opinionated John Garrett.

"We are the team to beat," declares Garrett, who for the third straight season, is handling the heavy goaltending burden for the Fighting Saints. "I believe that with the acquisitions of Dave Keon and Johnny McKenzie, we are the team to beat in the WHA."

Garrett, is a 5-8, 170-pounder whose neatly curved moustache has earned him the nickname Chi-Chi (after golfer Chi-Chi Rodriquez). "I've been watching Keon ever since I was a youngster — I hope he doesn't mind me saying that," the 24-year-old Garrett smiled. "He's always been a team leader on

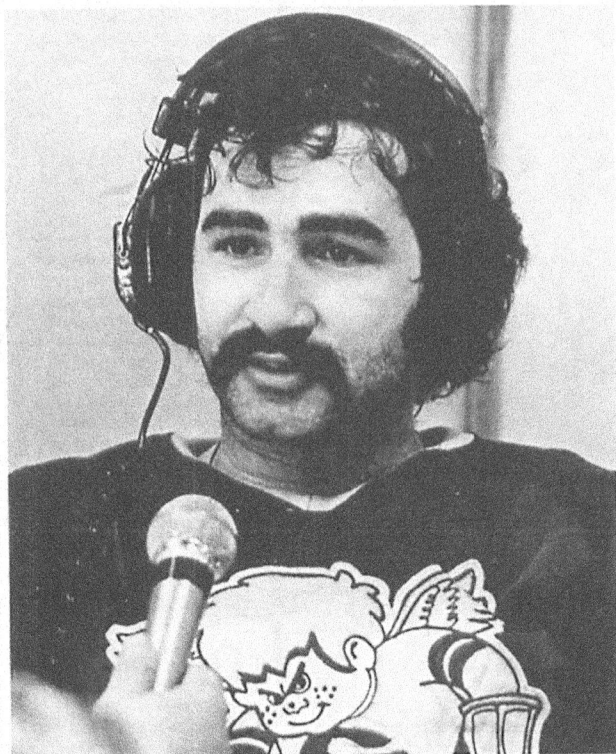

and off the ice. He's led the (Toronto Maple) Leafs to many Stanley Cups and there's no reason why he can't do it here."

"Keon knows how to steady down the younger players," says Garrett, "and he knows how to give the club a lift when it needs one." Johnny McKenzie? "He's always been aggressive and a digger."

Talking briefly about himself, Garrett says, "I'm shooting for another good won-and-lost record this season." In 55 games and 3,284 WHA regular-season minutes last season, Garrett granted 180 goals for a respectable 3.28 goals-against average. More important, he was credited with 30 victories. However, he wants to cut down from the 23 defeats he was tagged with in 1974-75. "I think I can win 30 and maybe more this season," he offers. He also wouldn't mind improving on his shutout record of last season, two.

But basically, Garrett is interested in seeing himself and his goalie partner stay healthy, and play and win their share of games.

Garrett has a pretty good "book" on WHA foes. After facing the league's top gunners for two seasons now, Garrett maintains that Winnipeg's Bobby Hull still has the league's hardest shot.

"But Frank Mahovlich has a good one, too, though he doesn't get it off as often as Bobby," Garrett adds. "In the playoffs last season, Quebec's Rennie LeClair had a big shot. And I know that Marc Tardif likes to fire right off the wing, and that New England's Wayne Carleton probably shoots more backhanders than 90 percent of the guys in the league."

Because of his comparatively diminutive size, Garrett plays a standup style, unlike the bigger boys who tend to be floppers.

"I've got to get out there and cut down those angles," he explains, "because I just can't cover that much of the net with my body. As far as my philosophy of goaltending goes, I try to act just a little nonchalant on the ice. I try not to let the pressure of the game get to me. I prepare myself for every game and try to keep my confidence up, even if things might not be going too well at the moment. It's easy for a goaltender to get down; the other guy might be playing more and you start thinking, 'What the hell am I doing here?'"

Some goalies, like Indianapolis' Andy Brown, one of the last maskless goalies in hockey, are virtual cheerleaders on the ice, talking it up to their teammates every minute. Not Garrett. That could lead to trouble, he believes.

"Not everyone likes to be advised by their goalie," he grins. "I know who to talk to on our club, and when. Some, like Ron Busniuk, seem to appreciate it. Others don't. Still others want to hear about it only in the dressing room between periods. Really, a goalie must know the psychology of who to talk to, and when."

Garrett also likes to observe that the caliber of the league has, "really improved. I don't think you can say enough about how all of the teams have worked so hard to add good players. Look at our management; they've gone all out to give us a winner, and they'll continue to do so. Look at how the Europeans have helped Winnipeg and Toronto, and of course who knows better than we do about what the Howes have meant to Houston?

And now, many of the top draft choices are starting to come with us. It's a league where a young player can plan a career. I definitely believe the WHA is here to stay now. Sure, we've had teams fold. But the NHL has some clubs with financial difficulties, too. We're a growing league and many of our clubs are doing well."

"GUEST SHOT"
TOM WEBSTER

*"All Tom Webster needs to be a superstar
is a little ink" — Gordie Howe*

Tom Webster

When Gordie Howe talks, people listen. The incomparable Howe has always spoken vis-a-vis his actions on the ice, so his statement made at a Boston press conference last season should not be passed over lightly. Gordie Howe is just not that kind of carte-blanche, kudo thrower.

To the brilliant New England Whalers' right-winger Tom Webster, it is a compliment of the highest order. It's kind of like receiving communion from the Pope, playing catch with Willie Mays, or getting picked up hitchhiking by Evel Knievel. For the relationship between Webster and Howe dates back to Tom's childhood, where the impressionable Webster idolized the great No. 9 of the then Detroit Red Wings.

But Webster's fondness for Howe later developed into something quite removed from this common childhood idolization. He later became Gordie's roommate and linemate with the Red Wings.

The Boston Bruins were the first to recognize Webster's tremendous talents. They ogled his 50-64-114-point season with the Niagara Falls Flyers, the leading scoring mark in the OHA for that 1967-68 season. Winning the Eddie Powers Memorial Trophy as the league leading scorer was a mean feat considering Tom was in pretty fair company. With Webbie on that junior juggernaut were Whaler teammates Rick Ley and Brad Selwood (Team Canada players), WHA stars John Arbour, Rosie Paiement, and Don Tannahill, and NHL stickouts Derek Sanders, Jim Lorentz, Don Marcotte, Jean Pronovost, Steve Atkinson, and Phil Roberto.

The highly touted native of Niagara Falls was lost to the Buffalo Sabres by the Bruins in the expansion draft of 1970. The Sabres, completely devoid of any goalkeeping talent, traded Webster to Detroit for veteran goalie Roger Crozier. With the Wings, Tom moved onto a line with a pretty fair center and right-winger, Alex Delvecchio and Gordie Howe.

"That was a great experience because both Gordie and Alex taught me two very important aspects of this game," Tom said. "Gordie taught me how to protect myself on the ice. And Alex taught me how to let the puck do the work in an offensive situation. Alex was probably the greatest example of this technique in hockey."

The tips paid a handsome dividend. Webster scored 30 goals with the Red Wings that season at left wing and exhibited many of the Howe methods. The brilliant season did not satisfy GM Ned Harkness, who proceeded to rudely dump Webster to the California Golden Seals for defenseman Ron Stackhouse.

After 12 games with the Seals and a very serious spinal fusion operation, Webster jumped Charlie Finley's crew and signed with the Whalers in July, 1972.

It was a brilliant coup for Whaler GM Jack Kelley. Paired with the artful dodger Terry Caffery, Webster and Caffery tore apart the league with dangerous offensive forays. All Webster did was score 53 goals and 50 assists for 103 points and a berth on the all-league team. And his centerman, the wispish Caffery, added 100 points.

And last season? Webster pumped home 43 more markers, despite missing 14 regular season games with injuries and countless other contests where he played at less than 100%. He finished with a 12-8-20 point mark in the last 15 regular season games. He then scored three playoff goals in the first two games against the Chicago Cougars, before crashing into a goal post which kayoed the remarkable Webster for the next four games in which New England lost three.

ON THE COVER: No. 12, veteran forward (left wing, center) Bob Barlow, who is captaining this year's Roadrunners club. Still has excellent speed, despite having more years behind him than any other on the club. Inspirational player, can lift team with his hustle.

Darryl Maggs — Survivor Par Excellence

By JIM MATHESON

Indianapolis Racer owner Nelson Skalbania sat on a stool at Teddy's Lunch recently and talked about running in between spoonfuls of hockey and money chatter.

"I never have got an athlete to take me up on my offer to run three miles," said Skalbania, who is a jogging nut.

"That's my distance . . . exactly where I'm comfortable."

"But I did run against the Racers . . . a mile and a quarter."

Skalbania, who is in better shape than most athletes through his running and racquetball workouts, beat all the Racers but two.

"I couldn't beat the little blonde-haired kid who played in Edmonton last year, Bobby Russell. Or Darryl Maggs."

The fact that he lost to Maggs isn't earth-shattering news. Even if

he's a big defenceman and not a fleet forward.

Maggs is a survivor, pure and simple.

If you don't believe it, check the Hockey Register.

He played in California for Charley Finley. In Chicago with the financially-strapped Cougars. In Denver where they had no money. In Ottawa where nobody really cared. And in Indy last year where they had to take pay deferments to meet some past bills.

Through it all, he's been a winner. Check last year's stats.

• Second in voting for WHA's best defenceman.

• Fourth in voting for MVP award.

• Seventy-one points, most for a blueliner.

• Averaged 40 minutes a game.

The accolades came pouring in last year for the 6'1", 195-pounder, who played junior hockey in Red Deer and Calgary. "In my mind, he WAS the most valuable player in the entire league," said former Racer coach Jacques Demers, now minding the store in Cincinnati.

That the rewards finally started coming is sweet music to Maggs' ears. Ever since he joined the WHA in 1973 with the ill-fated Cougars, he's had trouble making a name for himself. Maybe because he was playing on a team that was dying in the Windy City. Or maybe because he moved on to another loser in Denver after Chicago folded.

But most likely because he was overshadowed by former teammate Whitey Stapleton, who actually coached in Chicago. Whatever, he had to struggle for acceptance by the fans and media.

Mind you, that's not a new story. It's always been that way from the time Maggs was playing junior to the time he played college hockey in Calgary.

"I never really had pro aspirations," said Maggs, after a workout recently at the Coliseum. "It wasn't in the back of my mind . . . it wasn't the only thing I ever wanted to do."

He played Tier Two with Red Deer in the late '60s before moving up to Scotty Munro's club in Calgary late in the 1969-70 season. He played only 35 games of major league junior but unbelievably it was enough to get him drafted.

"I didn't even know there was a draft," recalled Maggs, looking back eight years to the time Chicago Black Hawks made him their fourth-round draft choice.

"I was a little ignorant of the situation, I guess. I thought you still belonged to a pro team when you were playing junior."

Still, pro hockey wasn't the pot at the end of the rainbow. Maggs wanted to go to school and play some hockey instead. "I wanted to go to U of Denver," he said, "but the deal fell through. So I ended up at U of Calgary."

It wasn't exactly the bigs. Maggs got an education in the classroom but didn't really progress on the ice.

"After one year there I had a plan to go and play in Vienna," said Maggs. "I decided to go to the Black Hawk camp for fun . . . to see where I stood." He stood rather high, even for a kid who'd played 35 junior games and 20 college contests.

He was immediately dispatched to Bobby Kromm's Dallas Black Hawks to team with Winnipeg Jet Barry Long. He wasn't there long. One year and he was in the Windy City playing some part-time rightwing for the Hawks.

Eighteen months later he was peddled to California Golden Seals for Dick Redmond and the playing rights to Indy centre Bobby Sheehan. When things went sour in Oakland, he wasted little time hopping to the WHA team in Chicago in 1973.

"It was interesting but a little shaky," said Maggs, as he recalled the financial struggles of the Cougars in a city weaned on the Hawks. The Cougars had lots of spirit with Stapleton, Oiler goalie Dave Dryden and Ralph Backstrom among others but they couldn't keep up with the flood of debts.

When they folded, he was sold to Denver. But, as luck would have it, the Spurs went belly-up too. The same happened in Ottawa and he was finally relocated in Indy late in the 75-76 season.

Then . . . this summer. More insecurity.

The Racers couldn't pay their bills and they died until Skalbania brought them back to life at the last moment.

"It was definitely a time to start scrambling," said Maggs, who was in a state of limbo like the rest of his Indy teammates.

"I had talked to Jacques (Demers) about going to Cincinnati. But things worked out."

After the first two and a half months, he's not scoring as much as he did last year but he's still contributing.

"When you're playing against Darryl you really don't concentrate on him as an individual," said Racer coach Ron Ingram, who looked after the rival San Diego Mariners last year.

"But he deserves more credit for his defensive ability. People notice his puck-carrying skill first. He makes the quick play and finds the open man as well as anybody in his own end.

"But, he's good on defence too — or has been until recently.

"He's an excellent player."

Maggs hasn't become jaded, either. His job is still fun.

"Maybe because I got such a late start and didn't play all those years of junior, I've benefitted," said Maggs.

"I really enjoy the game . . . it's not a drag at all."

Comment Corner . . .

To realize just how good Kent Nilsson really is, one has only to study the already exposed talent of the Winnipeg Jets forward.

He's big at 6 foot 2, 190 pounds, but he's also as fast a skater as there is in the World Hockey Association. He's so smart with the puck that even the admirers of Ulf Nilsson gasp at some of Kent's feats.

In the summer of 1974, when he knew he would eventually try professional hockey, Kent shot 1,000 pucks a day off a plywood sheet at a homemade net. Today his shot is being touted as the hardest ever seen in the WHA.

Even his opponents marvel at the talents of last year's WHA Rookie-of-the-Year. "Of all my years in hockey, I realize that

he's one of a kind," says Winnipeg coach Larry Hillman. "He seems so relaxed all the time he fools you. You wonder how someone so relaxed can be so swift on the ice."

Last season Nilsson loved to stand by the boards two hours before a game when the arenas are as quiet as a monastery and the ice is glistening white, and utter statements such as, "Tonight I'll score 2 goals and we'll win 8 - 3."

Teammates didn't argue, they merely grinned. "Kenta" they knew, was not just a windy rookie seeking attention. He delivered. It took the native of Sweden just

one month to prove to the Jets and the WHA that he's as good an offensive player as there is in the league.

No one had a better first month. He led the League in scoring for five weeks and by the end of his rookie season, he had 42 goals and 107 points, eighth best in the WHA. That came despite the month of December when he failed to score a single goal. But, like all multi-trained players, he bounced back strongly.

He ranked among the top 6 in the WHA in most goals, most power play goals, most assists, most first goals, most lead-producing goals and was ninth in the plus-minus ratings.

His only noticeable shortcoming is his backchecking. Nobody comes back harder but he still hasn't learned the fine art of backchecking.

Hillman says of his backchecking, "He's like a deer coming out of the forest with someone shooting after him."

★★★

"THE JOLLY GIANT"

Hull, in addition to being one of hockey's greatest talents, also is one of its gentlemen, and it should come as no surprise that he would say something to a kid fresh out of college. And it's not that Nugent is likely to go unnoticed much of any place.

The 22-year-old Notre Dame graduate, at 6-5 and 230 pounds, is just about the biggest man in hockey. Boston's Peter McNab is the same height, but about 20 pounds lighter.

Hull's opening remarks to the new guy on the street alluded to his size. "How 'bout giving me a foot (of Nugent's height)?" kidded the Golden Jet.

"How 'bout giving me 25 mph (off Hull's slap shot)?" fired back the rookie.

That concluded the repartee, but the rookie continued to give the immortal tit-for-tat in other ways as he checked him the remainder of the game, following him into corners and once deftly taking the puck away from him against the boards.

The kidding exchange with Hull on first meeting and the effective checking job he did on the Golden Jet make two points about Nugent: the first thing that hits you is his size. It's later that you notice he plays the game of hockey right well, too.

Pat Stapleton admits he didn't know what to expect from Nugent except size and willingness.

Despite his size, Nugent is no "towering inferno" and his "Mad Stork" nickname in college really isn't very appropriate. Off-ice, he is pleasant, smiling and easy going. On it, he goes about his business without looking for trouble.

That isn't to say that if crunch comes to punch, he's going to be headed in the other direction. He didn't get 85 penalty minutes in 23 collegiate games last year by turning the other cheek. And fans at Market Square Arena have seen him skate up to frisky opponents who have taken liberties with smaller Racers and suggest to them that if it was a fight they wanted, he was available.

There aren't many around who are willing to accept that invitation.

That's fine with Nugent. He's here to play hockey, not to goon it up. If a word to the wise is as effective as a right to the nose, the purpose is as well-served.

A surprisingly agile skater for his size, a checker of such skill that Stapleton uses him to kill penalties and possessor of a slap shot that really doesn't need to borrow any mphs from Hull, Nugent doesn't have to depend on his fists to earn a job with the Racers.

And it's his skills, not his size, that are the reason he was thrilled but not awed by going up against Hull. "I figure I belong here," he says.

It's the third period and the big kid hasn't been playing that badly in his professional hockey debut. In fact, he's already set up a goal and at the end of the evening he's going to be named his club's star of the game.

Now he comes over the boards for a shift, lines up at his right wing post and hears his opponent say something to him. He looks over — at Bobby Hull.

"It was a thrill," remembered the Indianapolis Racers' Kevin Nugent after the game. "I wasn't in awe of him or anything like that, but it was certainly a thrill to play against him.

"I remember my dad taking me to see him play when he was with the Chicago Black Hawks when I was just a kid. And here I was playing against him."

Mike Gartner:

For Cincinnati Stingers rookie standout Mike Gartner, playing hockey evolved naturally.

"In Canada, it's different," he explained. "Here (the United States), you automatically start playing football when you're 10 or 11. But in Canada, you automatically put on the skates and find out if you like hockey or not.

"My parents encouraged me but they didn't push me. I always wanted to be a hockey player and I had a dream that I would be a professional hockey player. When I was 15, I thought 'if I work at this, I've got a good shot.'

"It was a dream that at the time seemed so far-fetched, but then I worked at it."

Like many professional hockey players, Gartner began skating at an early age — three — prompted, he said, by an interest his mother had in figure skating.

Four years later, Gartner began playing organized hockey and developing the skills which would catch the attention of Stingers officials.

While he was honing his skills in hockey, young Gartner also began playing what is considered to be the most brutal of all sports — lacrosse.

Stingers captain Rick Dudley, himself an outstanding former professional lacrosse player, once referred to the sport as "diving championships without the water." Gartner concurred, but he did enjoy the sport.

Center Ice

WINDING UP — Rookie standout Mike Gartner gets set to fire on goal during his first game as a professional hockey player, October 7th, 1978. The Cincinnati Stingers beat the Pittsburgh Penguins of the National Hockey League, 6-4, in that game.

Young Man With A Future

"I really like the game," he explained. "I started when I was 9 years old and played until I was about 13. But once you get into junior hockey, they stress that and you have to quit what other sport you're playing and concentrate on hockey.

"It's the most rugged, brutal game there is. Even in the young leagues, the little kids are kicking the bleep out of each other. You have to be good and have a lot of guts."

Ironically, it was while Gartner was playing lacrosse that he first met Dudley, who plays left wing on the line that includes Dave Debol at center, and of course, Gartner on the right wing.

Gartner was 10 years old when he first met Dudley who, it seems, had a penchant for popsicles.

"My father was the head of a firm which ran a junior lacrosse team (Mississauga)," said Gartner. "As a lacrosse player Rick was my idol. I used to watch him play.

"In between periods, I used to bring him popsicles. When I came here, Rick knew my dad, but he didn't make the connection. It really floored him. It seemed kind of funny bringing him popsicles and than playing with him."

Lacrosse and hockey were not the only sports at which young Gartner excelled. He also played rugby, basketball, and football.

The North Collegiate High School (Barrie) team of which he was quarterback went to the district semifinals in his first year and the district finals the second year, when he was named the team's most valuable player.

It is conceivable that Gartner would have become an outstanding basketball player, for as a guard he averaged 15 points a game as a freshman. Yet something prevented that.

"I was 5-10 and I stopped growing," he said with a smile, "and everyone else kept on growing. That was the problem. They were 6-2, or 6-3."

Eventually, Gartner began playing junior hockey in Canada and became a standout for the Niagara Falls Flyers of the Ontario Hockey Association.

In his second year with the team, 1977-78, Gartner scored 41 goals and added 49 assists for 90 points in 64 games. One year later, at the age of 19, he is playing professional hockey, He talked about the difference.

"First, you have to make the adjustment in practice," he said. "It's as if you're in kind of a daze, the checking is much harder, the playing is much faster.

"And you have to think a lot quicker. There is really a big difference. You've seen these guys playing on tv for five or six years and you're playing against them. You have to forget about that and just play hockey."

Those who have seen Gartner play have been impressed by his style, his speed and puck-handling abilities, and they have also noticed he does not shy away from checking and taking a man into the boards.

During the two months he has been in Cincinnati, Gartner has made an impression on persons whose talk shows he has appeared on and the reporters who have written about

ALL-AROUND ATHLETE — Now a professional hockey player, Mike Gartner excelled at virtually every sport he played, including football, basketball, rugby and lacrosse.

him, for he exudes a maturity and confidence which belie his 19 years.

Through his first 15 games, Gartner had scored four goals and 5 assists for 9 points, figures which are not unimpressive for a man just a year out of the juniors. However, he would like to improve upon those statistics and discussed how he thinks he should accomplish that.

"I feel like I'm playing fairly well," said Gartner. "But I'm still not satisfied because I've been in a scoring slump.

"You just have to take it easy for a game. The goals will come if you just play your game and the rest will take care of itself."

There are many athletes in professional sports who set goals toward which they apply themselves. Did Gartner have any such goals?

"I really don't like to reveal my goals," he said. "But I know what I want to do. I want to prove to myself I can play professional hockey.

"I think I can. I'm not conceited. If you don't have confidence in yourself, nobody else will. I don't want to just play, and I won't be satisfied to be just another player."

For those who have seen Mike Gartner play, they know he is anything but just another player. ℮

INTERNATIONAL WHA PLAY

The first season of European infiltration opened a few North American eyes.

EUROPEAN CONNECTION

By Herb Holland

As did their ancestors at the dawn of Western civilization, the Vikings have once again discovered North America, bearing hockey sticks instead of battle axes and wearing plastic helmets without horns.

Hockey may never be the same.

The Nordic horde descended on the World Hockey Association last season, when seven Scandinavians signed with the Winnipeg Jets, two more with the New England Whalers and another pair of national stars defected from Czechoslovakia to join the Toronto Toros.

This season Phoenix has added two Finnish players, the Jets have signed two more Swedish players and the Indianapolis Racers have signed one.

Who knows what next year will bring?

The first season of European infiltration opened a few North American eyes.

Anders Hedberg, described by many as the best ever to play in Europe, scored 53 goals and set up 47 more for the Jets to capture Rookie of the Year honors and finish seventh in the WHA scoring race.

Linemate Ulf Nilsson, meanwhile, was fourth overall with 120 points, and was second only to scoring champ Andre Lacroix of San Diego in assists with 94.

Vaclav Nedomansky, the 31-year-old Czechoslovakian rookie, fooled goaltenders 41 times for the Toros.

In terms of swift skating, lightning-quick shooting, slick stickhandling and technical mastery of hockey, the European invaders positioned themselves well in the critical sight of North American hockey experts, possibly even showing up some six-figure major league wonders as somewhat less wonderful than their celebrated contracts.

"I wouldn't trade my European players for anything," says Winnipeg Coach Bobby Kromm, who admits he walked into a beautiful situation when he left Dallas of the Central Hockey League for Winnipeg at the start of the season. "Technically, they don't come any better. They are in such good condition and their attitudes so great towards their jobs that I'd love to coach an entire team of Scandinavians."

However the Europeans did show a major flaw in their maiden year in the WHA—they were easily intimidated by old fashioned goonery, something not in European rule books.

Europeans began to look over their shoulders after a while, and didn't seem to drop their gloves except by accident.

"When you do hit them, their first re-action is to come up with the sticks," says a well-known hockey scout. "And if you raise a stick in anybody's face, he's gonna get mad enough to jump at you.

"That's what's wrong with the way they play, more than anything else."

"Fighting? That is ridiculous. There is no fighting in Swedish hockey because it is not allowed. There is not even a five-minute fighting penalty in Swedish hockey," says Hedberg. "Kids do not fight in games at home. They do not practice fighting. They practice sportsmanship and still play a rough game.

"But many people over here think the only way to play against a European player is to be rough and tough. They then are upset when the penalty minutes are not even in the games. But we do not retaliate because a power play will help to win. That is retaliation enough.

"Also there are many Canadian players who do not retaliate or fight," adds Hedberg. "There are smart Canadian hockey players too, who do not take the stupid penalties.

"We are no different. We just do not like to fight. Some European players will retaliate with the stick. But not any different than the Canadian players."

WHA Referee-in-Chief Bill Friday has refereed many games in which some teams have tried to intimidate the European players as a game strategy.

"They honestly don't commit the same penalties," says Friday. "But it is pretty hard to keep a game with Winnipeg involved under control when other teams start taking runs at those Swedes and Finns.

"The other team's bench gets all hot and bothered about the penalties and the play gets a little chippy. Especially because of the stickwork involved sometimes."

Lacroix, the Mariners' explosive little center, is far from a brute on the ice.

"But there are some who say I play with a high stick," Lacroix says. "However, I cannot compare with some of them in Europe and now in the World Hockey Association.

"You might give them a stiff check or something like that, but, you know, you will never see them retaliate right off the bat. Somewhere down the ice, though, you can bet you'll get a stick behind the leg or something sneaky like that.

"It's not that they play any less chippy than we do," he says. "It's not that at all. They just do not get caught, which is why the games get so chippy when referees don't call them for the penalties."

That line gets old after a while, says Jet team captain Lars-Erik Sjoberg, who at 5-8 is a position defenseman reliant on technique rather than size and muscle to gain his advantages.

"You know, enough is enough," says Sjoberg, who also captained the Swedish National Team before joining the WHA. "After a while you start to give two-handers back to them. You begin to accept that as the only way you will get them to leave you alone.

"It doesn't hurt my way of playing to trade two-handers, but I don't think it should be that way at all. It is up to the referee to call down *continued p. 22*

than they are in Europe.

"The game is different because the ice surface is much, much larger in Europe, and that makes it more of a skating game, not a checking game. Checking in the offensive zone was not even allowed in international games until just a few years ago."

The European hockey rink, Bergman explains, is about 15 feet wider than the North American and has a semicircular goal crease, much larger than the North American rectangle.

"Because the ice is bigger, players can't really take runs at other players as easily," Bergman says. "Passes are to players further away from the boards because the goal is further away from the boards.

"You need to hip check much better, and strip the forwards of the puck in the middle of the ice better on the larger surface. And of course you have to skate more.

"But because the boards are further from the center of the action in Europe, players do not run each other. That's why there are no fights.

"Another reason there is no fighting is because it is not even part of the rule book," Bergman adds. "It is an automatic suspension from the league, not a major penalty.

"But if we get penalties, they are easier to kill on the bigger ice surface."

Bergman, Sjoberg, Hedberg and probably the rest of the Swedes and Finns in the WHA will rejoin the Swedish and Finnish national teams in September for the World Cup tournament. Canada, the United States, Russia and Czechoslovakia will field their best hockey teams, composed of amateurs or professionals, to settle once and for all the nagging question of "who's best?" which has been asked ever since the Russians shocked Team Canada in the first game of the now-famous 1973 series.

"I don't think anyone could object to our returning to play for Sweden for that tournament," says Bergman. "They are more or less professional over there, too. They might have jobs or are going to school but they get paid by the hockey federation, too.

"It is much like a scholarship. We went to school and played hockey for the school. They (the federation) gave us money for expenses and paid for our rent and food. It was from the team—not from the school like it is here.

"It is good because I have received a good education from it. Most of us here have good educations. We go to school most of our lives in Sweden. That is most important back home—it is good to get

dirty playing. I guess they don't think it hurts to take a two-hander.

"Maybe we sould give a ref a two-hander. Then he will begin to call them."

And so it goes...

Thommie Bergman was not the first European to play major league hockey in North America—a big Swede named Ulf Sterner played in the National Hockey League for a short time in the early 60s and then returned to Sweden where he supposedly became the dirtiest player in the national league.

But Bergman, a 6-3 scarecrow of a defenseman was the first European hockey player to jump the Atlantic Ocean suc-

cessfully, playing with the NHL Detroit Red Wings for three years before going to the Jets last year.

"Of course the prospect for better money was the major reason that I came to Detroit. I also wanted to be the first to make it in North America pro hockey," says Bergman. "However, I look at it this way: If I can't play here, I will have learned a new language and gotten some money, so my education has been broadened as well.

"Luckily for me, I could play here. But I noticed the difference in style of play right away. I don't think it is rougher here because players are rougher or dirtier

WHA

money for hockey but for me it is the good education that makes my life richest.

"Still we are not amateurs over there even by Olympic rules. But the Czechs or Russians are more professional than we were. Maybe even more than we are now. Maybe more than anyone else."

"Hockey is what we did," says Nedomansky, who demanded English lessons as part of his bonus for defecting to Toronto. "That is all. We were in the institute in Bratislava and we play hockey, go to class, study hockey and train.

"Hockey is what we did."

Nedomansky, his wife Vera, and son, Vaclav Jr., escaped to freedom from Berne, Switzerland while they were vacationing. He says he left because, at 30 years old, his time was limited in Czechoslovakian sports.

"Every time I ask them if I can leave to play professional hockey, they say, 'no, no, no, no,' " Big Ned says. "The sports directorate said I could leave maybe after two or three more years but I knew that would never be, since I was already 30."

Nedomansky says the Soviet-Czech method of developing athletes was the main difference between Eastern European and North American hockey.

"There we were all-around athletes. We would train as much on land as we would on ice," he says. "It made us better hockey players and stronger athletes altogether."

The training day would include soccer, gymnastics, acrobatics, classes in hockey theory, lots of cross-country track and then, workouts on the ice.

"It makes you a better athlete," Nedomansky says. "And we were better than the Russians in Czechoslovakia. They would just win the big games in Olympics. Now they win against the NHL and WHA.

"But do not think you'll see Russians coming over here like Richard (Farda, his Toro compatriot) and I," Nedomansky continues. "When I left there, it was because my family was together. They will no longer allow athletes to travel with their whole families.

"You can no longer take a holiday even with your entire families—they make you leave your wife or your kids behind. You do not dare to escape if you ever want to see them again. We were lucky to get away.

"And it is a shame, because I think the Russians could play over here. Some of them could, anyway."

"I don't know about the Russians because they are too political with their teams," says Lacroix, who skated with Team Canada II, the one composed of WHA players. "They did not play fair when we were over there.

"First of all, the Russians are not amateurs, they're pros—I don't care what anybody says. Then, and maybe this is most important, they wanted to be treated differently than other teams. For example, when we were in Moscow, the Russians said that if we didn't stop checking them rough they would pull their team off the ice.

"And you see, that is our national sport in Canada and to me there was too much politics there. They were trying to tell us how to play our national sport. And that really got to me."

Not to mention several incidents with official tilmekeepers in the Soviet Union, Lacroix adds.

"We found out from looking at the series (which the Soviets won, 4-1-3) that in the second-to-last game in Russia they took two minutes from the clock without us even noticing.

"And when we scored the tying goal in the last game, they ruled it was too late. There should have been 90 seconds left. But if they're going to be like that, we should not play with them.

"After all, it is OUR game, isn't it?"

September's tournament will tell all.

A Certified Czech Cashes In

Vaclav Nedomansky traded his homeland for cash and future considerations. By Wayne Lilley

For 10 years now, any kid over six feet who ever took a faceoff in a league higher than midget in Canada has been labelled the next Beliveau. Or maybe Esposito. Unfortunately, the main benefactors of all this talent have been the minor professional and industrial hockey leagues across the country. Professional hockey has a summary way of dealing with drumbeating agents and attaché cases full of press clippings.

There's been a reluctance on the part of hockey cognoscenti to make such comparisons of late. Thus, you must excuse the enthusiasm of Vaclav Nedomansky's interpreter, himself only six years out of Czechoslovakia, when he says, "They called him the Jean Beliveau of international hockey, you know, in Czechoslovakia." Nedomansky blushes at the comparison, dismissing it as the fervor of a countryman. But Buck Houle, the man who signed Nedomansky to a Toros contract and an undeniably shrewd appraiser of shinny talent, is undeterred by the hex. "He's going to be in the superstar class," says Houle with such assurance that the doesn't even bother trying to convince you.

Going to be? What does a guy have to do? Last year, playing for his Bratislava team in the Czechoslovakian League,

Nedomansky scored 46 goals and added 28 assists in 44 games. In his 10 years with the Czech club he scored 146 goals in 211 games in international competition. He was the captain and leading scorer on the national team for the last several years and was voted the most valuable player in the World Hockey Tournament last year.

Before 1972, it was easy to dismiss international hockey as second rate. After two Canada-USSR series, though, nobody does that anymore. Nor did Nedomansky ever consider international hockey all that inferior. It's just that having accomplished almost everything there was to accomplish in Europe, he wanted to realize what he says is a life-long dream—to have a crack at professional hockey.

"The Czech Ice Hockey Federation officials had been promising me for seven years that they wouldn't stand in my way if I wanted to go to North America and play professional," says Nedomansky, with the help of the interpreter. "But they kept putting it off and putting it off. I'm 30 and I was afraid that I would never get the chance." The suggestion wasn't as preposterous as one might think. In 1969, Jaroslav Jirik was released by the Czechs to play for the St. Louis Blues in the NHL. But Jirik, most observers agree, wasn't on a par with Nedomansky.

The story of Nedomansky's defection through Switzerland to Canada, of the covey of big league scouts from both professional leagues in North America making their offers through a Canadian agent, and of the coup by the Toros in snaring one of the most highly regarded hockey players in the world, is still shrouded in mystery. And for very good reason. "Let's not talk politics," says Nedomansky. "I still have parents in Czechoslovakia." The implication is that recriminations against the relatives of defectors aren't unknown in communist countries.

Even so, Nedomansky doesn't exactly reinforce the myth that everyone behind the iron curtain is held in strict bondage. There are, for instance, privileges for performance. "As a hockey player, I was allowed to vacation abroad," he says. "I've been to quite a few countries in Europe.

And this made it easier for me to get to Switzerland to contact people in North America."

So the Toros outbid all the competition for the services of the European star? Perhaps, but there were other considerations, Nedomansky claims. "I'd played against Billy Harris as a player and against teams he coached when he was in Sweden. I also knew Buck Houle from his days with Canada's national team. I respected both of them. But when I heard that the Toros signed Paul Henderson and Frank Mahovlich (whom he played against when both were with Team Canada 72), that clinched it."

There were also, it might be noted, a few dollars that changed hands during Buck Houle's furtive visit to Switzerland, though not as many, Big Ned insists, as he might have received from other teams had he chosen to play in Atlanta, New York or Buffalo.

Of course, it's on the ice that Big Ned is going to have to prove his value to the Toros. And as a rookie, he expects to be tried by opponents for durability as well as skill. "Hockey is hockey," he shrugs. "I know I'll have to adjust to the smaller Canadian and American ice surfaces but I'm not worried about the physical part of the game. In Czechoslovakia we tried to pattern our style after the Canadian game and that includes using the body." Nevertheless, getting in shape was a major concern both before and during the opening of training camp. At 6-foot-1 plus and a playing weight around 200 pounds, Nedomansky clearly has the physical attributes to play the North American game. And his pre-training camp regimen of running and skating was nothing new for him. "European players, especially those behind the iron curtain," he says, "play or practise for 10 months of the year. And they keep fit during the other two."

Despite the success of Nedomansky and teammate Richard Farda in making the jump from their Czechslovakian team to professional hockey with the Toros, don't look for a mass immigration of hockey-playing Czech and Russian athletes. Nedomansky expects Czech officials to be watching more closely for players taking vacations. And Bunny Ahearne, the czar of international hockey, is still bleating about the money—about $40,000 per player—that he feels should go the the European teams that lose players.

But the biggest step is on the part of the player, says Nedomansky. Quite simply, it's a decision that's irreversible. "I cannot go back to my own country," he says, a little wistfully.

The arrival of a rookie of Nedomansky's stature hasn't thrown the rival teams in the WHA into paroxysms of ecstasy. But his claim that "There are lots of players in Czechoslovakia that could play professional hockey," may set them drooling, particularly after seeing the big center in action in a tense match against the Soviet Union. Since the Russian invasion of Czechoslovakia in 1968, Nedomansky claims the Czechs have had a little extra to prove. He adds proudly that in the last five years, "The Czechs have won more games than the Russians" in matches between the two countries.

There have been reports that pressure off the ice can be just as powerful for a Czech hockey player as it is for a Russian. Nedomansky, it's said, wanted to play for the Brno team rather than the Bratislava team to which he was assigned by the Czech Ice Hockey Federation. When he threatened to quit if he wasn't given his wish, the Czech government countered with the threat of induction into the army for four years. It's enough to give a man pause. And enough to encourage him to play where he's told.

Aside from the attractions of playing for the Toros, Nedomansky says previous tours of Canada with the Czech team left him with a good impression of Toronto. And so far, he hasn't been disappointed. "My wife Vera and my son Vaclav Jr. are both pleased to be here and are adjusting well," he says. "We were all going to take a Berlitz course in English, but the hockey season interfered for me." At his present rate of progress with the language, says the interpreter, Nedomansky won't need any English course by the end of the season.

His preference for Toronto over other North American cities is guaranteed to gladden the hearts of the city fathers. His favourable response to his new home seems genuine, and it's very decent of Nedomansky to take the trouble to point out how happy he has been since his defection. In fact, it's the kind of diplomatic statement you might expect to hear from a guy like . . . well, like Jean Beliveau.

233

THE BEGINNING OF THE WHA
by/par Walt Marlow

LA NAISSANCE DE L'ASSOCIATION MONDIALE DE HOCKEY

From Bobby Hull to Frank Mahovlich.

The names in between read like a who's who of hockey: Gordie Howe, Pat Stapleton, Ralph Backstrom, Paul Henderson, Gerry Cheevers, Dave Dryden, Mike Walton, Wayne Connelly, Jacques Plante, Bruce MacGregor, Jim Harrison, Al Hamilton, J. C. Tremblay, Brad Selwood, André Lacroix, Rejean Houle, Marc Tardif, Serge Bernier, Darryl Maggs, Al Smith, Ernie Wakeley, Jim Dorey, Ted Green, Rick Smith, Mike Pelyk, Paul Shmyr, Harry Howell, Don McLeod, Wayne Carleton . . .

And many more.

Collectively, they represent the World Hockey Association, a league that, in a mere two winters, has achieved unprecedented success in the pressurized world that is major league sports.

As the WHA embarks on Year III of its historic journey, there is irrefutable evidence that those dreams of distinguished Canadian sportsmen like W. D. (Bill) Hunter, Ben Hatskin, Jim Pattison, John Bassett Jr., and Paul Racine will.

De Bobby Hull à Frank Mahovlich.

Entre ces noms prestigieux, on retrouve quelques-unes des grandes vedettes du Hockey d'aujourd'hui: Gordie Howe, Pat Stapleton, Ralph Backstrom, Paul Henderson, Gerry Cheevers, Dave Dryden, Mike Walton, Wayne Connelly, Jacques Plante, Bruce MacGregor, Jim Harrison, Al Hamilton, J.-C. Tremblay, Brad Selwood, André Lacroix, Réjean Houle, Marc Tardif, Serge Bernier, Darryl Maggs, Al Smith, Ernie Wakeley, Jim Dorey, Ted Green, Rick Smith, Mike Pelyk, Paul Shmyr, Harry Howell, Don McLeod, Wayne Carleton . . .

Et bien d'autres encore.

Toutes ces vedettes forment l'Association mondiale de hockey, une ligue qui, en deux hivers seulement, a connu un succès sans précédent dans le monde des ligues majeures où la pression est vive.

Au moment où l'AMH entreprend la troisième année de son essor historique, il est indubitable que les éminents sportifs canadiens, comme W.D.

Gordy Howe—Houston Aeros

Bobby Hull—Winnipeg Jets

indeed, have materialized far sooner than they, themselves, dare projected in their most optimistic moments.

They, along with a vibrant collection of their American counterparts, defied incredible odds to establish hockey's second major league.

"Our success and our future is apparent in the number of acknowledged stars and future stars that comprise the rosters of our 14 teams," says President Dennis Arthur Murphy, a virtuoso in sports organization who was the WHA's first visionary.

It was Murphy, the energetic 48-year-old Irishman reared in Shanghai, who, in concert with Edmonton's vigorous Bill Hunter and Winnipeg's verve Ben Hatskin, ignited the fuse that ultimately was to alter the structure of major league sport throughout North America. While hockey scientists the world over prophesied disaster, Murphy approached his task with evangelistic fervor—preaching the gospel of a new league to men of uncommon means in two countries.

They included the likes of Walter and Jordon Kaiser in Chicago, Nick Mileti in Cleveland, Jim Smith and Paul Deneau in Houston, Bernard Brown in Philadelphia, Lou Kaplan in Minnesota, Howard Baldwin and John Coburn in New England, along with Doug Michel in Ottawa, Hunter, Hatskin and Quebec's Racine, to be followed by Toronto's Bassett and Vancouver's Pattison.

Elimination of the reserve and/or option clause in contracts, which freed athletes from lifelong bondage to a single team, irrefutably represented the single most important act in the league's formation.

The momentous decision, rendered Nov. 8, 1972, by U.S. District Court Judge A. Leon Higginbotham in Philadelphia, freed Robert Marvin Hull and other distinguished major leaguers to function in the league of their choice.

Until then, of course, it was the Hull signing itself, on June 27, 1972, that skyrocketed the WHA into sports page prominence.

Hatskin, now chairman of the league's board of trustees and an instrumental force in bringing about this series with the Soviet Union, engineered the phenomenal coup with a $2.75 million contract for hockey's greatest left winger. The Golden Jet was now a Winnipeg Jet.

"Certainly that was the play that altered our early image," reflected Murphy, who first conceived the idea for the WHA in January of 1971. "The skeptics developed nervous disorders when Bobby came aboard."

The Hull acquisition, aside from the image impact, also touched off an avalanche of fresh

(Bill) Hunter, Ben Hatskin, Jim Pattison, John Bassett Jr. et Paul Racine, ont pu réaliser leurs rêves beaucoup plus rapidement qu'ils ne l'avaient eux-mêmes espéré.

En collaboration avec un groupe imposant de leurs homologues américains, ils ont triomphé des obstacles et ont réussi à établir la deuxième ligue de hockey majeure.

"Notre succès et notre avenir sont assurés par le nombre d'étoiles d'aujourd'hui et de demain qui se sont jointes à nos 14 équipes." C'est ce que déclarait le président de la ligue, Dennis Arthur Murphy, un maître de l'organisation de sports qui a le premier imaginé la mise sur pied de l'AMH.

En effet, c'est ce dynamique Irlandais de 48 ans, élevé à Shanghai, qui, en association avec l'énergique Bill Hunter d'Edmonton, et le fougueux Ben Hatskin de Winnipeg, répandit l'idée d'une nouvelle ligue parmi des hommes aux ressources peu communes dans deux pays. Parmi eux, nous citerons les noms de Walter et Jordon Kaiser de Chicago, Nick Mileti de Cleveland, Jim Smith et Paul Deneau de Houston, Bernard Brown de Philadelphie, Lou Kaplan du Minnesota, Howard Baldwin et John Coburn en Nouvelle-Angleterre, Doug Michel d'Ottawa, Hunter, Hatskin, Racine de Québec et finalement Bassett de Toronto et Pattison de Vancouver.

La suppression des clauses de réserve et d'option des contrats qui rompait les liens éternels qui unissaient les athlètes à une seule équipe, constitue certes l'initiative la plus importante qui ait marqué la création de la ligue.

La décision capitale, rendue par le juge A. Leon Higginbotham de la cour du district de Philadelphie le 8 novembre 1972, permettait à Robert Marvin Hull et d'autres athlètes connus des ligues majeures de jouer dans la ligue de leur choix.

Jusqu'à ce moment-là, la signature de Bobby Hull, le 27 juin 1972, avait à elle seule permis à l'AMH de défrayer la chronique des pages sportives.

M. Hatskin, maintenant président du conseil des fiduciaires de la ligue et qui a joué un rôle de premier plan dans la mise sur pied de la série avec l'URSS, a réussi un coup de maître quand il a fait signer un contrat de $2.75 millions au plus grand ailier gauche. La Comète blonde appartenait donc aux Jets de Winnipeg.

"C'est certainement ce geste qui a transformé l'image que nous projetions au début de notre existence, précise M. Murphy qui a songé à la création de l'AMH en janvier 1971. L'arrivée de Bobby dans nos rangs a embarrassé les sceptiques."

En plus d'influencer l'image de la ligue,

Marty Howe—Houston Aeros

Don McLeod—Houston Aeros

Gerry Cheevers—Cleveland Crusaders

J.C. Tremblay—Quebec Nordiques

signings, 28 within a period of a week. They included the likes of Gerry Cheevers with Cleveland, Ted Green with New England and Bobby Sheehan, now on the roster of the Edmonton Oilers.

The incomparable Gordie Howe, along with his two sons, Mark and Marty, had joined the ranks of the Houston Aeros to mark the first time in history of any major league sport that a father had played alongside of two sons.

"Howe's signing alone was a coup rivaling that of the Hull signing," reflected Edmonton's Hunter. "But for his two boys to join him, two future super stars, today stands as the most monumental event in the history of hockey. The chances of it happening again are a million to one."

Proclaiming that while there's a little snow on the roof, there's still fire in the furnace, hockey's living legend—21 months in retirement to the contrary—orchestrated the Aeros to the Avco World Trophy.

And like Hull in the WHA's baptismal year, Gordie emerged the MVP and a first team all-star. Not even son Mark, rookie of the year at 19, is convinced that his ol' man is 46.

A testimony to Howe's greatness was evident at the annual Charley Conacher Memorial Dinner in Toronto this past May when he modestly captured the audience with two standing ovations.

Announcing that hockey had become so much fun again that he would play another season, he attributed his MVP honors to the fact that he had sired two sons to cover up his mistakes.

Mistakes? All he did was score 31 goals and contribute 69 assists.

While it would be a friendly exaggeration to suggest that the WHA, in two seasons, has attained the stability representative of long established leagues, there are unmistakable signs for the unwavering belief of success exhibited by the league's 15 franchise holders.

The league's owners, their ambition showing like a petticoat under a mini-skirt, took giant strides over the past off-season in acquiring upwards of 20 outstanding Canadian juniors, seven of them among the top 10 graduates.

Certainly no one will deny that Pat Price and Ron Chipperfield (Vancouver Blazers), Dennis Sobchuk, Jacques Locas and John Hughes (Cincinnati Stingers), Gary McGregor (Chicago Cougars), Real Cloutier and Charles Constantin (Quebec Nordiques), Cam Connor (Phoenix Roadrunners), and Bill Reed (Michigan) are candidates for future stardom.

Add them to the rookie crop of a year ago, that

l'acquisition de Bobby Hull a incité une multitude de joueurs, soit 28 en une semaine, à se joindre à nous. Mentionnons les noms de Gerry Cheevers, avec Cleveland et Ted Green, avec la Nouvelle-Angleterre et Bobby Sheehan, maintenant des Oilers d'Edmonton.

L'incomparable Gordie Howe s'est joint, en compagnie de ses deux fils, Mark et Marty, aux Aeros de Houston, ce qui créait un précédent dans l'histoire des ligues de sport majeures. En effet, c'était la première fois qu'un père et ses deux fils étaient membres d'une même équipe majeure.

"La signature de Howe a été aussi spectaculaire que celle de Hull" précise M. Hunter d'Edmonton. Mais celle des fils Howe, deux futures super-vedettes, représente le geste qui a le plus marqué l'histoire du hockey. Il y a à parier un million contre 1 que cet exploit ne sera jamais renouvelé."

La légendaire vedette retirée depuis 21 mois déjà, a mené les Aeros à la conquête du trophée Avco. A l'instar de Hull, Gordie a été nommé le joueur le plus utile à son équipe et membre de la première équipe d'étoiles, à sa première saison dans l'AMH. Même son fils Mark, choisie recrue de l'année à 19 ans, n'est pas convaincu que son père est âgé de 46 ans.

Après avoir déclaré que le hockey était redevenu un grand plaisir, Gordie annonçait qu'il jouerait encore un an. Il a expliqué son titre du joueur le plus utile par le fait qu'il avait convaincu ses deux fils de réparer ses erreurs.

Des erreurs? Après tout, il a réussi à compter 31 buts et mériter 69 assistances.

Les propriétaires de la ligue masquent mal leur ambition et ont franchi des pas de géants au cours de la saison morte par l'acquisition de plus de 20 joueurs juniors canadiens de grand talent, dont 7 se trouvaient parmi les 10 joueurs les plus convoités.

Des joueurs comme Pat Price et Ron Chipperfield des Blazers de Vancouver, Dennis Sobchuk, Jacques Locas et John Hughes des Stingers de Cincinnati, Garry McGregor des Cougars de Chicago, Réal Cloutier et Charles Constantin des Nordiques de Québec, Cam Connor des Roadrunners de Phoenix et Bill Reed du Michigan ont le talent voulu pour devenir des étoiles.

Si vous ajoutez à cês noms ceux des jeunes qui se sont joints à nos rangs l'année dernière, tels les frères Howe, Wayne Dillon et Pat Hickey des Toros de Toronto, Michel Deguise des Nordiques, Tom Edur des Crusaders de Cleveland, Frankie Rochon des Cougars et John Garrett des Saints du Minnesota, vous constatez que la stabilité de la ligue est une chose acquise. La dernière grande vedette à se joindre à l'AMH

included the brothers Howe, Wayne Dillon and Pat Hickey of the Toronto Toros, Michel Deguise of the Nordiques, Tom Edur of the Cleveland Crusaders, Frankie Rochon of the Cougars and John Garrett of Minnesota's Saints and the case for stability is clearly evident.

The newest super name in the WHA cast, of course, is William Francis (Frank) Mahovlich, signed by the Toros June 20.

The league the detractors said would never make it, now owns the three most prolific goal-getters in the history of the game in the persons of Howe (817), Hull (708) and Mahovlich, who, at 533, starts the season a mere 11 back of the legendary Maurice Richard.

Of monumental significance this season is the fact that the WHA has established an all-Canadian division of Vancouver, Edmonton, Winnipeg, Toronto and Quebec. In essence, Canada now has it's own major hockey league for the first time in history.

The WHA's Western Division is comprised of Houston, Michigan, Minnesota, Phoenix and San Diego, while in the East it's New England, Chicago, Cleveland and Indianapolis, with Cincinnati taking up residence a year from now.

Meanwhile the Stingers, headed up by the aggressive Bill DeWitt, Jr. have assigned their signed players to other clubs in the league.

Indianapolis and Phoenix, plus the shifting of the New Jersey franchise to San Diego, represent the league's new look this season. Not to be overlooked, of course, is the new look in playing facilities, too.

Certainly Edmonton's new 16,000 capacity Coliseum will enhance the WHA's image, as will Cleveland's new Coliseum and Hartford's new arena which will become the home of the New England Whalers, who won it all in that first historic season.

"Our potential now is limitless," says Murphy, who first teamed with Hunter and the Canadian contingent five months into the league's talking stages. Thereafter, it was a story of perpetual motion.

"In those early days, Hunter was even more enthusiastic about the prospects of this league than we were," recalls Murphy. "We wanted four Canadian cities, and he knew of four who wanted us. Sure there were a few problems, but if you think you can create an 'instant' product without problems, then you've never tried to organize anything.

"Funny, how a lot of critics, people who should know better, said we'd never hit the ice. But the only critics that really count are the guys and gals who pay the shot.

"Our credibility is of their doing."

est, bien sûr, William Francis (Frank) Mahovlich qui a accepté l'offre des Toros, le 20 juin. Les détracteurs qui se plaisaient à dire que la ligue ne réussirait jamais doivent maintenant constater que ses équipes comptent les trois plus grands marqueurs de l'histoire du hockey: Howe (817 buts), Hull (708) et Mahovlich qui, avec ses 533 buts, n'est plus qu'à 11 de la marque établie par le légendaire Maurice Richard.

Il importe aussi de souligner un geste important que la ligue vient de poser: la création d'une division entièrement canadienne formée des équipes de Vancouver, Edmonton, Winnipeg, Toronto et Québec. En somme, le Canada possède maintenant, pour la première fois de son histoire, sa propre ligue de hockey majeure.

La division de l'ouest est formée des équipes de Houston, Michigan, Minnesota, Phoenix et San Diego et celle de l'est, de la Nouvelle-Angleterre, de Chicago et d'Indianapolis; à cette dernière, viendra s'ajouter l'équipe de Cincinnati, l'année prochaine.

D'ici là, les Stingers, sous la direction du dynamique Bill DeWitt Jr., ont affecté leurs joueurs à d'autres équipes de la ligue.

L'acquisition d'équipes à Phoenix et à Indianapolis de même que le déménagement de celle du New Jersey à San Diego représentent les nouveautés qu'offrira la ligue cette année. Il ne faudrait toutefois pas passer sous silence les nouveaux stades.

Le nouveau Coliseum d'Edmonton, pouvant accueillir 16,000 spectateurs, rehaussera certainement l'image de l'AMH, tout comme le nouveau Coliseum de Cleveland et le nouveau stade de Hartford qui logera les Whalers de la Nouvelle-Angleterre, qui ont raflé tous les honneurs lors de la première saison de la ligue.

"Notre potentiel est maintenant sans limite", a déclaré M. Murphy qui, pendant 5 mois, s'est joint à Hunter et aux représentants du Canada pour entamer les négociations qui allaient aboutir à la naissance de la ligue. Depuis lors, il a consacré toutes ses énergies à l'AMH.

"Au début, Hunter était encore plus enthousiaste que nous au sujet de la mise sur pied de la nouvelle ligue", rappelle M. Murphy. "Nous voulions compter quatre villes canadiennes dans nos rangs et il en connaissait quatre que le projet intéressait."

Il est étrange de constater que bon nombre de critiques qui devraient être mieux informés, avaient prédit que nous n'arriverions jamais à disputer une seule partie. Mais les seules critiques qui comptent sont celles qui sont formulées par les gens qui paient pour assister à nos parties.

"Ils ont suscité notre crédibilité."

Marc Tardif–Michigan Stags

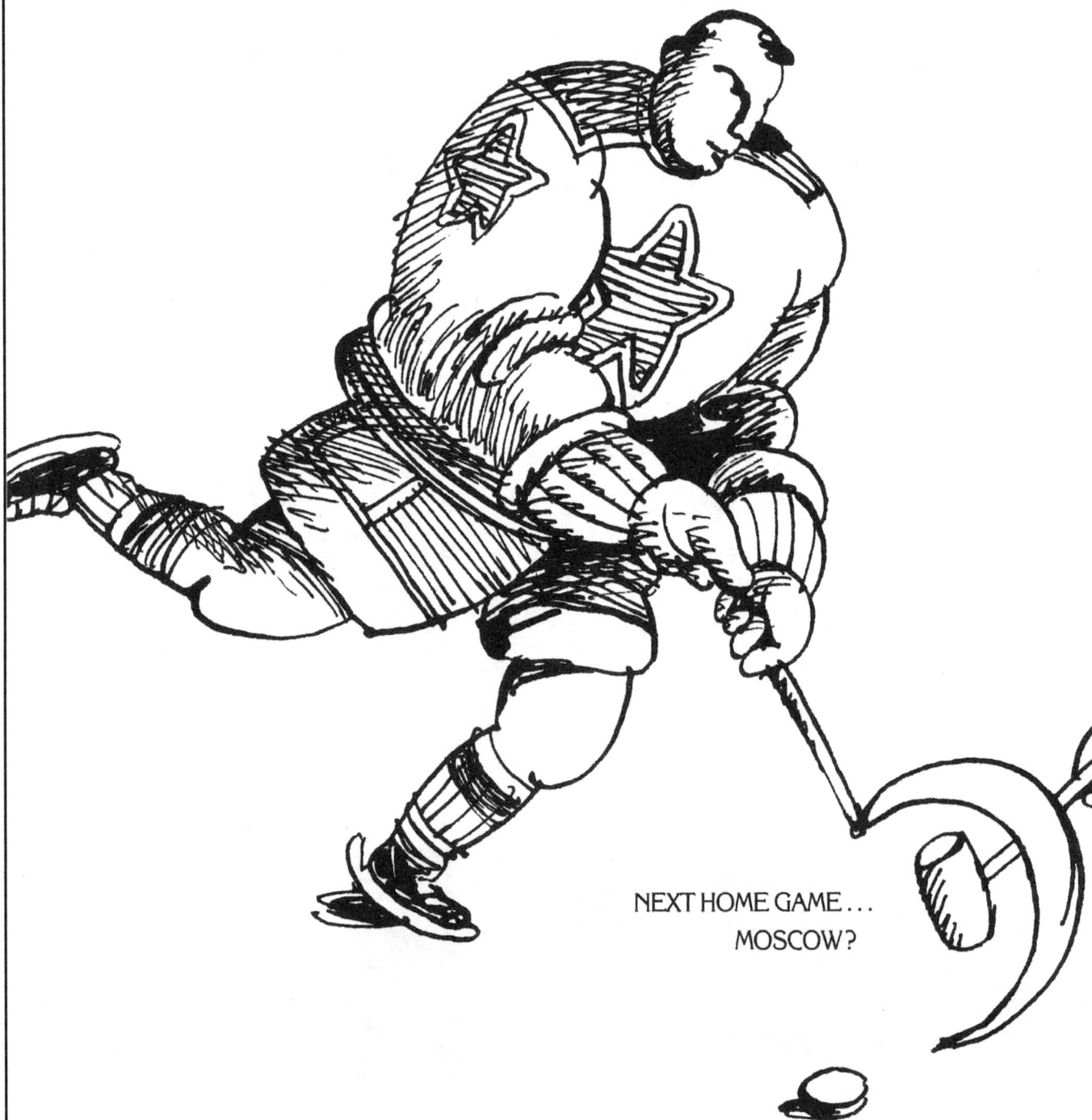

NEXT HOME GAME . . .
MOSCOW?

The Soviet Union and Czechoslovakia national teams have completed their respective tours of World Hockey Association cities and it's time to assess the impact of the league's latest and most ambitious venture into international hockey.

The figures produced by the 14-game series hardly tell the story, though they are revealing.

The WHA defeated the Czechs in four of six games, while the Soviets won six of eight games. The Soviets and Czechs got 59 goals and the WHA teams combined for 49 goals.

The series also drew nearly 150,000 fans and generated 10 sellouts. In several cases the games helped introduce major league hockey to many U.S. fans who have never seen the game before.

But that is what happened this year. What of the future?

This was not the first Soviet tour of North America. A Soviet national team played teams of professionals in 1972 and 1974 as part of Team Canada competition. During the 1975-76 season, two Soviet teams played four games each against National Hockey League teams.

It is likely we have not seen the last of the touring Soviet teams, either. It is good business for both parties. The only question is, who will the Soviets prefer to do business with?

Apparently, the WHA, the league whose survival has always been doubted, has the inside track. No NHL team has ever been invited to play in the prestigious Izvestia tournament, held annually in Moscow.

This year the WHA's Winnipeg Jets were and finished 1-2-1. And next year

NEXT HOME GAME...
MOSCOW?

another WHA team will compete in the tourney.

During a Houston press conference, WHA vice president Larry Gordon said the league has been asked to send a team again next year.

"We will probably send our league champion, with players from other teams in the league to bolster the roster. It was quite an honor to be invited this year and it is quite an honor to be invited to return," Gordon said.

To accommodate the league' representative, next year's schedule will be made up so that sufficient time for preparation, participation and winding down is available.

"We'll make sure our team has time to get ready and then isn't forced to jump right back into league play. We didn't want to have that situation this time, but it could not be helped," Gordon said.

The Izvestia tournament may not be the league's only try at the continental experience. League officials indicate that some league games may be played against European teams next year.

One league official, who asked to remain anonymous, said, "It makes sense. We can go over there and play to full houses, so our teams will be able to make some money. Attendance hasn't been that good in the early part of the season, anyway."

Before the series with the Czechs and Soviets began, Houston coach and general manager Bill Dineen said he favored international games that counted.

"What I'd like to see us do is play two games against the Finns, two against the Swedes, two against the Czechs and two against the Russians, with all the games counting in the standings," Dineen said.

"We could play some exhibition games, too, but I'd like to see us play games that count."

Even if it cannot be arranged that games in Europe become part of the WHA schedule, it is evident that international hockey is here to stay. Teams from the WHA have traveled to the continent the past three years for training camps, the Canada Cup tournament was a rousing success and the tours of the Czech and Soviet national teams were bonafide and legitimate successes.

A veteran hockey observer said, "Right now a lot of it (the attendance) is from curiosity. You hear a lot about the Europeans, especially the Czechs and the Russians.

"There are still a lot of differences in the styles of play, but that is going to change. The Czechs and Russians played more physically in the Canada Cup tournament, for example.

"The only real problem is time. It isn't easy to fly to Europe and it isn't easy for their teams to fly over here. And it costs a lot of money, too.

"I think those things can be worked out, though. It will be good for the game."

The talks seeking to overcome the obstacles have already begun. They began even as the Soviets were in the midst of their eight-game tour.

"There are a lot of things to be worked out. We had to rearrange our schedule this year and we would like to avoid that next year," Gordon said.

So WHA fans can prepare themselves for more games with an international flavor.

"I think one day we will probably see the Soviet Union and, say either Houston or Montreal playing for the world championship. It ought to be really something to see," the veteran hockey observer said.

Indeed it should. ●

WORLD HOCKEY ASSOCIATION

INTERNATIONAL SERIES '78

$2.00

"GUEST SHOT"
THE YEAR OF THE EUROPEAN

"Those two Czechs are going to give the other teams in this league a lot of grief," warns Toronto Toros' General Manager Buck Houle. "They're going to have to make a couple of adjustments but most of the adjusting will have to be made by our World Hockey Association opponents."

The Czechs are centermen Vaclav Nedomansky and Richard Farda, who defected from Czechoslovakia and signed contracts with the Toros in July.

They, of course, represent two of the 10 Europeans who'll be giving the WHA an international flavor this season. In addition to Nedomansky and Farda, there's the Abrahamsson twins, Thommy and Christer, in New England, while Winnipeg at last count had four Swedish stars in the persons of Curt Larsson, Anders Hedberg, Ulf Nilsson and Lars Sjoberg, and two products of Finland — Heikki Riihiranta and Veli-Pekka Ketola.

"I know the other teams will have trouble containing them," Houle added of his Czechs. "The other Toros are having trouble with them. What Ned and Farda will have to get used to are the excessive high sticks, hooks and trips that will be used to stop them."

Nedomansky, at 6-1, 205, is described as an excellent puck handler with muscle. Farda, on the other hand, at 5-9, 175, depends largely on speed to get the job done. Houle says he never stops backchecking and whenever there's a scramble on the boards for the puck he's in the thick of it.

"They're both very exciting players," said Houle. "Nedomansky has all the tools that spell super star."

The Czechoslovakians aside, however, the Toros apparently are on the brink of capturing Toronto.

"There's no doubt about it," says Houle with an air of unbridled enthusiasm. "We're attracting a lot of attention with this team ... but I'm not predicting a championship. Too many things can go wrong."

Season tickets have exceeded the 7000 mark, clearly an indication that the citizenry has discovered that the Maple Leafs aren't the only team in town.

Toro newcomers this season, besides the Czechs, include the likes of Frank Mahovlich, Paul Henderson, Tony Featherstone and highly promising amateurs Jim Turkiewicz and George Kucmicz, along with goaltender Jim Shaw from the American League.

Turkiewicz, to be sure, represented a major catch for the Toros. The 19-year-old defenseman, signed to a three-year pact, ranked among the top 20 juniors in Canada. He was Toronto's No. 1 pick.

"I'm impressed with his lateral movement and precision passing," said Houle. He moves the puck well and is potentially a great defenseman."

Up in Winnipeg, meanwhile, coach Rudy Pilous is offering high praise for his overseas imports, too.

And the one he's most pleased with, apparently, is Finnish centerman/left wing, Ketola (6-3), said to be in a class with the Soviet Union's Alexander Yakushev and Valeri Kharlamov.

"He gets better every day," said Pilous. "He's enthusiastic in practice, shoots a hard puck, is a wizard stickhandler in close. He's going to be just as good as Phil Esposito, and I'm not saying that just for publicity purposes. If we get the same results from him in games we are in for a very pleasant winter."

And of his Swedes, Pilous says:

"They're really something. When they first got here they came in and asked for ice time. We got them some — at midnight. They practiced by themselves. They have pride, they want to succeed."

In that regard, Pilous says the imports remind him of Canadian players of the past who thought the only way to succeed was through hard work, not through agents.

Riihiranta, a mobile defenseman, is exactly what he was billed to be, Pilous said. "He's a rugged individual who just has to acclimatize himself to our way of playing."

As for Larsson, 29-year-old all-star goaltender off Sweden's National Team, Pilous observed: "He has less to learn than his European colleagues. The nets are the same size wherever you go."

Coach Ron Ryan of the New England Whalers, one suspects, would echo Pilous' observations.

He, of course, has the Abrahamson twins — Thommy on defense and Christer in the nets. The latter is battling veteran Al Smith and Bruce Landon for the goaltending job, while Thommy, teaming with Paul Hurley on the blueline, has been nothing short of phenomenal with a plus 18 on the plus/minus system.

ON THE COVER: No. 4, veteran Howie Young, who last season successfully made the switch from defense to right wing and recorded career highs in goals (37) and points (69) helping lead the Runners to their second pair or WHL twin titles. One of the most popular players ever to skate at the Coliseum, Young was also cover subject of Sports Illustrated 11 years ago while playing for Detroit:

The Russians Are Coming

A mere three winters ago, hockey and Indianapolis weren't exactly synonymous. To the citizenry of Indiana, it was a game played in far off places, probably, no doubt, by equally far out people.

Today, with the emergence of the Racers, this town -- within a period of three months -- will have been exposed to the rival National League, the world champion Czechoslovakians and the Olympic champion Soviet Union.

You conclude that, the Racers, indeed, represent quite a platform for Indiana's cultural exchange program.

Both the Czechs and the Soviets are scheduled for Market Square appearances in late December and early January -- depending on when they can be worked into the WHA schedule.

International hockey, unmistakably, has reached a new level of sophistication. The recent Canada Cup series involving Finland, Sweden, the U.S., Canada, the Russians and the Czechs was the forerunner, hopefully, of an annual competition patterned after the World Cup soccer tournament.

The Czechs and the Russians used to call themselves the flowers of amateur livestock, refusing to engage in combat with Canadian and American professionals.

That, of course, was before they made the awesome discovery that the only difference between an amateur and a professional was that the amateur met you under the bridge at midnight and refused to accept credit cards and/or checks.

Following the Canada Cup tournament, in which the Czechs finished second to Canada and the Soviets third, it was established that both European powers were frustrated to the point of paranoia -- observing lamely that they didn't understand the bar customs.

It should be noted that the Soviets experienced little difficulty a year ago in a series of exhibitions with National League teams, winning the bulk of the contests.

"There are three million hockey players in the Soviet Union," observed Racer Coach Jacques Demers. "They're producing more players today than any country in the world. We'll have our hands full."

The Czechs will play six games with WHA teams in December, followed by the Soviet Selects who'll play eight games in January.

"We're honored at the opportunity to play them," added Demers. "Our tight-checking system could give them trouble. We'll give a good account of ourselves."

Meanwhile, Demers -- beginning his first full season as a major league coach -- is more pre-occupied with the task at hand.

"These pre-season games represent a barometer of our potential," he offers. "They're not life and death. Sure we want to win them. We're going to try like hell to win . . . that's what this game's all about."

What Demers is saying is that the real firing starts here Oct. 9 when the Racers open up with the Minnesota Saints.

Demers has proffered the view that the Racers, to claim another division title, must get off to a good start. "We played catch-up last season and survived. We lost only four of our last 20. That's doing it the hard way."

Two divisions make up the WHA this season, with the Racers in the East with New England, Quebec, Birmingham,

JACQUES DEMERS: Must be Most Selective

Minnesota and Cincinnati. Over in the West there's Winnipeg, Calgary, Phoenix, Edmonton, San Diego and Houston.

Parity is still the major trademark of the WHA. This year, particularly, there are no favorites and no underdogs. The Racers, going in, are as good as any team in the league -- including Bobby Hull's Winnipeg Jets.

Two years ago, in their baptismal season, the Racers were the kind of a team that could acquire a suntan running for a cab.

Today, as they rev up for Year Three, they are among the game's more abler practitioners.

Czechs, Soviets Eye Indy

Two years ago, a team of World Hockey Association selects — otherwise known as Team Canada — engaged the Soviet Union in an eight-game series and came away slightly tarnished.

It wasn't that the WHA played badly, with the likes of Bobby Hull, Pat Stapleton, Gordie Howe, Andre Lacroix, Marc Tardif, etc. It was just that the Russians played better — particularly on the Moscow end where they had a little local politics going for them.

While the WHA managed a win and two standoffs in Canada, they didn't fare too well in Bolshevik Territory, extracting a mere tie in four tries. Iron Curtain officials, it should be noted, have a nodding acquaintance with one-way trips to Siberia. Visiting teams in Moscow have been known to encounter elements like malfunctioning clocks, confused goal judges and referees who do not feel obliged to irritate the Politburo with unfavorable decisions.

Be that as it may, the WHA will try again — commencing next month when the Russians and Czechoslovakia make a 14-game tour of WHA cities, with the Winnipeg Jets participating in the famed Isvestia Cup tournament in Moscow Dec. 16-24.

It is the most ambitious undertaking yet of the International confrontations that started four years ago when Team NHL edged the Soviets in a celebrated eight-game series.

The Soviets got even a year ago, though, when their two touring teams went into NHL cities and captured the bulk of the contests — proving conclusively that the European system was geared to the major league level.

Then came the Canada Cup series this past fall involving Czechoslovakia, Finland, Sweden, the Soviets, U.S. and Canada. The Canadians, comprised of NHL players with the lone exception of Winnipeg's Bobby Hull, prevailed — bouncing the Czechs out in two straight in the final.

The Russians, by their own admission, were less than efficient, if not somewhat bewildered by the turn of events. One surmises that they mean to get even, in that they reportedly plan to send their "very best" on the WHA tour.

Indianapolis will see the Czechs here at Market Square Dec. 22 followed by the Soviets on New Year's Day. Tickets go on sale at the Arena box office Dec. 4.

You'll probably be exposed to the finest technical hockey you'll see all season. It may even get a trifle untidy, depending on how things have been going for the visitors in other WHA rinks.

The Czechs make their first North American appearance in Winnipeg Dec. 11, followed by stops in Edmonton Dec. 13, Calgary Dec. 15, Minnesota Dec. 17, New England Dec. 20 and finally Market Square on the 22nd.

The Soviet Union, penciled in for eight games, start off in New England Dec. 27, followed by Houston on the 30th. Then it's Indy town Jan. 1, Cincinnati the next night, San Diego on the 6th, Edmonton the 8th, Winnipeg the 10th and Quebec the 12th.

The Jets, with Robert Hull and all their European power, face Czechoslovakia in Moscow Dec. 16, Sweden on the 17th, the Soviets on the 19th and Finland on the 21st.

Originally, the Quebec Nordiques were scheduled for the Isvestia tournament, but backed off — presumably on the theory that they had everything to lose and nothing to gain.

The Nordiques do not feel too comfortable in the WHA Eastern Division race, what with Cincinnati's Big Yellow Machine pulling away and the fact that they're being seriously challenged by New England and the Racers.

Meanwhile, Hull — the Golden Jet — might well be making his first appearance of the WHA season in Indianapolis. At this writing, he was still sidelined with a broken wrist suffered in a pre-season skirmish with the St. Louis Blues.

Hull, perhaps the most vocal player in either league, says the only stumbling block to a WHA merger with the NHL is Alan Eagleson, who, as president of the NHL Players' Association, views himself as the self-proclaimed patron saint of the game.

BOBBY HULL

Says Hull:

"There are too many teams, too many players making too much — and some journeyman players not paid enough.

"The players need some sort of motivation to perform their finest for the fans — not a five-year, no-cut, no-trade contract. In the old days, if a guy didn't put out for two or three games he'd find his butt on the bench. Everyone's not giving a 100 per cent. It's gone too far the other way."

The meeting of the two teams marks the first occasion that a reigning championship professional team from North America has met its counterpart from Europe.

It is December 12, 1976. Winnipeg, Manitoba.

Czechoslovakia is beginning a six game odyssey through the World Hockey Association by playing the Winnipeg Jets.

The Czechoslovakians are the defending World Champions, European version.

Winnipeg Jets are the defending World Hockey Association Avco Trophy Champions.

Czechoslovakian stars like Milan Novy, Frantisek Pospisil, and Marian

Stasny, while not yet well known to fans in North America, are thought by hockey insiders to be among the finest hockey talents in the world, bar none.

The Jets, too, boast some pretty fair ice talent in players like Bobby Hull, Anders Hedberg, and Ulf Nilsson.

The meeting of the two teams marks the first occasion that a reigning championship professional team from North America has met its counterpart from Europe.

One game. Winner take all. It is only an "exhibition." But it's for the bragging rights to the world.

A Sunday afternoon sellout crowd of 10,033 is joined by television onlookers across Canada in watching the historic game.

Winnipeg triumphs, 6-5, by scoring six third period goals.

The scene shifts.

It is January 8, 1977. Quebec City, Quebec.

The Soviet National Team is concluding its eight game tour of the WHA with a match against the Quebec Nordiques.

The fabled Soviet Nationals. Karlamov, Tretiak, Mikhailov, Yakushev, Maltsev, Vasilyev, Lutchenko. All of the very best players from the nation that some are speculating might be the best hockey playing country in the world. In fact, some are calling this aggregation of Soviets the greatest team ever assembled.

This imposing array of Soviets is being challenged by the team that, some three months later, will supplant Winnipeg as the WHA Champions.

Starting with this season's competition, for the first time in the history of major league hockey, games against European powers are being counted in regular season World Hockey Association standings in North America.

Again a sellout crowd. Again a national television audience.

Again a victory for the WHA'ers, by the overwhelming score of 6-1.

Two isolated games, two victories. What did it all mean?

It meant that the WHA was one step closer to establishing a new order of International hockey competition. As one WHA General Manager prophesied prior to last season's International Series, "Someday soon we will be playing these teams on a regular basis.

"These games offer a glimpse of the future to our players and our fans."

The future is now!

International Series '78.

Starting with this season's competition, for the first time in the history of major league hockey, games against European powers are being counted in regular season World Hockey Association standings in North America.

Each of the eight WHA teams will be playing both All-Star teams from the Soviet Union and Czechoslovakia. A win or a tie in those games by the WHA clubs will earn them points in the standings just as if their opponents were New England or Houston.

And that is only the beginning of the WHA's International plans for the 1977-78 season.

For the second successive year, the WHA's Avco Trophy Champion has been invited to challenge for the Izvestia Cup, a tournament held each December in Moscow that is one of the world's most prestigious.

Last year, Winnipeg Jets became the first North American team ever invited to the Izvestia tournament.

Their performance justified their selection.

Playing against the National teams from the Soviet Union, Czechoslovakia, Sweden, and Finland, the Jets won once and tied once in four games, while scoring only two fewer goals overall than their opponents.

The emergence of Sweden as a serious challenger for the World Championship, which they nearly captured last Spring in Vienna, and the continued flow of top flight Swedish players into the WHA and NHL, shows the kind of hockey that can be expected when the Swedes visit Indianapolis, New England, Houston, Cincinnati, and Birmingham.

This year, the Quebec Nordiques will bear the WHA banner in Moscow. As their performance against the Soviet Nationals indicated, they, too, will be very competitive.

While the Izvestia will provide the first opportunity for the 1977-78 WHA to measure itself against the Soviet Nationals, it will hardly be the last.

The WHA will next meet the Nationals in Japan, of all places, where the Soviets and Winnipeg will engage in a three game mini-series, taking place in late December and early January.

Next on the docket will be the return confrontation between the Nationals and WHA clubs that will again take place on WHA ice. Record-setting sellout throngs greeted the Soviets on their eight stop trek through the WHA last season, and those fans thrilled to a brilliant display of hockey.

The WHA won only two of the eight games, those played in New England against the Whalers and in Quebec against les Nordiques, but five of the losses came in close, exciting games. Not at all bad considering that never before had individual clubs from North

America taken the ice against the full Soviet National machine.

Nevertheless, Round Two is upcoming, and the fans in Edmonton, Winnipeg, Quebec, Cincinnati, Indianapolis, and New England will undoubtedly enjoy all of the same excitement shared by those who were on hand for Round One.

After the Soviet National schedule is concluded on January 11, WHA fans will have two months to regain their composure and their voices before International Series '78 heats up once again. But heat up again it definitely will, because in March of 1978 two more of the top European hockey powers, Sweden and Finland, will march onto WHA ice.

The WHA has more than enough knowledge of Team Sweden's capabilities; for a few years now WHA players have been trying to chase down skating marvels like Anders Hedberg, Ulf Nilsson, Lars-Erik Sjoberg, Willy Lindstrom and Thommy Abrahamsson, all former members of the Swedish National Team. Given the scoring totals that the Swedes have compiled, the chase seems to have been largely unsuccessful.

The emergence of Sweden as a serious challenger for the World Championship, which they nearly captured last Spring in Vienna, and the continued flow of top flight Swedish players into the WHA and NHL, shows the kind of hockey that can be expected when the Swedes visit Indianapolis, New England, Houston, Cincinnati, and Birmingham.

Finland will be visiting the same five WHA teams, and their tour will coincide with that of Sweden. While Finland has yet to realize the success that the other European competitors have enjoyed, they are firmly entrenched with those three powers in forming the top flight of European hockey.

They too have provided the WHA with some talented performers, including Winnipeg's rookie goaltending sensation, Markus Mattsson.

Suffice it to say that by drawing on its best players, Finland can assemble a team capable of inspired hockey.

Put the whole package together — the tours by Czechoslovakia, Soviet Union, Sweden and Finland, as well as the Izvestia Cup Tournament and the Japanese exhibitions — and you have International Series '78. Thirty-four games in North America. Over forty games counting those abroad.

The picture that emerges is that of a World Hockey Association that is playing an increasingly important role in the World of The Sport. It is universally accepted that international competition is the wave of the future. The fans want the very best in hockey. The fans deserve no less than the very best. The fans are getting the very best ... from the World Hockey Association.

The Schedule

CZECHOSLOVAKIA

Fri.	Dec. 9	at Indianapolis
Sun.	11	at Quebec
Tue.	13	at Winnipeg
Wed.	14	at Edmonton
Fri.	16	at New England
Sun.	18	at Houston
Tue.	20	at Cincinnati
Wed.	21	at Birmingham

SOVIET ALL-STARS

Wed.	Dec. 14	at New England
Sat.	17	at Cincinnati
Sun.	18	at Indianapolis
Tue.	20	at Winnipeg
Wed.	21	at Edmonton
Fri.	23	at Houston
Mon.	26	at Birmingham
Wed.	28	at Houston
Fri.	30	at Quebec

IZVESTIA CUP TOURNAMENT
Dec. 15 - Dec. 22 Quebec at Moscow

JAPAN EXHIBITION TOUR
Dec. 29 - Jan. 1 Winnipeg vs. Soviet Nationals

SOVIET NATIONALS

Wed.	Jan. 4	at Edmonton
Thu.	5	at Winnipeg
Sat.	7	at Quebec
Sun.	8	at Cincinnati
Tue.	10	at Indianapolis
Wed.	11	at New England

SWEDEN

Fri.	Mar. 17	at Indianapolis
Sun.	19	at New England
Tue.	21	at Houston
Sun.	26	at Cincinnati
Tue.	28	at Birmingham

FINLAND

Sat.	Mar. 18	at Birmingham
Sun.	19	at Houston
Wed.	22	at Indianapolis
Sat.	25	at Cincinnati
Sun.	26	at New England

WHA HALL OF FAME

More 1972-1979 WHA game program covers

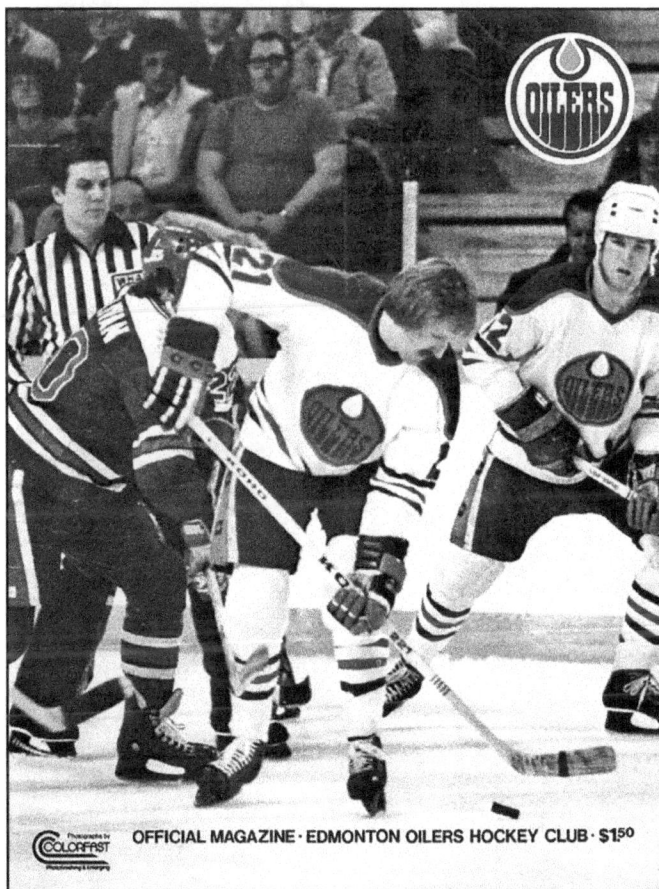

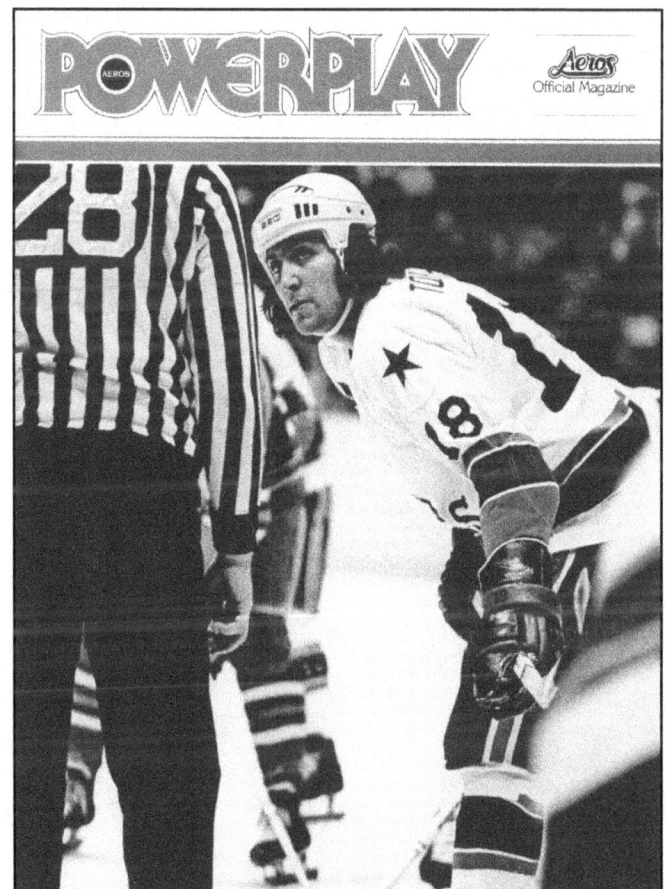

HOCKEY SPECTATOR

Preview Edition, 1972

the hockey spectator

Vol. I, No. 4   Preview, 1972   Price 50¢

WHA is on the ice

Ottawa's Marc Brunet (left) and goaltender Gilles Gratton watch errant Philadelphia shot. Philadelphia won, 3-1, October 1 in Ottawa before almost 8,000 fans.

Now there are two major leagues

The World Hockey Association takes its place as a second major professional league this week with home openers scheduled in 10 of its 12 cities.

Ottawa, bringing professional hockey back to the Canadian capital for the first time since 1934, and Cleveland, becoming one of a few select cities to have major league teams in four different sports, will share the distinction of hosting the first WHA games ever played. Ottawa's Nationals entertain the Alberta Oilers at the Ottawa Civic Centre and Cleveland's Crusaders meet the Quebeck Nordiques at the Cleveland Arena in a pair of 8 p.m. (Local time) games on Wednesday, October 11.

Gary L. Davidson, president and co-founder of the WHA, will drop the first puck at Cleveland. Donald J. Regan, general counsel of the league and a founding partner with Davidson, will officiate in the game at Ottawa.

"It's a very satisfying feeling to be this close to opening day," Davidson said. "All of our franchises are solid, and we're starting with a parity of competition that few leagues ever achieve.

"We realized we had undertaken an ambitious project in starting the WHA," he continued, "but there never were any doubts about it being successful. Hockey is the most exciting sport in the world,

and World Hockey is where the championships of the future will be."

Mayor Pierre Benoit of Ottawa and Mayor Jean Louis Seguin of Hull will be among the crowd attending the National-Oiler contest.

Hockey fans across Canada also will have an opportunity to watch the historic opener from the Ottawa Civic Centre. The game will be telecast live over the Canadian Broadcasting Corporation.

In Cleveland, the first of several hockey doubleheaders is planned. Cleveland's Barons meet the Providence Reds in an American Hockey League game at 5 p.m. with the Cru-

sader-Nordique game scheduled to be the feature.

Nick Mileti owns both the Crusaders and Barons, along with the Cleveland Indians baseball and Cleveland Cavaliers basketball teams.

He'll present fans attending the opening game with a souvenir glass mug, carrying the Crusader logo on one side and the words "World Premier Major League Hockey, October 11, 1972" on the other.

From October 11 on, there'll be no let-up. The WHA's 468-game schedule continues through Sunday, April 1, with each team playing 39 games at home and 39 on the road.

Here is the schedule of home openers:

Wednesday, Oct. 11 -- Alberta at Ottawa, 8 p.m.; Quebec at Cleveland, 8 p.m.

Thursday, Oct. 12 -- Winnipeg at New York, 7:30 p.m.; Chicago at Houston, 7:30 p.m.; Philadelphia at New England, 7:30 p.m.

Friday, Oct. 13 -- Houston at Los Angeles, 8 p.m.; Winnipeg at Minnesota, 7:30 p.m.; Alberta at Quebec, 8:05 p.m.; New England at Philadelphia, 7:35 p.m.

Sunday, Oct. 15 -- Alberta at Winnipeg, 7:30 p.m.

Tuesday, Oct. 17 -- Winnipeg at Alberta, 8 p.m.

Tuesday, Oct. 31 -- Winnipeg at Chicago, 7:30 p.m.

Bennett didn't think it was funny

By Frank Bertucci

PHILADELPHIA--Not only was the Miami Screaming Eagles franchise a joke, it turns out some of its draft selections were, too. Like John Bennett.

"I was playing in a league for college players in Culver City, Cal. last summer, when Les Patrick came in," Bennett relates. "He saw me working out and asked me why I was there. He told me he drafted me for Miami as a joke."

John Bennett wasn't laughing, though, and he wound up with the Blazers.

"I went to the Blazers' try-out camp in Roanoke, Va. That wasn't much different than college. But when I went to Sherbrooke to work out with the pros I knew the difference."

But he worked hard enough to earn a spot on the original Blazers roster, and he's been with the team all season, except for a two-week visit to Roanoke and the EHL. He was recalled in mid-December when John McKenzie left the team due to the death of his father.

"The travel was brutal in the Eastern League," says Bennett. "We had a 13-hour bus trip from Roanoke to St. Peters-burg, Fla. and had to play a game that night. I was dis-appointed when I was first sent down, but I had to give it a chance."

The Bennetts of Cranston, R.I., may be America's pre-miere hockey family. Harvey Bennett, John's father, spent some time in goal for the Bos-ton Bruins. John's older bro-ther Curt is with the Atlanta Flames, following stints with

the New York Rangers and St. Louis Blues. And Harvey, Jr. is at Boston College.

John joined the Blazers after graduating from Brown Uni-versity, where he majored in anthropology.

However, he never intended to live in the jungle with a prehistoric tribe of cannibals.

"I took anthropology because it was easier than economics," he admits. "It was pretty in-teresting, though.

"I wasn't really thinking about playing hockey profes-sionally until the Blazers con-tacted me. I think I would have gone to Europe and played on a team over there this year. Some friends of mine are with a team in Switzerland, and I probably would have joined them if it wasn't for the WHA."

Bennett has been filling in on both wings wherever he's needed. After 29 games he had four goals and six assists. (He had six goals and 13 assists for Brown last season, but had mononucleosis part of the year.)

John Bennett signed two con-tracts with the Blazers before this season. One was a major league pact, the other for a minor league. Les Patrick must be surprised at which contract is paying Bennett.

BLAZINGS...McKenzie's line with rookies Michel Plante and Michel Boudreau is hos-pitalized. Plante suffered three broken ribs (thanks to Dick Paradise) in St. Paul Dec. 26, Boudreau, who had been replac-ed by Pierre Henry, already was sidelined with twisted knee liga-ments.

Blazers John Bennett (20) and Don Burgess (8)

(Spectator Photo by Frank Bryan)

walt marlow

a big name in stripes

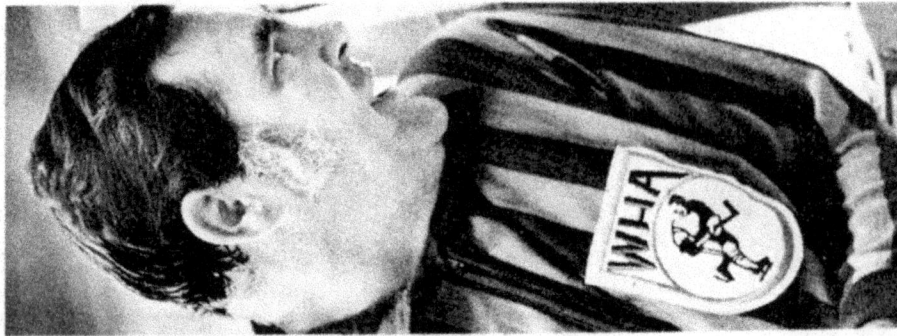

Bill Friday

LOS ANGELES--All a referee has to do is police 12 players traveling 20 miles an hour over 17,000 square feet of ice for 60 minutes with thousands of experts giving advice.

And while doing it, he's only required to remember 90-pages of a rule book. He has two seconds to make a decision. If he takes longer than that, he's second-guessing himself--a non-permissible luxury.

The life of an official can be a private hell.

When the WHA emerged, the signing of superstars like Bobby Hull, Gerry Cheevers, John McKenzie and J.C. Tremblay commanded much of the attention.

But an equally impressive signing was that of William Albert Friday, a veteran of 12 years in the National League. He, too, holds super star status.

As the WHA reached the halfway point in the schedule, Friday had worked in 45 games--about 10 more than he would have in the NHL.

The one big difference between the two leagues, he concedes, is the travel, and the fact that you work a little harder because of the overall experience, or lack of it, in the league.

"There's no alternate for experience," says Friday. "Certainly we have some inexperienced linesmen in our league. It puts a little added pressure on you. You watch their work closely and do a little teaching along the way."

Friday will tell you that a referee works just as hard as the players, possibly a little harder.

"You don't have anybody you can put the blame on when things go bad," he points out. "The player, he can always blame somebody else."

If Friday has one complaint, it's probably the fact that he's had to work when hurt, and that he's become almost a total stranger to his family based in Hamilton, Ontario.

"The body's getting a little tired," says the 39-year-old Friday. "I'm not 25 anymore, but you still like to maintain a high standard. This league is paying you good money, so you work hard."

No one will deny that Friday works hard, nor that he works

hurt. He's that kind of man.

He suffered a torn shoulder muscle during the first two weeks of the season climbing the boards. He gets needles, takes pills, but acknowledges that by working he's aggravating it. There's also the irritation of stretched knee ligaments.

As New Year's Eve approached, Friday had been home a mere three and a half days out of the last 33. He was looking forward to a few days with wife, Donna, and the Friday children, Bill Jr., 19; Larry, 17; Paul, 15; Donald, 13; and Diana, 10.

Friday's not only proud of his own wife, but all the mothers in the hockey world.

"You must have a dedicated wife in this business," he says. "Every game for us is a road game. At least a player can look forward to 39 home games."

But for all of that, Friday can see a great future for officials. Certainly a trifle better than when he broke in 12 years ago with an NHL contract that called for $5000. And he worked playoff games for nothing.

Last year in the NHL he reportedly was drawing $25,000--plus bonuses. His contract with the WHA is said to be in the territory of $50,000.

Likes WHA parity

"The WHA is great for the game, and great for anybody in officiating," points out Friday. "I would recommend to any young fellow who knows he doesn't have the ability to put the puck in the net that officiating can be a very lucrative career if he has the dedication and wants to work hard."

Is life in the WHA any rougher than that of the rival NHL?

"I don't think it's as rough as the National League," said Friday. "It's possible a little cruder, not as much finesse which makes it easier to officiate. They're a little cuter in the other league.

"Generally, I haven't had that many of what you'd class as real tough hockey games. I've had some, but out of 45 you're going to have a few. The general play has been good, and we've got parity. Nobody is running away with anything."

Friday, like any good referee, has learned to live with the loneliness and the criticism. But that doesn't mean he likes it.

Officials, at least those in the WHA, don't have the privilege of running to the news media, like a player or team official, and scream that they've been abused.

You wonder if maybe the rule that forbids an official to talk to the news media isn't an injustice to all parties concerned.

More often than not, the referee is the only man on the premises who knows what's going on.

Everyone else is seized with emotionalism.

Unknown commodity,
Gratton produces

By Vic Grant

WINNIPEG--A diamond in the rough for Winnipeg Jets is Jean Guy Gratton (pronounced Jan Gee).

Grats, as the players refer to him, was a major disappointment to club management through the first third of the Jets schedule but started to attain some of the shine that caught the eye of the Winnipeg recruiters when he was toiling with Hershey Bears in the American Hockey league.

Grats has earned himself a number of distinctions on the Jet club. He's the team's only bachelor, but he took the first step toward eliminating that distinction by presenting fiancee Nicole Boucher with a diamond as a Christmas present.

Grats is also the team's highbrow, meaning the only player who can pick up a 500-page book and read it from cover to cover. The subject of those books is usually four-legged because Gratton is also the only Jet to own a one-horse racing stable. He has a trotter (or should it be a pacer?) running in Eastern Canada and it must be earning money because each time he shows a result sheet to his teammates his horse finishes second.

Being the team's only bachelor makes the rightwinger somewhat of a loner, too. He'll spend most of his time on the road reading books and standing in phone booths. He finally decided it was cheaper to get

married than to pour coins into various booths around North America.

Gratton was the last Jet signed by player birddog Bill Robinson and he was signed unseen. What caught Robinson's eye was the statistical story last year in Hershey. Gratton played 76 games for the Bears last year and contributed 30 goals and 34 assists and, as far as Robinson was concerned, it warranted a World Hockey Association contract.

Signing any player unseen is dangerous and can sometimes prove a mistake. When Jets started the season there were second thoughts on Gratton's usefulness.

At first Gratton was inflicted with that malady that has ruined many a career...the footstep disease. Gratton was hearing footsteps around the corners of the rink and it was only through the kid-glove handling by coach Bobby Hull that pulled Gratton over the crisis period.

There were even thoughts of trying to trade Grats in that early going but Jets were up there battling for first place in the Division. But, Hull isn't one to take a piece out of a winning combination.

Gratton overcame his fear of the corners and he helped make a solid attacking unit out of centerman Danny Johnson and leftwinger Ab McDonald. Then, everything started to fall into place when Grats scored the first home-ice hat trick.

Up to that point Hull had been picking the spots for Gratton, using him more as a home player rather than in road rinks.

Another habit Gratton managed to shake was one of trying to stickhandle too much. There were times when he was set up in the slot and any sort of shot would have done the trick but instead he tried an extra deke. Finally, Jets told him what to do with his superfluous deke.

The day Grats scored his hat trick, all three goals came off blistering slap shots. Although his point total, 17 points off eight goals and nine assists, wasn't anything to get excited about after 41 games, Gratton was showing signs of what was to come. Jets are now prepared to wait.

JET DIBS--Gratton fired the winning goal in the Jets' Boxing Day victory over Chicago Cougars...Bobby Hull took his first major penalty of the year after a brief fistic exchange with Cougar tough guy Reggie Fleming...It was a one-punch victory and Fleming wasn't the winner...Hull's presence and worth in a Jet uniform is exemplified in the statistics... After playing 25 games up to the Christmas break, Hull had contributed seven power play goals, three game tying goals, two game-winning goals and one goal while his team was shorthanded. His total after only 25 games was 19 goals and 15 assists.

Winnipeg 'find' Jean-Guy Gratton

the hockey spectator

Two bright lights in Chicago

By Reid Grosky

CHICAGO—Two of the few things that have gone right for the Chicago Cougars this season are Ron Anderson and Jan Popiel.

It seems the rest of the league also has realized this because both players wound up playing for the West team at the recent All-Star game in Quebec.

Ed Short, Cougar General Manager, broke the good news to Anderson and Popiel in the locker room before a game. It was a nice Christmas surprise, although Short said the two all-stars at first thought it was strictly April Fool.

Anderson, a 6-0, 190-pound defenseman, confirmed his surprise afterward.

"I didn't believe him when he told me," Anderson said. "I pretty much thought all the former NHL guys would make it. I just placed my vote and forgot about it,"

Anderson's selection to the team was all the more noteworthy because the 24-year-old rookie has played while hurt all season. He injured his right knee in training camp, was in a cast for a week afterward, and missed the Cougars' first six games.

"It's not really painful anymore," Anderson said. "I stopped taping it a couple of weeks ago. I just haven't been able to strengthen it because of

the schedule we've had, and it tires very easily."

Anderson is a converted forward and just learning the defenseman trade, so more all-star votes should be accruing to the burly Cougar in future years.

Popiel, on the other hand, has been playing left wing most of his life. But still, like

Anderson, he was a little stunned by the All-Star honor.

"I was really pleased, but surprised to say the least," Popiel said. "There are a lot of good left wingers in this league,"

Popiel, it turns out, is one of the best, and the 25-year-old bachelor already has made a lasting mark with the Chicago

Ron Anderson

Jan Popiel

six. Popiel scored the first hat trick in Cougar history as part of his 16 goals and 19 assists during the 1972 portion of the season.

Born in Denmark, Popiel bore an uncanny resemblance to Mark Spitz (and some said to Derek Sanderson) before Cougar Coach Marcel Provonost made him shave his mustache

in training camp.

Now Popiel merely looks like a helluva hockey player, and he credits Pronovost, whom he played for at Tulsa, for much of his success in the WHA.

"I think he's helped because he knows my style of play," Popiel said.

Pronovost has Popiel skating on a line with center Bob Sicinski and right winger Rosaire Paiement. The trio has provided nearly a goal a game since its formation in December, and it gives Cougar fans something cheerful to look forward to in the New Year.

GOAL-MOUTHINGS -- The Cougars didn't plan it that way, but the distaff side of the team's front office all have something in common—a first name that ends in the letter A. There's Barbara (Office Manager), Cynthia (Ticket Sales), Donna (public relations), Joanna (program sales), Cymala (bookkeeping), Lo Juana (bookkeeping), and Tonya (group sales)..The week of the All-Star game, the Cougars obtained right winger Dick Sarrazin from the new England Whalers for cash and an undisclosed draft choice. ..Chet Coppock, the team's public-address announcer, performed a public service during one game by announcing the license number of a car whose owner had left on the lights in the parking lot. It took several seconds before Coppock realized it was his own car.

Once a right wing, always...

By Joey LeBourgeois

HOUSTON--Don Grierson has been playing right wing since he's been playing hockey. Now he's playing it for the Houston Aeros, and he's happy with the situation.

Working on a line with center Larry Lund and left winger Ted Taylor, one of Houston's All-Stars, Grierson has found that everything works well when you're together.

"We're really playing well together," says the 25-year-old, "and it's getting better all the time.

"Teddy's real strong. He can go into the corner and bring out the puck real well. Larry's a super stick handler, and he's strong, too. He can go into the corners just as well. I just skate around and shoot," Shooting is something Grierson has been able to do well all his life, although he has only eight goals for Houston this year.

Last year, his fourth in the pro hockey ranks, the North Bay, Ont. native played in 72 games for the Port Huron Wings of the International Hockey League. He scored 45 goals and had 32 assists for 77 points.

He had 28 points in 49 games in the same league the year before, and had 20 points in 43 games with Denver in the 1969-70 Western Hockey League season.

He's not a stranger to Houston, either. Grierson broke in as a pro with the Houston Apollos of the Central Hockey League in 1968, picking up 49 points in 59 games. Twenty-

two of them were goals.

"Last year was my best," says Grierson, "but this is just my fifth year. I've always had a good shot, and although I haven't broken any records this year I know I can do a lot better."

One of the things that Grierson thinks may be slowing him down is his attempt to keep down his penalty minutes total. Last year he spent 234 minutes in the penalty box, and so far this year it's just 37.

"I got in a few fights last year," he concedes. "But things are a lot different this year. You can't take that many bad penalties in this league.

"In the International League you could take a run at a guy and get away with it because it wouldn't hurt you that much if you got a penalty. Your team could still get out of it all right. Maybe not being able to do that has kept me down this year.

"Our line has been doing pretty well, though," he continues. "We pride ourselves on not letting too many goals be scored while we're on the ice. We've been fortunate in that it's really working out well. I don't know how many we've had against us, but it's not many.

"What we do is try to create as much action on the other end of the ice as we can. If you can get in on the defense fast, you've got a good chance to score.

"A lot of the defensemen in this league are inexperienced. They can all come up with the good play. . .there's a lot of

talent around. But a lot of times you can get them to mishandle the puck with some good pressure. It's working for us."

Another thing that's working for the Aeros, according to Grierson's coach Bill Dineen's try at using four lines. They only lost one of their first ten with the system in effect.

"What can you say bad about it?" he asks. "It's really paid off for us so far."

Grierson's also in favor of the overtime period the WHA uses, something the considers a great boon to the fans.

"The fans like to see a decision in a hockey game, and I'm all for it, too. It's kind of bad on the road, though.

"When you're playing away from home you have to really work for a goal, and it's hard to picture losing a game on a deflected screen shot or a tip in. But what the hell, I'd just as soon have it. It'll even out over the course of a year."

So will the Aeros, says the 6-foot, 185-pounder.

"I think we've got the best-balanced club in the league," he says proudly. "We don't have any superstars, but there's not a weak position on the team. We've got six good defensemen, two good goalies in Wayne Rutledge and Don McLeod (and another in Billy Hughes, who's our third) and good forwards.

"It puts us in a good position. Earlier in the year, when we had a lot of injuries, it didn't hurt us as much as it could have hurt another team.

We still had nothing but good hockey players left.

"Look what it did to Philadelphia when Derek Sanderson and John McKenzie were both hurt. We don't have to worry about losing a superstar with an injury, and with all our good players we're in better shape for it."

Aero right wing Don Grierson

January 19, 1973

the hockey spectator

If Bob Wall is a little confused . . .

By Terry Jones

EDMONTON--Bob Wall is a 10-year veteran of professional hockey. He's played on National Hockey League clubs in Detroit, Los Angeles and St. Louis. And only in his first season of pro hockey had he previously made an all-star team.

Wall is enjoying success with Alberta Oilers this season but should have been properly delighted when he was named to the World Hockey Association Western Division All-Star team.

But please excuse Bob Wall for being a little confused.

Wall was named the right winger on the second Western Division team or line.

"As far as I know, I've been playing defense all year," he said. "I find it a little strange. I'm lost to explain it. All the players had to fill out ballots.

"Maybe everybody remembers me from the Los Angeles Kings. I played a season on left wing there. It was mainly a checking line. They threw us together to play against all the big lines in the league. I scored 13 goals which made me happy because I certainly don't consider myself a goal scorer."

Wall says he doesn't even consider himself an offensive defenseman.

"I'm neither an offensive defenseman nor a defensive defenseman--I'm somewhere in between."

It's been that kind of a season for Wall.

He's found happiness in Edmonton, a city where he played Western League hockey with the Flyers in 1963. At the same time he's found something less than that with the club unable to get out of a two-month slump as the New Year was brought in.

"I like it here. It's sort of a relaxed atmosphere for my family for a change. My wife is curling for the first time since she was in high school and my kids have their first chance to play minor hockey. If we could only start winning games again, it would be just about perfect. It's given my kids a chance to be brought up as a Canadian. Heck, until this year, my kids (Bobby, 7, Danny, 5, and Cherylin, 2) haven't even experienced a Canadian winter."

Wall said he plans to join wife Margaret curling "when the club starts winning again.

"At this point we all have to concentrate on getting back on track. But once we get rolling again, I'd like to take up curling. I think it's good for a hockey player to have a recreational sport to fool around with and help take the tension off."

Wall said his impressive play this season is due largely to his gathering of confidence.

"Confidence is a big factor in this game. More than anything else, I think that's what makes Bobby Orr as great as he is. I'm no Bobby Orr, but I'm building some of that confidence up."

Oilers headed into 1973 in fifth place after flirting with the lead in the first month of the schedule.

"I don't know what happened," said Wall. "We're just not clicking properly. We've got a good strong team here right now. I don't think there is any question of that. We just have to do a little soul-searching and start to put things together.

"On paper we have a big league defense, as good as any team in the league and better than some in the NHL. Especially when you consider that Doug Barrie is playing forward when he's really a defenseman.

"We're getting good goaltending and our defensive record compares favorably with most teams in the league. We just can't seem to score any goals."

Such a situation is not entirely new to Wall. He had the honor of playing for Los Angeles Kings during a slump that lasted an entire season.

"It was three or four years ago. We set six records that year. Things like most games lost, least goals scored, most scored against.

"We've got to turn this thing around right now. I don't want to go through another year like that."

Oiler All-Star Bob Wall

WHA HALL OF FAME

Jets' good neighbor policy?

By Vic Grant

WINNIPEG--If nothing else, at least Winnipeg Jets treat the Alberta Oilers in a manner to which the Oilers are becoming accustomed.

When the World Hockey Association opened its doors for business before the first snowflake fell this year they tried to create natural rivalries.

They didn't have to create a rivalry between Winnipeg and Edmonton because it was already there. For how many years has Benny Hatskin been trying to beat Bill Hunter on a sheet of ice? Hatskin has beaten Hunter in some business tete-a-tetes, but Hunter has the monopoly on ice.

The Jets have met the Oilers six times in this hockey season and Hunter's team, the General Manager, has only lost one. That's only one of the reasons as to why Wild Bill likes playing the Jets, especially in his home arena, the ancient and decrepit Klondike Palace.

Jets have Bobby Hull and that assures a sellout in the Palace, something Oilers haven't had as a habit. So, Jets bring in the people and make the whole night a huge success by losing graciously.

Why do the Jets lose? It's no deep, dark secret that Jets would prefer to skate than hit and before the schedule is over this year that fact will cause some problems.

Oilers would run Jets out

Steve Cuddie

of most rinks in any league because the Oilers hit, at times like a 10-ton Mack truck. Jets, on the other hand, wouldn't raise a collective shoulder to lean up against a brick building, let

alone to knock down an opponent.

Discretion may be the better part of valor, but on a sheet of hockey ice? The Winnipeg team has three players who would fit

the mold of a hitter.

There's Steve Cuddie, the robust young defenseman who probably would skate into a tree mulcher to help his endangered goaltender. But,

Dunc Rousseau

Cuddie's only one hitter among five and a half defensemen and that's not enough.

Then, there Dunc Rousseau. Rousseau hits, but only every now and then. Rousseau, a left winger, is the only forward who does hit for Jets and that isn't enough either.

Then there's Brian Cadie. Cadle would probably run through a brick wall anytime Coach Bobby Hull asked him to, the only problem being Hull doesn't ask him very often.

Cadle's one of those hockey players who has to make up a lack in ability with 110 percent effort. Cadle's effort reaches that plateau all the time but he has weaknesses, the most glaring being his skating.

The only time Cadie's been getting on the ice as a Jet is when the cause is already won or lost.

What Jets need to come out of a midseason tailspin is a leader with moxiety not to mention muscle. If Jets had some such player(s) they probably wouldn't turn the other cheek to the likes of Jim Harrison, Doug Barrie, Ken Baird, Frank Sanders, John Arbour and Dick Paradise.

Minnesota Fighting Saints and the Oilers have caused Jets the most problems this season. The crux of those problems being physical.

The Saints are breathing hard after the Jets in the standings and have whittled a lead that once was in the big numbers down to a precious few.

February 2, 1973

the hockey spectator

Patenaude skates from oblivion

Oiler Rusty Patenaude

By Terry Jones

EDMONTON--Rusty Patenaude skated out of the oblivion that is the International Hockey League and hasn't stopped skating since.

At the All-Star Break in the World Hockey Association schedule Patenaude was an unlikely scoring star with Alberta Oilers. He'd picked away game-by-game, working his way to third in club scoring on hustle and desire.

"I'm not a goal scorer," he says.

"I consider myself a hustler. To be successful I have to hustle and go out and be consistent every night."

So far, he's getting the job done.

Patenaude was one of the few players to regularly draw the praise of Coach Ray Kinasewich and General Manager Bill Hunter during a month-long losing streak which saw Oilers drop from second to fifth place in the Western Division.

A former junior hockey star down the road a bit in Calgary, Patenaude is in his third year of professional hockey. He started his career in Amarillo, Texas and played last season in Fort Wayne, Indiana.

"I've always felt confident that I could play professional hockey and I felt that I hadn't been given a fair shake.

"I came to training camp in Edmonton with my mind made up that I was going to make the team if I had to fight and scrap every second to do it. I just

convinced myself that I was going to do it this year and that was that."

Now that he's more or less done it, Patenaude is reluctant to take much of the credit.

"I'm just happy to play regularly let alone be third in scoring on the club," he said.

"But I've got a heck of a center who deserves half the credit."

Ross Perkins and Patenaude were put on the same line early in the season and have managed to avoid the shuffling.

"We sit beside each other in the dressing room and I think we help each other off the ice as well as on it.

"We figure that if we score then we're really doing our job but that if we don't score, as long as we're not scored against, then we're still doing the job. We almost think like a checking line. If the coach wanted to make us one, I'm sure we'd be a good one."

Patenaude claims to be impressed with the first half season of the WHA.

"I didn't think the goaltending would be as strong as it is and I can't believe that the league is as evenly balanced as it is.

"Every game is a big game in this league.

"That's the toughest thing I've found about playing here.

You have to get yourself mentally up for every game. You really have to work on that because it's such a long season and the travel is so tough."

Patenaude figures the Edmonton surroundings have contributed in some way to his success.

"I really like it around Edmonton. As far as I'm concerned, it's the best place to play in the whole league.

"If there is one other spot that I wouldn't mind, it would be Minnesota.

"I'm an outdoorsman to begin with and I like to get outside after practice. I like the country around Edmonton and the country in Minnesota.

"I played some junior hockey in Moose Jaw, Sask. and I just hated it there. I wouldn't much like Winnipeg. I just don't like the prairies."

OIL SPILLS--Billy Hicke, President of the World Hockey Association Players Association, didn't make it to the first official meeting of the group because of asthma. . .Steve Carlyle and Doug Barrie are the other Alberta player reps in the association. .Bob Wall, the defenseman who was selected to the all star team as a winger, tried to talk coach Bobby Hull into letting him play on a line with him and Chris Bordeleau. . .Oilers had 15 home games in 30 days beginning Jan. 15.

It's always Bernie...

By Frank Bertucci

PHILADELPHIA--After finally evacuating the Eastern Division basement, the Blazers are finding fourth place harder to reach.

They ended their eight-game road trip at 4-4, but lost the last two vital games, to Ottawa and Quebec. Which left them seven points behind the Nordiques and New York Raiders.

Bernie Parent was in goal both nights for the Blazers. Bernie Parent is always in goal for the Blazers.

A syndicated hockey columnist recently rated Bernie among hockey's ten most overrated players. He has obviously not seen the Blazers play in 1973.

At the end of that trip Bernie had played 32 straight games. Since Dec. 1 when he recovered from his broken foot, his goals against average is 3.87. Since Jan. 1, it is 3.20, with two shutouts, one of which went 2:38 into overtime.

"I haven't played this much since I was 16," Bernie admitted.

Parent will not get much rest from here on since the Blazers have a long way to go before they're in the playoffs. And Bernie Parent has to be their most valuable performer.

"I don't think there's any extra pressure on me," he said. "I know I'll be playing every game as I'm ready for it."

While Parent was out for 11 games in November, the Blazers used four goalies, including Marcel Paille, who watches Bernie from the Blazers bench every game. And during that time, when Parent, John McKenzie and Derek Sanderson were injured, Danny Lawson for one admitted that Bernie was the most vital of the three.

"We really miss Bernie," he said at that time. "We have to have him playing behind us if we're going to do anything."

In the last month, Bernie Parent has been playing as well as he ever has as a professional, and has personally kept the Blazers in the playoff battle.

(Spectator Photo by Frank Bryan)

Bernie Parent plays ironman role for Blazers.

Kirk -- Rookie of the Year?

(Spectator Photo by Frank Bryan)

Nats found a bonanza in Gavin Kirk.

By Bob Mellor

OTTAWA--Until the WHA came along, Gavin Kirk wasn't sure there was any future for him in pro hockey--or at least the kind of future he wanted.

What the Toronto Maple Leafs were willing to offer him when they drafted him in the third round as an over-age junior graduate fell a long way short of his expectations. So after he thought it over through a training camp session that made him appear destined for a Central pro farm club, Gavin Kirk went back to school.

In the year he attended Loyola College, the WHA and Ottawa Nationals came along, and this time the offer was more acceptable.

Since the, the 5-11, 173-pound centreman has left little doubt that his future in hockey appears assured. In fact, his coach, Billy Harris, feels that Kirk is worthy of Rookie-of-the-Year honors in the WHA. Said Harris, "He's been the most pleasant surprise on the club."

Kirk has delivered in a manner not the club's leading scorer by a long haul, but he has developed into one of the most versatile and dependable performers on the team.

Kirk has been the sparkplug behind the success of Harris' most consistent trio, the kid line which includes Jack Gibson on the left side and Steve King on the right.

The unit is the only one on the club which Harris has found no reason to tinker with in a year fraught with problems, and he maintains that Kirk's dependable play at center ice is what makes it go.

Kirk had 12 goals after 56 games, but he'd been credited with assists on 25 more, and few of them could have been labeled 'cheapies'. He's tended to be overshadowed somewhat by his more spectacular wingmate, Jack Gibson of the booming shot, for whom he's helped set up 18 more goals.

But that hasn't been where Kirk's contribution stopped. He and his right winger, third-year pro Steve King, have been highly effective penalty killers.

That was one job Harris really hadn't expected to assign to Kirk. While he's a hustler and a puckhound--the kind who could get 28 goals and 40 assists in a 30-game college season him last before this year in junior hockey and hadn't thought of him as a checker.

"Somebody really did a job on him in teaching him how to check between the time I saw him play junior and he came to our training camp," said Harris.

When he discovered that unexpected bonus, Harris wasted little time making use of it.

Kirk says Frank Bonello, his old junior coach with the Marlies, had worked on his checking and helped him a lot. But he adds that the veterans on this club--particularly Brian Conacher--had taught him a great deal after he joined the Nationals.

"I had a lot to learn," he said.

Obviously, he's learned enough to draw quite a recommendation from a coach who doesn't hand out plaudits lightly. Not quite through his first pro season, Gavin Kirk should now have some idea about how he'll be spending the next few winters.

Fitting finale in Boston

By Dick Dew

BOSTON--It was strangely fitting that when the World Hockey Association's first playoffs came to an end, they did so in a barrage of goals, a wild, impromptu celebration, and a furor over a massive television boner.

The New England Whalers, the first champions of a rebel league that wasn't supposed to get on the ice, promptly hurled a challenge to the National League to play for the Stanley Cup.

Virtually overlooked in the Whalers' 9-6 elimination victory of Bobby Hull and the Winnipeg Jets was a rather startling domination by the first Avco World Trophy winners.

New England was posting its third straight 4-1 series victory in the playoffs, running a home ice winning streak to 11 games--including all nine Garden playoff appearances--and blanking the high-scoring Hull in the finale.

Al Smith, New England's winning goalie who rolled up a 12-3 playoff record and was clearly his team's most valuable player, joked that the score only showed "We have a better field goal kicker."

Smith, who among other things gloved a Hull slap shot from pointblank range in the windup, was joined in the new Whaler hero class by Larry Pleau and the veteran Tom Williams.

Pleau scored a hat trick in the finale, running his playoff goal total to an impressive dozen, only one short of the record set by Winnipeg's Norm Beaudin.

Williams, who turned 33 last month, wound up with four assists in the final game, setting up as many goals in spectacular fashion, and boosting to 17 his playoff point total, a remarkable effort considering he rode the bench for long stretches down the season.

Joining Pleau in an improbable assault on maskless Joe Daley were Tom Webster with a pair of goals, along with single

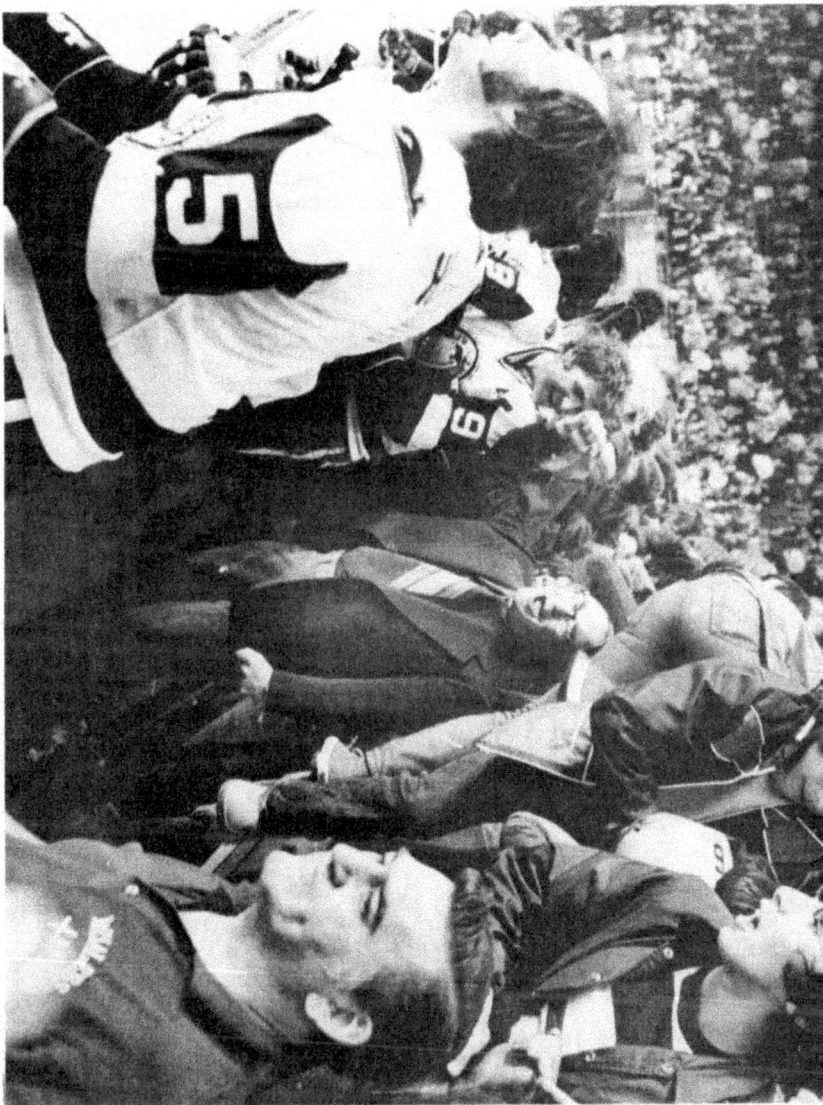

markers by Guy Smith, Rick Ley, Tim Sheehy and Mike Byers, the latter hitting an open net from 110 feet after Daley had been pulled with 3:27 remaining.

Beaudin ran his playoff scoring total to 13 with a pair before a Garden crowd of 11,186 while Danny Johnson, Milt Black, Bob Woytowich and Duke Asmundson checked in with singletons.

The cup clincher was a

strange, even peculiar contest in which the Jets enjoyed a fat, 42-27, shooting advantage and pulled themselves back from a three-goal early deficit to seriously threaten a comeback win as late as the five minute mark of the third period.

It was a Woytowich drive from the point with exactly 15:01 remaining that cut the Jet deficit to 6-5.

The threat was short-lived, however, as Pleau hit for his

second score of the game only 45 seconds later, capping a quick Whaler push triggered by Sheehy's interception of an attempted pass by a wandering Daley.

Pleau's first period goal was a shorthanded job on a solo sally after stealing at center ice. He added to his game winner and put the Avco Trophy on ice when he completed his hat trick at 7:31 of the third period, boosting the New Eng-

land lead to an insurmountable 8-5 and scoring twice in 1:47.

In addition to yanking Daley despite a three-goal deficit, the balding Hull even added to his already incredible ice time by going to defense during the waning minutes.

Tommy Williams (9) turns to congratulate happy Jack Kelley at moment of triumph.

(Spectator Photo by Earl Ostrom)

The 'Action Team' strikes

By Charley Hallman

ST. PAUL--Call Glen Sonmor and Harry Neale the "Action Team".

The Minnesota Fighting Saints' General Manager and Coach spent May at the salt mines and came out with a great deal of gold.

There are four new Fighting Saints--The Walton brothers (Mike and Bob), Rick Smith and Steve Cardwell.

Three have National Hockey League credentials. And Sonmor is convinced these four "and a couple more will give us the kind of help we are looking for to be first in the Western Division of the World Hockey Association."

The biggest catch was Mike Walton, the former Toronto and Boston star. Mike got off to the best start of his career with the Bruins last season, scoring 20 times in his team's first 25 games.

But a play accident in a hotel in St. Louis then put Mike out for two months and resulted in more than 200 stitches after he fell through a plate glass window.

Despite that, Mike wound up with 25 goals in 52 games for the Bruins after a 28-goal campaign the year before.

"Shakey should be a great one in our league," said Neale. "I'm going to play him until his tongue falls off. We're really relying on the Walton brothers."

Mike, at 28, is the oldest of the Saints' new players.

His brother, Rob "Shook" Walton, is 23--a year younger than Rick Smith and the same age as Steve Cardwell.

Last year, Rob led the Western League in scoring, pouring

in 40 goals and 61 assists for the Seattle Totems. Like his brother, "Shook" has a bit of a reputation as a rounder. But, that may be an advantage in St. Paul, where strange people have been known to not only survive, but thrive.

The Waltons were step two by the "Action Team."

Earlier, in May, the Saints put on the Smith-Cardwell show...and the two were very well received by the Twin Cities' media.

Smith, with five full seasons of NHL experience behind him, had his best year ever for California--canning nine goals and 24 assists from the left point.

"He means a great deal to our hockey club," said Sonmor. "Rick is a natural lead-

er, a proud man who has always been a winner. Bobby Orr has always said that Rick was his best defensive partner at Boston and it is apparently true if you look at the Bruins with Rick and without him."

Smith was dealt away from Boston two seasons back for Carol Vadnais, who hasn't really helped the Bruins the way Milt Schmidt thought he would.

Cardwell? Steve is one of those really talented youngsters the Pittsburgh Penguins had coming up.

Two seasons ago, Cardwell fired in seven goals and eight assists in the Pens' last 20 games and looked to be a new star at left wing.

But last year, he picked up an early injury and was sent

Rick Smith

Mike Walton

Steve Cardwell

to Hershey of the American League to play his way into shape. In 30 games with the Bears, Cardwell had 16 goals, 23 assists and 78 penalty minutes.

Then, in the AHL playoffs, Cardwell canned five more goals in just seven games.

"It was just a beautiful month for us," admitted Neale. "But we're not done yet. Other teams are doing good things. Look at Quebec! Dale Hoganson and Serge Bernier will make the Nordiques even stronger, especially if they land Rejean Houle and Michel Deguise.

"And Houston is bound to be strengthened by the Howes. Los Angeles got a super player in Marc Tardif. And Jim Hargraves will help Winnipeg," Sonmor says. "Everything is

looking great for the second WHA season. We hope to get some more talent in the near future but I'm certainly not ashamed to say we have the Waltons, Rick Smith and Steve Cardwell. Far from it, friends, we're in business."

Meanwhile the Fighting Saints announced Fred Grothe will return to the club as chief executive officer after Lloyd Leirdahl returned to private business.

Grothe, the most effective leader in Saints' history, said he will stay on indefinitely. SAINTS' NOTES: Goalie Mike Curran and center Keith Christiansen just returned to St. Paul from a month in the West Indies and Florida...

Ted Hampson won both the fishing and golf at the annual Stillwater Celebrity Derby. Members of the Twins, Vikings, North Stars, Saints and the University of Minnesota staff took part. Teddie hauled in a nine-pound walleye in the fishing contest...

Black Mike McMahon, Christiansen and Curran are conducting a hockey school in Bismarck, N.D., while Hampson and Mel Pearson have their annual school in Flin Flon, Manitoba...

Len Lilyholm had 5,000 people tour his mansion during a special neighborhood project aimed at restoring the Summit-University district of St. Paul. Lilyholm lives in a near-castle with winding spiral staircases near the famed Commodore Hotel...

Saints' executives have all but given up hope of signing Rick Middleton and Bob Gainey, the club's first two draft picks. The asking price for a rookie is $150,000 per year.

Webster leads Whaler flurry

By DICK DEW

BOSTON—They've already finished the toughest part of their entire schedule, they've made a marked improvement in their road record, and the New England Whalers are still ahead of their early pace of a year ago.

The Whalers, who won both the regular season and playoff titles in the World Hockey Association's inaugural campaign, staggered into a seven-day schedule break after a gruesome card.

They played nine games in 15 days including seven in ten days but came out of it with a 7-3-1 mark, a one point improvement on their 7-4 first season start.

"More important, we were 3-2 on the road and we got this heavy scheduling behind us, surviving it when we weren't really in prime shape," rookie Coach Ron Ryan exulted.

The Whalers capped their heavy run with their top gunner, Tom Webster, coming on like gang busters. He scored his fifth WHA hat trick against Los Angeles, running his four-game

total to six goals and piling up nine points in three games.

But despite Webster's hot streak, the Whalers desperately needed help from vet goalie Al Smith to run up a four-game winning streak to take on vacation with them.

Al, twice denied of shutout bonuses recently by one-time roommate Mike Laughton of New York, lost his third try when Gary Veneruzzo did him in.

"Smitty was sensational in the third period," Ryan said of Al's victory over Los Angeles as he officially lowered his goals against average below the 2.00 mark.

Ryan looked back over the rugged early run and cited several of his newcomers for adapting to the New England system. Don Blackburn and Al Karlander earned special praise as the Whalers survived a series of injuries and nagging physical problems that they didn't experience during their first year.

WHALE BITS: Terry Caffery, Rookie of the Year in the WHA last season, will probably miss

most of the season. After trying repeatedly to come back from knee surgery in the spring, Caffery was ordered to undergo new examination. Dr. Carter Rowe, otherwise known as the knee specialist who repaired Bobby Orr and Phil Esposito, was slated to perform repair surgery in early November... The club officially shifted John Cunniff to Jacksonville and brought up former New Hampshire star Guy Smith on a permanent basis... Reserve Goalie Bruce Landon was troubled by a split finger and was replaced by Gerry Gray, also from Jacksonville. Landon was expected back following the break, however... The Whalers drew only a disappointing announced crowd of 4,709 for a Chelsea Fire Fund benefit game... As nearly as can be determined, Jacques Plante's goaltending equipment is still lost in Boston Garden someplace. Plante, now coaching the Quebec Nordiques, asked his former Bruins employers for the gear but they have apparently been unable to locate it.

Tom Webster got fifth hat.

(Spectator Photo by Les Rosner)

OTHER STORIES

There's No Way Not To Ask THE Question:
WILL THE W. H. A. MAKE IT?

By Gerald Eskenazi

Like any new enterprise, the World Hockey Association may fall flat on its multi-colored puck. The key to the new league is a prosperous New York franchise and it doesn't look too prosperous at this point. Nevertheless, the WHA has what looks like five solid cities, some good people, a lot of money. Now for the players . . .

Dennis Murphy, left, co-founder of the WHL, announces the St. Paul franchise with owners Louis Kaplan, center, and Joe Lein.

Pat Brown, former Governor of California, is part owner of Los Angeles club.

There is something absurd —and yet appropriately symbolic—about the fact that the fledgling World Hockey Association plans to drop its black-and-white puck for the first time at Miami next October.

The absurdity, of course, is hockey in Florida. It just doesn't sound right. Imagine baseball in Anchorage in January. But the symbolism of it is pretty big. For when the puck is dropped, it will bring together the four corners of North America as a hockey-playing entity. Hockey no longer will be isolated and identified solely with specific areas. Enough people are willing to invest millions to prove the South will support the game that began on frozen lakes and rivers in Canada.

The big question now is simply: Will the WHA succeed? Another way of really putting the question is: Will hockey succeed away from the established urban areas it has proven so successful in? The answer must be: Yes. ·Of course, there are reservations. The easiest thing to do is laugh at a new venture, find fault with the principals, or the cities or the arenas. But that is not the point. You can't judge a new league by existing league standards. If you had, and if businessmen had, there would have been no American Football League or American Basketball Association.

It would, naturally, be just fallacious to reason that just because you're new means you're going to succeed—that just be-

cause other rival leagues got off the ground that the WHA will, too. It's a good idea to sit back and take a look at the WHA and what it proposes to do. Then maybe we can get an idea of just how it will get along.

First of all, the concept of a rival to the National Hockey League isn't a new one. Indeed, the NHL underwent its great expansion in 1967 specifically because it was faced with the possibility of another league being created. For the 25 years before 1967 there were only six teams in the NHL. It was the last remaining big-time sports league not to have expanded over that time. In fact, when you think about it, it does seem incredible that scarcely five years ago there were only six clubs in the NHL. But rumblings were heard then of the formation of a big-time league based on the West Coast, where there was no NHL representation. The old league wasn't happy about that. The league also was playing pretty nearly to capacity. How to get more revenue? Television. However, television only pays you if you deliver ratings. And there wasn't a good chance for big ratings on the West Coast, where there was no NHL to create the interest. So the league doubled in size—and in one swift stroke cut out a rival league, as well as opened a TV market.

When the league expanded again in 1970, bringing it two more clubs—both of which did fabulously at the gate—it was obvious that the markets weren't even beginning to be tapped. And who should decide to form a league to open those taps? Simple. Former executives of the ABA, who knew all about opposing an established league.

Three men got the new operation started—Gary Davidson, a lawyer from Santa Ana, Calif., who was the ABA's first commissioner; Michael O'Hara of Los Angeles, the first general manager of the ABA Texas Chaparrals; and Dennis Murphy, a Floridian, who

"If it weren't for me the Rangers wouldn't have a club in New York."
—Bill Hunter
Mr. Hockey of Western Canada

was the general manager of the Floridians of the ABA. They had made some preliminary talks in the middle of 1971 with prospective hockey purchasers. But no one got really excited about the WHA. Then in September O'Hara came to New York to line up a potential New York entrant—specifically, he was looking for someone to represent the league in the new Nassau Coliseum on Long Island.

What made the news was that O'Hara was meeting with William A. Shea, the dynamic attorney for whom Shea Stadium was named. Shea was advising Nassau County on the various ways it could get a big-league basketball and hockey team into its Coliseum—and give it a big-league image.

O'Hara made some mistakes. He really didn't know who wanted a New York franchise and his talk with Shea was set up in part because O'Hara boasted that Carl Braun, the former New York Knickerbocker star, was one of the principals interested in bringing hockey to Long Island.

Actually, all that Braun had done was simply talk to O'Hara. Braun and O'Hara had mutual friends who introduced the pair. Braun, a stockbroker, told O'Hara he might be able to put him in touch with some people who possibly might be interested. But O'Hara went ahead and told Shea that Braun was leading a delegation of Long Islanders who wanted a franchise.

Shea listened to O'Hara's pitch. After all, he had nothing to lose. "I'm smart enough to know the key to any new league is the Coliseum," Shea said. He also knew that the NHL would be watching the situtuation very closely—and Shea wanted an NHL team for the

Coliseum. Obviously, he was using leverage. He successfully got the NHL thinking: "Well, if we don't give him a franchise, a rival league will."

Why the big deal about New York? I might be accused of chauvinism, but I believe—strongly —that a New York team is essential to any professional sport venture—especially a new league. Look at how the AFL rutted around for years until the Jets came of age with a move to Shea Stadium and the acquisition of

Joe Namath. The Jets play in the communications capital of the world. Once they had a Namath, the AFL was talked about all over the United States. The magazines that matter, the television networks, the foreign and national correspondents, the wire services—all are based in New York.

Without a place to play for its New York club, the WHA nevertheless decided to go ahead with the major announcement of its formation. At a meeting charged with rampant optimism in New

Herb Martin of Miami stands in front of soon-to-be completed Executive-Arena Center which will seat 16,000.

York in November, it announced that 10 of its 12 franchises had been awarded. It also said that it hoped for the remaining two franchises to go to a southeastern city (Atlanta) and to New England. But the remaining two went to Hamilton, Ontario, and New England. Atlanta was already gobbled up by the NHL.

Most of the teams were in major population centers. But they had another common denominator: Either there was no rink to play in, or the one available

wasn't that majestic. Here's a run-down.

New York—In the WHA brochure, the New York entrant listed as its arena: "The Nassau County Coliseum (hopefully)." Neil Shayne, the team's president, is suing because he can't get his team in the municipally owned building. It looks as if Shayne's club may have to go somewhere else because of NHL expansion.

Chicago—Actually, the team will not play in Chicago, but in a suburb northwest of the city.

There are no big-league rinks in the area, although the owners of the club insist one will be put up as part of a sports complex.

San Francisco—The club here is talking about the 12,000 seat Cow Palace, which was unacceptable to the NHL and is the reason why the NHL expanded to Oakland rather than San Francisco. The owners of the WHA franchise here also are talking about a new arena.

Los Angeles—As far as United States fans are concerned, the

board. The club is talking about playing either in the Long Beach Arena (14,200 seats) or the Los Angeles Sports Arena (14,700).

Ohio—This is really Dayton. When a team is in a city that doesn't have a big-league image, it takes the name of the state. This is what's happening here. There is no major-league arena right now. The owners are talking about playing in a building that, when it's finished, will be called the Dayton Arena and will seat 14,000.

St. Paul—There actually may be a major league team in St. Paul—and not Minneapolis-St. Paul, or Bloomington. However, the arena isn't finished yet. It's called the St. Paul Civic Center and will seat 16,000.

Winnipeg—The Winnipeg Arena, according to the club's management, seats 11,300. It can be expanded, they say, to 14,000 by 1973. It is a proven hockey town.

Calgary—The Calgary Stampede Arena holds 8,500 fans, and plans are supposedly underway to inlarge the seating to 14,000.

Edmonton—The Arena holds only 5,800—not big-league by any standards. Management insists a 20,000-seat building will be ready for the 1973-74 season.

Hamilton—This Ontario city is just a stone's throw from the Maple Leaf Gardens but the club is looking to construct a new building, hopefully in time for next season—but doubtful.

New England—This franchise is looking to set up in Boston (it has been offered some dates by the Bruins), but most likely it will flounder around the New England area for awhile.

The bare statistics of the above wouldn't encourage many people to start such a venture. However, as I noted before—don't use your major-league standards to judge whether it will succeed. In the first place, the people behind the league appear to be fairly substantial. Many of them have long hockey backgrounds. The big hockey name is Bill Hunter of Edmonton, who is the league's director of player personnel. Hunter is known as "Mr. Hockey of Western

Ben Hatskin, owner of the Winnipeg club.

271

WORLD HOCKEY ASSOCIATION Previews

By Rick Pearson

Once upon a time there were six little men, each of them with a house built of bricks.

Because their houses became so popular, they built and sold six more houses. But these six houses were made of sticks.

"Don't worry," they said to the six new home owners, "the sticks are just as good as the bricks."

But after a long winter, the houses made of sticks were never as strong as the houses of the original six little men.

Despite the problems, there was even more demand for houses. So, the six little men (with the second six buyers sharing in the booty) built four more houses. These were houses built of straw.

"Don't worry," they said to the four newest residents, "the straw is just as good as the sticks."

Then, a new builder came on the scene and constructed a dozen three-bedroom ramblers with full basements and nice wooden siding.

"Don't worry," said the new builder. "Our houses may not be quite up to the caliber of bricks, but they're certainly going to be better than sticks or straw."

Born because of the potentially incredible explosion in hockey interest, and because of the National Hockey League's rampant expansion and resultant depressing lack of parity, the World Hockey Association begins play in October.

The new league has its players, its arenas and its money. It has Bobby Hull. It has John McKenzie. It has Bernie Parent. It has Derek Sanderson. It has Gerry Cheevers. It has J.C. Tremblay. And it will probably get a lot more before the first puck is dropped.

Not bad for a league a lot of people said was never going to get off the ground.

The league promises fans a faster game. It has virtually discounted the red line to open up passing and scoring. It will play 10 minutes of sudden death to reduce the number of tie games. It has signed many players, some young, some not-so-young. But it must begin somewhere. And it is beginning at a level most thought unattainable for a hockey league.

WHA President Gary Davidson, the 37-year-old Southern California attorney who, along with Dennis Murphy (now president and general manager of the Los Angeles Sharks), who put the league together, said last spring, "I see the WHA reaching parity with the NHL within three years, and I'm talking about the top NHL clubs. I see a European division and an Asian division coming within the next four years."

Last December, such a statement would hardly have been taken seriously. But now, the things Davidson says have a ring of prophesy. After all, he and Murphy also founded the American Basketball Association and their track record is getting more and more formidable each day the WHA grows.

Parity has been a primary objective of the WHA since its inception.

With everyone starting from zero, they all had an even chance to win the league championship. Or finish dead last.

A unique draft held in February distributed the players. There were no distinctions of playing level. Everyone was in the same pool—NHLers, minor pros, juniors, collegians, Europeans, amateurs and free agents.

Players were selected on the basis of their ability and, most important for the WHA, the likelihood of their joining the new league.

Then, the signing derby began.

Toronto goaltender Parent was the first NHL player to make the move. He agreed to terms with the now-defunct Miami Screaming Eagles late in February. When the Miami franchise was reclaimed by the league because of its owner's inability to come up with a suitable playing arena, Parent dropped into a state of limbo.

The Miami franchise subsequently was purchased by two New Jersey businessmen, James Cooper and Bernard Brown, and moved to Philadelphia. Part of the agreement was that the Blazers would receive rights to pick up Parent's fat contract.

But by that time, Parent was actually the 50th player to sign with the WHA. He had pushed the door open by signing with Miami and others had followed.

Hull, who was the 95th player to sign, pocketed $1 million cash. He'll get another $1.75 million from Winnipeg

Jets' owner Ben Hatskin over the next 10 years. The first million came from WHA Properties, Ltd., a conglomerate of WHA clubs.

Like Hull in Winnipeg, McKenzie is player-coach in Philadelphia. McKenzie became available after he was left unprotected by the Boston Bruins in the NHL expansion draft.

The maneuver left McKenzie irked at the Bruins. So, Cooper made a deal with Quebec for the rights to the former rodeo rider and signed him. In fact, the Bruins have been virtually knocked out of NHL contention by the WHA. The new league has grabbed Sanderson for $2.65 million and Cheevers and Ted Green.

In the package with these great stars are many other potentially top-level hockey players. Their names are scarcely household words, but part of the excitement of a new league is seeing it develop its own heroes.

The WHA is divided into two divisions, with each team playing a 78-game schedule.

With four Canadian and eight American teams, here's a breakdown of the setup:

EAST—New York Raiders, New England Whalers, Philadelphia Blazers, Cleveland Crusaders, Quebec Nordiques and Ottawa Nationals.

WEST-- Chicago Cougars, Minnesota Fighting Saints, Winnipeg Jets, Alberta Oilers, Los Angeles Sharks and Houston Aeros.

Each team will play a 4-and-4 home and away series within its own division and a 3-and-3 series against teams in the other division. One 5-and-5 series will be scheduled between natural rivals.

Gary L. Davidson
President, WHA

Natural rivals have been designated as New York and New England, Philadelphia and Cleveland, Quebec and Ottawa, Chicago, and Minnesota, Winnipeg and Alberta and Los Angeles and Houston.

The **New York Raiders** are the second of three major league hockey teams in Fun City. The WHA picked New York late in October. Almost a month later, the NHL plopped an expansion franchise in Long Island.

Originally, the WHA's New York franchise had hoped to play in the Nassau County Coliseum on Long Island, but the NHL's machinations prevented entry.

So, the Raiders proceeded to rent Madison Square Garden and by August were among the WHA leaders in announced player signings.

General manager Marvin Milkes, a veteran of 26 years in professional baseball and two first-year organizations (Los Angeles Angels and Seattle Pilots), found the WHA and the Raiders right up his alley.

Included in the list of signees were NHLers such as defenseman Brent Hughes of Philadelphia, goaltender Gary Kurt and right wing Norm Ferguson and Bobby Sheehan of California and center Ron Ward of Vancouver.

The Raiders also signed the WHA's first black player, right wing Alton White of Providence of the American Hockey League. White has averaged 28 goals and 63 points per season since turning pro in 1965-66.

Camille Henry, one of the all-time New York Ranger favorites, is the Raider coach.

New England, which will play 19 games in Boston Garden and 20 in Boston Arena, has erstwhile Jack Kelley, former coach at Boston University, as coach and general manager.

The first two signings by the Whalers were center Larry Pleau of Montreal and defenseman Brad Selwood of Toronto. Since then, the list has been embellished with other outstanding young hockey players, such as goaltender Bruce Landon; centers Tim Sheehy, Terry Caffery and John Danby; wings Dick Sarrazin, Kevin Ahearne, Tom Webster and defensemen Bob Brown, Jim Dorey, Ted Green and Rick Ley.

The Whalers' front office is one of the WHA's most dynamic and, combined with the hockey interest in the Boston area and the ability of Kelley, the New England club shapes up as possibly the strongest organization in the WHA.

With energetic Jim Cooper leading the

Hull's signing with the WHA's Winnipeg Jets was the decisive factor in throwing the world of hockey into turmoil.

way, the **Philadelphia Blazers** have been hustling to make up lost ground.

Dave Creighton, who played 12 seasons in the NHL with Boston, Toronto, Chicago and New York, and was general manager at Providence, was hired as general manager.

In addition to player-coach McKenzie and goaltender Parent, the Blazers signed Derek Sanderson, center Andre Lacroix, who had been traded by the Philadelphia Flyers to the Chicago Black Hawks.

Then, the club added other players: defenseman Ron Plumb of Oklahoma City, center Brian Campbell of the Black Hawks, right wing Don O'Donoghue of Baltimore and right wing Richard Campeau of Sorel in the Quebec Junior Hockey League.

The Blazers will play their 39 home games in the Philadelphia Civic Center, which can accomodate 9,000 for hockey.

In Cleveland, the Crusaders are the fourth sports franchise owned by Nick Mileti, a 41-year-old attorney.

Mileti also owns the National Basketball Association's Cleveland Cavaliers, the Cleveland Indians of baseball's American League and the Cleveland Barons of the AHL. He plans to continue operating the Barons as a development club for the Minnesota North Stars, completing the final season of a three-year contract.

Part of Cleveland's adoption of the rescinded Calgary franchise was that each of the WHA clubs gave the Crusaders the rights to one proven NHL performer and one minor leaguer or junior hockey player.

Because they were the 12th franchise to be solidfied, the Crusaders started well behind the field in player signings. However, they went out and grabbed Gerry Cheevers.

Home for the Cleveland WHA team will be the 9,500-seat Cleveland Sports Arena, but the elegant new Midwest Coliseum, with 18,000 seats, is expected to be ready for the WHA's second season.

Les Nordiques de Quebec shook off the frustration of a late start and bridged the credibility gap in one fell swoop.

Les Nordiques brought in financier Paul Racine as trustee and president of the club and then added Jean Lesage, former Prime Minister of Quebec, as a member of the board of directors.

Since then, things have started happening for the Nordiques. The players started coming after the club named Maurice Fillion, who coached the Quebec Remparts to the Memorial Cup two years ago, as chief scout. He then went out and got J. C. Tremblay from the Montreal Canadiens. The great Maurice "Rocket" Richard was then signed as coach.

274

John McKenzie left the Bruins of the NHL on a sour note to take the role of player-coach of the Philadelphia Blazers where his Boston Teammate . . .

Derek Sanderson signed a reported multi-year contract for $2.65 million.

Two centers, both with NHL experience, signed. They were Michael Parizeau of Philadelphia and Renald LeClerc of Detroit. A pair of promising CHL left wingers--Mike Archambault of Dallas and Bob Guindon of Fort Worth--also signed.

Then, Les Nordiques concentrated on home-grown talent in the Canadian Junior and Intercollegiate ranks.

Les Nordiques will play in the 10,000-seat Coliseum de Quebec.

The Ottawa Nationals signed Hull first. Garry Hull, that is. Garry is the 28-year-old youngest brother in the Hull family. He attended a Chicago Black Hawk training camp several years ago, but turned down a contract to play in Dallas so that he could remain in Canada. With a team in Ottawa, Garry, a left wing like his brothers, decided to give professional hockey a try.

The Nats also signed wingers Bob Leduc of Providence of the AHL and Ron Climie

of Kansas City of the CHL.

Ottawa had money problems in the early going, and was unable to plunge into the signing battle until its problems were resolved.

Ottawa Civic Center, with 9,300 seats, will be the home of the Nats.

In the West Division, the **Chicago Cougars** were another of the foot-draggers in the beginning. The problems in Chicago were due to recurrent changes in the ownership picture.

The first group couldn't stand the financial gaff, and the second group never quite got it all together. But, the third set of major investors appears the final salvation of the Cougars.

Two wealthy real estate developers, brothers Jordon and Walter Kaiser, who own Sports Centers International, invested in the club at a cost approaching $1 million.

The Cougars are ticketed to play in the

Chicago International Amphitheatre, which seats 9,000 for hockey.

The first player announced as signed was Bob Kelly, a left at the Philadelphia Flyers, who subsequently signed a second contract with the Flyers.

The Cougars then announced center and right wing Rosaire Paiment of the Vancouver Canucks, a player the Black Hawks had sought via trade for some time. Left wing Ricky Morris of Laurentian University also came to terms with Cougars.

Then, the Cougars made a move many in the WHA had been waiting for--they hired a coach. Marcel Pronovost, a four-time all-NHL selection during 20 NHL seasons, 15 with the Detroit Red Wings and five with the Toronto Maple Leafs, was the man.

Pronovost, 42, had been coaching the Tulsa Oilers of the CHL.

Rabid hockey country makes every-

The Bruins also lost the services of Ted Green to the New England Whalers, where the defenseman will close out his career.

Andre Lacroix, Philadelphia

Gerry Cheevers, Cleveland

J. C. Tremblay, Quebec

Winnipeg Jets' owner Ben Hatskin is the man responsible for the acquisition of Bobby Hull.

thing look rosy for the **Minnesota Fighting Saints.** They also will play in one of the class arenas in the league, the new St. Paul Civic Center, with 16,180 seats for hockey.

Glen Sonmor, a talkative sort who gets things done, is the Fighting Saints general manager and coach. The former University of Minnesota coach set about to put together an aggressive hockey team. His early signings indicate he will succeed.

Among the signees are defensemen John Arbour of St. Louis, Terry Ball of Cincinnati, Dick Paradise of Tidewater, Frank Sanders of the U.S. Olympic team and George Konick, a free agent who served a brief stint in the NHL and was MVP in the 1970 World Cup.

Up front, the Saints will send Wayne Connelly of Vancouver, George Morrison of Buffalo Jim Johnson of Los Angeles, Billy Klatt of Oklahoma City, Mike Antonovich of the University of Minnesota, Terry Ryan of the Hamilton juniors and Bob MacMillan of St. Catherine's into the attacking zone.

MacMillan, a first round selection of the New York Rangers in the junior draft, was the first junior player signed by the WHA.

In goal, Minnesota will have either of two great former U.S. Olympic goaltenders. Mike Curran, who starred in Sapporo, and Jack McCartan, who led the U.S. to a gold medal in 1960 in Squaw Valley.

Players with some local ties were in great demand for the Saints. Virtually all of their signees fit, somehow, into the local hero category.

Bobby Hull, of course, is the big name in **Winnipeg.** And in the WHA, for that matter.

Hull's presence has caused some concern among the rest of the WHA clubs. The Jets are going to be tough to beat with that guy, no question about it.

Also on the Jets list of signees are Danny Johnson of Detroit, Norm Beaudin of Cleveland, Milt Black of Dallas and Dunc Rousseau of Baltimore.

Bob Woytowich, a veteran NHLer, was the first defenseman signed.

In goal, the Jets may have the depth to be the toughest in the league with Ernie Wakely of St. Louis and Joe Daley of Detroit.

Jets owner Ben Hatskin promised "a couple NHL linemates" for Hull. Hatskins promises have a tendency to be good.

Winnipeg Arena, with 11,300 seats, will be home for the Jets.

Bill Hunter, the oil country orator who heads the **Alberta Oilers,** was instrumental in helping create the WHA. But

277

In goal, the Jets should have the most depth with the jumping of
Ernie Wakely from the St. Louis Blues along with
Detroit's Joe Daley.

now he is just another owner, an owner with a great potential market in Edmonton and a list of accomplished players.

Ray Kinasewich, a former coach of the Edmonton Oil Kings junior team (which Hunter also owns), is the Oilers' coach.

At his disposal, Kinasewich will have the likes of Al Hamilton of Buffalo, Bob Wall of Detroit, Doug Barrie of Los Angeles, Ed Joyal of Philadelphia and Jim Harrison of Toronto.

From minor hockey, Hunter landed Ross Perkins of Fort Worth, Brian Carlin of Springfield, Roger Cote of Cleveland, Bob Falkenberg of Tidewater and Jim Benzelock of Dayton.

Hamilton, Barrie, Joyal, Perkins, Falkenberg and Harrison all once played for the Oil Kings.

A major league arena is one of the Oilers' problems, but the city has said it plans to build a 16,000-seat arena. For now, the Oilers will operate out of the 5,800 capacity Edmonton Gardens.

Under the guidance of the vibrant Dennis Murphy, the **Los Angeles Sharks** are actually making some Los Angelinos start paying attention to hockey.

Murphy first hired Terry Slater, a "tough guy" by reputation, as his coach. Slater, who had been coaching at Des Moines of the IHL, drafted heavily from

the minors in the WHA player selection meeting.

"We're going to win right away," Slater declared.

Murphy then went out and signed top minor pros and a sprinkling of NHLers.

Among the early signings were defensemen Bart Crashley of Dallas, the first choice of the New York Islanders in the NHL expansion draft, Jim Niekamp of Tidewater, Jerry Odrowski of St. Louis, Jim Watson of Buffalo and Larry Mavety of Salt Lake City.

The forwards signed early included J.P. LeBlanc of Dallas, Tom Gilmore of Tide-

WHA

Alton White, New York, should be the first black to make it big.

water, Joe Szura of Baltimore, Gary Veneruzzo of Denver, Earl Heiskala of San Diego, Steve Sutherland of Port Huron, Mike Byers of Buffalo, Bob Liddington of Phoenix, Mike Jakubo of Columbus and Bob Whitlock of Phoenix.

In goal, George Gardner, who began last year as the Vancouver Canuck's regular goaltender but was injured at midseason, will wear the Shark's red and black.

Also a possibility in goal is one of the three European players signed by the Sharks, Joseph Gale of Yugoslavia.

Centers Rudie Hitti of Yugoslavia and Zoltan Horvath of Hungary complete the European trio.

The Sharks have two home arenas, the L.A. Sports Arena, where they will play 34 games, and the Long Beach Auditorium, where the remaining five are scheduled. The Sports Arena seats 14,700 and the Auditorium 11,325.

In **Houston,** where the original Dayton franchise landed, the Aeros are seeking players in much the same manner as the Sharks. Coach Bill Dineen's background

is minor league, though five of his 18 years in professional hockey were spent in the NHL.

Three of the first 11 Aeros signed were NHLers. Defenseman John Schella came from Vancouver, as did left wing Ted Taylor and center and right wing Murray Hall.

From the WHL, Dineen's old habitat, came goaltender Wayne Rutledge of Salt Lake City, defenseman Dunc McCallum and right wing-center Brian McDonald of San Diego, defenseman Gord Kannegeisser of Denver and left wing Andre Hinse of Phoenix.

Two AHLers decided to join the Aeros—center Gordon Labossiere of Cleveland and Keke Mortson of Cincinnati. Don Grierson of Port Huron of the IHL also signed.

Sam Houston Coliseum is the home of the Aeros. Located in downtown Houston, the Coliseum has a 9,300 capacity for hockey.

Twelve teams, 14 arenas and plenty of hockey players . . . there is not much left to do but drop the puck and see what happens.   •

WHA FEATURE

By Rick Pearson

It happened in football, back in 1960, when the AFL was busy trying to get off the ground. The merger with the 'Big' league came ten years later, but it came. And with it came a list of established heroes, who were soon to find their names and accomplishments in the records of the NFL. As for hockey's WHA . . . the new league has been born and is on its way to an apparently fruitful life, along with its list of star-studded performers, whose feats will be long remembered

Forgive the reference to professional football in a hockey magazine, but there is a parallel to be drawn. Monday, December 11, of last year, Don Maynard of the New York Jets surpassed Raymond Berry, fabled wide receiver of the Baltimore Colts, to become the National Football League's all-time leading pass-catcher.

So what? So Maynard's first 10 seasons as anything resembling a starter were played in the old American Football League, before the interlocking schedule and the birth of the American Football Conference of the NFL. What has happened then, is that despite the laughter and the predictions of doom for the AFL in its early days,

each Maynard reception now is valued the same as each catch Berry ever made.

So, let us subtract no lustre from the accomplishments of those who labor in this, the World Hockey Association's first season. Someday, none will draw a distinction between a Bobby Hull goal in the WHA and a Bobby Hull goal in the National Hockey League. It is inevitable, and it haunts the NHL as inexorably as age shadows Clarence Campbell.

Continuing the story of Don Maynard, he came out of Texas Western a whippet-fast running back, lasted one year with the New York Giants, was cut after coach Allie Sherman suggested

he "shorten his strides," and went to the Canadian Football League. A year later, the AFL came along and Maynard was back in the Big Apple with the old New York Titans.

Now, 13 seasons later, Maynard is the premier pass receiver in NFL history, so says the record book.

The point is that evaluating talent is perhaps one of the most difficult tasks human beings undertake. Because it is such a subjective matter, it usually is characterized by mistakes.

Some of those in the WHA represent such flat-out goofs by the NHL.

J. C. Tremblay, center, of the Quebec Nordiques was a star with
Montreal of the NHL and now is shining again down the river.

RON WARD, for instance. In 1971-72, Ron Ward played expressly defense and killed penalties for the NHL Vancouver Canucks. By the middle of the next season he was the WHA's leading scorer, reaching the 50-point plateau December 11, ahead of Phil Esposito's 76-goal pace of

Vancouver general manager Bud Piole told Ward he probably wouldn't make the Canuck roster for 1972-73, so Ward decided to sign with the New York Raiders of the new league. The day after Poile's comment, Canuck coach

Hal Laycoe tried to persuade Ward to remain an NHL minion. "What did they offer you?" asked Laycoe. "Maybe we can match it." Ward stared back at the coach. "No, Hal, you can't. The Raiders offered me a chance to play hockey." Raider coach Camille Henry made a center out of him and the rest, as they say, is history.

RON BUCHANAN was something of a scoring hot shot in the Western Hockey League, but remained about as far from the NHL as Denver is from Gander, Newfoundland.

The Cleveland Crusaders signed

the gangly center and almost since 'Day One' of the WHA, he has been the Crusaders' leading scorer. He is 6-3, 178 pounds and has been called, at one time or another, The Splendid Splinter, The Sorcerer, The Kid, Mr. Wizard and the Thin Man. Someone also suggested Pencils, for the size of his legs. His scoring pace in the first third of the season virtually assured him of making the top 10. He also turned in one of the WHA's first four-goal performances, beating former NHL goaltender Les Binkley in a game at Ottawa in mid-November.

WAYNE CARLETON was something of a fatty in the NHL, playing for the Bruins at 230 pounds two years ago. Routed to Oakland in the intra-league draft, he played unhappy and ballooned to 245 pounds. He got 17 goals and 14 assists and was determined, "There was no way I was going back." Carleton had been contacted by Buck Houle of the Ottawa Nationals. Houle managed the 1964 Memorial Cup team that launched Carleton into pro hockey.

Now, fat left wing Carleton is a skinny (195) center and one of the Nats' most productive scorers. "I signed for what I thought was really good money. I wanted to show them—and particularly Buck Houle—I was worth it." So far, he has.

WAYNE CONNELLY's career record reads like the itinerary for an NHL tour—Montreal, Boston, Minnesota, Detroit, St. Louis, New York (for one day) and Vancouver. But his blistering slapshot and the immense popularity he gained as a Minnesota North Star made him a highly desirable player for the new Minnesota Fighting Saints franchise. He immediately took his place as one of the Saints' steadying veterans and top scorers and figures to see an end to the gypsy existence he once knew.

The Saints have another who never could get the NHL to give him more than a quick glance. **MIKE CURRAN,** the left-handed goaltender who amazed the world as he led the 1972 U.S. team to a silver medal at Sapporo, had several looks from NHL clubs. "They didn't offer enough money to spend time kicking around the minors," says Curran. The NHL clubs didn't think enough of his abilities, apparently. After Sapporo, though, the Fighting Saints went after the native of International Falls, Minn., and signed him. Despite a slightly shaky start, "Lefty" is now one of the three best goaltenders in the WHA Western Division. The Winnipeg press started calling him "The Zero Kid," because of his propensity to throttle the Jets in the early going. Gifted with an incredibly fast glove hand, Curran plays better the more the opposition shoots at him. He

stopped 41 Winnipeg shots for his first shutout and 37 Houston Aero attempts for his second.

The Aeros found a diamond in the minors in **GORDON LABOSSIERE,** a former North Star farmhand who didn't figure in Wren Blair's plans. The rangy center, who likens his position to a traffic cop, teamed with NHL veterans Murray Hall and Ted Taylor to form Houston's Action Line, a trio that virtually carried the Aero offensive load as the WHA came out of the starting gate.

JIM HARRISON labored in the trenches for the Toronto Maple Leafs, playing center behind Norm Ullman and Dave Keon, almost never seeing a turn on the power play. But the last half of the 1971-72 season he probably was the Leafs' best player. Bill Hunter of the Alberta Oilers thought Harrison was a guy to build a team around, and signed him for the WHA. Notorious for slow starts, Harrison was convinced by Oiler coach Ray Kinasewich it was all in his head. Mind over matter being what it is, Harrison roared from the opening faceoff into a battle with Ward, Bobby Sheehan and Chris Bordeleau for the WHA scoring lead. Then his knee lost a confrontation with a goalpost in mid-November and he missed a month. But, he seems certain to verify Hunter's judgment.

Winnipeg picked up a couple of bright lights. **CHRIS BORDELEAU,** who had been Bobby Hull's center in Chicago, stepped out scoring goals at a furious pace. His antics made Winnipeg fans wonder if they even needed Hull. **NORM BEAUDIN,** another Minnesota North Star castoff languishing at Cleveland, was pleased for a chance in the WHA. He nearly matched Bordeleau's output and alleviated a Jet preseason problem of supposed weakness on right wing.

A pair of unsung goaltenders stepped to the forefront in the WHA—**PETER DONNELLY** of New York and **SERGE AUBRY** of Quebec. Donnelly had retired from hockey at the ripe old age of 19 and gone back to college, seeking an engineering degree. Then the WHA was born. "I was out of hockey for three years," says Donnelly.

Ron Ward, New York Raiders

Wayne Connelly, Minnesota Saints

Jim Harrison, Alberta Oilers

WHA

Bernie Parent of the Philadelphia Blazers, here gets some help
from Ron Plumb. Parent was the first player the WHA got
from the NHL.

"I was going to the University of Detroit for a degree in electrical engineering when I began to hear talk about the new league they were trying to form. I felt I'd like to give it another try. That's how I wound up with the Jersey Devils last season. If they hadn't started the WHA, I never would have come back."

BLAZERS TWICE

Donnelly's performance made him the Raiders' frontline goal-tender, ahead of NHL veteran for-mer California Golden Seal Gary Kurt. Donnelly had special fun with the Philadelphia Blazers. The first two times he faced them, he shut them out, 5-0. Both games came on Sunday afternoons, and both were at Madison Square Garden.

Aubry started the season challenging Gerry Cheevers for the title as the new league's best goal-tender. He kept the surprising Quebec Nordiques in second place in the WHA Eastern Division through much of the early going. Only the Cheevers-led Cleveland Crusaders were playing better than the Nordiques. The Nordiques then developed a distressing lack of ability to win on the road, dropping eight of their first 10 away from home and both the club and Aubry dipped a bit in the statistics. A spectacular netminder, Aubry drew more than a little attention for his ability to accumulate penalty minutes. Once,

Gerry Cheevers, Cleveland Crusaders, is proving to be the best goalie in the WHA.

he dumped a pitcher of water on referee Ray Thomas after Thomas had issued him a game misconduct. He remains Les Nordiques' stopper in the battle for a playoff spot.

The Los Angeles Sharks scored a real coup when they convinced young **BART CRASHLEY** that the WHA was his future. The 26-year-old rushing defenseman who already has drawn the inevitable comparison to Bobby Orr, was the first choice of the New York Islanders in the most recent NHL expansion draft. He played last year for the Dallas Black Hawks of the Central Hockey League. His big chance, so to speak, came during the 1967-68 season with Detroit.

"I was teamed with Gary Bergman," Crashley recalls. "I would work a full shift one night and nothing the next. Sid Abel and

Baz Bastien were in charge. They told me that if I carried the puck across the blue line they'd bench me. That wasn't my style of play." A good part of the reason Crashley chose the WHA was that the Islanders didn't have a coach at the time. "I didn't want to get into another Sid Abel situation," he says. "I knew how Terry Slater (Sharks' coach) felt about my style of play. I figured he'd let me play my game." Crashley has been one of the Sharks' top scorers and is considered by many the WHA's best young defenseman.

Relative obscurity was hardly the prior residence of many of the WHA's other stars.

JEAN CLAUDE TREMBLAY, once the reputed turtle neck sweater king of the NHL when he was with Montreal, was also one of the league's best defensemen. In

French-speaking Quebec, his signing with the Nordiques was tantamount to the announcement Derek Sanderson was coming to Philadelphia. Wise and skilled, J.C. served to anchor the kids who make up the Nordique roster and also became the WHA's highest scoring defenseman and an instant all-star.

GERRY CHEEVERS took $200,000 per annum of Crusader owner Nick Mileti's money and proceeded to live up to his end of the bargain. Mileti envisioned Cheevers the cornerstone of the Crusaders. He was more like the entire wall. No goaltender was stingier or more spectacular. His wandering style brought fans to their feet, and only an offensive slump by his teammates brought the Crusaders down from first in the WHA East, a position they had held since opening night. He is every bit the goal-tender he was with the Boston Bruins. No better, no worse. But in his case, status quo suits Mileti just fine, thank you. Just fine.

JOHN "PIE" McKENZIE came from the Boston Bruins to the Philadelphia Blazers, chiefly because of his ability to fire a team. He broke his arm in a preseason game and, to a great degree, the Blazers' horrid start was due to the absence of the feisty little ex-rodeo rider. After he returned, and after the club's personnel began to jell, the Blazers began to look like the hockey team most thought it ought to be.

Perhaps the Blazers and the WHA's biggest disappointment was **DEREK SANDERSON** (see cover). Sanderson took his $2.5 million and decided he didn't want anything to do with Philadelphia or vice-versa, depending on whom you believe. At presstime, Sanderson was trying to get back to Boston or allegedly to the Raiders.

New England Whaler general manager-coach Jack Kelley had his eye on **TOM WEBSTER** for some time. "I scouted him quite a bit in junior because I thought he'd be a great college player," says the former Boston University coach. Webster, who scored 67 points for the Detroit Red Wings in 1970-71 before being traded to the California Golden Seals early the next season, is coming off major back surgery. The injury was so complex many doctors doubted he would ever play again. Yet, his recovery has been complete and his big shot easily is among the five fastest in the WHA. Kelley had been prepared to give Webster a little time, considering the injury, but Webster was almost 100 per cent from the first time he donned skates at training camp.

BOBBY SHEEHAN was expected to be a folk hero in New York He was California's leading scorer in 1971-72 and had a reputation as a high liver off the ice. He seemed the kind of athlete New Yorkers would love. His rink-long dashes and early season WHA scoring burst fulfilled the prophecy. He started the season with long, long locks, but relented to teammates' pressure and visited the barber. After the shearing, he got even hotter. He slumped briefly, but rallied at mid-season.

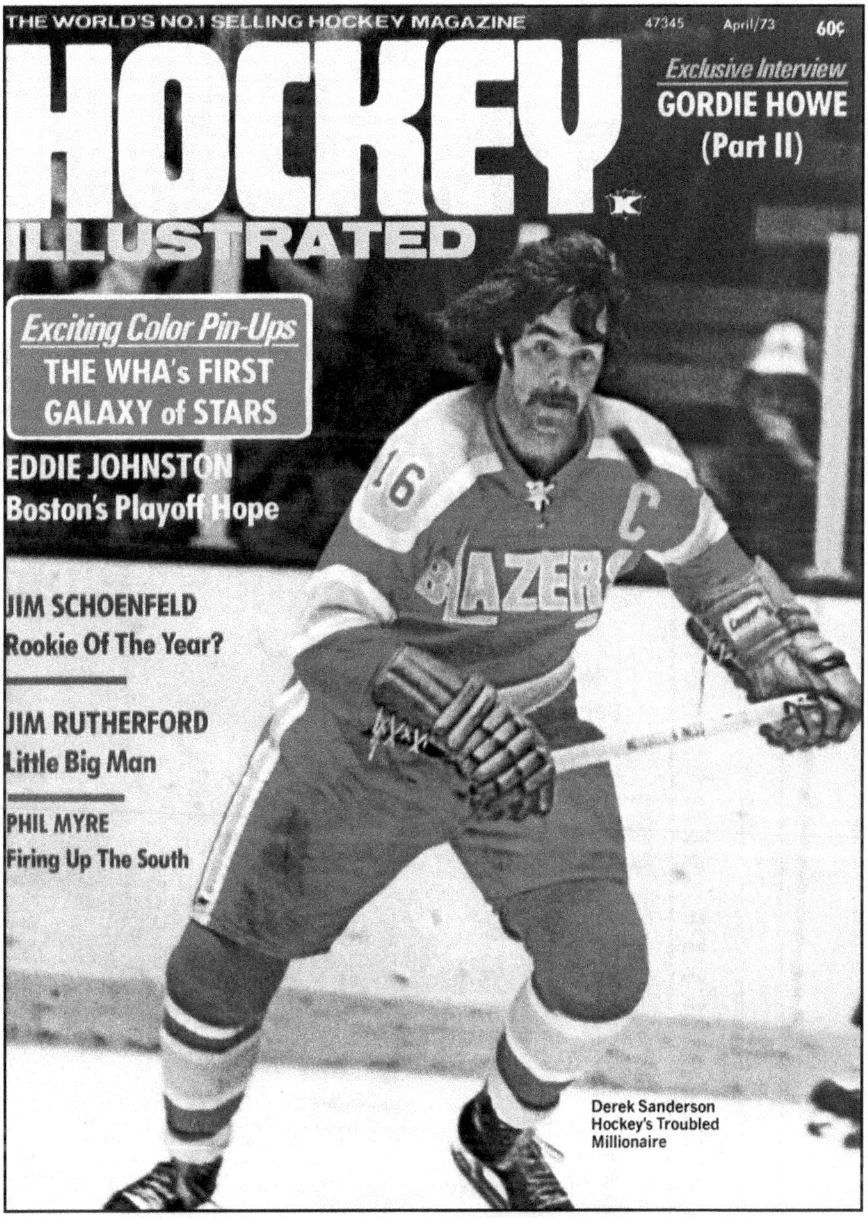

THE WORLD'S NO.1 SELLING HOCKEY MAGAZINE   47345   April/73   60¢

HOCKEY ILLUSTRATED

Exclusive Interview
GORDIE HOWE
(Part II)

Exciting Color Pin-Ups
THE WHA's FIRST GALAXY of STARS

EDDIE JOHNSTON
Boston's Playoff Hope

JIM SCHOENFELD
Rookie Of The Year?

JIM RUTHERFORD
Little Big Man

PHIL MYRE
Firing Up The South

Derek Sanderson
Hockey's Troubled
Millionaire

And there is, of course, the game's reigning legend—**BOBBY HULL.** Forced to delay his WHA debut because of pending court action, Hull finally got onto the ice November 8. A bit out of shape at first because of the hassle, he eventually responded in the expected manner and, by Christmas, had climbed into the WHA's list of top 10 scorers. What can be said about Hull that has not already been said a hundredfold? He is it, the symbol of the WHA, the eternal Golden Jet. If he plays the full five playing years of his Winnipeg contract, he seems certain to emerge as hockey's all-time leading scorer . . . and no fair saying 604 were NHL goals and the rest WHA goals. Let's not forget Don Maynard.   •

17-YEAR-OLD POSSIBLY 'BEST PLAYER IN WORLD'

Racers Get Top Canadian Junior

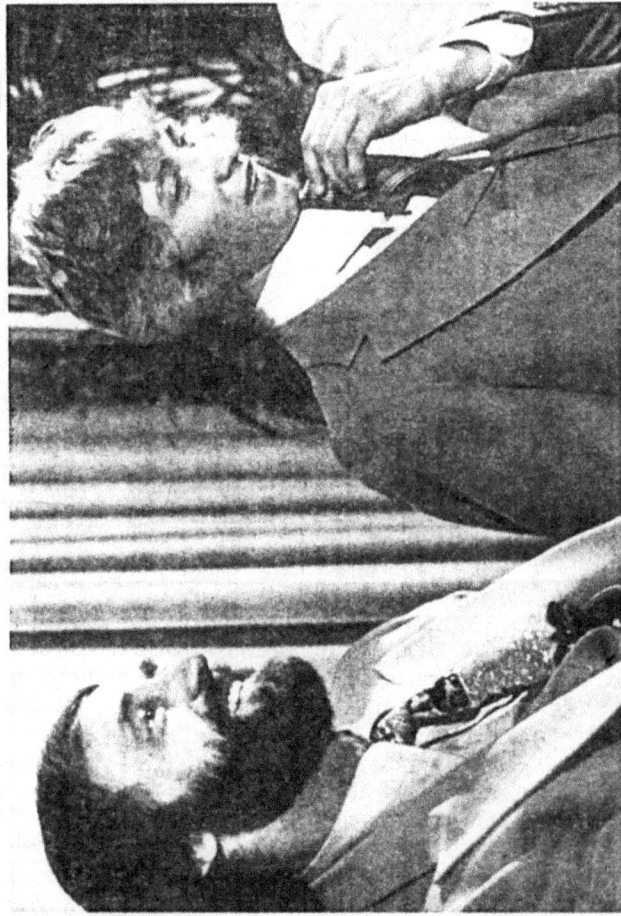

By JOHN BANSCH
Assistant Sports Editor

Nelson Skalbania has scored a major triumph in his battle to become a leading figure in the world of professional hockey.

The wealthy owner of the Indianapolis Racers made his move Monday by announcing the signing of 17-year-old Wayne Gretzky to a seven-year personal services contract estimated to be worth around $2 million.

Considered the finest junior skater to emerge from Canada since Bobby Orr and said to have the same potential as Gordie Howe and Bobby Hull, the youthful centerman is ticketed to perform with the Racers in the upcoming World Hockey Association season.

Unless there are complications which prohibit Gretzky from playing here, he will be the highest-paid player in the league, according to Skalbania.

LAST WINTER he scored 70 goals and 112 assists as a member of the Sault Ste. Marie Greyhounds in the Ontario Hockey Association. He then went on to lead all scorers in the world junior tournament which included teams from Russia, Czechoslovakia, Sweden and Finland.

Skalbania termed Gretzky the world's best junior center and possibly the "best player in the world." Gus Badali, the Toronto-based agent who negotiated the transaction, observed, "Wayne has unbelievable puck sense, he mesmerizes the opposition," and he predicted "the poorest player on the Racers will score 30 goals if he's on Gretzky's line."

The signing was announced at about the time the rival National Hockey League opened its summer meetings at Montreal. It is expected the NHL will issue a statement against the signing since it has a rule which prohibits its teams from signing juniors until they reach 20 years of age.

Skalbania could care less.

"WE HAVE BEEN raped," he said in reference to WHA players who have jumped to the NHL. Included among those who have changed leagues are Anders Hedberg and Ulf Nilsson, two former Winnipeg stars now with the New York Rangers. "If we expect to maintain the caliber of play we have had in the WHA, we can only resort to raiding the underage juniors."

There have been reports the NHL will "invite" Edmonton, Quebec, New England and Winnipeg to join the older league next winter. Skalbania's latest move could force Indianapolis to be considered.

Asked about the situation, the Racers owner was vague. He did say "the dollar amount (of the signing) makes it serious on our part." However, he would not say the signing was an attempt to torpedo any talks because Indianapolis was not mentioned in reports of possible new NHL teams.

The signing will also be the subject of much discussion throughout Canada, according to Badali. "This move has the same impact as the signing of O.J. Simpson with Buffalo did in the United States."

SKALBANIA SAID the acquisition of Gretzky "precludes my going to Houston." It had been rumored that Skalbania would attempt to purchase the financially distressed Houston franchise and possibly move it to the NHL. "Right now no changes are contemplated in the Racers situation," he added.

Gretzky, a long-haired blond who somewhat resembles tennis star Vitas Gerulaitis, said he is "very excited" about playing for the Racers.

"This is a very big challenge," added the slender skater, who said his 5-11, 155-pound frame may be his "biggest downfall."

The newest Racer admitted he "may be a little small" for professional hockey, but he doesn't foresee the opposition "taking 60-foot runs" at him in the WHA like they did in Canada.

Gretzky has been labeled a "slow" skater. Badali says that's not true. "Wayne is very fluid and at times it just appears he's slow," asserted the agent.

A NATIVE of Brantford, Ont., Gretzky began skating when he was 2 years old. When he was 8 he was already being touted as the next great Canadian superstar. At 11 he scored 378 goals in 68 games. He was a legend before he was a teen-ager.

Gretzky still has one year of high school to finish. Racers officials will seek to enroll him in summer school when he returns to Indianapolis in a couple of weeks.

Now that Skalbania has signed Gretzky he must turn his attention to hiring a coach. The Racers owner skirted the issue.

Pressed as to the status of naming a coach, he said the search is "narrowing down." Is Jacques Demers, former Racer coach among the candidates? "No comment," was the reply. When will a coach be named? "Soon," Skalbania said.

TOP JUNIOR PROSPECT — Wayne Gretzky, considered the finest junior skater to come out of Canadian junior hockey since Bobby Orr, adjusts his tie as he is introduced to the news media Monday at the Columbia Club by Indianapolis Racers owner Nelson Skalbania. The 17-year-old center was signed by Skalbania to a seven-year personal services contract and is expected to give the Racers more scoring punch. He scored 70 goals and added 112 assists last year with the Sault Ste. Marie Greyhounds of the Ontario Hockey Association. (UPI Photo)

courtesy The Indianapolis Star

When the Racers began to spring leaks—soon after their formation in 1973—it wasn't long before the franchise was swamped by red ink.

RACING TO OBLIVION

by Keith Bellows

IN THE SUMMER of 1945 the U.S.S. *Indianapolis* steamed into harbor on the West Pacific island of Saipan, unloaded two A-bombs destined for Hiroshima and Nagasaki, then headed for home. She never made it: Japanese torpedoes sent her to the bottom of the Pacific. More than three decades later, that ship's namesake would be the site of another wreck—the W.H.A.'s Indianapolis Racers, a team that broke up amid confusion, bankruptcy, lawsuits, disillusionment and shattered dreams. The Racers, whose demise followed that of the World Team Tennis' Indianapolis Loves by only a few weeks, were the 21st team to join the W.H.A.'s long, sad roster of failure: the Minnesota Fighting Saints, the Calgary Broncs, the Ottawa Civics, the Miami Screaming Eagles, the Phoenix Roadrunners, the Denver Spurs, the Philadelphia Blazers—and on and on. The main characters in what became Indianapolis' front-office soap opera were a genial ex-Chicago Black Hawk, a Canadian real-estate magnate, a soon-to-be-superstar and a bunch of fair-to-middling hockey players. And the city of Indianapolis.

FROM THE DAY a group of ambitious businessmen founded the Indianapolis Racers—on September 14, 1973—the franchise was destined to chart stormy waters. In a city best known for its 200-lap racing extravaganza, it would seem that hockey's thrills and spills would never be a match for the colorful world of the race track. Or for basketball and football, the sports of tradition in the Hoosier State. "Hockey has a future here," says Bill Neal, the Racers' former public relations director. "It's the baby sport in this area. If nourished, it will grow." Neal, and the others involved with the franchise, point to a potential market of one and a half million fans—fans that in four and a half years of operation the club never reached.

Exactly one year to the day after the franchise was chartered, the spanking new $20-million, 16,040-seat Market Square Center opened its doors, and the club began losing money—at a $1-million-a-year clip. To be sure, there was a solid core of 3,000 to 5,000 fans (how many depends on who you talk to). But to break even, the team had to draw an average of 10,000 per game. And, yes, there were record crowds (16,040), twice in April 1975, when the Racers were bowing to the New England Whalers, two games to one in the first of only two playoff appearances. But the house was often papered and, even with that, the club's best average attendance (in 1975-76) never exceeded 9,000. Most ex-Racer staffers say that Indianapolis will only support a winner. "Otherwise," says former Racer goalie Gary Inness, "Indianapolis will never be a hockey town."

On the ice, the Racers were consistently mediocre, beginning with their 1974-75 fourth-place finish (18-57-3), through their best season (1976-77: 36-37-8), right up to the end when they closed the hatch with a 5-18-2 record, a result that newspapers still uncharitably include in the W.H.A. standings. Their all-time record ended up a dismal 118-202-25.

Speculation that the Racers were doomed increased with each succeeding year. Racer personnel turned over faster than the checkout staff at a fast-food outlet. Coaches came—and went—with alarming rapidity: Gerry Moore, Jacques Demers, Bill Goldsworthy, Ron Ingram, Pat Stapleton. In the Racers' first three seasons alone, the team had no fewer than 62 regulars on the roster, yet only seven played all three seasons; 34 played only one.

The lack of continuity angered the fans, who desperately needed to identify with their team. Despite what ex-Racer employees call "good media coverage," the hardcore support soon began to ebb away. By the beginning of the 1977-78 season, the franchise was listing so badly there seemed little hope of salvaging it. Enter Nelson Skalbania.

A millionaire Vancouver real-estate tycoon, Skalbania was accustomed to making money and to making it quickly—he snapped up Toronto's Dufferin Mall for $24 million and sold it less than a minute later for a $1-million profit. Skalbania is an engineer by training, a solitary figure given to running the marathon, the ordeal of the loner. He is always on the run: Known to leap up in the middle of W.H.A. trustees' meetings and head for the racquetball court, he admits that in the past three years he has been in his Vancouver office only one day in four.

Although he claims that $50 million in debts more than offsets his $35 million in assets, Skalbania is not a frugal man. The ceiling of his Vancouver living room is gold. He has homes in Edmonton, Maui and Puerto Vallarta (Mexico), and a floating condominium off Majorca. Moored in the Mediterranean is his 600-ton yacht, *Chimon* (Little Canoe). He owns Renoirs, Monets and Picassos, and four Rolls Royces, including a 1928 Phaeton convertible. Appropriately, it was used in the film *The Great Gatsby*. "I buy everything," Skalbania has said, "but everything I buy is for sale."

Skalbania has all the instincts—and, apparently, weaknesses—of a gambler (he and Edmonton Oilers owner Peter Pocklington often settled mutual debts at the backgammon board). Approached by a group of adventurers, he refused to fund the raising of the *Titanic*. Instead, he found his own wreck—the Racers.

At the start, Skalbania believed the team could be profitable. And he saw an opportunity to slip into the N.H.L. should the W.H.A. be successful in one of its many merger bids. Ultimately, though, Skalbania couldn't resist a deal: When the Racers' owners offered him a 51 percent controlling interest for a dollar, he bit. The remaining 49 percent remained in the hands of two minority owners. Skalbania also agreed to cover the club's losses, and therein lay the rub.

The consensus is that Skalbania had no inkling of the seriousness of the Racers' situation, though a look at the

track record should have tipped him off. Says Bill Neal: "I don't know how much thought Nelson put into the takeover. It was just a whim, I guess."

Evidently, the attendance figures that Skalbania examined were suspect, a result of the team's giveaway ticket program. Management was chaotic and inept. "They had all these guys working in the front office," says former Racer and one-time Maple Leaf Blaine Stoughton, "but none of them were doing anything." The Racers'

player personnel was weak, and the team was laboring for still another new coach, Ron Ingram. "Nelson," says Pat Stapleton, a veteran of both the Racers and the Chicago Black Hawks, "was in deeper water than he knew."

Nonetheless, he persevered as the club chugged to a 24-51-5 record the first year. That he rarely turned up to see them play (he saw only 10 games) was perhaps understandable given their ineptness, but it soured both players and fans. "Hockey isn't like

real estate," says W.H.A. director of public relations John Hewig. "It needs strong, committed, local ownership." Skalbania himself expressed a desire to be in Indianapolis, if only "to watch my money being lost."

Still, Skalbania seemed nothing if not committed—at least with his wallet. After receiving a positive initial response to his request for local investment, Skalbania vowed to keep the franchise afloat for at least another year—"come hell or high water." He appointed Pat Stapleton as coach-general manager and gave him complete control over hockey operations. In July 1978, Skalbania began negotiations with friend and Birmingham Bulls owner Johnny Bassett to merge the two franchises in Indianapolis — and give the Racers some fresh players. Skalbania brought in a new management team headed by Bill Neal. And, in a personal Lear Jet high over Alberta's Rocky Mountain foothills, Skalbania made the deal he believed would save the Racers: He signed 17-year-old Wayne Gretzky, the hockey marvel who had scored 70 goals and 112 assists in his first and only year of junior A hockey, to a seven-year, $1.7-million personal services contract.

But, to paraphrase Murphy's Law, everything that can go wrong, will. And it did in Indianapolis. The local investors reneged on their promise of aid (if any was actually tendered) and the Bulls deal fell through. The management group so hastily thrown together wasn't fully operational until late August, too late to launch a significant promotion campaign. "There had been a lot of mismanagement the year before," says Neal. "But we never got a chance."

As for Gretzky, he formed the basis for what Racer publicity there was, and a 1,500-strong Great Gretzky Fan Club sprung up. But most people were unimpressed by the untried junior who was too young even to sit in a bar with his teammates. "Most people here didn't know Wayne Gretzky from Adam," says Neal. "He didn't carry all the hoopla he would have in a Canadian city."

While Pat Stapleton pared and shuffled his roster as best he could, he desperately needed players. He couldn't get them: Skalbania felt he had done enough to land Gretzky. "Sure, Nelson gave me complete control," says Stapleton, "but if you don't have any dollars there's not much you can do."

Skalbania nevertheless expected the team to get off to a good start. And, say many former Racers, had they done so the fans might have responded. Unfortunately, they didn't — on both counts.

As if to tempt fate, last October the W.H.A. kicked off its seventh season on Friday the 13th. Fate was more than tempted. In the first two minutes of the Racers' first game, No. 1 goalie Eddie Mio was sidelined when a Bobby Hull slap shot caught him between the eyes. Before a crowd of 11,271 (who took advantage of a two-for-one deal), the Racers collapsed 6-3 to the Winnipeg Jets. The next night, before a crowd of 5,031, the Racers were humiliated by the Birmingham Bulls 9-3. The Racers got off to a 1-4-0 start. No matter how hard the players tried, the fear of losing their jobs fueled their ineptness. Indeed, it wasn't hard to smell rotting franchise. Blaine Stoughton had wagered with his teammates that the Racers wouldn't last the season.

For Nelson Skalbania, payday meant an $80,000 headache; for the players it meant another team meeting. "We had four paydays and four team meetings," says former Racer Dave Inkpen. "At the first, we were told that Mr. Skalbania was sick and tired of losing money, and that there would be drastic changes." The changes, they were told, would assure the franchise's future. Everyone would be paid — eventually.

Meanwhile, the players were fed a steady diet of rumors. "There were so many stories going around that no one knew what the truth was," says Gary Inness. "People were playing one off against the other, and the players were caught in the middle."

Afraid to capsize an already sinking ship, the team made few demands — despite grueling 12-hour bus rides from Indianapolis to Cincinnati to Buffalo to Montreal to Quebec City, and meal money that sometimes never materialized. "It was depressing," says Inkpen, "but we played as hard as we could. What else could we do?"

Skalbania's first "drastic change" involved Gretzky. Desperate for funds, a situation made critical by the Canadian dollar's 18 percent slide in value against the American, Skalbania sold Gretzky, winger Peter Driscoll and goalie Eddie Mio to the Edmonton Oilers for $850,000. Gretzky, then not even in the W.H.A.'s top 25 scorers, had played only eight games for the Racers, scoring 3 goals and 3 assists (by late January he was the league's No. 10 scorer with 22 goals and 22 assists). Next to go was defenseman Kevin Morrison and the Racers' disgruntled scoring leader Richie Leduc, who were shipped to the Quebec Nordiques for draft choices that would never be claimed.

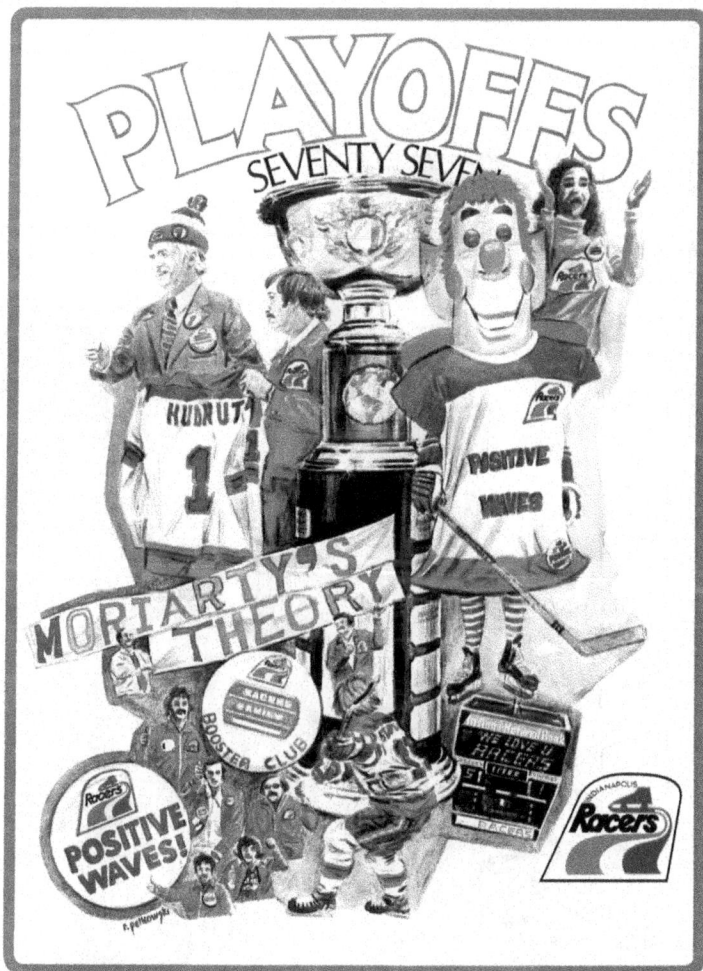

Skalbania had already axed the practice of handing out free tickets (Market Square Associates, the entity that controlled Market Square Center—and concessions and parking—was the only one making money from them, anyway) and attendance had dipped still further. Frustrated, Skalbania berated the fans for their poor support. Says Inkpen: "He was a fool by kicking what supporters he had in the teeth." On one of his rare appearances in Indianapolis, Skalbania turned his fire on the players, saying that he hoped they would play better hockey if they "were worried about putting food on the table."

But Skalbania's tantrums only made things worse. On December 15, shortly after a 7-4 Racer loss to New England, he gave his players an unpleasant Christmas present: their freedom. Even then, he did it by proxy, letting Gordon Robson, his representative, tell the world what everyone knew anyway: that the Racers' situation was "hopeless." In a telex message, an embittered Skalbania said: "The incentive to keep writing checks to cover the cost of playing hockey in Indianapolis seems ludicrous. The almost total lack of support from those in the city who would benefit from the continuance of hockey in Indianapolis leads me to believe I am nothing but a damned fool." The Racers were finally, in Skalbania's words, a "quivering corpse." "A week before Christmas and all of a sudden no paycheck," laments Inness. "It hurts a lot. You start scrambling."

Although most players were prepared for the end, it was still a shock—especially, perhaps, to Byron Baltimore, a former Racer who only a week earlier had been traded back to his old team by Cincinnati.

For players like 34-year-old Ken Block, a veteran of two previous W.H.A. foldings, the Racers' demise marks the end of their hockey careers. Even for 24-year-old Dave Inkpen, third star of the Racers' last game, the future remains uncertain. Picked up by the New England Whalers, he is shaken and glum. "I don't know what's going to happen to me. New England has a tight club and they're winning. They're sending me down to Springfield [of the A.H.L.]. I just don't know what I'll do . . ."

Few players have expressed bitterness. Says Inkpen: "I just think we all felt cheated of honesty. No one ever gave us the straight story."

As for the future of Indianapolis hockey, it too is uncertain. Bill Neal and Pat Stapleton are valiantly trying to put together a team for possible entry into the International Hockey League or Central Hockey League in a bid to, as Neal says, "build up the hockey spirit that was destroyed by the death of the Racers." That will take some doing. Seething at what they call deceit, 3,000 Indianapolis season ticket-holders have brought a $20-million class-action lawsuit against Skalbania, the Racers and the W.H.A., claiming they are owed $275 to $300 per seat for the Racers' remaining and never-to-be-played 26 home games.

Players and front-office people alike refuse to hold Skalbania responsible for that death, preferring instead to credit him with prolonging the franchise's life. "He was a businessman first and a hockey fan second, or at least that was somewhere in his list of priorities," says Inness, who gained a berth with the Washington Capitals. "But you have to sympathize with him—to a point. His losses were colossal, his heart was in the right place. He just didn't know how to deal with people. He loved confusing them. And he made a lot of mistakes." More to the point was an Indiana newsman's belief that Nelson Skalbania was a genius at buying and selling and an idiot at operating.

Despite the blow to its prestige, the W.H.A. has gained by losing the Racers, which had become another land mine on the road to a possible W.H.A.-N.H.L. merger. So tight is the six-team league now that at this writing only 17 points separate the top and bottom clubs (45 points are betwixt first and last in the N.H.L.).

So the Indianapolis Racers soon will be another forgotten disaster, an enormous tax exemption for Nelson Skalbania. And the man who tried to save a franchise will turn his attention to the Nevada gold mine he has just bought (potential production: $6.9 million annually at current world prices). Or to the next batch of lucrative office towers that comes along. When he stops running, he can ponder the dollar that cost him a million. And perhaps pop open the product of his British Columbia brewery: Pacific Gold.

Which is a lot easier to stomach than Indiana Red. 🏒

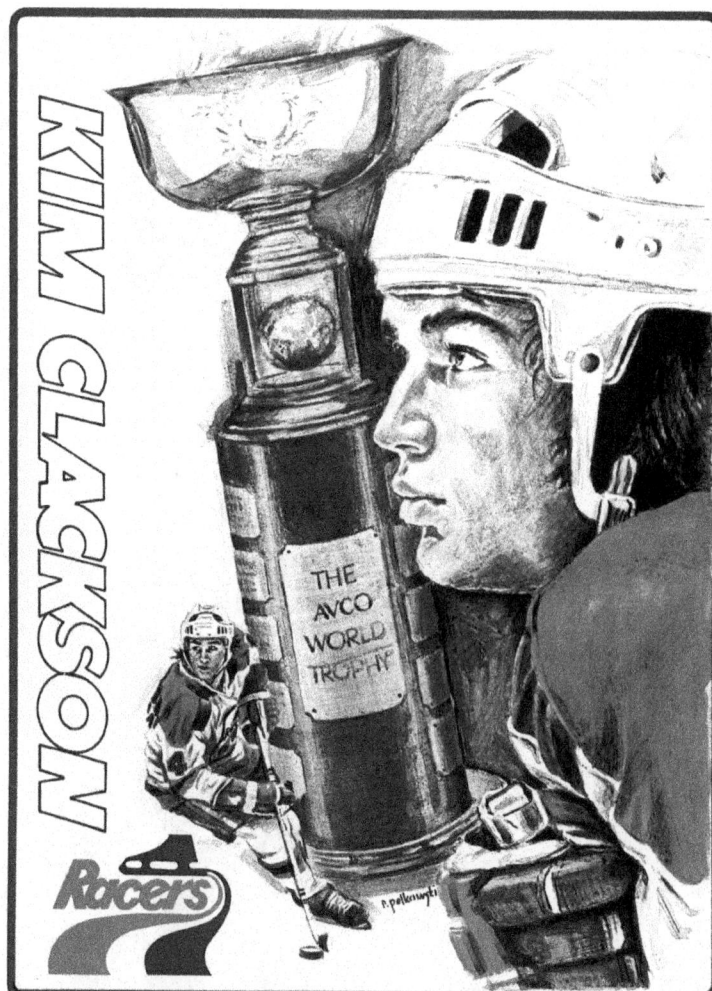

KIM CLACKSON

THE AVCO WORLD TROPHY

Racers

ABOUT THE WHA HOF
& THE AUTHOR

ABOUT THE WHA HOF & AUTHOR

The World Hockey Association Hall of Fame is an independent organization of hockey historians, journalists and former WHA coaches, players and management who are dedicated to honoring the 1972-1979 major league.

Voting for the Honored Members of the WHA Hall of Fame was completed in 2010 and 2012. Induction ceremonies were completed throughout North America, featuring such WHA luminaries as Gordie, Mark and Marty Howe, Bobby Hull, Anders Hedberg and Ulf Nilsson, Pat Stapleton, Andre Lacroix, and many others.

The WHA HOF also conducts WHA reunions, film screenings, and seminars throughout the USA and Canada.

Visit the online archives of the WHA Hall of Fame at **www.WHAhof.com** and see our official display at the United States Hockey Hall of Fame Museum in Eveleth, Minnesota.

Author Timothy Gassen is president of the World Hockey Association Hall of Fame, and an acknowledged expert on the history of the WHA. He has written, produced, and directed the more than 12 hours of WHA video documentaries for the WHA Hall of Fame DVD and Blu-ray Disc series.

His other books on the World Hockey Association include "The WHA Hall of Fame: A Photographic History Of The Rebel League 1972-1979," published by St. Johann Press. It features many previously unpublished WHA photos and a complete league history. He is also author of "Positive Waves: a history of Indianapolis Racers hockey 1974-1979," and editor of the "1972-1979 WHA Media Guides" book, published by the WHA HOF.

Gassen has won Arizona Press Club Awards for his hockey coverage, and he's served as a college hockey team media director, a college and pro hockey radio man and TV broadcaster. He has also been a longtime columnist for hockey magazines and the Arizona Daily Star newspaper. This is his sixth book.

Visit the author's company Web site at **www.purple-cactus.tv** and the WHA Hall of Fame at both **WHAhof.com** and **whaRACERS.com**

SUPERFANS

WHA Hall of Fame President Timothy Gassen started at the top -- at the top of Market Square Arena, from 1974-1978, cheering wildly for his WHA Indianapolis Racers hockey team. Along with fellow high school students Dave and Bill Pickering, they were the infamous "Racers Superfans."

Here is their story, from -- yes, you guessed it -- a 1977 Racers game program.

Volume 1, Issue 14
December 15, 1977

CONTENTS

SUPERFANS IN ACTION

The Racers are tied, there's a faceoff, the organ music fills Market Square Arena and suddenly from the top of the building comes this loud, "Thump, Thump, Thump."

"Superfans" are in action, trying to stimulate their heroes into scoring the goal that will win another World Hockey Association game.

Who are the "Superfans", those cushion-crashing, wooden block-knocking, super-sign making young people who say they wouldn't trade their "bird's-eye" view for any other in MSA?

They are brothers Dave (19) and Bill (15) Pickering, Tim Gassen (16) and Alex Waddell (18), and they want it known "we are the only Indianapolis-based" top-of-the-building Racer fan group.

"The Rafter Rats are Chicago-based, and they only come on weekends," said Dave Pickering, who wears a red-white-and-blue Racer cap, Racer jersey and red cape with "Superfan" on it to all home games.

Dave, who attends night school at Marshall High School, has a season ticket.

SUPERFANS IN ACTION

"It's the best seat in the place," said Dave, holding up his ticket stub that said aisle 18, row XX (the very top one), seat 1.

Dave and Bill, a sophomore at Warren Central, began "Superfans" at the tailend of the 1975-76 season when the Racers, spurred on by their "Positive Waves" theme, won the Eastern Division title.

"Superfans" are proudest of their sign that says "Positive Title Waves." It was their first and is always hung in the No. 1 position on the wall behind their "bird's-eye" view.

Tim, a junior at North Central, became a "Superfan" at the start of the 1975-76 season. Alex, a North Central senior, joined just recently.

The group has about as many sound effects as some of the old-time radio shows. Bill's specialty is banging together wooden blocks. Dave slaps together two old cushions that go "Thump, Thump, Thump." Tim whacks away at an old can lid that might not make it through another season.

"Superfans" came up with a new gimmick recently. They got a plastic helmet with a red light on the top similar to a police car's when it's flashing. "We turn it on when the Racers score," said Dave.

"Superfan" art work has quite a variety:
"Go Racers
Racers #1
In Indy"
"Do It
To 'em"
"What A
Claude:
No. 20"

The group was especially pleased when new Racer Bill Goldsworthy scored a goal in his first game in MSA. "Superfans" had a sign on the wall that read "Goalsworthy."

There are other signs the "Superfans" hold up at different times.

"When the Racers score, we hold up a sign that says, 'Super Shot,' " said Dave. "When the other team scores, we hold up a sign that says, 'Lucky.' "

There's also a sign that looks like an eye chart. It says, "A bad call by the referee."

"It's used more than any other sign," said Dave, with an obvious partisan smile.

Indianapolis Racers Magazine is published by the Indianapolis Racers Hockey Team, owned and operated by Hockey World Ltd. Price: One Dollar and Fifty Cents ($1.50) per issue. All rights reserved. Reproduction without the expressed written permission of Hockey World Ltd. is prohibited. Address all correspondence to Editor, Indianapolis Racers Magazine, 151 North Delaware Street, Indianapolis, Indiana, U.S.A., 46204. Printed in the U.S.A. by Image Builders / Allied Printing.

Editor: Don Wahle   Art Director: Bruce Neckar   Assistant Editor: Leo Kovach

WHAhof.com